HOW PEOPLE MATTER

Mattering, which is about feeling valued and adding value, is essential for health, happiness, love, work, and social well-being. We all need to feel valued by, and add value to, ourselves, others, co-workers, and community members. This book shows not only the signs, significance, and sources of mattering, but also presents the strategies to achieve mattering in our personal and professional lives. It uses research-based methods of change to help people achieve a higher sense of purpose and a deeper sense of meaning. Each chapter gives therapists, managers, teachers, parents, and healthcare professionals the tools needed to optimize personal and collective well-being and productivity. The volume explains how promoting mattering within communities fosters wellness and fairness in equal measure. By using the new science of feeling valued and adding value, the authors provide a guide to promoting happier lives and healthier societies.

Isaac Prilleltensky is an award-winning academic and former Dean of the School of Education and Human Development at the University of Miami, USA, where he currently serves as Professor and Vice Provost for Institutional Culture. He also has published 11 books and over 130 papers.

Ora Prilleltensky is a former assistant clinical professor and the former Director of the major in Human and Social Development at the University of Miami, USA. She is a wheelchair-user and has published a book in 2004 about her research on motherhood and disability. She has worked in a variety of clinical settings and has co-authored three books on the promotion of well-being.

D0988779

Advance Praise for *How People Matter*

This deeply illuminating volume is essential reading for those interested in mattering, meaning in life, happiness, and mental health. The authors provide a wonderfully comprehensive, integrative overview of mattering in a wide variety of life domains and its power to positively transform our love relationships and ourselves. I warmly recommend this groundbreaking book as the go-to resource for students, professionals, researchers, and the general public interested in better understanding how to approach the topic of mattering and how to use the useful insights provided by the authors in order to reach a happier and more meaningful life.

Mario Mikulincer, Founding Dean, Baruch Ivcher School of Psychology, Interdisciplinary Center (IDC), Herzliya; author of *Human Learned Helplessness* and *Attachment in Adulthood: Structure, Dynamics, and Change*; editor of the Herzliya APA Series on Personality and Social Psychology.

***

In this brilliant book, Isaac and Ora Prilleltensky elevate the notion of mattering, a concept that is perfectly suited for our times. In contrast to the individualistic ethos of the "Me Culture," mattering focuses on adding value to others, culminating in a "We Culture." This book is written in a personal, evocative, and passionate way, relating meaningful encounters with the authors and people in their lives as well as with critically needed ideas. The book reads like a fascinating novel that illuminates and enlightens while also creating the framework for a more authentic life and a more just world in which people feel called to contribute.

David Blustein, Duganne Faculty Fellow and Professor, Lynch School of Education and Human Development, Boston College; author of *The Importance of Work in an Age of Uncertainty*; editor of *The Oxford Handbook of the Psychology of Working*.

***

It is difficult to describe all that the Prilleltenskys have accomplished with *How People Matter* With gentleness and humor, the book embraces big, important elements under the heading of mattering: love, political action, Black Lives Matter, meaning in life, meaning to each other. They show the inseparability of social currents from our own well-being as they incisively describe contemporary "me culture"; they introduce illuminating new concepts like "wellfair" and the building of a "caring sector" in society; they offer clear, helpful strategies for putting their concepts to work in our lives. Loving, funny, brilliant, honest, and open, the Prilleltenskys emerge as the kind of friends that we all wish we had. Their work is liberation psychology for everyone.

Laura Smith, Teachers College, Columbia University; author of *Psychology, Poverty, and the End of Social Exclusion.*

***

How People Matter is a wonderfully detailed user's guide to help people feel valued for what they do and actually add value with what they do. It combines discussion of relevant research with lots of very practical tips that will help us lead more useful, productive, and fulfilling lives. There is a valuable lesson on almost every page.

Barry Schwartz, U. C. Berkeley; author of *Why We Work* and *Practical Wisdom*, among other books.

***

A book on mattering or feeling valued and adding value is timely and immensely critical. This book deepens our understanding of the power of dignity and self-worth and calls us to action as individuals and as a "collective we" to enhance mattering for all. It spans the arenas of mattering for the self, for relationships, for work, and for communities, giving us frameworks and tools to spur understanding and action. It marries concerns for wellness and fairness at all levels and offers inspiration and actions to make their fusion a reality. The book is both practical and wise, integrating diverse streams of social science to make mattering a process we can appreciate, understand, and act upon.

Jane Dutton, Robert L. Kahn Distinguished University Professor Emerita of Business Administration, University of Michigan; author of *Awakening Compassion at Work.*

***

This book is a joy to read and I did not want it to end. It should go a long way toward making mattering a bigger focus in the academic community and in people's lives. But what most comes through these pages is the heart and humanity of Isaac and Ora Prilleltensky. They remind us that mattering, like life, is about people, and it represents a way forward during a time when a way forward is perhaps needed more than ever.

Gordon Flett, York University, Toronto; author of *The Psychology of Mattering*.

***

Feeling good by doing good has the ring of a self-help cliché. There is a healthy dollop of self-help in this entertaining and beautifully written book – but there is also so much more. Adding value to others and oneself is a credo for how to create a better society, one that fosters good relationships and well-being. And it is all based on evidence that takes us from the individual, relationships, and work to what needs to happen in society. Psychology in a very social perspective – grand.

Sir Michael Marmot, Institute of Health Equity, University College London; author of the *The Status Syndrome: How Social Standing Affects Our Health and Longevity* and *The Health Gap: The Challenge of an Unequal World*.

***

Chock full of science and real-life stories, *How People Matter* beautifully illustrates practical steps to cultivating a more meaningful life. Isaac and Ora do a masterful job of balancing the need for wellness with the importance of fairness in creating a more harmonious world where we can all truly become happy together.

Suzie Pileggi Pawelski, MAPP, and James O. Pawelski, PhD; coauthors of *Happy Together: Using the Science of Positive Psychology to Build Love that Lasts*.

***

Through *How People Matter*, Isaac and Ora Prilleltensky make a critical and timely call: to pursue meaning, to balance rights and responsibilities, to seek both wellness and fairness, at home, at work, and in social life. It is a judicious appeal for our troubled times.

Julio Frenk, MD, MPH, PhD, President, University of Miami.

***

What a great book on mattering! The authors have a real gift for turning complex academic ideas into something that many people can understand and apply to their own lives. This volume puts the very important issue of mattering center stage and gives us tips on how we can all get a bit more mattering in our own lives or in the lives of others. The mattering wheel is a great resource around which we can plan actions ourselves to Increase what we do to ensure that everyone matters. Leave the bookshop with a fabulous gift. After you have read this book, the importance of mattering will be yours forever.

Angie Hart, University of Brighton, United Kingdom; author of *Building a New Community Psychology of Mental Health: Spaces, Places, People and Activities.*

***

In their insightful and compelling book, Isaac and Ora Prilleltensky offer us a path out of our current crisis of self-absorption and self-obsession. They do this by teaching us how to balance our concern with our own well-being with actions that promote the well-being of others, and by helping us recognize that all of us – especially those whose skin color, income, birthplace, or disability status differs from our own – *matter.*

Mark Pancer, Professor Emeritus, Wilfrid Laurier University; author of *The Psychology of Civic Engagement.*

***

This is a book of our time. Isaac and Ora Prilleltensky have provided us with an excellent guide for what we can do about the mess we find ourselves in. They have provided an exceptionally clear explanation of why so many experience so much angst and what can be done about it. The Prilleltenskys help us understand why it is critical to matter as an individual, in our families, in our relationships, in our work, and in our communities.

The Prilleltenskys have provided excellent step-by-step guidance and activities that lead to greater personal skill and ability to impact one's own life and the lives of others. An example is the BET I CAN method in which they instruct the reader on developing understanding of Behaviors, Emotions, Thoughts, Interactions, Context, Awareness, and Next Steps. The presentations are easy to grasp and come with specific guidance on developing mastery of each of the concepts. Well-developed examples, vignettes, and case studies are presented that provide the reader with a clear understanding of how to incorporate steps of learning into the practice of living. *How People Matter* will be an excellent addition to a book club list. Anyone interested in learning more effective approaches to improving life, love, work, and community will benefit greatly from this fantastic book.

Arthur M. (Andy) Horne, Dean Emeritus and Distinguished Research Professor, College of Education, University of Georgia; coauthor of *Bullying Prevention: Creating a Positive School Climate and Developing*

Social Competence; coeditor of *Realizing Social Justice: The Challenge of Preventive Interventions.*

***

How People Matter is a timely challenge to the notion of self-absorption that threatens our humanity and our planet. An in-depth explanation of personal and political dimensions of mattering within the arenas of self, relationships, work, and community is skillfully integrated with practical guidelines for finding balance between valuing the self and adding value in all these arenas. This inspiring work can be applied in any context to facilitate transformation toward wellness and fairness for all.

Dr Ansie Elizabeth Kitching, Associate Professor in Educational Psychology, Faculty of Education, University of the Western Cape, South Africa.

***

Ora and Isaac's poignant new book helps the reader construct what makes life worthwhile: the capacity to feel valued and to add value in our intimate relations, at work, and in society. Ora and Isaac document how we can navigate from a "Me Culture," primarily individualistic and hedonistic, to a "We Culture," communitarian and transformative. They address how to overcome powerlessness and helplessness, offering specific strategies like the BET I CAN method to change our thoughts, emotions, and behaviors. Their aim is to develop a culture where we can pursue values such as autonomy and freedom that increase our own well-being as well as values such as compassion, empathy, generosity, and justice that promote the well-being of others. I am sure this book will be a seminal text in helping America complete the French revolution, promoting not only individual freedom but also equality and fraternity. It has done too much of a good job promoting liberty. America now has to focus more on equality and justice, promoting a culture balancing wellness with fairness, rights with responsibilities, feeling valued with adding value to others.

Donata Francescato, former Community Psychology Professor (Sapienza, Rome), current Co-Director of the Association for Individual and Community Development (ASPIC); author of twenty-three books on interventions to promote individual and social change, published in Italian, Spanish, Portuguese, French, Chinese, and Japanese.

***

With their new book *How People Matter*, Isaac and Ora Prilleltensky join the ranks of Martin Seligman and Brené Brown as brilliant scientists and teachers who translate what they have learned into accessible and practical advice. By exploring the role of mattering to self, to others, at work, and within a community, the Prilleltenskys provide a thoughtful road map for how adding value and feeling valued leads to a fulfilling life.

Julie Haizlip, MD MAPP, University of Virginia Schools of Nursing and Medicine.

***

Increasing employee engagement and creating inclusive environments are hot topics on corporate "to-do" lists. But many leadership teams struggle with how to accomplish these goals and how to know what initiatives will make a cultural impact. The psychological concept of mattering can provide a road map for leaders looking to develop productive and positive energy in their organization. In this fascinating and extremely practical new book, the authors provide a great resource for leaders to create an environment where employees feel seen, heard, and appreciated and where they can make a contribution to the enterprise. This is creating an environment where people feel they are valued and their work is valuable. This is mattering, a topic every manager should master. Let Isaac and Ora be your guides!

Rebecca Lamperski, Executive Director, Learning & Development, Comcast University.

***

Far from a typical self-help book of instructions, the Prilleltenskys have graced us with a humble, thoughtful, and instantly appealing analysis of what it means and what it takes to become ever more human, ever more connected to family, friends, coworkers, and community. Filled with personal stories of kindness and brilliance, this book makes the reader enjoy the ride as much as the reward. People who develop a healthy personality appreciate and exercise free choice. So should you. Be kind to yourself. Choose to read this terrific book. I promise it will greatly affect your heart and mind. Time spent reading, reflecting on, and appreciating the wisdom, lessons, and suggestions within the pages of this delightful book will inspire and repay the effort. In valuing yourself and adding value to others, you deserve to use this time. Together, we may all continue to grow our hippocampus and our humanity.

Peter A. Gorski, MD, MPA, Professor of Pediatrics and Humanities, Health & Society, Wertheim College of Medicine, Florida International University; Professor of Public Health, Miller School of Medicine, University of Miami.

***

As we all go through the global pandemic together, it is clear that we must embrace the collective "We" rather than the self-centric "Me." *How People Matter* shows us how we can make the transition from an individualistic to a communitarian culture. From managing the self to maintaining our relationships through effective emotional regulation, importance is given to understanding the contexts of our lives. By using numerous anecdotes, case studies, and authoritative research, the authors bring to us an in-depth look at mattering and its relationship to our health, happiness, love, work, and society. This book is undeniably a most helpful read for everyone. What makes it extra special is the strategies described to enhance the various domains of one's life. The simple tips outlined and the description of the steps are alone worthy of your time. Buy it. Read it. Transform. Matter.

Sangeeta Bhatia, PhD, Associate Professor, Department of Psychology, Gargi College, University of Delhi, New Delhi, India.

***

Using humor, research, and real-life examples, Ora and Isaac Prilleltensky deftly lay out the foundation of why mattering is so important to well-being and happiness. Here they offer a practical approach to how we can feel valued and add value in all areas of life. This book is not only timely but also necessary for personal and systemic change.

Karen Guggenheim, social entrepreneur, co-founder of WOHASU Foundation and World Happiness Summit.

HOW PEOPLE MATTER

Why It Affects Health, Happiness, Love, Work, and Society

ISAAC PRILLELTENSKY

University of Miami

ORA PRILLELTENSKY

University of Miami

CAMBRIDGE
UNIVERSITY PRESS

CAMBRIDGE
UNIVERSITY PRESS

University Printing House, Cambridge CB2 8BS, United Kingdom

One Liberty Plaza, 20th Floor, New York, NY 10006, USA

477 Williamstown Road, Port Melbourne, VIC 3207, Australia

314–321, 3rd Floor, Plot 3, Splendor Forum, Jasola District Centre,
New Delhi – 110025, India

79 Anson Road, #06–04/06, Singapore 079906

Cambridge University Press is part of the University of Cambridge.

It furthers the University's mission by disseminating knowledge in the pursuit of
education, learning, and research at the highest international levels of excellence.

www.cambridge.org
Information on this title: www.cambridge.org/9781108839013
DOI: 10.1017/9781108979405

© Isaac Prilleltensky and Ora Prilleltensky 2021

First published 2021

A catalogue record for this publication is available from the British Library.

Library of Congress Cataloging-in-Publication Data
NAMES: Prilleltensky, Isaac, 1959– author. | Prilleltensky, Ora, 1959– author.
TITLE: How people matter : why it affects health, happiness, love, work, and society / Isaac
Prilleltensky, University of Miami, Ora Prilleltensky, University of Miami.
DESCRIPTION: Cambridge, United Kingdom ; New York, NY : Cambridge University Press,
2021. | Includes bibliographical references and index.
IDENTIFIERS: LCCN 2021001942 | ISBN 9781108839013 (hardback) | ISBN 9781108969246
(paperback) | ISBN 9781108979405 (ebook)
SUBJECTS: LCSH: Respect for persons. | Values. | Social integration. | Interpersonal relations. |
Well-being.
CLASSIFICATION: LCC BJ1533.R42 P75 2021 | DDC 179/.9–dc23
LC record available at https://lccn.loc.gov/2021001942

ISBN 978-1-108-83901-3 Hardback
ISBN 978-1-108-96924-6 Paperback

We dedicate this book to our sister and sister-in-law, Miriam (Cachi) Prilleltensky and Myriam Rapoport, for making the world a better place by helping people matter.

Contents

Figures

Acknowledgments

We would like to acknowledge the generosity of Barbara Mautner, who endowed the Erwin and Barbara Mautner Chair in Community Well-Being at the University of Miami. The Chair has enabled Isaac to work on several scholarly projects associated with this book. The University of Miami also provided Isaac with a sabbatical, during which much of the work for this book was done.

We received constructive criticisms from Gregory Elliott from Brown University in the United States and Angie Hart from the University of Brighton in the United Kingdom. Gordon Flett from York University in Canada provided us with his latest writings on mattering, which have been very helpful to us. Some of Isaac's former students in the Masters of Applied Positive Psychology program at the University of Pennsylvania shared useful materials on the topic of mattering with us. Rebecca Lamperski generously facilitated published and unpublished articles on mattering that she had been collecting. David Yaden provided us with an early copy of an influential paper on mattering in the workplace that he coauthored. Julie Haizlip also shared valuable insights on mattering from her research at the University of Virginia. In addition to these students at UPenn, Mike Scarpa, a doctoral student in the Community Well-Being program at the University of Miami, has been a great intellectual partner in studies on mattering.

Our colleague Cengiz Zopluoglu, now at the University of Oregon, has provided great statistical advice on some of our mattering studies. We also appreciate our scholarly collaboration on mattering with our Italian colleague Salvatore Di Martino. Our partners in the Fun for Wellness project, Adam McMahon and Samantha Dietz, from the University of Miami, and Nick Myers, now at Michigan State University, helped us develop and test the BET I CAN model of change. Tania Rodriguez from the Office of Institutional Culture at the University of Miami provided assistance with the list of references. Donner Valle helped us with graphics. We are deeply indebted to all the colleagues around the world who read the book and offered supportive comments, including Sangeeta Bhatia, David Blustein, Jane Dutton, Donata Francescato, Gordon Flett, Julio Frenk, Karen Guggenheim, Peter Gorski, Julie Haizlip, Angie Hart, Andy Horne, Ansie Kitching, Rebecca Lamperski, Michael Marmot, Mario Mikulincer, Mark Pancer, Suzie Pileggi Pawelski, James Pawelski, Barry Schwartz, and Laura Smith. Four anonymous reviewers also provided useful critique.

Our sister-in-law, Myriam Rapoport, has had many wonderful conversations with Ora over the years about meaning and mattering. Miriam Prilleltensky, Isaac's sister, has been a great listener, thinking partner, friend, and supporter. Ora also appreciates the caring and support of her brothers, Oded and Hanan Rapoport, and her special bond with her niece Yael Rapoport Gov-Ari. Our son, Matan Prilleltensky, the smartest member of our own family, was a sounding board throughout the process, providing great insights, poignant commentary, and much-needed comic relief.

At Cambridge University Press we received fantastic assistance from David Repetto and Emily Watton. We also very much appreciate the careful editorial review of the manuscript by Wade Guyitt. We gratefully acknowledge permission from John Wiley and Sons to reproduce Figure 1.1 and a few segments from the following publication: I. Prilleltensky (2019), "Mattering at the intersection of psychology, philosophy, and politics," *American Journal of Community Psychology* 65(1–2): 1–19.

Last, but not least, we would each like to acknowledge the love and support we received from our coauthor.

Introduction

We, the authors, have been married for nearly forty years. Since meeting in 1982 we've lived in thirteen houses in six cities in four countries. We've also remodeled a few houses to make them wheelchair accessible, and every single time the contractors drove us insane. We bought and sold fifteen properties in three countries, and, thanks to Isaac's financial acumen, we have a nearly perfect record of always losing money on real estate.

Surprisingly, we've found time to do other things together. For example: we coauthored four books on well-being that almost killed us. We also co-taught a class for twelve semesters; and every semester Ora insisted that Isaac upgrade his lectures, even though the students seemed to like them just fine. We lived through four graduate degrees and two doctoral dissertations. Combined, we've had a total of fifteen jobs. We also ran together two randomized controlled trials of an intervention consisting of 152 activities that we designed. Ora has censored dozens of Isaac's humor columns for fear that he might lose his job. We also raised an amazing and highly spirited child who could argue about the fairness of bedtime before he was toilet trained. And we did all of this without ever having a single argument.

You probably don't believe us, do you? You *shouldn't* believe us. Of course we argued! In fact, we argued endlessly about this book. But despite Ora's search for perfection, and Isaac's many imperfections, we are still truly happily married.

When we think about what we're doing right, there are three things that keep us together. First, we make each other *feel valued*. Second, we help each other *add value*. Third, we cuddle in bed. (In this book we deal only with the first two factors, because Ora thinks it is too embarrassing to talk about anything we do in bed.)

When it comes to mattering, however, we have learned not only from each other but also from our son. Matan taught us an important lesson when he was three years old. This was in Winnipeg, Manitoba, thirty years ago.

Winnipeg has the distinction of being one of the coldest cities in the world. While the contrast with the warmth of Tel Aviv could not be starker, we decided to move to Canada in 1984 to pursue graduate studies. Despite its freezing temperatures, Winnipeg turned out to be a great place to raise a family. Matan was born there in St. Boniface Hospital in 1987. We bought our first home there in 1990. It was in River Heights, next door to Torah Academy, where two wonderful teachers, Morah Pam and Morah Darcy, ran a fantastic preschool program. Most mornings Isaac would walk Matan to preschool, but occasionally, when he had an early morning meeting, Ora would take him. Although Ora uses a wheelchair full time now, she was still able to walk short distances at the time.

One morning Ora walked Matan next door to the school before heading off to work. It was the dead of winter, and the temperature outside was minus twelve Fahrenheit. Ora slipped on a hidden piece of ice and fell down. She tried to get up, as she was still able to do at the time, but the ground was too slippery. Matan, three years old, became very distraught at the sight of mommy on the ground, unable to get up on her own. He wanted to help her as he had seen daddy do at home. Ora explained that he's too little to do that, and she did all she could to reassure him that one of the drivers passing by will stop to help. It all happened in a matter of seconds, but for Matan it seemed like eternity. Eventually, Ora was helped by a driver who spotted them despite the high banks of snow. Matan was visibly upset that he could not help. He was too small to help, but he was big enough to feel frustrated.

Safely at home at the end of the day, Matan and Ora told Isaac what had happened. The distress no longer there, Matan was nonetheless bothered by the incident. "But I didn't help you up," he kept repeating. Ora sat him on her lap and explained that he did the best he could. A little later, Matan came up to Ora with some of his little toy cars. He wanted to play what had happened. "One car goes by, and doesn't stop. Another car goes by and doesn't stop. Another car goes by and stops." He demonstrated with his cars as he spoke. Going along with his game, Ora said: "This must be the nice lady who came to help us." Matan raised his head from his cars, looked at Ora with his big brown eyes, and said: "No mommy, this is me when I am big. I get out of the car and help you up."

Connections that help us feel valued and add value impact our health, happiness, love, work, and society.[1] The consequences of mattering or not mattering can be seen everywhere, at every age.[2] The lack of mattering often results in depression, suicide,[3] and even aggression and xenophobia.[4]

The suicide rate in the United States rose 33 percent from 1999 to 2017. In 1999 the rate was 10.5 per 100,000. By 2017 it had gone up to 14. In rural counties, the rate increased 53 percent.[5] Depression affects 322 million people around the world.[6] This is the equivalent of the entire population of the United States. The rate of depression in the United States has gone up from 2005 to 2015 from 6.6 percent to 7.3 percent. Among teenagers, the rate has increased from 8.7 percent to an alarming 12.7 percent.[7]

Lack of engagement at work is rampant. Around the world, 85 percent of workers are either not engaged or actively disengaged at work. The cost of having so many workers psychologically absent is approximately $7 trillion.[8]

Nationalism is on the rise around the globe, presenting a serious threat to liberal democracies.[9] We are now facing a democratic recession.[10] A few countries that embraced liberalism in the 1990s, such as Hungary, Turkey, Thailand, and Poland, went back to authoritarianism in the last decade.[11] China and Russia are undemocratic in their own ways. Brexit and the election of Donald Trump confirmed the turn toward nationalism in the English-speaking world. In Europe, xenophobic parties gained strength in France, Germany, Austria, and the Netherlands.[12]

What do depression, disengagement at work, and divisive movements around the world have in common? They all reflect lack of worth and lack of mattering. People who suffer from depression, workers who feel alienated, and citizens whose identity is threatened feel devalued. They feel that their lives, work, and identity do not matter. While some respond to this situation by internalizing feelings of despondence, others overcompensate by nurturing feelings of superiority and joining nationalistic movements headed by authoritarian leaders.[13] Indeed, it is not only rates of depression that have gone up but those of narcissism as well. The proportion of teens endorsing the statement "I am an important person" has risen from 12 percent in 1963 to 80 percent in 1992. Among college students, scores on the Narcissistic Personality Inventory have gone up 30 percent from 1979 to 2006.[14]

Inequality has also reached unprecedented levels. The wealth of the eight richest people in the world, $440 billion, is the same as that of half the world, 3.5 billion people. In the United States, 85 percent of the entire wealth of the country is owned by 20 percent of the population. The bottom 40 percent, in turn, own just 0.3 percent of it. When it comes to compensation, in 1960 a chief executive earned approximately twenty times as much as the average employee. In 2018 this number was 354.[15]

Despite mounting evidence concerning global warming, governments and citizens alike continue to ignore the consequences of bequeathing to our kids an uninhabitable planet.[16] What do narcissism, inequality, and indifference to global warming have in common? They are expressions of the belief that some lives are worth more than others. Narcissists are obsessed with their own value, the elite is utterly indifferent to the well-being of the poor and racial minorities, and elected officials are sacrificing future generations. They all feel that their own sense of mattering, here and now, is more important than the rest of the world. In some cases, people who feel forgotten by elites support populist politicians who promise to restore to the masses their lost privileged status.[17] For people who feel like they don't matter, joining a nationalistic movement presents a tantalizing opportunity to regain prestige and feel superior.[18]

Feelings of being devalued or overvalued, in relationships, at work, and in the world, are among the most serious threats facing us. They derive from a failure to foster mattering. The results can be disastrous for individuals and society as a whole. When disaffected masses feel that their identity is devalued in society, they respond in one of two ways. They either turn toward nationalism and extremism, as in the case of xenophobic movements, or they protest to defend their rights, as in the case of Black Lives Matter and the LGBTQ movement. Discrimination against people with disabilities gave rise to the Americans with Disabilities Act (ADA), while the oppression of Blacks in the United States gave birth to civil rights legislation. These are but two groups who felt excluded – that they did not matter. The passing of the ADA and the Civil Rights Act sent the message to millions of people that they did matter. But their gains have been tenuous.[19]

Prompted by the killings of innocent Black men and women, many of them by the police, today we witness a resurgence in the fight against racism. The recent killings of George Floyd, Breonna Taylor, and Ahmaud Arbery, among other Black men and women, reflect deep and entrenched institutionalized racism: the belief that an entire group of people matters less.[20] As Isabel Wilkerson has amply documented in her 2020 book *Caste*, the United States created, and for centuries upheld, a caste system in which Blacks are kept at the bottom of the social hierarchy. This was alternately done through brutal repression and violence such as lynching, through the legal system, and through the dissemination of racist ideologies.[21] The response to racism cannot be just individual. It must be collective, societal, and structural. Oppression, the antithesis of mattering, will not be eliminated by the hope that some people will become enlightened.[22]

The cumulative effects of disadvantage and racism are in full display in times of crisis. The COVID-19 pandemic has shown that Blacks and Latinx die at much higher rates than Whites, demonstrating, once again, that discrimination has enduring and lethal repercussions.[23] When people don't matter, individually and collectively, fatal consequences ensue. Social action is required to fight racism and oppression. This is why in this book we go beyond the personal and the psychological aspects of mattering. We also address its societal and political aspects.

Mattering consists of feeling valued and adding value. By feeling valued we mean being appreciated, respected, and recognized. By adding value we mean making a contribution and making a difference in the world. We feel valued by, and add value to, self, relationships, work, and community. In the best of times, feeling valued and adding value create a virtuous cycle. In the worst of times, they form a vicious one. It is hard to feel valued by others when you don't add value to them. Racism, discrimination, and oppression work against feeling valued and opportunities to add value.[24] This is exactly what the Black Lives Matter movement is fighting against.

Mattering is essential for happiness, health, autonomy, self-acceptance, well-being, purpose, mastery, and growth.[25] These may be seen as positive personal outcomes, but mattering is also crucial for justice and community well-being.[26] When we balance feeling valued with adding value, when we reach an equilibrium between adding value to ourselves and adding value to others, we are building a healthier society. Research shows that people report more satisfaction with society when they experience high levels of tolerance, trust, civic engagement, and nonmaterialism.[27] All of these factors contribute to mattering at the same time that they enhance social contentment.

When we feel valued by ourselves, we fulfil the need for self-acceptance.[28] When we add value to ourselves, we meet the need for self-determination.[29] By feeling valued by others and by enriching their lives, we cultivate love.[30] The act of adding value at work fosters mastery and competence.[31] Making a contribution to the community promotes a sense of belonging.[32]

When these needs are met, we experience personal, relational, occupational, and social well-being. When these needs are thwarted we develop one of two types of problems: devaluation or narcissism. We feel either invisible or invincible; ignored or grandiose.[33] These conditions result in internalizing disorders such as depression or anxiety or externalizing symptoms such as violence and entitlement. The fact that today we suffer from so much depression, disengagement, divisions, narcissism, inequality, and ecological entitlement derives from a particular culture, a "Me Culture." In this culture, "I Matter" is more important than "We Matter."

In a "Me Culture" people are guided by one mantra: "I have the right to feel valued and happy." The self-centered nature of this philosophy focuses on what is good for me and what can make me happy. The COVID-19 pandemic has shown, in stark relief, the rampant individualism of the "Me Culture" – people ignore basic safety measures that would protect the collective. Instead of wearing masks, people claim infringement on personal liberty. Instead of showing solidarity toward fragile neighbors, they care about their own need to party first.[34]

But if the "Me Culture" is the problem, what's the solution? We need to cultivate a new philosophy of life where "We all have the right *and* responsibility to feel valued *and* add value, to self *and* others, so that we may all experience wellness *and* fairness." We call this a "We Culture." Whereas the "Me Culture" is primarily individualistic, hedonistic, acquiescent, and ameliorative, a "We Culture" is communitarian, purposeful, challenging, and transformative. Had we all embraced the latter, we could have avoided much of the ravages of the coronavirus pandemic.[35]

Our culture is obsessed with feeling valued and feeling happy. This infatuation with ourselves, bolstered by selfies, personal branding, and access to megaphones such as social media, is deceiving at best.[36] The way to matter is not to turn ourselves into commodities for sale. Rather, the way to matter is to pursue meaning by adding value to self and others, making others feel valued, balancing rights and responsibilities, and seeking wellness with fairness.

Without fairness, there is a limit to how much wellness we can promote in individuals, organizations, and societies.[37] Women, African Americans, people with disabilities, and many other minorities cannot flourish unless they experience fair treatment at school, work, and the community. To fully matter, we must combine fitness with fairness. Yes, we must develop skills, work hard, cultivate grit and resilience; but in the absence of fair opportunities minorities will not experience mattering. We must create a *wellfair* society, one that embraces not just wellness but also fairness.

Mattering exists in the microcosm of relationships and work but also in the macrocosm of social policies. Countries that promote economic fairness and equality achieve much better results in health, mental health, trust, education, safety, social mobility, and life expectancy. Similarly, people in countries that promote fair policies in health, education, labor market inclusion, and wellfair in general report higher levels of life satisfaction. Fairness makes people feel like they matter not just as family members or colleagues but also as citizens.[38]

Mattering faces a serious challenge in the future. When robots and artificial intelligence eliminate millions of jobs, people will need to find alternative ways to make money and meaning. We must build the caring sector and the green sector. With rising life expectancy, many of us will require help as we age. Robots cannot replace love and caring. In a caring economy, day-care providers, home health-care workers, and teachers would be paid living wages. In addition, we must create green jobs and must consider a universal basic income program that will guarantee all of us the provision of essential resources.[39]

The profound sense of worthlessness affecting millions of people is causing a great deal of personal and social misery. The suffering ranges from depression and suicide to entitlement, xenophobia, riots, and mass shootings. Lack of mattering is felt at home, at school, work, and in the community. If you are affected by relationships, workplaces, or cultures that denigrate people, you can do something about it. We need nothing less than a mattering revolution, and you can be part of it. The mattering revolution must begin now, and it must begin at home, in the workplace, and in the community. You can fight depression and disengagement by making other people feel valued and helping them add value. You can build a society where equality and fairness replace nationalism, discrimination, narcissism, and neglect of global warming. By showing that you care about others, in the present and in the future, you will find a sense of meaning and mattering. We invite you to explore the signs, significance, sources, and strategies of feeling valued and adding value.

PART I

Understanding and Promoting Mattering

CHAPTER I

The Mattering Wheel

She had just experienced the greatest disappointment of her life: she could not marry the love of her dreams. Heartbroken, in desperation, she ran away, leaving everything and everyone behind. After many trials and tribulations, including a very dangerous journey, she arrived sick and penniless to a new town. There, Jane Eyre found respect and appreciation from the community. As a teacher, she *felt valued* because she *added value* to her pupils and their families. She felt welcomed. This is how Jane described her new life:

> I felt I became a favourite in the neighbourhood. Whenever I went out, I heard on all sides cordial salutations, and was welcomed with friendly smiles. To live amidst general regard . . . is like sitting in sunshine, calm and sweet; serene inward feelings bud and bloom under the ray. At this period of my life, my heart far oftener swelled with thankfulness than sank with dejection.[1]

Charlotte Brontë published *Jane Eyre* in 1847. In that passage, she captured an essential part of mattering: feeling valued. Over forty years later, across the pond, William James, the great American philosopher and psychologist, described the opposite experience – feeling devalued – as follows:

> If no one turned round when we entered, answered when we spoke, or minded what we did, but if every person we met "cut us dead," and acted as if we were nonexisting things, a kind of rage and impotent despair would ere long well up in us, from which the cruelest bodily tortures would be a relief; for these would make us feel that, however bad might be our plight, we had not sunk to such a depth as to be unworthy of attention at all.[2]

Astute observers of the human condition, Brontë and James were describing the feelings associated with the first part of mattering: *feeling valued* or *devalued*. Matan, our son, showed us earlier how important it is to also add value. Matan's story, as well as the writings of Brontë and James, illustrate the two sides of mattering: feeling valued and adding value. So far, these two experiences have been studied in isolation, but in fact they are two sides of the same coin: mattering. You may feel valued, but if you don't have opportunities or skills to make a meaningful contribution, to yourself or others, your life is incomplete. The same goes for adding value. You may be able to help yourself or others, but in the absence of feeling valued, something important is missing. This is why this book brings together these two symbiotic components of mattering.

Feeling valued and *adding value* are not only complementary but highly interdependent. Together, they create virtuous or vicious cycles. Marginalization and exclusion engender frustration, alienation, and even aggression, which make it very hard to gain positive regard. Appreciation, on the other hand, leads to self-confidence, mastery, and the desire to make a difference. This, in turn, will make you feel valued.[3]

It's not hard to relate to these experiences. They need not be dramatic events. Thinking back, have you ever felt *devalued* by your relatives, boss, or peers? Have you ever been ignored at a party, at work, or in the community? Has anyone excluded you from a group? If not, you're lucky, but if such things have happened, you know these experiences hurt. They hurt because they threaten your sense of mattering; and if they happen often enough, research shows, they shatter your psychological and physical well-being. Indeed, the experience of exclusion has been linked to serious consequences, ranging from stress and depression to suicide to mass killings.[4] In some instances, as in the case of Christian Picciolini, who became a skinhead to find acceptance, marginalization leads to joining extremist groups.[5] There, the excluded again experience a sense of belonging.

In contrast to experiences of exclusion, if you've ever *felt valued*, or had an opportunity to *add value*, you know how good it feels to matter – so much so that your health and happiness go up every time you experience these positive emotions. In fact, you live longer and feel more fulfilled when you experience them regularly. You get a sense of meaning, importance, and satisfaction in knowing that your actions make a difference in somebody's life.[6] As leading social motivation researchers put it, "giving can create a warm glow of happiness, boost self-esteem, increase self-efficacy, and reduce symptoms of depression. It predicts improvements in physical health and even how long people live. It can strengthen social relationships, creating and strengthening social bonds and fostering the sense that one can make a valuable contribution to others."[7]

When it comes to adding value, we can learn a great deal from people who dedicate their lives to service. Whereas givers in general tend to be healthier than nongivers, some givers live longer than others. Those who experience more positive emotions live longer than givers who do not report as much positivity. This was discovered in a fascinating study spanning over six decades.[8] The famous Nun Study involved an examination of the lives of 678 members of the American School Sisters of Notre Dame. All sisters born before 1917 were asked to participate in the study. When the study started in the 1990s, all participants were between 75 and 102 years of age.

In a letter sent to all the sisters on September 22, 1930, the Mother Superior requested that each sister compose an autobiography; their average age at this time was twenty-two. Six decades later, researchers at the University of Kentucky were able to retrieve 180 autobiographies from nuns in the Milwaukee and Baltimore convents. As part of a careful review, the investigators scored them as having positive, negative, or neutral content.

The analyses revealed that the higher the level of positive emotions in the text, the lesser the risk of mortality in both convents. As the authors note, "for every 1.0% increase in the number of positive-emotion sentences there was a 1.4% decrease in the mortality rate."[9] When the researchers divided the nuns into four groups – sorting them according to the presence of positive emotion sentences, the number of positive emotion words, and the number of different positive emotions – they discovered that the highest group had lived between 6.9 and 10.7 years longer than the lowest group. When they compared the group in the top quartile with the one in the bottom on positive emotion sentences, the highest lived 6.9 years longer. When they compared top and bottom quartiles on the number of positive emotion words, the difference was 9.4 years in favor of the highest group. Finally, when they compared highest and lowest groups on the number of different positive emotions, nuns in the top group lived 10.7 years longer.

All things considered, we can see that generosity plus positivity provide a considerable boost to health and longevity. While generosity is first and foremost a gift to others, happiness is primarily a gift to ourselves. In both instances we are adding value, first to others and then to ourselves. Both gifts are necessary for mattering. If we want to enjoy the benefits of meaning and mattering, we must do both: help others and help ourselves.

Mattering motivates not only people of faith but everybody. It is a universal drive. Consider now the following stories, which we cover in more depth later on:

- Shirin, an immigrant health-care worker in Miami, goes above and beyond the call of duty to perform her job with care and grace despite low pay

- Talking to a colleague about a fantasy, Joseph Molesley, fictional character in *Downton Abbey*, proclaims: "Imagine, Molesley, valet to the Earl of Grantham!"
- Ronald, a senior executive with a very high salary, feels slighted because he was passed over for a promotion
- Ramón Antonio Gerardo Estévez changes his name to Martin Sheen
- Alicia Garza cofounds Black Lives Matter
- Muhammad Yunus, social entrepreneur, creates the Grameen Bank in Bangladesh to help poor people and goes on to win the Nobel Prize
- Oprah Winfrey recalls as a formative experience how her father wanted every guest at their house to feel like they matter
- Linda Tirado, in her recent book *Hand to Mouth*, describes in great detail the indignities associated with being poor and feeling like she doesn't matter

All these people, and many others you'll encounter in the book, are motivated by the *need to matter*, a pervasive phenomenon. Some seek to feel valued and add value, like Shirin, Molesley, and Alicia. Others, like Ronald and Linda, fear being devalued. Martin Sheen wanted to conceal his Hispanic origins, also due to fear of being devalued. Yunus and Oprah's father understood the need to provide people with dignity; they were motivated by the need to add value.

A great deal of human behavior can be explained by the need to either feel valued or add value, the twin engines of mattering. Some behaviors are driven by the *pursuit of a positive experience*, like feeling valued (Shirin, Molesley) or adding value (Yunus, Garza); while others are driven by the *avoidance of a negative experience*, like feeling devalued (Ronald, Linda).

Everyday interactions at home, school, work, and the community involve mattering. These interactions can be as short as a millisecond but as memorable as a slap in the face. A strange look from your boss can send you straight into rumination land: "Is she not happy with me? Did I do something? No wonder she did not invite me to the meeting about the ACME account. I wonder what's going on." We fear shame, rejection, and ostracism; and we crave recognition. We are not even aware of how much our behavior is dictated by the fear of exclusion and the need for inclusion.

It is not surprising that mattering to one's family would protect us from risks and threats. In one of the most comprehensive studies on mattering, a social psychologist at Brown University, Gregory Elliott, examined the relationship between mattering to one's family in adolescence and two types of problems: antisocial and self-destructive behaviors. The study, which included over 2,000 teenagers, confirmed the fundamental importance of mattering and the risks associated with its absence.

Elliott defines mattering as the perception that "we are a significant part of the world around us."[10] For him, mattering consists of awareness, importance, and reliance. Awareness implies that others notice our presence and that we are not invisible. Importance refers to the fact that we are the object of someone's caring and concern. They worry about us when we are down and celebrate with us when we are up. We are part of their lives. Reliance, in turn, means that other people have faith in us and come to us for help when required. We feel needed and valued because we have something meaningful to offer. Awareness and importance fit very well with the aspect of mattering we call feeling valued. Reliance, in turn, parallels our notion of adding value – in this case, adding value to others.

Confirming his predictions, Elliott's study found that lack of mattering in one's family resulted in both antisocial and self-destructive behaviors. With regards to the former, he argues that teens will do anything to feel like they matter, including dysfunctional acts of defiance. Faced with indifference and disregard from their own families, teens "force mattering by acting in outrageous and often undesirable ways."[11] The findings showed that, as a sense of mattering in the family decreased, violence against others, vandalism, truancy, theft, and carrying weapons increased sharply. According to Elliott, it is better to get negative attention than no attention at all. His results, as well as the school shootings seen in recent years in the United States, prove the point.

But lack of mattering can also result in self-destructive behavior. In the same study, it was found that adolescents who matter to their families were far less likely to binge drink, use illicit drugs, and plan or attempt suicide. Clearly, mattering is a protective mechanism – and not just in childhood and adolescence. Its protective qualities persist throughout the life cycle.

We all strive to feel like we matter, and we fear being ignored. Unfortunately, too many people feel devalued and don't know how to add value, either to themselves or to others. To address this need, we present in this book not only the nature, sources, and consequences of mattering but also ways to matter, to yourself and others.

Mattering is not a matter of divine intervention. It is achievable through actions, skills, and practice. These are habits and capabilities you can learn and for which there is a lot of research support. With this book you will be able to learn how to make changes in your life, relationships, work, and community. Chapter 4 introduces a set of skills that will be applied to these four domains to make your life more meaningful.

As you might have gathered, mattering is both *psychological* and *political*. It is psychological because it affects your behaviors, emotions, and thoughts: it is about *what you do, how you feel,* and *what you think*. But mattering is also political. It is political because it entails *power dynamics* capable of thwarting your sense of mattering, at home, in the office, or in the community. And let's be clear: politics is not only what happens, or doesn't happen, in Congress or city council; politics is what happens every time a person uses power to get his or her way.

You may be familiar with the more common and overt forms of power, such as threats, punishment, rewards, and the use of force. But you need to be aware of subtle forms as well. These involve manipulations, emotional blackmail, silent treatment, judgmentalism, guilt tripping, mind games, sarcasm, and various forms of exclusion. There is, indeed, a long list of put-downs available to people who want to belittle you. Politics is everywhere.[12]

To cope with power imbalances and achieve an even distribution of mattering between you and others, we must seek an equilibrium between freedom and fairness, between our own well-being and the well-being of others.[13] Your spouse may be very concerned about his or her own mattering, but what about yours?

Cultures that extol personal importance above all else lead to obsessive self-preoccupation.[14] Paradoxically, this incessant interest in oneself results in meaninglessness and pathological attempts to gain praise and recognition. In the end, there is suffering for the self-obsessed and agony for everyone else. Compulsive preoccupation with one's status, prestige, and looks results in alienation from others and the eventual destruction of mattering for everyone concerned. This is why we propose a shift from a "Me" to a "We Culture."

In the current "Me Culture," many people espouse a narrative that says: "I have the right to feel valued by others so that I may experience wellness." This is a limiting view of mattering that is very prevalent. In the "We Culture" we propose, the narrative is different: "We all have the right *and* responsibility to feel valued *and* add value, to our self *and* others, so that we may all experience wellness *and* fairness." We argue that the dominant "Me" discourse is 100 percent right about 50 percent of the problem. We must balance the current focus on rights *with* responsibilities, the current emphasis on feeling valued *with* adding value, the betterment of self *with* betterment of others, and the pursuit of wellness *with* the pursuit of fairness.

We need a new narrative about mattering. Many advocates of mattering are stuck in a "Me" narrative that is not helpful. This book will present a counternarrative that will help society move toward a culture of balancing wellness with fairness, rights with responsibilities, feeling valued with adding value, and narrow interests with the common good.

Creating a "We Culture" requires paying attention to psychological and political factors. This is because psychological and political forces affect us throughout the lifespan, from birth to old age. When children feel neglected, they develop emotional problems that prevent them from adding value.[15] When adults feel devalued, they respond mostly in one of two ways: depression or aggression.[16] While some overcome adverse conditions in healthy ways, many become despondent, and others become entitled, with insatiable needs for attention. These reactions might be considered psychological problems. But when certain groups feel marginalized due to the color of their skin, gender, sexual preferences, socioeconomic status, age, or disability, it is not just a psychological but a social problem as well.[17] In the 2016 elections in the United States, many regarded White working-class males as the most forgotten group. That was the group that got Donald Trump elected.[18]

Despite the significance of mattering as a social issue, very little has been written on the subject. To fill this gap, we explore mattering in *self, relationships, work,* and *community* (see Figure 1.1). At the personal level, we explore the healthy and unhealthy dimensions of mattering. We will review the sources and consequences of healthy mattering, such as secure attachments, self-compassion, creativity, and self-efficacy; and the unhealthy side, such as depression, anxiety, aggression, entitlement, and narcissism.

At the interpersonal level, we discuss how relationships can nurture a sense of mattering or can diminish it through neglect and abuse. At the workplace we deal with engagement, since studies show that about two-thirds of workers are disengaged.[19] This is a failure by management to make workers feel appreciated and offer them pathways for meaningful involvement. Bullying in the workplace is a ubiquitous threat that will also be covered.

Finally, at the social level, we discuss healthy and unhealthy cultures. We will see how some communities foster mattering for everyone, while others erode it through division and inequality. The latter are mostly "Me Cultures." We will analyze recent events triggered by distortions in mattering, such as school shootings, racism, and the narcissism epidemic. We will also examine responses such as Black Lives Matter.

Rooted in scientific evidence of how people, organizations, and communities change, each section of this book will provide an opportunity to initiate transformation in your own life. Hopefully, these changes will help you achieve a higher sense of purpose – and a deeper sense of meaning.

Figure 1.1 The mattering wheel
Reproduced with permission from John Wiley and Sons.

Virtuous and Vicious Cycles

The first thing to note about the wheel in Figure 1.1 is that mattering is at the very center, supported by two experiences: *feeling valued* and *adding value*. By feeling valued we mean feeling worthy, acknowledged, and appreciated. By adding value we mean making a meaningful contribution, to yourself and others.

The second important feature of the wheel is that it contains eight sectors. The left-hand side has four sources of *feeling valued*; the right-hand side four beneficiaries of *adding value*. The four sources of feeling valued are self, relationships, work, and community. Naturally, they are all fluid and related. Experiences at work impact our self-esteem and nurture our aspirations. When Joseph Molesley, a footman in the *Downton Abbey* series, exclaimed "Imagine, Molesley, valet to the Earl of Grantham!" he was relishing the thought of a promotion and the prospect of higher status. We regard ourselves as more or less competent depending on the feedback we receive from our boss and colleagues. Molesley judged his worth based on the position he occupied on the hierarchy at the castle. He is not atypical. This is in line with the socio-meter theory of self-esteem, according to which self-esteem is "a marker of one's relational value to other people."[20] In Figure 1.1 we see this dynamic represented by the outer arrow. It shows the influence of feeling valued by others on our own sense of worth.

Jane Eyre, in Brontë's novel, was embraced by her new community. She felt welcomed and admired for her teaching abilities. Her students loved her. But, needless to say, not all of us experience gratitude from our neighbors. Some of us are fearful to express our opinions; even reticent to use our names. Martin Sheen, like many minorities, knew that his Hispanic name, Ramón Estévez, may present a barrier to his acting career. Other famous actors have felt the same. Krishna Bhanji became Ben Kingsley, Issur Danielovich Demsky adopted the name Kirk Douglas, and Joseph Levitch became known as Jerry Lewis.

What happens at home, at work, and in the community affects our self-perception. These actors were strong and resilient. But for every success story such as Martin Sheen, many others have succumbed to discrimination based on weight, race, color, gender orientation, disability, or just accent. In short, feeling valued is not just something that happens in our head. It happens at the intersection of our identity and the external world.

But mattering is not just about feeling valued. We have a profound need to make a difference in the world.[21] Unless you are pathologically self-centered or highly influenced by the dominant "Me Culture," you will feel a need to connect with others and make a difference in their lives. We want to add value to ourselves, others, work, and community. Shirin, a refugee from Iran who experienced discrimination because of her faith and gender, gracefully helps other people to get on with their lives. She can do anything around the house, and whatever she does she does well, with a smile, humor, and warmth. We know because Shirin worked with us at our house for a long time.

Muhammad Yunus went to Vanderbilt University, our former employer, to get a PhD in economics.[22] Yunus is a rock star at Vanderbilt, and every time he returns to campus it's a big celebration. We were still working there during one of his visits. Yunus became famous because he helped the poor in his native Bangladesh. He spent a lot of time with farmers, especially women, in rural areas. He wanted to understand their plight. Despite hard labor and long hours, most farmers were exceedingly poor. Once Yunus understood that they were poor because they were indebted to loan sharks, he went on to create the Grameen Bank, which provided loans with decent interest rates. His work lifted millions of people out of poverty, and he went on to win the Nobel Peace Prize. Yunus added value to his community and his country. He did so with ingenuity and tenacity. Like Yunus, most of us want to make a difference. Connecting with loved ones and with a higher cause makes us feel alive.

To fulfil this need and aspiration, we need to nurture self-efficacy, or the belief that we can make a difference in the world.[23] We explore how to foster this belief throughout the book.

Self, relationships, work, and community are arenas of mattering. We add value to ourselves and others through *acts of wellness* and *acts of fairness*. Shirin makes people feel well. Yunus brings fairness to the poor. Both support a "We Culture."

We should point out that the *work* segment in the mattering wheel, a big source as well as beneficiary of mattering, *does not refer only to paid employment, but to your main occupation.* Many people work but they do not receive financial compensation. You may be a stay-at-home parent, full-time student, or volunteer at a local hospital. For our purposes, these activities constitute your work. In short, mattering refers to paid or unpaid work, either at home or outside. If you invest a lot of time in parenting, studying, or working at the office, what happens while you are engaged in these endeavors has a lot to do with mattering.

Something else to note about the wheel: *all eight components are important and require attention.*[24] Exactly how much attention depends on your stage in life. But in principle, we should devote some time and effort to all of them. If you are a full-time student trying to finish a degree with a load of twenty-one credits, you naturally need to invest more time in yourself and your studies. But if you are a young mother with a three-week-old baby, you are investing more in your child than in yourself. This is expected, but at some point parents want to have an adult conversation and stop changing diapers.

We should aim to achieve two types of balance in mattering. *The first balancing act is between feeling valued and adding value.* The two must be present to experience mattering. A life of complete sacrifice without any appreciation is unsustainable and frustrating. Our ultra-social nature requires connection and a degree of affirmation. By the same token, a life of complete self-absorption is isolating at best and harmful at worst. You just have to witness the narcissism epidemic to realize that feeling valued, without adding value to others, is a dangerous path for individuals and societies. This is why there cannot be individual or collective mattering without balancing the need to feel valued with the moral imperative to add value, not just to the self but to others. This is why mattering cannot be devoid of values and responsibility.

There is a fundamental distinction between "feeling good" and "doing good." If we focus exclusively on "feeling good," we will seek mostly opportunities for hedonic pleasure, self-aggrandizement, and adulation. We will surround ourselves with sycophants. "Doing good" requires making a contribution to the community. Narcissists are not necessarily concerned with "doing good," and to the extent that they are, it is to bring attention to themselves. They are primarily concerned with feeling good. Our culture exalts winners and celebrities and foments self-admiration with selfies and self-branding.[25] It is all about feeling good. In moderation, we all need to feel good about ourselves, but the evidence suggests that a little restraint is in order. Otherwise, the culture of "me first" will never give way to a culture of "we first."

The second balance required in the mattering wheel *is among the four sources of feeling valued, on one hand; and among the four sources of adding value, on the other.* This means that we should feel valued by, and add value to, our self and others. By "others" we mean people in close relationships, at work, and in the community. Maintaining equilibrium among the four sources of mattering is important because we cannot rely just on one. Other people may show care and affection toward us, but nothing matters unless we care for ourselves too. On the other side of the wheel, adding value only to yourself will lead to selfishness.

The mattering wheel is a prescription for personal meaning and social harmony at the same time. By balancing attention between self and others, we maintain a dual focus on feeling good and doing good, on one hand, and between rights and responsibilities on the other.

This brings us to a few assumptions about this wheel that you should know about. The first one is that *human beings have a limited amount of psychological energy* to devote to any of the eight parts.[26] Think of it as an investment diversification approach. You have a certain amount of money (or psychological energy), to be invested in certain funds (aspects of mattering), and if you invest all of it in one bucket, there will be none left for others. Diversification requires a portfolio with some capital, financial or psychological, in different funds. We must pay attention to ourselves, others, work, and community.

The second assumption is that *the eight sectors are interconnected.* Too much investment in any one might detract from others. Workaholics provide a very good example. If you ignore your own needs and those of your family because you are always adding value to work, what you will get is not mattering but stress, burnout, and possibly a divorce. If you invest all your mental energy in adding value only to yourself and ignore the well-being of others, don't expect much caring in return. *We aim to have a virtuous cycle* where the benefits of feeling valued will lead to adding value.

When others make you feel like you matter, you are more likely to have confidence to play an active role in their lives. The more assets you bring to your community, the more likely you are to receive positive feedback, engendering a positive feedback loop.[27] Psychologists Jennifer Crocker, Amy Canevello, and Ashley Brown recently put it this way: "giving increases social integration and connection, which bolsters the sense that one is valued by and valuable to others .... Giving support increases people's sense that they have value to and can make a difference for others ... leading to a sense of belonging and connectedness."[28] But *vicious cycles are also possible.*[29] Growing up under conditions of neglect, where your worth is questioned, will likely result in timidity and self-doubt. Such characteristics do not bode well for making a contribution to anybody. What's more, they can lead to disease, dysfunction, and early death. Feeling valued as a child is one of the best predictors of health and wellness as an adult. Feeling neglected is one of the best predictors of disease and dysfunction.

The extent of the connection between abuse and family problems in childhood and disease in adulthood was discovered in a landmark study in the mid-1990s.[30] The Center for Disease Control partnered with Kaiser Permanente in San Diego to examine the relationship of health risk behaviors and disease in adults to exposure to abuse and family dysfunction in childhood. Over 9,500 people participated in the study. Participants were asked about early experiences of emotional, physical, or sexual abuse. They were also asked about violence against their mother in the home as well as living with people who were substance abusers, mentally ill, suicidal, or ever imprisoned. All these conditions were termed exposure to adverse childhood experiences (ACEs).

The results showed that, compared with people who had no exposure to adverse experiences, people who were exposed to four or more adverse experiences had a four- to twelve-fold increase in risk of drug abuse, depression, suicide, and alcoholism. Moreover, they also had a two- to four-fold increase in smoking, self-reported poor health, and sexually transmitted diseases. Finally, they had a 1.4 to 1.6 increase in severe obesity.

In general, the study showed that the more adverse childhood experiences people had to endure, the higher their risk for heart disease, cancer, chronic lung disease, liver disease, and skeletal fractures. These are all leading causes of death. Needless to say, when you are preoccupied with alcoholism and afflicted with serious diseases, you have less bandwidth to contribute to others and to yourself. This study provides strong evidence that feeling devalued, a clear result of abuse, neglect, and family dysfunction, is predictive of limitations in our ability to add value. Depression and suicidal ideation, experienced by many participants who were exposed to neglect, are the opposite of self-love and the antithesis to adding value. Alcoholism is so all-consuming that it limits how much people can contribute to others. In fact, alcoholics exact an incredible toll on their families.

You may be wondering: What is the mechanism through which feeling devalued gets translated into disease? The researchers asked themselves the same question. What happens is that, when you are faced with constant psychological pain, you turn to behaviors and substances that would soothe the agony. You turn to smoking, for instance, or drinking. While immediately helpful as pain relievers, chronic use results in disease, suffering, and premature death, as shown in the study. The authors explain the turn to dysfunction this way:

> Coping mechanisms appear to center on behaviors such as smoking, alcohol or drug abuse, overeating, or sexual behaviors that may be consciously or unconsciously used because they have immediate pharmacological or psychological benefit as coping devices in the face of the stress of abuse, domestic violence, or other forms of family and household dysfunction. High levels of exposure to adverse childhood experiences would expectedly produce anxiety, anger, and depression in children. To the degree that behaviors such as smoking, alcohol, or drug use are found to be effective as coping devices, they would tend to be used chronically.[31]

While this study focused on childhood and family environment, the negative consequences of feeling devalued are also very much part of the workplace and life in the community. Field studies and laboratory experiments show that when adults are excluded from a group they also respond with anxiety, anger, and even aggression.[32] Their self-esteem goes down, and they are hesitant to get involved due to fear of rejection. The less you get involved, the fewer the opportunities to add value and to get recognition in return. This is why throughout the life cycle it is crucial to help others feel valued. The mattering wheel can serve as a guide. In fact, the mattering wheel can help in two ways: through promotion and prevention.

The experience of mattering promotes health and happiness, but it also prevents personal *devaluation*, relational *disconnection*, work *disengagement*, and community *disintegration*. These four problems define the crisis of our time: the crisis of not mattering, or mattering only to ourselves. *Devaluation, disconnection, disengagement*, and *disintegration* of the social fabric is a burning issue.

The four Ds can be seen everywhere, and their consequences are devastating, for individuals and the community as a whole. Too little personal worth results in the high prevalence of depression we are currently witnessing around the world.[33] Too much personal worth results in the narcissism epidemic that has been well documented.[34] Disconnection is seen in high levels of isolation, loneliness, relational breakdowns, and extramarital affairs.[35] The costs of work disengagement in the United States, Europe, and other OECD countries is in the hundreds of billions of dollars.[36] Declining social capital and increasing inequality and segregation point to community disintegration.[37]

The four Ds stem from deficits or distortions of mattering. Countries,[38] communities,[39] and corporations that take mattering seriously are healthier and happier.[40] We ignore mattering at our own peril.

In synthesis, the mattering wheel is about two fundamental needs – feeling valued and adding value – and four arenas – self, relationships, work, and community. What happens in one arena affects the others. What happens on one side of the wheel affects the other. All eight segments of the wheel are interconnected. Mattering consists of breathing life into all parts of the wheel. All require energy and verve. It is up to you to fill the parts with your signature strengths, values, and skills. The rest of the book combines the science of mattering with the science of change. It is up to you to translate these lessons into action.

CHAPTER 2

Feeling Valued

Kenji Yoshino, a graduate of Harvard, Oxford, and Yale, knows only too well the human need for belonging and the universal fear of rejection. As a gay man in an unwelcoming society, he did not live an authentic life for many years. This lack of authenticity expressed itself in three phases: the wish to convert, the struggle to pass, and the need to cover. *Conversion*, *passing*, and *covering*, as he came to call them, were efforts to assimilate into an oppressive society.

The need to belong, and the fear of being ostracized, led Yoshino, and many other gay men, to hide their identity. Today, Yoshino is a professor of constitutional law at New York University School of Law and the Director of the Center for Diversity, Inclusion, and Belonging. His book *Covering* recounts his own struggle to fit in, as well as those of other minorities.[1] This desire has forced many people to do none other than change their names, as we saw earlier.

Growing up Jewish in Argentina, I, Isaac, had my own troubles with my last name. Before I escaped the fascist dictatorship in 1976, I had to obtain, like all thirteen-year-olds, my official ID card. To do so, I had to go city hall, stand in line, and wait for someone to call me by my last name to issue the document. I vividly remember the anticipatory fear of the looks I would get once the clerk would attempt, in vain, to pronounce "Prilleltensky." Amidst all the Gonzales, Rodriguez, and Pereira, Prilleltensky provoked great curiosity indeed.

As I suspected, when I got up from my chair dozens watched intently my approach to the counter. Objectively, there should have been no shame or fear in having any last name, except that I associated my own with the graffiti adorning the walls outside city hall: "Be a patriot, kill a Jew." Jewish youngsters like me were a clear target in the anti-Semitic campaign of the military dictators.

For some people, context can make it exceedingly hard to belong and remarkably easy to feel anxious. Due to survival, social, and existential reasons, humans are driven by two fundamental needs and two primal fears:

1. The need to feel valued
2. The need to add value
3. The fear of being devalued
4. The fear of being helpless

The Need to Feel Valued

This need derives from three motives: *survival, social,* and *existential.* The attachment of a newborn to his or her caregivers is very much a survival need. Without the love and care of parents, a baby cannot survive. The social need is expressed in the desire to belong to a group and to derive relational value from associations with friends and family. Finally, the existential motive operates through dignity and fairness. These three sets of motives are separate but complementary. They are all important. Let's see why.

Attachment

Peter, Molly, and Sara have three things in common. They love to play, they don't particularly like strangers, and they are one year old. Each of them is about to enter a room full of toys with their mother. But after a few moments she is going to leave them with a stranger. The stranger is a member of a research team studying how kids respond to the "stranger situation test." The researchers wanted to see how toddlers respond to being left alone with a person they don't know. As we shall see, each one of the toddlers reacted differently. What does that say about them? But first, let's see three typical responses.

Upon entering the room with his mother, Peter sees interesting toys that call his attention. But in addition to toys there is something else in the room: the stranger. While his mother stayed in the room, Peter was happy to explore the environment and play with the toys. However, when she leaves Peter in the room with the stranger he begins to whimper, making his way to the door. At this point he is no longer interested in the new toys. When his mother returns a few moments later, he greets her with out-stretched arms and a big smile. He is quickly comforted by his mother and is happy to keep on playing.

This situation is repeated with one-year-old Molly. Her mother also leaves the room for a few moments, leaving her with the stranger. Molly reacts like Peter. She fusses and whimpers. She protests the fact that her mother is leaving the room. She is very unhappy. But unlike Peter, when the mother returns, Molly is not easily consoled. She continues to fuss and arch her back in displeasure. She is no longer interested in the toys. She is invested in her temper tantrum.

Next comes Sara. Like the other kids she is drawn to the toys. She is aware that her mother is leaving the room, but she seems unperturbed. The toys seem more important than staying with a stranger. Sara is not too concerned when the mother leaves, but she does not acknowledge her upon her return either. She seems indifferent to her mother's comings and goings.

Toddlers like Peter, Molly, and Sara were part of Mary Ainsworth's studies on infant attachment. The American-Canadian psychologist was interested in how kids might respond to the "stranger situation test" and what that might say about them and their families.[2] She discovered that most kids fall into three categories. Peter represents the majority of infants, about 60 percent, who are *securely attached* to their parents. These toddlers may cry and complain when the parent leaves the room but are happy when they return. Furthermore, they are easily soothed. Trust in the relationship provides them with a sense of security. As a result, they are free to explore the environment around them. Infants like Peter cope well with the temporary anxiety created by the absence of the parent.

Babies like Molly, in turn, were labeled by Ainsworth *anxious-ambivalent,* and they comprise about 15 percent of the population. Infants like Molly learn early in life that they cannot rely on consistent care that is in tune with their needs. Their primary caregiver is inconsistent: at times available, at times distant. Sara belongs to the third group of kids, called *avoidant.* These babies, about 23 percent of the population, have experienced unresponsive and even rejecting caregiving. They have internalized that they cannot faithfully rely on their caregivers to attend to their needs.

Mary Ainsworth built on the work of John Bowlby, an eminent British psychiatrist, psychologist, and psychoanalyst, who formulated attachment theory to explain how interactions early in life can result in individual differences.[3] They argued that the quality of bonds we form with our caregivers early in life is highly influential in the quality of relationships we form later in life. Moreover, the type of attachment we experience with caregivers is going to impact our overall outlook on life.[4]

His theory postulated that a primary caregiver's behavior toward the infant is going to affect the child's view of the world and of herself.

A caregiver, usually a parent, who is emotionally responsive, sensitive, and available to the child is going to foster in the infant a view of him- or herself as worthy, lovable, and secure and an outlook that the world is generally a safe place. If problems occur, they will believe, other people close to me will be there for succor and support. This type is called *secure attachment* and reflects how Peter behaved in the experiment.

Securely attached children feel comfortable with themselves and take steps to explore the world around them. Moreover, they are able to regulate their emotions and solve problems. Unfortunately, not all families provide their babies with responsive, attentive, and affectionate care. Some are rejecting, while others are inconsistent.

Children who are insecurely attached to primary caregivers tend to develop one of two problematic forms of attachment: *avoidant* or *anxious*. Those who grow up feeling rejected tend to avoid close relationships and are afraid to get too close to others. They develop *avoidant attachment* style and downplay their own personal needs, like Sara. They are reluctant to engage with others in mutually supportive relations due to fear of rejection, reminiscent of earlier relationships characterized by neglect or dismissal. If they disclose personal vulnerabilities, they may get hurt because others will not show empathy or concern for their plight.

Infants with *anxious attachment* style, like Molly, have experienced inconsistent parenting, not knowing what to expect from caregivers. When parents are unpredictable or emotionally unavailable, children do not know what to anticipate, creating uncertainty. This lack of predictability is confusing and generates anxiety in children, who respond with clingy behavior. As these children grow, they worry about rejection and abandonment. They struggle to feel a sense of mattering.

Mario Mikulincer, Isaac's closest college friend, became a world authority on the topic of adult attachment. Incidentally, the two of us, Ora and Isaac, met at his house in Israel, where he hosted a drama club, almost 40 years ago. We left for Canada to pursue graduate degrees while Mario stayed in Israel, where he developed a thriving career as one of the most respected psychologists in the world in the field of personality and social psychology.

In his recent book with Philip Shaver, they define attachment security as "a felt sense, rooted in one's history of close relationship, that the world is generally safe, other people are generally helpful when called on, and I, as a unique individual, am valuable and lovable, thanks to being valued and loved by others."[5] They go on to claim that attachment security "provides a psychological foundation for easing existential anxieties and constructing an authentic sense of continuity, coherence, meaning, connectedness, and autonomy."[6] The consequences of either type of insecure attachment are grave. As Mikulincer and Shaver observe, "insecurely attached people harbor serious doubts about their self-worth and self-efficacy. They lean toward hopeless and helpless patterns ... are susceptible to rejection, criticism, and disapproval; and suffer from self-criticism and destructive perfectionism."[7]

Needless to say, attachment matters for mattering. Studying attachment in adults, Theodore Robles from UCLA and Heidi Kane from Wayne State University found that various forms of insecure attachment result in problems related to stress, excessive cortisol release, sleep problems, and even skin repair and eating disorders. For people with avoidant attachment style, a national representative sample discovered that they are more prone to experience arthritis and a host of chronic pain issues. Those with anxious attachment style had higher prevalence of stroke, heart attack, high blood pressure, ulcers, and headaches.[8]

These unhealthy outcomes derive primarily from early relationships that failed to provide the infant with a secure base, a healthy self-image, and a loving relationship. Extreme deprivation and neglect result in failure to thrive – and even death. As John Bowlby claimed, attachment is a survival need. Most children who experience insecure attachments survive physically but suffer psychologically. Without a secure attachment, children do not feel valued, and without feeling valued their sense of mattering is shaky at best. Parents who fail to provide a secure attachment are too invested in themselves to see the needs of their infants. These parents, in turn, may be the victims of a "me first" culture in which their own parents neglected them.

Knowing that their parents will be there for them in case of need, securely attached children feel free to explore the world, try things out, and form new relationships. In moments of doubt, they can go back to their parents or just invoke their presence. These children feel more valued and enjoy greater self-determination.

When our son Matan was just over two years old, we took him to a playground where he met some older kids. Feeling slightly threatened by their presence he was quick to tell them that *my daddy is over there*. Better safe than sorry!

Parents of securely attached children are able to balance their own needs with the needs of their kids. They achieve an equilibrium between their rights as individuals and their responsibilities as parents. They foster a "We Culture" in their own families.

Belonging

If the first reason for needing to feel valued concerns survival motives, the second one pertains to social drives. The need to belong is closely related to the need to matter.[9] Both derive from the need to validate our identity, and our existence, through interpersonal affirmation. In a landmark paper, psychologists Roy Baumeister and Mark Leary (1995) called the need to belong and the desire for interpersonal attachments a "fundamental human motivation."[10] They suggest that "belongingness can be almost as compelling a need as food."[11] These authors suggest that the need for group membership also has evolutionary roots.

If secure attachment to the mother accounts for the need for survival early in life, affiliation to a collective guarantees protection against enemies, scarcity, and natural disasters. However, belongingness is not just a protective mechanism, it is also a means of flourishing.[12] People form bonds for defensive as well as growth-promoting aims. There seems to be a natural inclination to seek memberships in collectives. Indeed, people are willing to invest considerable time and effort in forming and nurturing social bonds. We are evolutionarily programmed to seek a "We Culture." What we currently witness in the "me first" culture is a distortion of what humans need to thrive.

When our family moved to Australia at the beginning of the millennium, we knew very few people. But that situation did not last long. Matan, who was twelve at the time, had twin passions for soccer and chess. Thanks to his hobbies we met remarkable people and made wonderful friendships. When Isaac took him to Caulfield Park in Melbourne to register for soccer with Maccabi, our social situation made a complete 180-degree turn. We went from isolated newcomers to welcomed new members of a warm, receptive, and inclusive community.

As we stood in line to register, Isaac heard two men speak Spanish with a distinctive Argentinean accent. Isaac approached them to introduce ourselves, and within two minutes of knowing us they invited our family to a Shabbat dinner three days later. Luis Ladowsky did not hesitate to welcome us into his home and to introduce us to a wonderful group of friends. We felt instantaneous belonging. Some of them were Argentinian Jews like Isaac, others were Israeli émigrés like Ora.

Luis, a master community builder, along with his wife, Gabriela, had created a warm and welcoming group. At his house we met several other families who showed care, compassion, friendship, and reciprocity. We felt like we belonged. We had found a group of people who practised belonging every day. We made lifelong friendships with many of them.

The way our Australian group nurtured belonging was very structured. Every Friday we would get together at somebody's house for Shabbat dinner, and our kids would play together. We spent time together during holidays and Bar Mitzvahs. We went for walks and exercised together. We shared the excitement and the struggles associated with immigration. We exchanged information and helped each other adjust to the new country. Although Isaac was the community psychologist and Luis was the IT guy, Isaac learned a lot from Luis about how to build a caring community.

Just like us, people all over the world yearn for connection and a sense of community. Joining clubs and teams is associated with positive affect. The same goes for friendship and marriage. We seek affiliation, group membership, and family ties, even if it increases financial and occasionally parental stress.

The need to belong to a couple, family, or group is evident by the sense of loss that ensues from separation. This is clear in summer camps, college graduations, retreats, conferences, or family reunions. People mourn the separation and promise to stay in touch.

When we left Australia, we grieved the loss of our tight connections. Although we stay in touch through social media and the occasional transoceanic visit, it is not the same. The loss of belonging is painful and sometimes acute. The dissolution of marriage through divorce is one of the most difficult experiences people go through.

Just as belonging is a powerful tonic for well-being, exclusion is toxic for health. As Baumeister and Leary observed, "being accepted, included, or welcomed leads to a variety of positive emotions (e.g., happiness, elation, contentment, and calm), whereas being rejected, excluded, or ignored leads to potent negative feelings (e.g., anxiety, depression, grief, jealousy, and loneliness)."[13]

The negative consequences of exclusion and loneliness extend to the physical realm; so much so that mortality rates are higher for divorced, single, or widowed individuals. Fatal heart attacks are more common among lonely people, as are tuberculosis and cancer. Loneliness has also been associated with lower levels of immunity, such as natural killer cells, and higher levels of stress hormones like cortisol. It is also highly correlated with depression, unhappiness, and ill health. Among the elderly, isolation is related to higher mortality rates and increased risk for cognitive decline and heart attacks.[14] In the United Kingdom, loneliness has become such a problem that the government has recently appointed a new minister to deal with the issue.[15]

It is worth noting that people do not need a vast network of support to reap the benefits of belonging. As Baumeister and Leary observed, "people seek a limited number of relationships, consistent with the view that the need to belong is subject to satiation and diminishing returns."[16] This is what makes isolation so tragic. People do not need many acquaintances to fight loneliness; very few suffice. When partners die, or children move away, some people are able to substitute one source of love and belonging for another. That is how humans adapt to loss and grief. Yet, for some, finding new friends and lovers prove a serious challenge. The instinct to survive and the desire to belong help explain the need to feel valued. No less important is the longing for dignity.

Dignity

When Oprah Winfrey received the first Bob Hope Humanitarian Award at the Emmys in 2003, she told the following story about her father, who owned a barber shop. During holidays a lot of poor people would come to him for free haircuts and money. In many cases, these people would join Oprah and the family for dinner. When Oprah would ask her father, "Dad, why can't we just have regular people at our Christmas dinner?" her father used to say: "They are regular people. They want the same thing you want." Upon reflection, Oprah said: "At the time I thought he was just talking about dinner, but I have since learned how profound he really was because we are all regular people seeking the same thing. We all just want to know that we matter."[17]

Dignity is the backbone of mattering. The *Merriam-Webster Dictionary* defines dignity as "the quality or state of being worthy, honored, or esteemed." The feelings of being recognized, acknowledged, included, and respected for who we are or what we know provide us with dignity. They make us feel human.

To feel worthy, we have to feel that we are equal to others and that we deserve to be treated with respect.[18] We have to experience fairness in relationships, at work, and in society. Moreover, we have to be fair to ourselves. We cannot experience dignity without fairness.

We seem to be wired for fairness. As human beings we are hypersensitive to fairness transgressions – so much so that lack of fairness and rejection register in the brain as physical pain.[19] But the opposite is also true. As social neuropsychologist Matthew Lieberman notes, fairness feels like chocolate in the brain. We seek fairness and pursue dignity. We know right away when someone makes us feel valued and when someone is dismissive. We have highly developed radars for dignity.

From children's exclamations of "it's not fair" on the playground to feeling dissed by somebody at work, evidence of our sensitivity to injustice is everywhere.[20] The psychological wound inflicted in unfair treatment is very painful. We feel deprived of our humanity when we are dismissed, ignored, or devalued.

Some people have an enhanced sense of identification with all humanity, which leads them to heroic acts to protect the life and dignity of others. Chiune Sugihara, a member of the Japanese embassy in Poland, lost his job after he provided thousands of visas to Polish Jews during the Holocaust.[21] People like Sugihara display profound concern for dignity, not just their own but also for those who suffer.

Researchers from Europe and the United States show that insults to our dignity come in different ways: from pity to invisibility, bullying, and upward social comparisons.[22] Any insinuation that we are less than other people ignites circuits of frustration and anger. These assaults need not be intentional, but they are hurtful nonetheless.

After Isaac lost his parents in a car accident when he was eight years old, he became the subject of pity. People meant no harm, but the sensation of being less than other people on account of a tragedy did not sit well with him. Adults were especially bad at this. In Spanish, he was often called "pobrecito," which more or less translates into "poor soul." Kids his age, in contrast, were much more attuned to his feelings, and they never made him feel inferior or marked for life. His friend Beto, in particular, made him feel respected and appreciated – that he still mattered despite the loss of his parents. They kept playing soccer, pretending to do homework together, and visiting often. He was always welcomed at Beto's house, and indeed he spent many days there, feeling like the friendship was the one place where he did not feel pity.

As Ora and others have shown in earlier studies, people with disabilities are also often the subject of pity.[23] They are made to feel that their lives are not really as worthy as the lives of able-bodied people. The "tragedy" replaces the person, and the person becomes the disability, as opposed to the disability becoming a part of the person. These experiences cheat people of their dignity.

Ora has had multiple experiences of being asked why she's in wheelchair by complete strangers. The last time was a few months ago in the elevator in our building. The man asking the question explained that he thought he could help since he's a doctor. Waiting to board a flight together, airline personnel have asked Isaac "Can she walk to her seat or does she need an aisle chair?" rather than asking Ora who was right next to him. Ora handles these situations skillfully and assertively, but these micro-aggressions do take a toll. Dignity is not something one should have to fight for.

Constant exposure to social inequality, in a culture that extols material success, is a serious threat to dignity. It is a reminder that other people are worth more than me. These upward social comparisons, research shows, are especially pernicious for poor people. They are always primed to think that they do not measure up because they don't have the education, language, houses, cars, watches, clothes, or gadgets other people have. The social cues are everywhere, from TV commercials to social media.

To add insult to injury, some people treat the poor with utter disdain. In her compelling account of living in poverty, *Hand to Mouth: Living in Bootstrap America*, Linda Tirado discloses some of the indignities she was subjected to, among others, by bosses and government representatives. "I've rarely had a boss who gave me any indication that he valued me more highly than my uniform ... The problem I have isn't just being under-valued – it's that it feels as though people go out of their way to make sure you know how useless you are."[24] Reflecting on her interactions with various welfare officials, she emphasizes that some were highly empathic, while others were awfully rude. Asking for help, she recalls, made her feel less than human.

But make no mistake, it is not only the poor who suffer indignities. Most of us have experienced it in one form or another. It happens when the boss puts you down in front of your colleagues, when parents humiliate their kids, and when government officials make you feel subhuman. It happens in offices, families, and communities, and every time it does it erodes our humanity and enhances our dysfunction. Stress hormones flood our system and resentment ensues.

Experimental and field evidence shows that efforts to regain dignity come in two flavors: healthy and unhealthy. Some individuals build on personal assets and social resources to become resilient. Others, in turn, become more impulsive, sacrifice long-term goals for immediate gratification, seek refuge in gangs, and even resort to violence. They are trying to achieve dignity but in destructive ways. In the words of a former gang member: "When I was 18, I thought it was cool to be a gang banger. Everyone gave you respect, girls were always around and money was easy."[25]

Like a secure attachment and a sense of belonging, the need for dignity is an essential part of feeling valued. These desires meet, respectively, sur-vival, social, and existential needs. Evolution has led us to seek not only survival and connections but also a feeling of humanity, which is what dignity is about. Unless we feel valued, by ourselves and others, we cannot feel like we matter.

Pathologies of Mattering

Mattering can be overdone. We can obsess about our own importance and need to feel valued. So much so that some people behave pathologically. By pathological we mean dysfunctional: hurting self or others, consciously or unconsciously. One such pathology is behaving in ways that draw attention to yourself at the expense of others. Due to insecurity, frustration, previous neglect, entitlement, or just plain hubris, some people exhibit unrelenting self-importance, pomposity, and egotism. It is all about them. They are the embodiment of the "me first" culture. These qualities are distortions of mattering. This is a case of too much of a good thing. Feeling valued, by self and others, is good only in good measure, but for some people the only way to matter is to be number one, always and everywhere. They thrive on adulation and cannot tolerate criticism.

You can recognize this pathology in a number of ways: incessant talk about themselves, affording others little recognition, taking up too much air time, showing no interest in other people's lives, feeling entitled, praising one's accomplishments, and lacking empathy. These people are calculating and uncaring. The official term for this irksome behavior is, you guessed it, narcissism.

Psychologists Jean Twenge and Keith Campbell[26] have conducted extensive research on this personality type. It won't surprise you to learn that narcissism has been on the rise for the last four decades, with steep increases in the last fifteen years. In a major study of 16,275 college students who completed the Narcissistic Personality Inventory, considerable growth has been observed from 1979 to 2006 in the number of students identifying with behaviors related to narcissism. In fact, one in four college students who completed the inventory by 2006 answered most of the questions in the direction of narcissism. This represents a 30 percent increase from the previous two decades. When Twenge and Campbell updated their study in 2008, the sample of students went up to 49,818. With more data, the researchers discovered that by 2008 the numbers of students identifying with narcissistic tendencies has gone even higher. Using data from the University of South Alabama in 2009, a full third of US college students were showing narcissistic traits. As a point of comparison, in 1994 only one in five students exhibited these characteristics.

In reviewing data from a population of fourteen to sixteen years old, the researchers noted a dramatic change from 1951 and 1989. The item in the questionnaire was simple: "I am an important person." In 1951, 12 percent of teens agreed with the statement. By 1989, more than 80 percent of girls and 77 percent of boys agreed with it.

When it comes to adults, a conservative estimate is that one in four would experience clinical symptoms of Narcissistic Personality Disorder by age 65. What these numbers show is that you are very likely to encounter narcissists at work and in the community – if you don't already have one at home.

As Twenge and Campbell demonstrate, narcissists are manipulative, self-centered, exploitive, and uncaring. In many cases, they use people for self-aggrandizement, while others are disposed of with ease when no longer serving that function. They often acquire trophy spouses but abandon them when a better one comes along. Not surprisingly, victims of narcissists often report feeling used.

A measure of self-centeredness might be expected in young children, but it is quite distasteful and dysfunctional in adults. We are quite amazed at the lack of self-awareness some people exhibit in interacting with others, even if they are not narcissists. We have been to hundreds of cocktail parties, dinners, social events, and work meetings where we met some really fantastic people and some totally clueless ones. Perhaps you have come across some pathologically overvalued folks at work or even in your own family.

At first, if you are not aware of what is going on, you might leave an encounter with such people feeling a little down, confused, or frustrated. If you feel that way, watch out for cues of *self-overvaluation*. Does he talk too much? Does he ever ask you about yourself? Does he keep referring to personal achievements, possessions, or special connections he might have? Or is she showing off? Does she put you or others down? Does she ignore you in the hallways? If some of these patterns are recurring, you may be dealing with a case of self-overvaluation – a prototypical "me first" type.

Since life is short, you may wish to limit the amount of time you spend with these people. If you are stuck with them at work, you may have a serious problem. You may need to call their attention to these behaviors. If the person is a superior you may need to invoke their boss. Later in the book we will deal with strategies to manage conflicts affecting mattering. For now, it is useful to begin paying attention to these patterns in others and, ahem, yourself.

The Fear of Being Devalued

We are motivated by the pursuit of pleasure and purpose and by the avoidance of pain. Feeling valued is the first half of the mattering equation. Before we explore the other half, adding value, we need to explore the pain of being devalued. Just like we can feel appreciated by ourself and by others, so we can suffer from devaluation by ourself and others. Just as we seek attachment, belonging, and dignity, we are afraid of exclusion, injustice, and inequality. They are serious threats to our sense of mattering. Exposure to any of them is enough to cause significant psychosomatic turbulence.

Exclusion

Our friend Ronald (not his real name) was passed over for a big promotion. Little did he know that his indignation goes back thousands of years – a time when social rejection posed a serious threat to survival. In tribal communities, exclusion meant an existential risk. Alone, you couldn't feed yourself or defend yourself against mastodons. The pain of exclusion was not just a psychological threat but a physical one as well. Evolutionary theories link our fear of exclusion to primitive dangers.[27]

While getting the promotion would have enhanced Ronald's self-concept, its denial by no means threatened his existence. Still, the social pain is just as real as physical pain. Psychological and brain studies show that feelings of rejection activate the same neural system as physical pain.[28] In evolutionary terms, both social and physical pain are alerts of impending threats – a call to action.

We no longer face extinction by the menace of prehistoric beasts, but the fear of exclusion still reverberates in our psyche nonetheless. Our ultra-social nature impels us to live in groups, and the slightest threat to our sense of belonging can unleash chains of psychological, and even physical, damage in ourselves and others.

We can learn a lot about exclusion from baboons, who live in very hierarchical societies.[29] Low-status baboons exhibit signs of arterial clogging and other physiological damage, the result of excessive secretion of stress hormones. This is the body's response to threat. Low-status baboons face the wrath of the big baboons that dominate a clan.

While most of us living in modern cities do not fear baboons, our egos often sustain considerable wounds. Ronald had a great job and enjoyed the respect of his colleagues, but he could not bear the thought of being ignored for a position for which he was eminently qualified. He perceived the discourteous behavior of management as an insult to his knowledge and expertise in the field. He had shown that he can do the job and had been tested many times. In his mind, he deserved at least an interview. He felt ignored and justifiably upset. Some research shows that we are prone to assess our worth not just in terms of inclusion and exclusion but also in terms of winners and losers.[30] For Ronald, the whole experience reinforced his perception that he was both an *outsider* and a *loser* within his own organization.

Exclusion is an umbrella term that encompasses ostracism and rejection.[31] The former works by making people feel ignored, the latter by telling people they are not wanted. Both can be blatant or subtle. Not surprisingly, you can feel marginalized in multiple ways.

Passengers flying economy – or cargo, as our son refers to it – are often aggrieved by the privilege of those flying business. They have to wait until the elite class board the plane, and then they have to trudge through the sumptuous quarters of the rich on their way to discomfort.[32]

In Miami, we don't have to fly to feel like second-class citizens when travelling. The authorities installed in the I-95 some express lanes that require extra payment. Having travelled through that lane many times, we can estimate that there are probably a hundred cars stuck in the regular lane for every car breezing through the paying lane.

Some acts of exclusion are deliberate, such as bullying in school or the workplace; but some are innocuous, such as ignoring people in the elevator or the hallways. Nowadays, exclusion is also felt online. Removal from a WhatsApp or Facebook group can damage our social standing and self-concept. Failing to respond to an email on time can also be perceived as undermining the sender.

The disapproving gaze of your boss, let alone an open rebuke in front of colleagues, can start a process of self-doubt leading to feelings of rejection, anger, and depression. Needless to say, some people are more resilient than others to signals of disapproval and marginalization, but they all threaten our well-being nonetheless.

Some common forms of ostracism include avoiding eye contact in public spaces, keeping someone out of the loop, giving someone the silent treatment (including e-silence), and speaking a language others do not understand.[33] Exclusion is everywhere, and so are its noxious effects.

We crave inclusion and belonging so much that marginalization hurts us to the core. Exclusion generates feelings of inferiority, anger, humiliation, sadness, and shame. Feeling devalued and dehumanized are often the case.

Our basic needs for control, meaning, self-esteem, and belonging are usually threatened, and many people react aggressively and antisocially.[34]

What's more, the victims tend to engage in self-defeating behaviors, eating more unhealthy foods, taking more risks, and having problems with self-regulation overall. They are less kind to themselves and others. In a variety of studies, victims of exclusion were less likely to help others and donate money. In addition, people subjected to short-term exclusion perform poorly in cognitive tests like the GRE. The outcomes of long-term exclusion are also quite severe. They include a feeling of meaninglessness, helplessness, alienation, and depression. Suicidal ideation and actual suicide attempts have been documented. Reduced immune function and increased rates of eating disorders and sexual promiscuity have also been reported. Chronic exclusion has often led to school violence.[35]

In a study of fifteen school shootings, it was found that in thirteen cases the perpetrators were the victims of bullying or social exclusion.[36] As Williams, a leading researcher in the field, observed, "ostracized individuals report a feeling of invisibility, that their existence is not even recognized. In this case, a desire to be noticed may supplant a desire to be liked .... In order to be recognized (either positively or negatively) by the largest audience, it may be far easier to achieve this sole goal by committing a heinous act than by behaving prosocially."[37]

How people respond to rejection, exclusion, and ostracism depends on a number of factors, including length of exclusion, perceptions of intent, the value people place on the particular relationship, and, most importantly, the fairness of the situation. The more unfair the exclusion is perceived to be, the more aggressive the response is likely to become. When the victims place high value on the relationship, the exclusion is short, and the behavior is not interpreted as malicious, many people respond to exclusion by trying to regain affiliation with the group or the person. In this case people will respond prosocially. But if the marginalization is perceived as unjust, the person is more likely to react antisocially.[38]

There also seems to be a difference between the types of threat the person experiences while suffering from exclusion and the response that ensues. When our sense of belonging is threatened, most people seem to react in prosocial fashion, trying to restore the relationship. However, when our sense of control or the meaning of our life are under attack, antisocial behaviors are more likely. The assault on our sense of control and our dignity precipitate hostility. This finding relates to lack of fairness. Undermining our sense of fairness, control, meaning, and dignity become intolerable because they question our very own humanity.

In addition to prosocial or antisocial responses to exclusion, there is a third one: socially avoidant. This makes sense. Why risk another rejection? The irony is that by isolating themselves these people are bound to suffer the consequences of loneliness, which are very harmful. Isolation has been linked to depressed immune function, poor physical and mental health, and premature death.[39] In all its forms, feeling devalued is devastating to our well-being and our sense of mattering. A number of Black authors have recently documented the horrific consequences of systematic exclusion on their community, which is unabated.[40] But in addition to exclusion, there seems to be a particularly pernicious effect to being the subject of injustice.

Injustice

What is it that hurts so much about experiences of injustice? It won't surprise you to learn that it is the feeling of disrespect.[41] Since we are highly status-conscious and very concerned with social standing, acts of injustice make us feel inferior. We feel undermined and disrespected. It is an insult to our dignity and to our rightful claim to respect. Feeling disrespected is feeling devalued. In the offender's eyes, we matter less than they do. More than anything, acts of injustice make us feel that we matter less and that our emotions and thoughts count less than other people's. In some cases, these acts of injustice make us feel that our entire humanity counts less. Our existence is undermined and minimized. Wilkerson has recently documented the sophisticated ideological, legal, religious, and economic stratagems that superior castes have put in place throughout history to make sure that Dalits, Blacks, and Jews, among others, feel inferior and devalued.[42] Lack of mattering is the phenomenological embodiment of injustice.

We fear injustice not only because we may get the short end of the stick but also because our voice is suppressed and our entitlement to respectful treatment is violated. Whatever piece of the pie we get is a question of distributive justice. What role we have in making the allocation is a matter of procedural justice. Outcomes of decisions are obviously important, since they can determine whether we get a scholarship, a loan, or a raise. But no less important is the fairness of the process. So much so, in fact, that people are more willing to live with untoward consequences when they feel the process was fair and their voice was heard. Granting people an opportunity to express their opinions is a sign of respect – their views matter.[43]

Part of procedural fairness is accountability. We are entitled to know why certain decisions were made. We are owed an explanation, especially when these decisions have a big impact on our lives. We seek fairness at home, the office, and the community. Every decision made that is going to affect us requires a measure of procedural fairness, from the movies we choose to watch to the house we buy to the school we pick for our children. Family decisions require input from all participants.

People feel disrespected when their voice, needs, efforts, or sense of equality are ignored. Disregarding any of these four considerations leads to a sense of injustice. Dismissing your views sends a signal that you don't count, thereby undermining procedural justice. Neglecting your needs conveys the message that your wants are not as important as others'. Failing to take your efforts or knowledge into account says that you are not really valued here. Finally, treating you as less than equal is an assault on your dignity.

Our friend Ronald felt particularly offended by the fact that his knowledge and expertise were obviated in favor of other candidates. The message he got from upper administration was "we don't care how much you know, how much you have done, or how hard you have worked here for many years – you are not good enough for this position." His voice was suppressed because he was not given even the courtesy of an interview. His needs for recognition were thwarted, all his previous efforts and knowledge were ignored, and he was made to feel inferior.

In terms of mattering, the messages were unequivocal: your views don't matter, your needs don't matter, your efforts don't matter, and ultimately you don't matter. Needless to say, there might have been better candidates for the position, but, given the circumstances, it was particularly hurtful that he did not even get an interview.

Ronald is well-to-do and highly respected by his colleagues. Other than the missed opportunity, he enjoys many perks at work: a high salary, lots of freedom, dedicated staff who report to him, and great benefits. All in all, he had many things going well for him, and he eventually recovered from the blow.

Linda Tirado, in contrast, was the subject of disrespect at work, and, since she was poor and needed government support, she was also the target of contempt by government workers. Without any legal protections for the workplace, her boss ignored her need for time off for medical or family reasons. Without any regards from welfare officers, she was made to feel less than human. Her voice did not matter. Her circumstances did not make a difference. Linda's account of working for minimum wage is full of injustices, big and small, that many people in her circumstances endure.[44]

Compared to Ronald, she was at the other end of the economic ladder. Even though both suffered from lack of distributive and procedural fairness, Linda had far fewer resources for coping. Ronald still wore expensive clothes to work, enjoyed great medical care, had savings, and enjoyed respect from colleagues. Linda was humiliated by inconsiderate managers, made to feel insignificant by callous government representatives, and did not have medical insurance. No wonder she was upset.

Disrespect leads to anger and aggression. Insult is the principal factor in eliciting anger. Insults are regarded as unjust because they deprive people of dignity.

Victims of injustice feel that a psychological contract has been violated.[45] This contract consists of implicit expectations of fair play between people and institutions. Suppressing voice, ignoring needs, disregarding effort, cheating, and magnifying inequality are felt like breaches of contract. Whatever you feel, think, or know doesn't matter.

Following an injustice, our sense of mattering can be restored, at least partially, by sincere apologies.[46] When offenders accept responsibility and express remorse, the victim regains a measure of self-respect. In the absence of an apology, or restorative justice of some kind, victims of injustice will engage in retaliation to protect and preserve their dignity. In a "We Culture," people take responsibility for their transgressions and pay attention to fair play. In a "Me Culture," people privilege their own wellness, even if it entails violations of fairness.

We fear exclusion and injustice because they make us feel devalued and inferior. There is good reason to fear them because they can happen everywhere: at home, at work, in the community, in intimate relations, and in dealing with institutions. The risk of being dismissed is pervasive. This is why we now turn to inequality.

Inequality

While Ronald belongs to the upper class, and has many more resources than Linda, he still feels the sting of inequality from time to time. This is because inequality is both objective and subjective. Although he is quite wealthy and possesses material resources, compared to the person who took the job he coveted he feels inferior. In other words, status is not just absolute but also relative. By economic and educational measures, he has nothing to complain about. By occupational aspirations, he feels less than the successful candidate.

We are forever comparing our wealth, looks, education, occupations, and possessions.[47] We are comparing machines. This is also a vestige of evolution. In ancient times, the one with higher status procreated more and ate more. If you were a lower-status baboon, you had to watch out for your safety, lest a dominant ape steal your food and your date.

Whatever advantages might have accrued to the strong in prehistoric times, it was probably nothing compared to the spectacular wealth that the upper class enjoys today. Now there is so much more to envy: clothes, watches, cars, houses, gadgets, phones, education, and even silicon body parts.

With inequality reaching unprecedented levels in the United States, the opportunities to compare are just about everywhere. They are overwhelming, and they affect us all.[48]

Rationally, you may say to yourself that you have enough and that you are not affected by your surroundings. Upward comparisons, you may think, is for idiots. You wish! Our rational talk has no chance against our affective brain. It is just hard to train ourselves to ignore signals of inequality, especially when so many people flaunt their privilege.

Rationally, people want to live in a society where economic disparities are kept in check. That much was discovered in a study where people compared two wealth distribution graphs. One was from the United States and the other from Sweden.[49] The participants did not know that these graphs belonged to actual countries. Over 90 percent of people preferred the Swedish model, where there is much more economic equality, and that went for Democrats as well as Republicans. The vast majority of people preferred a flatter economic distribution. This is what we might want, but this is not what we have, certainly in the United States, which is among the most unequal wealthier countries.

Day in and day out we are reminded of our place in the pecking order, at home, at school, at work, and in society. We engage in comparisons automatically and unconsciously. As Payne, a leading researcher in the psychology of inequality, put it, "we can end up feeling inferior or superior without any awareness we were doing any comparing at all."[50] We might add that the consequences of these comparisons are not always pretty. They affect our thinking, our feelings, our health, and our happiness, not to mention levels of crime and overall community well-being.

If you experience lower social status, the first mechanism affecting our health is the stress-response. In efforts to protect ourselves from the indignities of poverty, the capriciousness of our boss, or plain lack of control over our lives, our bodies secrete cortisol. In the short run, stress hormones like cortisol help our system repel threats. They prime us for fight or flight. They pump us. The problem is that prolonged exposure to inequality requires chronic stress reactions that result in inflammation and diminished immune function. Stress reactions are good in small doses. Large doses inflict long-term harm to our bodies. This is why poor people die younger and get sick more often than the rich.[51]

The second mechanism affecting our well-being is risky behaviors. Inequality divides people into those with more and those with less. Some are regarded as losers and some as winners. The more inequality there is, the more people feel needier because, in comparison with the well-off, they lack all kinds of things.

To level the playing field, some people behave in risky and impulsive ways; they take short cuts, such as gambling. There is a lot of evidence that inequality leads to risky behaviors, not just in the poor but also among the middle class. The result of engaging in risky behaviors, such as gambling, is that inequality breeds even more inequality because people take risks that rarely pay off.

In a study comparing the extent of risky behaviors involving sex, drugs, and money across states, Payne found that "inequality was a strong predictor of risk taking, which in turn was a strong predictor of health and social problems."[52] In international comparisons, wealthy countries with higher levels of inequality experience more crime, mental illness, obesity, infant mortality, and premature mortality than rich countries with less inequality. In a comparison of twenty rich countries, the United States fared the worst.[53]

Exclusion, injustice, and inequality make us feel that we matter less than others. Being devalued is associated with a series of negative outcomes, ranging from depression to aggression to a whole host of medical and social problems. This is the bad news. The good news is that there are proven ways to help people feel like they matter, at home, in relationships, at work, and in the community. In Chapter 4, we will review a series of strategies and skills that can be learned. Later, throughout the rest of the book, we examine their relevance and application in different aspects of your life.

CHAPTER 3

Adding Value

The Need to Add Value

To matter, it is not enough to feel appreciated and recognized. Being valued is a necessary but insufficient condition for mattering. To feel fully human, and to matter, we need skills and opportunities to add value, to make a contribution, to ourselves and others.[1] In short, we need to move from a "Me Culture" to a "We Culture." In the latter, we pay attention to wellness *and* fairness, to personal interests *and* the common good, to feeling valued *and* adding value, to rights *and* responsibilities.

Having a voice is crucial in judging the fairness of a situation.[2] It is also essential in adding value. It is part of being noticed. We can't add value without voice and visibility. We need to be present, physically and psychologically.

There are numerous ways to make a contribution. We can offer gifts of the heart, the head, and the hand.[3] We can provide emotional support, ideas, or tangible help. When it comes to adding value to our own lives, we can increase our happiness, study new things, find meaning in life, and develop physically and spiritually. There are really countless ways to make our life more exciting, goal-oriented, virtuous, and passionate, and it is up to each one of us to discover what actions will make that happen.

Needless to say, our opportunities are influenced by the environment we live in. Some social ecologies are more supportive than others, but the aspiration to add value remains, regardless of the particular context. This is why we devote later a great deal of attention to changing conditions, not just understanding their impact.

The needs to make a difference, to master the environment, and to express ourselves are well ingrained in all of us. We yearn to be in control of our destiny and to learn new skills. This is obvious in child development. Babies relish the opportunity to feed themselves, while toddlers marvel at

45

the art of walking. The glee of conquering challenges is there for all to see. As we grow, we continue the search for new skills and paths to potentiate our talents. Most of all, we want to make a difference, in our lives and the lives of others.

Two well-established psychological theories attest to the universal need to add value: self-determination and self-efficacy. These two drivers can be applied to a variety of domains, from relationship-building to sports, from learning a new language to performance at work. Both reflect something fundamental about human beings: our motivation to be engaged, express ourselves, manifest our agency, and have a purpose. When these needs are thwarted, we matter less.

Self-Determination

Shirin came to the United States as a refugee from Iran. There, she was a member of the Baha'i faith, a persecuted minority. As a woman, she did not enjoy the privileges of her brothers, who were sent abroad to the United Kingdom and the United States to study. Her former husband did not wish to grant her a divorce, despite an unsatisfying relationship. She lost all she had when she decided to come to the United States.

Shirin has three kids, and before escaping Iran she made sure that her two sons and her daughter were safely relocated to the United States. Unlike her parents, who favored her brothers and afforded them prospects she did not have, Shirin made sure that her daughter was well looked after.

When she came to the United States Shirin experienced a decline in socioeconomic status. Whereas she was middle class in Iran, here in Florida she had to work for low wages for a home health-care company. We were privileged to meet Shirin because she helped us with various things around the house. She worked for a company that Ora contracted to provide us with some help. Although her pay from the company was not great, Ora always found a way to compensate her properly for her enormous help to us.

For us, Shirin embodies self-determination, the drive to lead a self-directed life. Although she grew up under oppressive conditions, as a woman and a persecuted minority, she very much took charge of her life and looked after the well-being of her kids under adverse circumstances. She sought and obtained control of the direction of her life.

Shirin is intelligent, capable, affectionate, helpful, and funny. We just loved having her around. Eventually she left Miami to help one of her kids who had a baby. Being the extraordinarily dedicated mother that she is, she felt the need to be close to her family. She is very much enjoying looking after her grandson. All her kids are doing very well in the United States. They all studied and have good jobs.

Although she is obviously smart and talented, Shirin was working at a low-paying job because of the difficulties that beset many immigrants. She sacrificed a lot for her kids, working double and triple shifts, driving from house to house as a home health-care worker. Yet she enjoyed helping others and making a difference in people's lives. Her positive presence lit up the room. She derived genuine pleasure from helping people in challenging circumstances. For her, adding value was second nature. Despite her own troubled history, she had an amazing predisposition. She mattered a great deal to all the people she helped, and that made her feel like she had a purpose in life.

Shirin embodies the three human qualities captured in self-determination theory: she was *autonomous, capable,* and *relational.* According to Ryan and Deci,[4] the famed psychologists who developed the theory, we thrive when we experience autonomy, competence, and high-quality relationships. The satisfaction of these needs predicts wellness and vitality.

Autonomy refers to the ability to behave according to our values and interests. When we experience autonomy, we pursue a course of action that is determined by us, free from psychological or physical coercion. We lead a life that we believe is worth living, not the life that someone or something imposed on us. We feel that we matter when we experience autonomy over our decisions and actions.

Competence is a manifestation of our need to master the environment and feel effective. Without competence we cannot make a difference. To function productively in the world, we need to know how to perform certain actions that are grounded in knowledge. But to operate effectively, we need more than formal education – we need to know how to manage ourselves and how to manage other people. Although these are called soft skills, we can hardly think of more sturdy skills than knowing how to deal with self and others.

To matter, we have to feel competent in some areas of life. None of us are experts at everything, but all of us must feel good at something. This something can be parenting, soccer, teaching, carpentry, or surgery. The area of expertise can be as varied as human predilections, but to matter we must feel that we are making a contribution in some area of life: at home, at work, or in the community.

The third pillar of self-determination theory is relatedness, which speaks to the need to establish meaningful and supportive social connections.

Without them we feel lonely, like we don't belong and we don't matter. Shirin is a master relationship builder. She exhibits empathy, caring, and compassion. She is affectionate and warm. If we just concern ourselves with our own advancement, we neglect the need to add value to others, which is a central part of mattering.

An obsessive focus on the self, at the expense of prosocial behaviors, typically derives from efforts to compensate for earlier deprivations. Environments that thwart our needs for autonomy, competence, and relatedness lead to dysfunction. Materialism and status-seeking behaviors reflect insecurities based on early experiences of rejection or neglect. Antisocial behaviors usually emanate from controlling and cold environments, while perfectionistic tendencies are efforts to get love through displays of competence.[5]

Healthy environments are those that support personal choice and autonomy, encourage skill acquisition, and show love and affection. Unhealthy settings exact unrealistic demands, pose overly challenging tasks, and fail to provide warmth and affection. Growing up in healthy environments facilitate thriving and flourishing. Growing up in unhealthy ones predisposes people to negative outcomes such as obsessive pathologies, self-preoccupation, depression, conduct disorders, impulsivity, and in certain cases eating disorders and paranoid personalities. The impact of context cannot be overstated, for it can lead to pathological efforts to matter – or internalization of messages that we will never matter.[6]

Self-Efficacy

To get from perceived need to action, we have to believe that we can make a difference. Self-efficacy is the belief that we can take action to achieve certain outcomes.[7] Self-efficacy is essential to adding value to our lives and improve the well-being of others. When self-efficacy generalizes across fields, we can say that we are self-confident. Without the belief that we can make a difference, we cannot get out of bed, finish a degree, polish our resume, go for a jog, or eat more vegetables.

The confidence in our ability to achieve goals makes us resilient in the face of adversity. We are better able to cope with stress and vulnerabilities. When applied to health habits such as physical activity and proper nutrition, self-efficacy predicts longer, healthier, and happier lives.[8]

Like autonomy, competence, and relatedness, self-efficacy can be nurtured or impeded by more or less favorable environments. Albert Bandura, the progenitor of this influential notion, identifies different sources of self-efficacy. The first one is experiences of mastery. Nothing like success to bolster our confidence. But achievements must be based on challenging tasks that require perseverance. Accomplishing easy tasks does not build resilience. Perseverance in the face of adversity builds self-confidence and grit.

The second way through which we build our own efficacy is through exposure to successful role models. If John can do it, I bet I can do it too! If John made it through great determination and perseverance, perhaps I can do that too!

Social persuasion is another way to build our self-efficacy. But this should not be confused with vacuous praise. Good teachers structure situations for learners where the latter can experience progressive success. By scaffolding opportunities for success, good teachers show students that they can do it.

Self-efficacy can be general as well as specific. Some people may doubt their prowess in the physical arena but exhibit great confidence in intellectual pursuits. Self-efficacy can also be enhanced, as our research team recently demonstrated in a study to promote wellness. Exposure to an online program we created, Fun for Wellness (www.funforwellness.com), resulted in improved self-efficacy in the wellness domain. Other studies have demonstrated improvement in self-efficacy in scholarly, sports, and occupational realms. In short, self-efficacy is essential for mattering, and more importantly, it can be bolstered.[9]

Autonomy, competence, and self-efficacy can be applied to many pursuits that provide us with a sense of meaning. The need for self-determination requires self-efficacy. Needs require competencies, and competencies lead to activities that produce meaning.

Meaning

Viktor Frankl acted according to his principles.[10] Despite imminent danger, he chose to stay in Vienna to look after his parents. Although he could have fled to the United States, he made a decision to remain in Austria. A few months after he let his US visa lapse, he was sent to Auschwitz in 1942.

Fifty years later, in the preface to the 1992 edition of his famous book *Man's Search for Meaning*, Frankl, a Jewish psychiatrist, recounts the dilemma he faced. Had he immigrated to America, he could have continued to develop his thriving career. But doing so would have meant abandoning his mother and father. He chose responsibility over opportunity. He paid dearly for his choice: several years in concentration camps. He embodied a "We Culture." In the concentration camp, he felt it was his responsibility to look after other prisoners. He derived meaning by focusing not only on his own survival, but in helping others. His life had meaning because he mattered to the many inmates he was helping. He had a clear role adding value to others, who, in turn, made him feel valued. In line with his experience, recent studies suggest that mattering may be the most reliable predictor of meaning in life.[11]

Before the war Frankl had been working on a book on the pursuit of meaning. When he returned from the extermination camps, he wrote *Man's Search for Meaning* in nine days. By then, his wife and parents had perished in the hands of the Nazis. He credits his own survival to the love for his wife, his commitment to his work, and to the meaning he attached to his experiences. He needed to survive the horrors of the war to bear witness and share with the world what had happened.

During the Holocaust, under dehumanizing conditions and ignominious treatment by the SS, he was kept alive by two dreams: to be reunited with his wife, and to continue his work. He transported himself to a better future, a future that gave him hope. The moment his fellow prisoners gave up hope, he knew they were going to die. Many of them died of exhaustion, starvation, or disease. Those who were not assigned to slave labor were murdered in crematoria. Against all hope, he tried to infuse hope among his friends, but few could be heartened.

Man's Search for Meaning became an inspirational best seller, with more than twelve million copies in print. The book was translated into twenty-four languages. The main idea was that under any circumstances people can make a choice to act with dignity and responsibility. The evil Frankl suffered was *beyond* his control, but his reactions to it were *within* his control. This concept gave birth to logotherapy, a system of healing through the search for meaning.

It is difficult to ascertain how many could endure what Frankl did, even if they did have a goal, a meaning, and a purpose. But the lesson was clear. For most of us, who are not facing the horrors of the Holocaust, the choice to take responsibility for our actions must not be squandered. He took responsibility for his parents when he could have escaped. He then took care of his fellow inmates when he was close to starvation himself.

None of us can really tell how we would have behaved under these conditions. Frankl might have been one in a million. But his point was that even under *favorable* conditions, people often relinquish responsibility. His message was that we have an obligation to ourselves and others. That obligation is to add value – in other words, to find meaning in pursing personal and prosocial goals. Frankl would argue that this responsibility holds regardless of the toxicity of the environment.

Meaning comes in many forms, and is derived from many sources. Most thinkers agree that having a purpose in life provides a sense of meaning.[12] In addition to mattering, Frankl was motivated by a clear purpose; to bear witness, to finish his book, to be reunited with his family. Purpose can relate to personal, interpersonal, or social aspirations. Raising a family, finishing a degree, following a tradition, acting according to one's values. These are examples of personal goals. Showing caring and compassion are instances of relational pursuits. Fighting injustice and discrimination combine passion with purpose. Nelson Mandela was in prison twenty-seven years for his convictions. These are all instances of adding value, to ourselves and others.

Meaning is derived from actions, in the pursuit of goals, based on justifiable values. If excellence is a value, we shall strive to do our work with distinction. If fairness guides our lives, we shall fight injustice at home, at work, and in the community. If your goal is to be an exemplary parent, your actions shall be guided by nurturance and patience. It is not always easy to keep your cool with your kids, but the meaning derived from being a good parent justifies the effort (we think).

The connection between actions and values is essential. Actions devoid of values don't build meaning, while values devoid of action remain abstractions. For some, meaning derives from esthetic, creative, and artistic pursuits; for others, from devotion to a particular faith. For many, meaning ensues from the relationship with the people we love.

In *Meanings of Life*, psychologist Roy Baumeister claims that we derive meaning from a sense of purpose, self-worth, a value-system, and efficacy.[13] These elements are synergic. Purpose provides a direction, values justify our actions, and efficacy makes it all happen. Self-worth has dual roles. It generates action and, in turn, benefits from action. Feeling valued motivates us to engage in even more prosocial behavior, which is going to reward us with satisfaction and recognition. The pursuit of self-worth without a value-system and a sense of purpose feeds right into the dominant "me first" narrative.

The role of efficacy and control cannot be underestimated. Exercising control is at the heart of adding value. We add value by exerting control over our actions and the environment. Frankl could not direct the course of events in the concentration camp, but he could control his reactions to it. Mandela was in jail for nearly three decades, but within the confines of his cell he could control his behavior, establish an exercise regimen, and maintain mental sharpness.[14] Both men were guided by a dream of liberation. In the direst of circumstances they regulated their feelings, thoughts, and behaviors, as much as humanly possible. This sense of control was vital for survival.

Judith Heumann, a disability rights activist, had to fight two colossal bureaucracies:[15] first, with the New York City school system, after they denied her a license to teach because she used a wheelchair; second, with the federal government to pass legislation to facilitate inclusion of people with disabilities. She organized the longest takeover of a government office in the history of the country. Heumann showed remarkable determination and tenacity in her pursuit of better lives for people with disabilities. She resisted tremendous pressures and exerted great leadership in the pursuit of her goals. Her actions helped to spark the movement that would eventually result in the legislation of the Americans with Disabilities Act. She was guided by a clear set of values. She found meaning in her purpose. She mattered to the community of people with disabilities.

If Judith Heumann helped ignite the disability rights crusade, Rosa Parks played a central role in the civil rights movement. She made history when she went to jail for refusing to cede her seat to a White man in the first row of the Black section of the bus on December 1, 1955. That was not the first time that Parks had shown great determination to fight discrimination in Montgomery, Alabama. In 1945 she became one of the few Black members of the community who was registered to vote. She had been denied that right twice before because the registrar had failed her in the obligatory test. These acts were not sudden rebellion. In June 1955 Parks had participated in a summer workshop at the Highlander Folk School in Monteagle, Tennessee. She had also been the secretary of the Montgomery chapter of the NAACP from 1943 to 1956.[16] Like many other Black women, she added value to the fight against injustice and oppression; she found meaning in liberation work. Her work mattered to millions of African American citizens.

Many women played essential roles in humanizing the treatment and education of vulnerable people like migrants, farmworkers, minorities, and the poor. Women like Jane Adams, Dorothy Day, and Victoria Earle Matthews before them fought the educational, criminal justice, and welfare systems to procure compassionate care for people who were deemed not to matter.[17] Their lives mattered to the many they helped – just the way supporters of the Black Lives Matter movement find meaning in honoring the lives of George Floyd, Breonna Taylor, and Ahmaud Arbery.

Very few achieve recognition the way Parks, Adams, Day, Heumann, Frankl, or Mandela did, but most of us are engaged in meaningful activities nonetheless. We experience meaning when we focus on our work, teach our children values, or support our friends. Indeed, many people experience meaning, and the more they enjoy it the better off they are.[18] People who report having a sense of meaning in life claim that life has significance, that their lives makes sense, and that they have a clear purpose. Those who report a high sense of meaning are usually happier, have more life satisfaction, are more engaged at work, and have a sense of control over their lives. In contrast, those who report little meaning in life experience more negative affect, depression, anxiety, suicidal ideation, substance abuse, and workaholism. The data are clear: we must find ways to add value and to derive meaning. We must translate values into action.[19]

The belief in our ability to make a difference is crucial for adding value and making meaning. *How* we add value, and to *what* we add value, depends on values such as caring, equality, solidarity, autonomy, and kindness. But before going any further, we should clarify the two meanings of the word *value* in this context. When we talk about *adding value*, we refer to making a contribution, making something or someone better. We can add value to a relationship by investing time and interest in the other person. We can add value to a social cause, fight climate change, and promote racial justice.

On the other hand, when we talk about values such as *freedom, fairness,* and *equality,* we refer to ethical principles that guide our behavior. Some people may adhere to the value of White supremacy, but this would not fit our definition because it is not an ethical value. Others may claim that selfishness is the only way to get ahead, but this would not fit our description either. Ethical principles are supposed to advance personal, relational, and communal well-being at the same time. They are not supposed to advance the personal at the expense of the communal. Different cultures privilege either the individual or the common good. And some societies fluctuate over time. In the United States, the last three decades have seen a steady retreat from the common good, but a healthy society requires that we add value to ourselves and others: not one or the other, but both.[20] This is why the mattering wheel prescribes a balance between personal and communal goals. It is the only way to build a sane and just society.[21] Meaning, then, must be derived from the pursuit of personal and communal values, the essence of a "We Culture."

There are *approach* and *avoidance* motives for pursuing personal and communal goals at the same time. An *approach* motive generates some good; an *avoidance* motive prevents something bad. On the *approach* side, the pursuit of personal goals makes us happier, fulfilled, focused, and engaged. The pursuit of common goals, in turn, generates feelings of belonging, solidarity, friendship, and reciprocity.[22] There are bene-fits in approaching both goals, individual and social, together. By adding value to others we are helping them and helping ourselves at the same time. Generosity works both ways, for the giver and the receiver.[23]

There are also good reasons to avoid the single-minded pursuit of exclusively private or communal goals. The exclusive interest in private pursuits can easily degenerate into selfish behavior, while the exclusive quest of communal aims can suppress autonomy. Too much compliance with preordained traditions and norms can easily undermine self-determination. This is why many people leave oppressive cults and cultures; they are suffocating. It is a delicate balance to achieve, though. Rigid communities suppress freedom, but too much freedom can erode the common good.

The genius of the French Revolution was to offer values that bridge between personal and communal good. Liberty, equality, and fraternity correspond, respectively, to personal, communal, and relational values. Liberty is analogous to autonomy and self-determination. Equality speaks to the need to foster a community where everyone has the same worth. Fraternity, in turn, is the bridging value. If we care about each other, and we care about the community as a whole, we should uphold relational values like fraternity, solidarity, and belonging. Healthy societies pay attention to all of them. Equality without liberty robs people of their unique identity, whereas liberty without equality sends the message that certain groups are not as valued as others. Fraternity, in turn, reminds us to create bonds of solidarity and mutual help. There is no belonging without fraternity. Whereas freedom and equality may be regarded as human rights, fraternity represents human connection. Rights, without bonds of warmth and affection, create walls. Fraternity, instead, creates bridges. The mattering wheel functions at its best when we pay attention to the trium-virate of liberty, equality, and fraternity.

When individuals and corporations are not subjected to any kind of limits they can engage in selfish, destructive behavior.[24] This tendency is exacerbated when fraternity is absent. The erosion of social capital and neighborhoods accounts, in part, for the polarization between values of freedom and principles of justice. One political camp focuses on justice, while the other concentrates on personal liberty. To reconcile the two tendencies we need more dialogue, which, in itself, is a way of adding value to ourselves and society.

The Fear of Being Helpless

We dread helplessness and hopelessness because they prevent us from adding value. We fear them because they threaten our sense of mattering. Much like a sense of control is vital for wellness, loss of control is inimical to it. The feeling that no matter what we do we cannot change a particular outcome, for ourselves or others, is distressing, disturbing, and demoralizing. Loss of predictability increases stress and the feeling that we don't matter. To learn how to prevent, and eventually overcome, these feelings, we need to understand helplessness and powerlessness.

Helplessness

In the movie *I, Daniel Blake*, the main protagonist suffers a heart attack. Doctors forbid him to return to his carpentry job, and he is required to go on welfare. Although the movie takes place in England and shows the impersonal treatment he gets from British officials, the story could be anywhere that people come into contact with bureaucracies, especially those that stigmatize recipients of services.

Daniel applied for certain benefits and was rejected. During the movie he struggles with helplessness and hopelessness as he tries, in vain, to get a hearing with the "decision maker" to appeal the judgment. It is painful to watch how Daniel becomes depressed over the lack of control over his life. Bureaucrats ignore doctors' orders, force him to look for jobs when he is not physically ready, and demean him time and again. Daniel sells most of his possessions to get by while waiting for financial support from the authorities.

Eventually Daniel gets a hearing and a lawyer guarantees to him that he will win the case. However, Daniel has a second heart attack and dies just before he walks into the appeal. The outcome is terribly unfortunate – but not unpredictable. Helpless people get sicker and depressed in response to uncontrollable environments.[25]

Helplessness ensues when people are confronted with uncontrollable events. If you are trying to change a situation but nothing is changing no matter what you do, you are going to feel despondent and helpless. This phenomenon has been extensively studied, and its relation to depression is well-established. Further studies on hopelessness demonstrate that the presence of negative thoughts about yourself exacerbates the impact of the situation even further. What's more, there is evidence that self-deprecating beliefs are tied to early experiences of emotional abuse.[26]

The loss of control creates an overall psychological sense of loss. People feel anxious, confused, and incompetent. This condition can be created in laboratory situations where research participants are given unsolvable tasks like puzzles. After the experiment is over, participants are told that they were tricked into believing they were incompetent, but the temporary descend into depression is very noticeable nonetheless.[27]

Outside the lab, if you are exposed to helplessness-inducing situations chronically, the outcomes are not just temporary despondence but serious mental and physical problems. In the landmark Whitehall Studies involving thousands of British civil servants, Michael Marmot discovered that lack of control predicted no less than premature mortality.[28] Thinking and feeling that you have less control than others can result in compromised immune systems, more cortisol, more inflammation, and overall more sickness.

Since these studies were conducted in a highly stratified environment, Marmot was able to show that the less control you have, the more disease you experience. When you divide the workforce into four status groups, as Marmot did, it turns out that the second group from the top experiences double the rate of disease as the top, the third group about three times as much, and the last group about a fourfold increase. This natural experiment showed that there is actually a social gradient of disease and distress. The more status you have, the more control you possess over your life, and the more protected you are from all kinds of threats afflicting your well-being.

Gone are the days when the boss claimed that he – and most bosses are still a *he* – suffered more stress than his employees. Yes, managers have decisions to make, but overall they have much more freedom and latitude than the rest. Yes, administrators have a lot of demands placed on them, but they exercise much more control over their lives than the people they command will ever know.

Some events create helplessness in traumatic ways, such as hostage situations, but many others are much less dramatic. A dismissive gaze, an ignored email, and a sarcastic comment send you the clear message that you are not valued. Persistent and pervasive negative feedback on your work is telling you that you cannot add value: that no matter what you do, it does not matter much at all.

Of all the threats to mattering, helplessness is one of the most serious ones. Feeling that you cannot help yourself or others escape pain and suffering has enduring negative effects. Helplessness and lack of control are magnified by powerlessness. Perceived lower status engenders powerlessness, which, in turn, ignites hazardous chain reactions, from making you feel devalued to dying prematurely.

Powerlessness

Power can be used for good or ill. Power can be objective, as in the control of tangible resources; but it can also be subjective. The perception of power plays a huge role in health and well-being. We are forever comparing ourselves to others on various matters of status: beauty, wealth, education, connections, occupation, and possessions. We do this automatically and without even noticing. People react differently to encounters with rich or poor people. Some may pose a threat to our own status and prestige; some may enhance it. When we compare ourselves to people we perceive more powerful we assume a defensive posture, trying to protect our dignity and self-esteem.[29] If our self-concept is secure, we are not easily threatened by interactions with more powerful people. Therefore, we use the opportunity to enjoy a good conversation, learn about the other, and build new connections. However, this is only half of the equation. The other party is responsible for making us feel at ease or ill at ease. If our conversation partner engages in self-aggrandizing, name dropping, or other types of entitled behavior, even our most secure selves will take a hit.

Individuals are not equal on all measures. Some are more accomplished in one domain than others: some are taller, while others may be faster. What leads to a sense of powerlessness is not these obvious differences but rather how they are played out. Encounters characterized by equalizing efforts reduce the perception of power differentials. If you hold a senior position in the company and come into contact with assistants, you have a chance to maximize power differentials or strive for an egalitarian relationship based on how you treat others. The key is to engage in mutually enhancing relationships where both sides show positive regard, ask questions, listen genuinely, and express caring. Power differences will never be completely erased, but there are better and worse ways to manage them.

The problem is that the more people acquire power, the less virtuous they become.[30] As they accumulate titles, money, and signs of prestige, the more entitled they behave. Studies have shown that powerful people violate rules more often, are less courteous on the road, display ruder demeanors, and overall tend to ignore the needs of others. In short, they diminish the dignity of others while basking in the glory of their privilege. As they augment their importance, they weaken others.[31] They embody a "Me Culture."

Power-plays are ubiquitous. They happen at home, at school, in the playground, in the office and at cocktail parties. An easy sign of pomposity and self-importance is how long people talk and what they talk about. If your partner is engaged in a monologue, rather than a dialogue, you may be in the presence of someone powerful, clueless, or both. Poor people tend to be kinder, more empathic, and more compassionate. Powerful people tend to be arrogant and pretentious. Of course there are exceptions, but there are also rules, and studies confirm the rules.[32]

Exposure to chronic powerlessness – at home, at work, or in the community – can lead to mental and physical wounds.[33] If you belong to a minority, or if you are poor, you face more threats, and if you do you are going to experience more stress. Acts of discrimination, small and large, create hypervigilance, which, in turn, leads to the release of cortisol and a plethora of damaging physiological reactions. Reduced physical, cardio-vascular, intellectual, and sexual performance often accompany chronic exposure to stress. Anxiety, depression, and panic attacks are more common among the poor.[34]

If you are poor, you are likely to live in a noisier, more polluted, and more dangerous part of town. A constant state of stress results in damage to certain regions of the brain involved in planning and goal pursuit. As Dacher Keltner recently put it, "powerlessness undermines the individual's ability to contribute to society .... . Powerlessness robs people of their promise for making a difference in the world."[35] This outcome derives from preoccupation with illness and reduced band-width. If you are afflicted with digestive, immune, respiratory, and cardiac problems, not to mention discrimination, you are going to have less cognitive and emotional resources to engage with others in the community, which, paradoxically, is going to increase isolation.

Helplessness and powerlessness emerge when we cannot add value. The lack of either control or status unleashes negative chain reactions that diminish our dignity, self-worth, and capacity to make a difference. To matter, we must find ways to make a difference, conquer self-efficacy, advance autonomy, and minimize helplessness and powerlessness. These are dynamics affecting all of us in our role as either promoters or blockers of mattering. To embrace the former and resist the latter, we need to acquire some skills. To them, we now turn.

CHAPTER 4

Ways to Matter

There are many ways to matter, but some are better than others. We want you to be as efficient and successful as you can in the pursuit of mattering. This is why we introduce in this chapter seven levers that can help you feel valued and add value. These levers are based on scientific studies of how people change, achieve goals, and improve their overall well-being.

The levers you are about to learn are the result of a challenge we posed to ourselves: If we had to teach people effective strategies to improve their lives, what would they be? We had rules for this exercise. We could not come up with a list of twenty-five things because nobody can remember twenty-five things. Instead, we had to come up with a short, memorable list of strategies. Research shows that most people can retain seven things at a time, so seven was our upper limit. Also, the strategies had to have science behind them: they had to have been tested in real-life scenarios, with positive results. The strategies had to be applied to a wide set of issues and challenges. Finally, since people change in different ways, we had to offer a menu of options that could appeal to various appetites. Some people engage in a process of change by interpreting events in new ways, while others achieve goals through behavioral means. Some rely heavily on other people; others go it alone. We knew that no single theory of change could account for individual predilections or, for that matter, help all people. As a result, we had to integrate the best of multiple approaches. This exercise gave birth to the BET I CAN method.[1]

BET I CAN stands for *B*ehaviors, *E*motions, *T*houghts, *I*nteractions, *C*ontext, *A*wareness, and *N*ext steps. When it comes to mattering, you can easily see that it involves all the BET I CAN levers. For instance, we can add value by doing something (behaviors), relating to people in certain ways (interactions), and shaping the community where we live (context). In turn, we can feel valued through emotions or thoughts. Our plans to add value, or feel valued, as the case may be, always require awareness of our situation, and next steps.

We first tested the BET I CAN model in a randomized controlled trial (RCT) with healthy adults. The goal of the study was to teach people how to use the BET I CAN levers to improve any of the following aspects of their well-being: *I*nterpersonal, *C*ommunity, *O*ccupational, *P*hysical, *P*sychological, or *E*conomic (I COPPE). The results were very encouraging.[2] We discovered that people who use our BET I CAN intervention (see www.funforwellness.com) report greater satisfaction with their interpersonal, community, psychological, and economic well-being. Participants also engaged in more concrete activities to improve their interpersonal and physical well-being. Finally, participants also reported higher levels of self-efficacy, which is the belief that you are capable of making meaningful changes in any of the I COPPE domains of life. This study, which included 479 adults, showed that it is possible to generate meaningful changes in well-being and self-efficacy by using the BET I CAN model.

We then tested the BET I CAN model in a second RCT with a population of 667 people with obesity.[3] The results were also positive. With this group, there were reports of better physical and community well-being after the intervention. Participants also reported improvements in their occupational and psychological well-being. The latter was mainly due to enhanced feelings of self-efficacy in these domains. Of crucial importance to this group, after thirty days of using the BET I CAN strategies, participants achieved greater self-efficacy in the physical activity domain, which, in turn, led to greater physical activity thirty days after the intervention ended. Finally, participants reported better physical and mental health status.[4]

Across the two studies with 1,146 participants, we learned that the main way people improve their well-being is through self-efficacy. We found that growth in the belief that they can achieve desirable goals was crucial for improving their health and wellness. But we didn't just tell people to use their behaviors, emotions, or thoughts to improve their self-efficacy. That would not have helped. We had to break down the BET I CAN levers into specific skills. Each letter of the BET I CAN model encompassed two skills. This is what we taught our research participants in the two studies:

Behaviors
- Set a Goal
- Create a Positive Habit

Emotions
- Cultivate Positive Emotions
- Manage Negative Emotions

Thoughts
- Challenge Negative Assumptions
- Write a New Story

Interactions
- Connect
- Communicate

Context
- Read the Cues
- Change the Cues

Awareness
- Know Yourself
- Know the Issue

Next Steps
- Make a Plan
- Make it Stick

Our studies, as well as many others, demonstrate that BET I CAN skills can be successfully applied to improve well-being and self-efficacy. We learned that BET I CAN improves interpersonal, community, occupational, psychological, physical, and economic well-being. These are all crucial aspects of mattering. One of the main ways to matter is through the cultivation of interpersonal well-being. The same goes for occupational and community. If we feel capable in the occupational sphere, we are very likely adding value to our work. If we feel satisfied with our community, we are enhancing the chances of mattering to our neighbors.

We can add value to ourselves by creating positive habits, such as regular exercise. We can feel valued by connecting and communicating warmly with others. We can add value to our work by changing negative cues in the environment, such as norms of disrespect. You can alter your surroundings to make them healthier. For instance, you can remove junk food from your cupboards to avoid temptations. (Changing food cues is a very good strategy for losing weight, by the way.)[5] Every single one of the fourteen BET I CAN skills can be applied to a mattering goal. The goals can be directed toward self-improvement, organizational effectiveness, or social change. Let's see how.

Behaviors

Do you feel like you matter? Do you help others to feel like they matter? Do your habits support mattering? To feel valued by, and add value to, our self and others, we must engage in certain behaviors. Thinking about mattering is not enough. People come to love us and to trust us through our actions, not our thoughts. We feel capable and agentic through specific behaviors.[6] Positive routines can fight helplessness and foster belonging, meaning, and self-determination. The question is how? The answer is through setting goals and creating positive habits.

Set a Goal

To enrich your life through mattering, you have a few options. If you go back to the mattering wheel in Chapter 1, you can see that there are eight important segments to choose from. To make life easier, let's start with choosing to focus on either feeling valued or adding value. Once you have picked one of the two, the next step is to focus on one of the four important entities of life: self, others, work, or community. Let's say you picked adding value to others. Your goal is to make a particular person feel good about him- or herself. It may be your mother, whom you don't call often enough; or your girlfriend, who feels neglected due to your crazy schedule. Or perhaps you want to add value to yourself. Or maybe you want to add value to the community by joining a social cause, such as one promoting the rights of gender minorities, the fight for a living wage, or the battle against climate change.

There is really no shortage of ways to add value and to feel like you matter. Notice, however, that mattering does not mean heroic efforts to save humanity. While some people achieve great transcendence through bravery and courage – Rosa Parks, Ella Baker, Dr. Martin Luther King, Nelson Mandela, Gandhi, Cesar Chavez, Rigoberta Menchu, Muhamad Yunus, Malala Yousafzai – most of us feel a sense of mattering by engaging in simple acts of kindness and competence. Society absolutely needs giants of justice, but it also needs caring human beings who may never achieve fame. The goal is to achieve not prominence but mattering, and mattering can be attained by looking after someone frail, teaching kindergarten, or being a great carpenter. The last thing we want is to create a mattering neurosis: the worry that, if you don't achieve some kind of celebrity status, you are a failure. Nothing could be further from the truth.

Everyone wants to matter, and everyone can achieve it in vastly different ways. Our aim here is to help you achieve a goal that will make you feel like you matter, to yourself and others. Our aim is not to feed the frenzy of fame, which is so much part of the "Me Culture."

Studies show that there are five simple rules in formulating goals. They apply to general as well as to mattering goals.

Make it meaningful. The first rule is to set a goal that is authentic and congruent with your values.[7] Do not pursue a career just because your parents want you to. You may find yourself making a lot of money and being miserable. One of our son's friends is a very successful lawyer who makes a lot of money and absolutely hates his corporate job.

To make a goal meaningful, we assume that you know what you want and that you know what you stand for. This is no simple feat – especially in light of social pressures that tell you what to think – but totally necessary. If your goal is to become a great chef – even though this may not be a popular career choice among your friends or family – then that may be a way for you to feel like you matter. You cook for other people, you make them feel good, and they thank you for it.

An authentic goal is one that is congruent with your values and not with someone else's. Before pursuing a certain path in life, ask yourself the following two questions:

- Is this what I really want?
- Is this an ethical choice?

If you answered both affirmatively, chances are you picked an authentic and defensible goal. Some goals are hard to achieve, such as getting a graduate degree or becoming an excellent violinist, but knowing that this is what you really want will help you overcome barriers. By establishing a clear link between your long-term goal and your short-term actions will motivate you to stick with it. Ask yourself who you are doing this for? Is it for your kids, for your spouse, for the community, for yourself? Images of a better future, for you and for them, will make the goal sustainable.

Make it SMART. There is a difference between your long-term goal and your near-term steps.[8] You have to break down the long-term goal into small sub-goals. You don't get a degree by saying "I will study hard for the next four years." You need a plan to tackle each course, each assignment, and each test.

Whether you want to add value to yourself through a new diet, savings plan, or meditation routine, you need to identify one specific step towards that goal. Without a concrete plan of action, your goal will remain illusory. This is why you need to make your goal SMART: *S*pecific, *M*easurable, *A*ttainable, *R*elevant, and *T*ime-Bound.

Make it real. Having a meaningful and SMART goal will help, but let's be real: setbacks are bound to occur. It is best to plan for barriers and impediments along the way. The more prepared you are for stumbling blocks, the easier it will be to get back on the horse. Studies show that having a contingency plan for addressing barriers will help you achieve your goal.[9] If you cannot go the gym on Thursday due to an unanticipated work meeting, plan to go on Friday. Contingency plans help with persistence.

In the real world, there are many competing demands for your time and attention. Having an implementation plan, with specific times and places in which you will engage with the desired behavior, will greatly enhance the chances of sticking to your goal. Your goal may be to complete an assignment, go to the gym, call your mother, take your boyfriend on a date, read a book, or practice your guitar. It really doesn't matter what the specific goal is. The more you make your steps toward your goal automatic, the easier it will become.

There is a lot of empirical evidence that specific implementation plans facilitate engagement with goal-oriented behavior. Examples include going for a much-dreaded colonoscopy, recycling, getting a flu shot, and finishing assignments. The more specific the plan (when, where, what, for how long), and the more detailed the contingency plan (if X, then Y), the higher the likelihood of success.[10]

Make it positive. Certain addictions and negative behaviors may get in the way of your mattering goal. You cannot find time to spend with your family if you are a workaholic. You cannot find time to study Spanish if you are addicted to social media. Research shows that instead of framing goals as the reduction or elimination of a negative behavior (less time on Facebook and Instagram, fewer drinks, less junk food), it is better to frame your mattering goals in the positive: more time with family, more time to relax, becoming proficient in Spanish.[11] Think what your life would be like if you achieved your mattering goal. How will you feel? How will your family feel? Framing the goal as the healthy opposite of your problem behavior will be more inspirational than aiming to curtail an addiction.

Make it about the process. Once you have framed a SMART and meaningful goal in positive terms, and you have made concrete implementation plans, it is time to focus on the process. The process is the system of working toward your goal. If you follow the system – at this time and place I will engage in this specific behavior for a certain period of time – the goal will take care of itself.

If you focus obsessively on the outcome you may get discouraged. You do not master Spanish in a week, nor can you run a marathon because you exercised for ten consecutive days. If you focus on the process and the system you put in place, outcomes that are within your control will eventually materialize. Do not get discouraged if it takes a little time.[12] If you want to make a change in the world, focus on what you can do and what is within your control. Some changes, like reversing climate change, will take a long time. The same goes for eliminating inequality. Identify a SMART goal that you can work on, make it meaningful, and make it real. That is our best bet for contributing to others, work, and the world. If you can say to yourself the following, you probably found a good goal:

- I am fully engaged with my goal
- I feel great about doing it, even if it's difficult from time to time
- I see how my goal relates to my values and my identity as a person
- This is important to my sense of mattering in the world

In contrast, if you can say to yourself any of the following, the goal you set may not be the best for you:

- I think this is what my family wants me to do, not really what I want to do
- I feel social pressure to do this
- I don't think this is really me
- I don't see how this relates to my values

Create Positive Habits

Good habits are repeated actions that bring about predictable positive results.[13] The best way to achieve some of your mattering goals is to make helpful habits. Many of us have started something, like spending quality time with our kids every day, but few of us continue. There is a joke, often attributed to Mark Twain, that quitting smoking is easy; indeed, he did it a thousand times. Like him, many start quitting, but few stick with it. Many start exercising, few keep it up. Many start volunteering, not many return. The trick is to turn a positive behavior into a habit, not into a false start. How can you turn a phone call to your mother into a routine? How can you say a good word to your employees on a regular basis and not just during festive occasions? There are two principles that have proven useful in maintaining positive habits.

Know your habits. Most habits, good and bad, happen automatically and outside of our awareness. We brush our teeth automatically after we get up. This is a good thing. We snack on junk food every day: doughnuts, cookies, and potato chips are just irresistible. That is a bad thing. They are there, so we eat them. To eliminate your bad habits (ignoring emails from your colleagues, procrastinating on work assignments, eating junk food, yelling at your kids) and reinforce good ones (showing kindness and respect to your colleagues and family, eating mainly fruits and vegetables, learning new things), you have to become a detective. Find out what things you do automatically and how they relate to your goal (saving more for retirement, becoming more productive and compassionate, volunteering in the community, eating more veggies).

Keep track of your daily behavior. Like a detective, you are after clues. What situations elicit a positive habit? Under what circumstances do you engage in negative habits? To do that, you need to know your ABCs.[14] *Behaviors* are usually preceded by an *Antecedent* and followed by a *Consequence*. These are the ABCs of habits. If you plan on responding to emails after dinner, but as soon as you get on your computer you go on social media, the antecedent is social media, and the ensuing behavior is procrastination. You may experience a momentary good consequence – satisfying your curiosity about the whereabouts of friends and celebrities – but the long-term consequence of procrastination is not good. To alter a habit you can modify the antecedents. Make sure there is no social media when you get to the computer. This is a way to suppress a negative behavior. Put your gym clothes next to your bed so that you remember to exercise every morning. This is a way to augment a positive one.

You can also work on consequences. If you feel good about sticking to your workout routine, reinforce yourself. You can tell yourself that you are becoming the person you want to be: healthy. If you made an effort to listen attentively to your employee's concern, celebrate the fact that you are becoming an empathic boss. You can also reward yourself in other ways. Get up and go for a walk if you just worked for an hour straight.

Some rewards for negative habits are so tantalizing, however, that it is better to avoid the antecedent altogether. The cookie jar on the kitchen counter, the automatic notification of a sale at your favorite store, a text from your best friend – these cues release dopamine in your brain, a powerful neurotransmitter that turn us into reward-seeking machines. It is better to control the antecedent than fighting your willpower. The chocolate fudge cake in front of you will win every time.

When it comes to mattering, you can conduct a mattering audit of your life. Out of the eight regions of the mattering wheel, is there one where you feel particularly vulnerable? Is it work, or is it your relationship with your spouse? Are you experiencing self-determination, mutual respect, fairness, and a sense of community in your life? To feel valued and to add value we need to be engaged. First, we must be engaged in meaningful activities that nurture ourselves. Second, we need to be engaged with others in mutually supportive ways. Engagement starts with concrete habits, such as asking your wife how she is feeling at work and listening attentively to your friends.

To sum up, set a mattering goal, like making someone else feel valued, and make it meaningful, real, and SMART. Focus on the process and frame your new habit in positive terms. Know your automatic habits, and know the antecedents, behaviors, and consequences associated with it.

Emotions

Emotions play an important role in mattering because they can promote either a positive or a negative loop. The presence of positive emotions can make you feel valued by yourself and others. This, in turn, will generate more positive feelings. The presence of negative emotions, on the other hand, can make you feel unworthy and prevent you from adding value, either to yourself or to others. The less you add value to self or others, the fewer the opportunities to feel like you matter, and the higher the likelihood of experiencing yet more negative emotions. A few examples can illustrate these loops.

Practicing mindfulness, recognizing your strengths, expressing gratitude, savoring good moments, and finding the silver lining in difficult situations will result in positive emotions. You will feel good that you are present and aware of your gifts. You will get an emotional high by expressing gratitude to a friend or former teacher. These positive emotions will make you more creative, social, happy, and intelligent. These are distinct ways of adding value to yourself, those close to you, your work, and the community. In addition, you will feel valued by yourself because you have just inventoried your gifts and positive attributes. The more you feel valued by yourself, the more likely you are to contribute to the happiness and mattering of others. So positive emotions are a fabulous resource. But beware of negative emotions.

Negative emotions such as rejection, fear, failure, disappointment, and anger can diminish your sense of mattering in two ways. First, you are not adding value to yourself or others by acting angrily or feeling depressed. Second, you are feeling unworthy because you failed an exam, did not get a promotion, or were dumped by your boyfriend. If you are not feeling good about yourself, chances are you will not make a contribution to yourself to get out of a bad situation. So, negative emotions can be really toxic if they are not properly managed. When the effects of positive and negative emotions on mattering are taken as a whole, we realize that we need to find avenues to cultivate positive and manage negative emotions.

Cultivate Positive Emotions

There is a lot you can do to increase your sense of mattering. Cultivating positive emotions will not only improve your sense of mattering, but it will also be fun. Positivity is associated with happiness, health, generosity, empathy, and better outcomes overall in relationships and work.[15] Positive emotions can broaden our horizons, make us more creative, and help us with problem-solving – excellent mattering pathways. Negative emotions, on the other hand, will constrict our thinking. If you are feeling really angry or fearful, all your psychological energy goes to the person or situation creating adversity; not much is left for innovative thinking about your problems.

Consider positive emotions as fuel for your intellectual, social, and psycho-logical engines. The more you experience them, the higher the likelihood of mattering. There are a few ways to cultivate positive emotions.

Celebrate your strengths. All of us have strengths. We rarely pause to take stock of our gifts, yet it is an important exercise. Recognizing strengths, in yourself and others, is associated with higher levels of happiness, increased productivity at work, enhanced performance, and lower levels of depression.[16] Yes, we should try to correct weaknesses, but it is more powerful to focus on strengths. There are a few things you can do to elicit your strengths and celebrate them:

- Compile a list of your positive attributes and describe how you use them
- Recall in detail a situation in which you used one of your signature strengths
- Consider new ways in which you can apply your strengths
- Think about ways in which other people benefit from your strengths

Creating an inventory of your strengths and reflecting on them will help you feel valued. It will remind you of the many contributions you make to the world. You may be generous, kind, creative, courageous, organized, athletic, or conscientious. You may excel in relationships, intellectual pursuits, humor, music, or tennis. Whatever you excel at, take a moment to cherish your virtues.

Develop an attitude of gratitude. Expressing gratitude is the quintessential mattering exercise because it contributes to someone else's well-being, and in doing so you are also helping yourself.[17] Both giver and receiver benefit fiom expressions of gratitude. Sending a letter to a former teacher who helped you, appreciating the meal your husband prepared, and thanking a colleague for a job well done are simple acts of gratitude. The more that goes into it, the better. The more details you describe in your expression of gratitude, the greater the benefit. Don't just say thank you in a robotic voice. Refer to particular events or acts that you are grateful for. There is more than common sense behind this recommendation: there is scientific evidence. Expressions of gratitude are good for your health and wellness and for your interpersonal well-being. It is also associated with kindness toward others, empathy, and forgiveness.

Benefits derive not just from expressing gratitude to someone else but also from simply writing things you are grateful for in a journal. Even counting your blessings is helpful. People who engage in these practices report higher levels of life satisfaction. In one study, participants were organized into three groups. The first one was asked to keep a gratitude journal. The second was asked to list daily hassles. The third group did not receive any intervention whatsoever. Compared to the other two groups, the journal group were more energetic, exercised more, reported fewer physical ailments, and were more hopeful.[18] The following can help you increase your positive emotions:

- Take a few minutes each week to recall the things that you are grateful for in life
- Write a letter of gratitude to someone who has helped you
- Call a relative or a friend and thank them for something they did on your behalf

Savor the moment. Pause, pay attention, relish and enjoy the moment. A focus on regrets of the past or worries about the future can rob you of opportunities to savor the present.[19] As John Lennon wrote in "Beautiful Boy," a song about his son, "life is what happens to you while you're busy making other plans."

You don't have to wait for an idyllic vacation to relish the moment. There is a lot of research on the benefits of being present-oriented and savoring the little things in life, from your first cup of coffee in the morning to your baby's smile. Savoring is the act of extending and intensifying the pleasure of an experience. Focus on it, eliminate extraneous distractions, and think about how beautiful this moment is. Although it doesn't have to be anything grandiose, it does help to spice up your routine with surprise and variety.[20] When planning a special event, you can enjoy the anticipation, delight in the moment, and reminisce about it in the future. Consider the following:

- Recall a beautiful experience you recently had and identify what made it special
- Think about an exciting upcoming event and share your enthusiasm with someone who can partake in your joy

Find the silver lining. We cannot go through life without adversity. When it strikes, many people show not only resilience but also a remarkable ability to see the silver lining.[21] Post-traumatic growth and benefit finding describe the capacity to discover something positive in hardship.[22] Divorce, illness, and the death of a loved one impose on us a heavy toll. Yet it is possible to find something positive in them. People report becoming more empathic, resourceful, and grateful as a result of adversity. In addition, they report a heightened appreciation of life's precious moments and an ability to let go of minor aggravations. Consider the following:

- What can you learn from people who experience serious loss but remain optimistic in life?
- Have you or someone you know experienced growth as a result of a hardship?

By celebrating your strengths, expressing gratitude, finding the silver lining, and savoring the moment, you can add a healthy dose of positive emotions to your life. When you do that, you are becoming happier, healthier, kinder, and smarter; and your sense of mattering in the world goes up.

Manage Negative Emotions

Managing negative emotions is crucial for our well-being. A good place to start is a Native American legend.[23] In the story, a Cherokee grandfather is teaching an important lesson to his grandson. "A fight is going on inside me," he said to the child. "It is a terrible fight and it is between two wolves." He continued by saying: "One is full of anger, envy, sorrow, regret, greed, arrogance, self-pity, guilt, resentment, inferiority, lies, false pride, super-iority, and ego." The other wolf, he said, is "full of joy, peace, hope, serenity, humility, kindness, benevolence, generosity, truth and compassion." After listening attentively to the elder, the grandson asked: "Which wolf will win?" His grandfather answered: "The one you feed."

The wisdom of the elder has been confirmed in empirical studies documenting the negative effects of rumination, and the positive effects of understanding, acceptance, and self-compassion.[24]

Understand your emotions. Emotional literacy consists of the ability to identify and label different emotions. Are you angry? Disappointed? Frustrated? Rejected? Content? Happy? The more we are able to differentiate among the range of positive and negative emotions, the better our response will be. Understanding what is going on inside us is the first step in regulating our affect.[25] Instead of reacting impulsively in anger or self-dejection, labeling emotions can help us analyze their origins and consequences. Once you know what you are feeling, you can monitor your typical responses. What do you usually do, think, and feel when such emotions take a hold of you? Where are they coming from?

If you manage to study your emotions the way a scientist would, you would be better able to control their repercussions. Instead of gyrating inside your body and soul like a storm, with regular practice these emotions can be accepted and tamed. You don't have to be a victim of your emotions. You can prevent these negative feelings from hijacking your brain by growing self-awareness. Understanding can lead to acceptance and constructive action.[26] Instead of using drugs, alcohol, or food to blunt negative emotions, you can learn how to deal with them. You don't have to blame or isolate yourself. Take time to grow your awareness and practice acceptance.

Practice acceptance. We all experience negative emotions from time to time. It is part of being human and being alive. Pretending they don't exist, or that you are not affected by them, will only intensify their grip on you. Once you have learned to label your different emotions, you can practice accepting them. A proven strategy to accept your negative emotions is through mindfulness. This approach claims that negative feelings and thoughts can be accepted rather than feared or fought.[27] Identifying, labeling, observing, and accepting your negative emotions are effective ways to control their consequences. What you need to control is your behavior, not necessarily your emotions. It is okay to feel angry, but it is not okay to act violently. It is okay to feel rejected, but it is not okay to drink to oblivion. The act of acceptance will help you be more in control of your emotions, thoughts, and actions.

Take action. You know the kind of things that will not be productive: acting out, addictions, rumination, avoidance, denial, and isolation. What constructive action can you take in the face of an emotional storm? You can start by setting a good goal, the way you learned earlier in this chapter. The goal can be to analyze the antecedents, behaviors, and consequences associated with negative feelings. You may recognize unhealthy antecedents in your environment. Perhaps you are involved in a toxic relationship that needs to end.

Maybe your work is making you sick. Do you work in a highly stressful environment? What behaviors and feelings follow these antecedents? Do you feel depressed, angry, unworthy?

Sometimes the best thing to do is to change the antecedents. If you do that, the negative feelings will dissipate. Instead of sinking into dejection or rumination, you can create a list of possible solutions to the situation. Being proactive and taking control of the situation is a key ingredient in healthy coping. Generate as many possible solutions as you can, and consider their pros and cons. If you change the antecedents and the behaviors, chances are you will get a different outcome.

While you are in the midst of an emotional storm you may not be able to act so rationally as to generate lists of pros and cons. In that situation, you can practice mindfulness meditation and acceptance. In addition, it is good to get social support. Call someone you trust, someone who knows how to listen nonjudgmentally. Social support is essential in coping with adverse situations. Some things you will be able to change; some others you may need to live with, such as a chronic condition, as in the case of Ora, or the fact that Isaac lost his parents when he was eight years old. When change is not possible, acceptance is desirable. The trick is to know the difference, as expressed in the serenity prayer: *God, grant me the serenity to accept the things I cannot change, the courage to change the things I can, and the wisdom to know the difference.*

To summarize, negative emotions are inevitable, but your reactions to them are not. You can be in control of your emotions by analyzing their antecedents, practicing acceptance, and seeking support. The more we take these steps, the more we interrupt the vicious cycle of negativity and unworthiness. If we don't intervene, some folks will become helpless, while others will become ruthless. In either case, mattering goes down. Needless to say, in some cases these strategies will not suffice, and you will need professional help. If you feel that way, do not hesitate to reach out for help. Sometimes we require external assistance to get unstuck. In that case, seeking professional counseling is the most constructive action you can take.

Thoughts

Humans are interpreting machines. We are constantly interpreting ourselves, the environment around us, and other people's actions. We are thinking machines, but we are not infallible machines. In fact, our thoughts and perceptions are often distorted. What we think does not always resemble the facts on the ground. Despite evidence to the contrary, if we fail a test we may think we are a failure. If we don't get the job we wanted, we may arrive at the conclusion that we are incompetent. If we are ignored in the hallway of our dorm by an acquaintance, we think we are unpopular. There may be a lot of evidence that we succeed most of the time in tests, that we do pretty well at work, and that we have a wide social network, but sometimes thoughts play tricks on us and we tend to believe them, even if there is evidence to the contrary.

Negative thoughts such as *I'm a failure*, *I'm unlovable*, and *I'm incompetent* can diminish our sense of mattering really fast. Thankfully, psychologists have learned a great deal about how to challenge negative assumptions and how to write a positive story about ourselves.[28]

Challenge Negative Assumptions

An email from your boss that she wants to meet with you can increase your anxiety. What have I done wrong? If your friends are getting together without you, you jump to the conclusion that they are excluding you because they don't value your friendship. But what if your boss wants to meet with you to praise your work and ask you to mentor a junior colleague? Or what if your friends are getting together to organize a surprise birthday party for you? In both cases your faulty attributions caused unnecessary anxiety. But in both cases you were wrong. To prevent misleading appraisals we need to learn how to challenge negative assumptions.

Consider multiple interpretations. The first task is to realize that thoughts are not identical to reality. We can interpret situations in multiple ways. If you are caught up at work and need a little challenge, you will welcome a new assignment. But if you are behind, the new task may be considered a curse. What you think changes from situation to situation. What others think of you and the world is also context-dependent. The acquaintance who ignored you in the hallway may have just gotten a text from her mother that her brother is in the hospital. She might be reasonably preoccupied with her sibling's condition. Your acquaintance was not responding to you but rather to the situation. In other words, there isn't a single version of reality, and we need to be open to multiple interpretations.[29]

Check the evidence. The second step is to check the evidence for your negative thoughts. Are you really incompetent because you did not get the job you applied for?[30] Have you considered the fact that 450 people applied for the job and that some of them have much more experience than you have? Have you forgotten that you were promoted three times in the last seven years? What about the fact that you ended up first in your class in college? If earlier we asked you to act like a detective, now we are asking you to act like a lawyer. Ask yourself what is the evidence for your negative thoughts. Do these events really mean that you are incompetent and unlovable? Upon closer examination of the facts you realize that your interpretation is incorrect. Catching a bad thought is important because it can interrupt a negative loop. Negative thoughts often lead to negative emotions and negative behaviors: my friends are getting together without me because they don't like me (thought); I feel sorry for myself (feeling) and am not going to initiate contact with them ever again because they are inconsiderate (behavior). A perception of rejection leads to feelings of dejection, which, in turn, leads to isolation.

Recognize cognitive errors. Because of depression, anxiety, or earlier experiences of failure or rejection, some people are prone to biased thinking. They tend to interpret events in a negative light, filtering out alternative explanations.[31] These people often commit one or more of the following cognitive errors:

- *Catastrophizing*: expecting the worst possible outcome of an event
- *Shoulding*: constantly telling yourself that you should be doing something and criticizing yourself for not doing it
- *Overgeneralizing*: thinking that one setback will affect all aspects of your life, for the rest of your life
- *Polarizing*: engaging in all or none thinking. If my project is not perfect, it is worthless!
- *Filtering*: perceiving yourself and events around you through a negative filter and ignoring positive experiences
- *Labeling*: applying negative labels to yourself and others (lazy, inconsiderate, stupid), instead of thinking that you or someone else just made a mistake
- *Personalizing*: thinking that other people's behaviors have something to do with you
- *Emotional reasoning*: thinking that your emotions are a reflection of reality. If you feel anxious, there must be real danger around the corner. If I feel stupid, I must be incompetent.

Relate differently to your thoughts. Just like negative emotions are inevitable, some negative thoughts are also unavoidable. However, this doesn't mean that we have to believe these thoughts any more than we have to believe our emotions. In fact, thoughts, like emotions, are only mental events that flow through our mind. They cannot harm us unless we let them.[32] If we relate to our thoughts as mental events as opposed to literal truths, we can see that they come and go and that we can even accept them without getting hurt. We can get some emotional distance from our thoughts and analyze them the way a scientist would – as a phenomenon worth exploring, as opposed to a monster to run away from.

Write a New Story

To make sense of our lives, we create stories. Sometimes the stories are positive, as when we create a narrative of mattering: I feel valued most of the time, and I add value to myself and others. When one or both of these elements are absent from our story, however, we are likely to feel despondent or disappointed with ourselves.

Storytelling is a way to organize our thoughts, experiences, and feelings in coherent ways.[33] We link social and mental events in a sequence to give them meaning. The good thing about stories is that they help us organize the world in meaningful ways. For example, we link daily routines with our identity and our goals. So, instead of questioning the existential meaning of having to go to work every day, we tell ourselves a story that we are conscientious, that we have certain goals in life, and that these goals require investments of time and effort in a job. We tell ourselves that we contribute to charity because we are caring people. We link our identity with our actions and thoughts in ways that allow us to function effectively. It would be very chaotic to question every action, every thought, and every chore. Instead, we create grand narratives about ourselves, others, and the world, and these help us go about our business.

When the narratives help us feel valued and add value, everyone benefits. But when our stories fixate us or others in dysfunctional patterns or identities, it is time to consider a new story. To author a new story about your life, it is useful to challenge negative assumptions. Consider the following scenario. A friend of ours grew up in a house of Holocaust survivors. Her parents went through the war and experienced horrendous trauma. As a result, their ability to parent was impaired. They were not able to create a nurturing environment for their child. They conveyed messages of inadequacy to their daughter. She could never be good enough for her parents. As a result, our friend grew up with a story that she will never be good enough, period.

If you hear denigrating messages often enough, you internalize them and they become part of your story. A voice within your head tells you *I'm unlovable, I cannot do math, I'm uncaring, I'm inconsiderate, I don't know how to prepare a meal, I will never amount to anything.* When you review all

the negative messages that people punish themselves with, often unconsciously, they fit neatly into two categories: *I'm not a worthy person*; or *I'm
incompetent.* Think about all the prejudicial messages that circulate in our
culture: *Girls cannot do math, Jews cannot be trusted, immigrants steal our
jobs, poor people are lazy,* and the like. Research and history tell us that
minorities often internalize these messages, perpetuating an oppressive
story.[34] It is much easier to think that poor people are lazy than questioning
structures of injustice. It is much simpler to blame women for not being
assertive than to challenge male dominance.

We all play a role in storytelling. When we don't challenge stereotypical
stories about ourselves or others, we play the role of a passive audience,
providing tacit consent. *Qui tacet consentit* is a Latin phrase meaning
"whoever keeps silent consents." If you don't challenge oppressive narratives about yourself or others you are relinquishing your moral obligation.
You cannot let dominant figures in your family or community colonize
your mind with stigmatizing notions. You have to author a mattering story
about yourself and others. There are psychological ways to do that.

Question the dominant narrative. Similar to challenging negative
assumptions, we have to question the grand narrative that shapes our
lives.[35] In the Italian movie *Happy as Lazzaro*, a tobacco landlord manages
to isolate sharecroppers from the rest of the world, keeping them in virtual
slavery. When by chance a policeman comes to the village to investigate
a possible crime, he looks in disbelief at the condition of the poor farmers.
When he questions them about their condition, they reply that they *belong*
to the marquise, and they have to follow her orders. It never occurred to
them that they can escape or contemplate another life. In many ways, a lot
of us fail to imagine a more empowering scenario.

The first step in challenging the dominant narrative is to *separate the
problem from the person.* In the movie, sharecroppers could not separate
poverty from their personhood. They thought that their decrepit conditions had to do with their personal and communal deficiencies.
Abused children and oppressed people often think that they *are* the
problem. Instead of locating the problem in the *external* world (abusive
parent, systemic poverty, human rights violations), they come to believe
that they *embody* the problem. Children are especially vulnerable to this
automatic pairing of problem with person.

Find exceptions to the negative story. To persuade yourself and others that
the problem is different from the person, find exceptions to the narrative. If
the dominant conversation is that you are unlovable or incapable, think of
situations in which you defied the stereotype.[36] Are there situations in

which you demonstrate strength and ability? The more exceptions you find to the oppressive story, the better able you are to challenge convention and compose a healthier narrative.

The fact that you have a problem does not mean that your entire life is problematic, or that *you* are problematic. Consider situations in which you were able to resist or overcome the problem.

- What precisely did you do to resist the problem or stereotype?
- When and where did this happen?
- Who benefited from your actions?
- What enabled you to behave in ways that made you feel like you matter?

By finding exceptions to the negative story you begin the process of re-authoring your life. Is it true that you cannot do anything? Is it true that you don't deserve to be loved? The very act of contending with oppressive conditions is an act of dignity. Finding exceptions to totalizing depictions of yourself as either unworthy or incapable provides evidence that you are resilient and have strengths. As Toni Morrison said in her book *The Source of Self-Regard*, we find meaning in agency.[37]

Imagine a better future. Just like writers compose various scenarios for their characters, you can imagine a future free of your burdens. What would that look like? What would it feel like to get rid of this affliction? This visioning exercise is crucial. You may come to the realization that *it is not you who is the problem, but the situation.* You may be entrapped in an oppressive relationship, or you may be the subject of social injustice. What would it take for you to leave such a relationship? What can you do to challenge lack of fairness?

Act a new story. Ultimately, competence is realized in actions and not just in thoughts. If you wish to act according to your values, you will have to take some concrete steps. If you value self-determination, you will have to do something to break the chains of oppression.[38] If you value fairness, you will have to do something to protect the rights of vulnerable people. Granted, acting a new story is much harder than imagining a better future, but to make the task doable you can use proven techniques to help you with setting goals and creating new habits. You do not have to wake up one morning and tackle all the challenges in your life at once.

Interactions

Mattering is mainly about interactions. When you look at the mattering wheel in Chapter 1, you can see that six out of the eight segments of the wheel have to do with other people – feeling valued by, or adding value to, others, work, and community. The nature of these interactions will determine, to a large degree, how we value ourselves and what we do to grow as human beings.

Some people destroy relationships because they are narcissists or aggressive. But many others ruin relationships simply because they lack skills. Being a nice person is definitely not enough. We know plenty of kind and caring people who are clueless about how to maintain, let alone nurture, a satisfying and reciprocal relation. We start with communication skills because without them there is not much chance of building a firm connection.

Communicate

By now you've heard all the research about the importance of verbal and nonverbal communication. What you haven't heard much about is the importance of pressing the pause button before you even begin to interact with someone else.

Pause and edit. Being the reactive creatures that we are, interactions trigger in us all kinds of responses. Depending on our level of affect regulation, we may consider our responses carefully or react impulsively. Most of us react automatically to perceived slights or minor offenses. Many people alternate between defensive and offensive mode. Their goal is to win an argument as opposed to having a meaningful conversation.

If you think of your life as a movie, and you are the director, one of the most useful things you can do is press *pause* before you respond to other people and *edit* the movie. Your first impulse may be to say "you are an idiot for thinking that" or "you always, always, always, make the same mistake." If you could press the pause button on the movie of your life and edit the scenes, you would probably want to delete impulsive outbursts and find better ways to dialogue. Some couples especially are hooked into negative communication patterns. They do not even see the repercussions of their sarcasm or derision. It is all automatic, and it happens in a split second.

Being able to press the pause button and edit your responses is what psychological flexibility is all about.[39] If you are able to monitor your responses, as opposed to acting automatically like a robot, you would consider some of the following:

- What response will reflect my values?
- How will the other person respond to my reaction?

- Why do I get upset every time my wife raises a particular issue?
- What is my goal here, to win an argument or to build a lasting relationship?
- How can I edit my response so that I avoid needless escalation of conflict?

At every juncture in the conversation, there is an opportunity to take control of your reactions. Your exchange with your friend may not have started well, but that doesn't mean that you have to keep adding fuel to the fire. Also keep in mind that the pause button applies not only to what you say and how you say it but also to your body language and facial expressions. Knowing about the importance of nonverbal communication in theory is no guarantee that you will apply it in practice.

Listen carefully. People often focus on what they are saying, or will say, in a conversation. They are so focused on their own speech that they fail to listen to the other person. Being a good listener is absolutely essential to nurture satisfying relationships.[40] When you grant other people an opportunity to express their views without judgment, you are giving them the gift of mattering. How simple and how scarce! Good listening is in very short supply in families, workplaces, and society as a whole. Instead of engaging in a mutually enriching experience, many people concentrate on scoring points for their brains or self-image.

A few simple skills can make you a better listener:

- Ask open-ended questions, such as "tell me what it was like working on the project" or "what went through your mind when that happened?"
- Give people uninterrupted time to tell their story
- Stay with the story and do not ask distracting questions
- Refrain from judgment

Express yourself. In reciprocal relationships both parties have an opportunity to express their views. If you want the relationship to be healthy, you will pause and edit your listening as well as your talking. You always must have two goals in mind: to express your views and to build the relationship at the same time. If you only care about the former, the latter will suffer, and vice versa. The trick is how to add value to yourself, the other person, and the relationship at the same time.

Starting with "I" statements is a very prudent beginning. Instead of saying "you are always late and it makes me furious" you can say "I prefer to be on time and would appreciate it if next time we could plan accordingly." Also, refrain from character assassination. Instead of saying "you are just beyond repair" to your sister, you could say "when you do this I feel really frustrated." You can assert yourself in respectful ways. Remember, your goal is to be heard and build bonds of connection at the same time.[41] To be heard, you must refrain from putting the other person on the defensive. Once that happens, the chances of a healthy conversation, let alone a resolution, are greatly diminished.

Master the art of feedback. Regardless of your level of tolerance, empathy, and kindness – and despite your best efforts to be nonjudgmental – from time to time you will have to give feedback to a colleague, a family member, or a friend.[42] Some rules will help you achieve the dual goals of making your point and maintaining the relationship:

- *What*: Think carefully about what you want to say. Be specific and discuss behaviors as opposed to character flaws.
- *When*: Select a time that is conducive to dialogue. Refrain from giving feedback when either person is rushing or other circumstances prevent full attention.
- *Where*: Find a place with some privacy, especially if the feedback you are about to deliver concerns performance issues
- *How*: Balance critical observations with appreciation for contributions the other person might have made to you or others

Pausing, editing, listening, asserting yourself, and providing feedback are building blocks in the creation of mattering relationships. Ultimately, the goal of communicating in ways that enhance mattering is to strengthen bonds of connection.

Connect

The previous skill set dealt mainly with verbal communication, but there are many ways to connect that are nonverbal. A touch, a gaze, a wink, a hug, or a dismissive gesture speaks volumes. The following ways to enhance mattering in relationships must incorporate both verbal and nonverbal approaches.

Show interest. If you wish to build rapport with someone you must show interest in the other person. Remember, it is not all about you! Ask open-ended questions, listen nonjudgmentally, and celebrate other people's accomplishments. You cannot show interest unless you literally show up. If you want to nurture close connections with your friends, you have to invest time and effort. You have to invite them to your house and call them. If the interest is all in your head it is as good as null. To show interest you must show up.

Share vulnerability. It is hard to build a relationship without being vulnerable. You have to bring your whole authentic self to the relationship, and that includes fears and failures. Although this may be one of the most challenging aspects of building a relationship, it is also one that can pay off with big dividends. Showing weakness and vulnerability foster intimacy.[43] Some people find it easier to provide support to a suffering person than to celebrate his or her achievements. It is very dispiriting to share good news that falls on deaf ears. Never miss an opportunity to congratulate someone who is celebrating a promotion, winning a race, or finishing a degree. Ask them specific yet open-ended questions about their journey, and be an active partner in their joy. Do not pass up an opportunity to show interest and concern.

Seek and give support. Mutual support is a characteristic of strong relationships. You cherish accomplishments, but you also lend a shoulder in difficult times. It is essential that both parties are able to ask and provide support. Support must be bidirectional.[44]

In brief, we must build connections based on nonjudgmental listening, constructive feedback, assertiveness, and authentic vulnerability. Never miss an opportunity to cherish somebody else's accomplishments, and be ready to give and get help.

Context

Willpower is overrated; context is underrated. When it comes to behaviors, much is made of grit and tenacity, while little is made of environmental cues and influences.[45] Yet contextual cues are strong determinants of behaviors, emotions, and thoughts. We pretend that our decisions are based on rational thinking, without much external interference, but nothing could be further from the truth.[46] Cues are all over the place, and they have a big impact on our sense of mattering. Cues can be subtle or blatant, physical, or psychological.[47] In essence, cues are signals that communicate messages to us. "Likes" in social media are cues revealing how popular people are. Similarly, images on Instagram and Facebook trigger us to compare ourselves to others who may be wealthier, sexier, or smarter. In fact, a number of studies have shown that, when exposed to profiles of people regarded as more successful, the self-esteem of the viewer goes down. Moreover, the higher the frequency of social media use, the lower the self-esteem.[48]

When teachers unconsciously lower expectations of minority students, they are sending a message that some groups are not as talented as others.

Excluding a colleague from a project is a sign that he or she is not valued. These may be subtle psychological messages, but there are also blatant ones. Buildings without ramps tell people with disabilities that they don't matter. Dilapidated schools tell students that they are not as valued as other kids in the "good" part of town. From discrimination to a thumbs-up on Facebook, cues are everywhere, and they can diminish or enhance our sense of mattering.

Read the Cues

We are both recipients and generators of cues. We are constantly exposed to signs of social comparison and peer pressure, but we are not only consumers of cues: we are also producers. This is why it's important to read the cues that come our way – and those that we emit to the world. Some cues are negative and some are positive. For example, a reminder via a phone app to call your friend on her birthday is a helpful cue. You put it there so you won't forget. For a person trying to quit drinking, going for happy hour with friends to a bar may not be a great cue. It is usually pretty hard to resist temptation when everybody else is engaging in the behavior you are seeking to avoid. Willpower usually loses to environmental cues.

Monitor inputs. If you are trying to lose weight, it is not a good idea to go to a Chinese buffet when you are hungry. Your hunger pangs feel as if they are killing you, and the external circumstances make you salivate – bad combination.[49] You have to be able to read internal (hunger pangs) and external cues (150 different dishes to choose from) while trying to stick to a healthier diet. If you want to exercise daily, put your gym clothes next to your bed to remind you to do this first thing in the morning. This is a cue to get active.

Our judgment is clouded by physical aspects of the environment, such as color, weight, height, temperature, and touch.[50] If you are holding a warm cup of tea, you are more likely to judge another person as warm than if you were holding a cup of ice tea. Rationally, the temperature of the mug should not shape your perception of other people, but it does. You are also more likely to judge someone as sexier if she is wearing red.

Monitor outputs. But we are not only passive recipients of contextual influences: we also generate cues, positive and negative. We may neglect someone through errors of omission or commission. Not making time to read a bedtime story to your daughter is an act of omission. It is a cue that is telling her "daddy's work is more important" or "the football game takes priority." Errors of commission take the form of active exclusion of someone from your team. Since we are hypersensitive to social rejection, both types of output must be monitored carefully. You can make someone feel devalued in multiple ways – verbally or nonverbally, through acts of omission or commission – but you can also make them feel valued with the help of cues.

Change the Cues

Sending a thank-you card may seem insignificant in the great scheme of things, but thousands of employees sending notes of appreciation to their coworkers amounts to culture change. To make it simple to do so, Isaac's team created an application called "ThankU" at the University of Miami. Since its introduction, thousands of ThankU cards have been exchanged. Many had good intentions before, but it was never as easy or convenient as it is now. We introduced a simple cue to educate faculty and staff about the importance of making people feel valued. With the recipients' consent, an automatic copy of the digital card is sent to their manager as well. Managers love getting kudos about their employees. It makes them look good. We made a simple change, from paper thank-you notes to electronic ones. We changed the cue, and we changed behaviors.

In general, we can affect mattering by altering three types of cues: people, places, or things.

Change cues related to people. If you want to add value to yourself and the community, join a group of volunteers and people you admire in some social cause. Make sure to surround yourself with role models. Their behaviors will serve as reminders to do the right thing. When we internalize moral role models, they can guide us with difficult decision-making. When we identify with just, ethical, and courageous people, we can metaphorically ask "what would Beth or James do in this situation?"

Change cues related to places. Since our willpower is no match for contextual cues, you have to arrange your environment to make it easy to accomplish your goals. If you are trying to lose weight or become more productive, you can design your kitchen and your office in ways that align with your objectives. It is far easier to bring home only healthy foods than fighting with your willpower every time you open the cupboard and see the potato chips or chocolate bars. You can become the architect of your kitchen. Put a bowl of fruit on the table. Cut up veggies and have them ready for snacks. Put cues to remind you to eat healthy and avoid junk foods.

If you are easily distracted at work and are trying to finish a task, design your environment for productivity.[51] Turn off email alerts while you are concentrating. Put your mobile phone away. Clean your desk. Remove clutter. Close your door for some quiet time. Set a timer to work for forty-five minutes straight before you get up for a stretch. It is amazing how much you can accomplish by changing minor cues.

Change cues related to things. Smell, light, sound, and text can be subtle but powerful determinants of behavior. If you are trying to save money, using passwords such as "frugal" or "bankrupt" on your Amazon account will curtail frivolous spending.[52] If you want to build an egg nest, tell your employer to deduct a certain amount directly from your paycheck. If you don't want to pay interest on your credit card, create an automatic payment from your bank account. Citrus smells encourages doctors to wash their hands more often. Blue lights suppress melatonin, helping us fall asleep. Soft music can help us relax while exposure to narcissistic politicians can raise our blood pressure. It is better to control all these cues than to let them control us.

Awareness

To reach higher levels of mattering and well-being, we need to know our values and reflect on our behaviors, emotions, thoughts, interactions, and context. We have to ask ourselves if our demeanor corresponds to the values and principles we believe in. In theory we may be all for reciprocal relationships, but in practice we may care only about our egotistic pursuits. Is there alignment between our values and our actions? We call this exercise *knowing yourself.* While crucial, this is only one part of awareness. The other part is *knowing the issue.* If your employees are not feeling valued, take the time to learn what is going on. If you are bothered by inequality and discrimination, learn about the root causes of social injustice. There is no substitute for knowing yourself and knowing the issue.

Know Yourself

Sooner or later, in your quest for mattering, you are going to have to ask yourself what you stand for. You will also have to ask yourself if your mindset and behaviors are aligned with your values. None of the previous skills will do much good if you don't engage in a little self-reflection.

Know your values. The pursuit of meaning and mattering flows from the pursuit of values.[53] Values are ethical principles that guide our behavior. Without a clear set of values, we don't know how to tell right from wrong. If truth is not valued in society, we will live among liars. If compassion is not valued, we will live among callous people. If justice is not valued, we will live with intolerable levels of inequality. Life is not only brutish without guiding values, but also very confusing, since any course of action is as good as the next. Values serve as criteria for action.

Stop for a moment and reflect on the values you cherish the most. Are they things like freedom, fairness, integrity, honesty, compassion? You may not have asked yourself this question lately, but it's a crucial step in fostering a sense of mattering. What are the top five values that guide your decision-making? After you generate this list, try to place these values into two categories: values for my own well-being, and values for the well-being of others.[54] Self-determination, autonomy, and freedom belong in the former, while values such as compassion, empathy, generosity, and justice correspond to the latter. The former promote your sense of mattering, while the latter advance it for others.

Upon reflection, you may discover that most of your values lean toward the self or others. If you focus too much on the self, you risk narcissistic tendencies. If you concentrate too much on others, it may be at your expense. The key is to balance attention to self with attention to others. As noted earlier, the brilliance of the French Revolution was to create a set of values that foster personal (liberty), community (equality), and relational well-being (fraternity) at the same time.

Once you are clear and honest about which values you cherish the most, you can then ask yourself if your behaviors match your values. This is part of the value of integrity. Do you walk the talk? Do you believe in kindness but are dismissive of others? Do you value empathy but rarely have time to listen to your sister's concerns? Do you cherish self-determination but often find yourself blindly following the crowd? Do you practice self-compassion? You may be compassionate toward others but not toward yourself, or vice versa.

As a result of this exercise you may discover one of two things: that your behaviors are congruent with your values; or that they are not. If they are concordant, your sense of mattering will grow over time, since you will be contributing to self and others. If your behavior is incongruent with your values, you have the choice to ignore the tension or do something about it. If you ignore it, somebody will suffer the consequences. You may suffer because you may behave in either domineering or submissive ways. Others may hurt because they may be the subject of your controlling demeanor, or because they may be deprived of your contributions.

Know your wellness. You have to be honest when you evaluate your behavior against your values, but also when you assess your overall well-being. Are you satisfied with your life? Do you derive satisfaction from your relationships? Is your job meaningful and rewarding? Are you a stress ball? Are you depressed or isolated? Do you feel welcome in the community? There are many reasons to bury your head in the sand. Often it is very painful to acknowledge that the choice of your major in college was the wrong one or that your relationship with your boyfriend is about to end. The pain of admitting that life is not great is often paralyzing. This is what keeps many people from taking steps toward higher levels of health and wellness. To avoid the discomfort, we often distort reality.

Know your defenses. Earlier experiences of failure, rejection, or abandonment exert tremendous influence on us. Some of them are so scary that we tend to repress them and ship them to the unconscious. We run away from the pain associated with them. Instead of confronting negative feelings, we vanish them. While this may be helpful in the short term, refusal to deal with them will result in even more pain in the long run. Our unconscious is a huge reservoir of repressed memories and fears. When we ignore these monsters, they come up from the basement in uncontrollable ways. Better to control them than let them control us.[55]

Earlier experiences of failure may prevent us from applying for a more interesting job. Past betrayals may have taught you that you can trust no one. Because of histories of parental neglect or rejection you may be afraid to get close to people. The prospect of a new rejection may be too much to bear. Maybe you learned to protect yourself by being aggressive. If you perceive a disagreement with a colleague as a form of disrespect, you may respond sarcastically. In most cases, these behaviors are meant to hide vulnerability.

Of all the monsters inhabiting your unconscious, vulnerability may be scariest one.[56] We do all we can to escape it. Despite obvious pain and suffering, people will go to tremendous lengths to pretend that everything is okay because they don't want to be seen as weak. This denial has serious consequences. We become depressive or aggressive. In the process, we isolate ourselves. This is why it is essential to practice mindfulness and acceptance. Without them, we will be forever running away from vulnerability. We are in denial.

Denial is the refusal to admit that you have a problem. This often characterizes people with addictions. While they do all they can to pretend that they are in control of their gambling or drinking, they incur debt, inflict untold suffering on others, and ruin their careers. To deal with unpleasant feelings, we ascribe to other people negative motives that we harbor ourselves. We project onto other people our own feelings of jealousy or envy. Sometimes, instead of dealing with vulnerability and painful events, such as a separation, we theorize about the importance of freedom and independence.

Rather than admitting the wound associated with a separation, we rationalize that he or she was not a good match for us anyway. For others, the agony of taking responsibility is so aversive that they constantly blame others for failed deadlines. In all these cases, we are trying to protect ourselves from pain, vulnerability, or responsibility. We blame others, pretend everything is okay, and come up with excuses why these events are really not a big deal. To some extent, and from time to time, these defenses are adaptive, but frequent and prolonged use result in dysfunction.

One way to know your values, your wellness, and your defenses is to conduct a personal checkup. You are used to going to the doctor for a physical once a year. You take your car for an oil change and a tune up once in a while. You check your bank account online. You monitor how your pension plan is doing. You weigh yourself once a week to keep your waistline in check. Your emotional well-being deserves no less. You can set aside time every week – or every month, like the first Sunday of the month – to reflect on your values, wellness, and defenses. Are you running away from vulnerability? Are you betraying your values? Do you need a tune-up?

Know the Issue

The previous exercises will raise your awareness about your psychological well-being. You also need to raise your awareness about external circumstances affecting your emotional health and the well-being of others. Sometimes, it is not us but rather the situation that is causing misery. Although many people blame themselves for their pain – a tendency perpetuated by our hyperindividualistic society – there is often something in the environment generating pain and suffering. Oppressive relationships, domineering partners, tyrannical bosses, discrimination, and human rights violations do not require an emotional tune-up but rather social transformation.

Since many powerful interests benefit from the societal status quo, there is great resistance to change.[57] Instead of changing social conditions, it is much easier to blame victims for their "flawed character or behavior." Instead of challenging inequality, it is much easier to blame poor people for "being lazy." Instead of challenging chauvinistic norms, it is much easier to blame women for "seductive behaviors" when there is date rape.

Next Steps

Nothing of the foregoing really matters unless you make a plan and make it stick. It all boils down to having an achievable plan to promote personal, relational, and communal mattering. This is a two-step solution. First, design a strategy based on the various skills you learned. Second, make your engagement with new behaviors, emotions, and thoughts sustainable.

Make a Plan

This is the time to focus your efforts and integrate all the skills we reviewed in this chapter. Any aspect of mattering can be defined as a goal. If you wish to be more productive and add value to yourself and the workplace, you can use the SMART principles to set a good goal. If you wish to improve a sense of mattering in your romantic relationship, you can build on the skills of connect and communicate: become a better listener, refrain from judgment, ask open ended questions, celebrate the other person's accomplishment, and show empathy.[58]

To get started, go back to the mattering wheel in Chapter 1. Choose one of the eight slices in which you wish to grow your sense of mattering. Is it feeling valued at work? Is it adding value to yourself? Once you have done that, set a SMART goal and be as specific as possible. Start with defining your goal as a specific behavior that will become a positive habit. Devise implementation intentions by stipulating the time and place of the desired behavior. Then, leverage the positive emotions associated with making the first step. Challenge negative assumptions about yourself (I can never lose weight; learning Spanish is not for me; I will never get a promotion; I will never pass chemistry) and create a new story about your sense of mattering. Build on your strengths and savor your achievements. Recruit friends and relatives to help you, and become the architect of your environment to plant helpful cues in your house. Become aware of your habitual responses.

Make It Stick

Many people start new behaviors on January 1: a new diet, a new exercise regime, reading more, spending more time with your partner, learning Spanish, drinking less, turning off social media at 8 pm, and the like. The problem is that few people persist. The success rate is very low.[59] The question then becomes: how do you make these new habits stick? Many people are familiar with the SWOT analysis. We will make use of it here as a form of prevention.

SWOT stands for strengths, weaknesses, opportunities, and threats. Strengths and weaknesses pertain to our skills, abilities, and personal resources. Opportunities and threats exist in the outside environment.

A new job with prospects of career advancement is a great opportunity. One threat to exercise and healthy living is a crazy schedule at work. You are constantly eating fast food and never quite manage to make it to the gym. How can you maximize strengths and opportunities and minimize weaknesses and threats? And if you do encounter barriers, what contingency plans can you put in place? If you cannot exercise on Tuesday evening, what's the backup plan?

To make changes sustainable, you can practice the GREASE method.[60] To instill positive habits in your life you need to make changes *g*radual, *r*ewarded, and *e*asy. In addition, you need to find *a*lternatives to unhealthy behaviors, you need to be *s*upported by family and friends, and you need to get *e*ducated about the issue you are tackling.

- *Gradual*: Take small steps, one at a time. Set realistic and achievable goals. Don't try to run a marathon if you have not exercised in months, or years, or ever. Start with a walk around the block and gradually increase. Years ago we used to drink coffee with sugar: one teaspoon for Ora, two for Isaac. We gradually reduced it until we eliminated sugar altogether. Isaac has since eliminated coffee as well, and Ora is drinking more decaf. James Clear, the author of *Atomic Habits*, advocates a technique of 1 percent improvement every day.[61] Over time, the compound interest of these gains become meaningful and rewarding habits. In sports, some teams use the 1 percent rule. Grow your performance by 1 percent every season. Before you know it, your team will be winning. Pat Riley introduced that method in the summer of 1986 with great success with the LA Lakers. He called it Career Best Effort, or CBE. To improve performance by 1 percent over an entire season seemed eminently doable, and improve they did. The Lakers won two back-to-back NBA championships in 1987 and 1988.
- *Rewarded*: Praise and reward yourself for achieving small wins. Tell yourself you are becoming healthier, more compassionate, or more productive. Go for a walk or watch an episode of your favorite show. Celebrate your achievement by sharing it with friends: "Hey guys, I started running today."
- *Easy*: Make it simple for yourself so that you can experience success quickly. Go for small wins. The more you experience self-efficacy in the short term, the more likely you are to stick with the new habit. Even if you spent five more minutes every night with your kids, you are contributing to a reservoir of positivity.
- *Alternatives*: Always have an alternative available for the behavior you want to replace. If you crave something sweet in the afternoon, always

carry a piece of fruit with you. It is healthier than sugary soda or a chocolate bar.

- *Supported*: Enlist your friends and relatives in your cause. Tell your friends that you are trying to change something – that you are trying to be more productive, so ask them to forgive you for not joining them for happy hour. If you want to volunteer at an animal shelter, ask friends to join you.

- *Educated*: Learn and inform yourself about the issue you want to tackle. If you want to lose weight to get healthier, don't jump on the first bandwagon diet you see on TV. If you want to be a better leader at work, learn about the research on leadership and avoid gurus that have never led anything other than a successful speaking career. Learn from people with real-life experience.

In summary, when trying to stick to a new habit, tell yourself and others that you are becoming the person you want to be. This is an identity-based reinforcement, the best kind. You get excited and motivated by writing a new story about yourself. At the beginning, make it easy to achieve success so that you experience self-efficacy. If you are trying to eradicate a negative behavior, such as chewing your nails, try squeezing a stress ball instead. Remember to enlist helpers. Tell your friends and relatives that you are changing and that you want their support. What's more, you can try doing something together. If you are after more family time, find a game that everyone enjoys. Finally, educate yourself about the issues involved, and distinguish between personal and external issues. In the subsequent chapters, we call upon all the levers of change to elevate our sense of mattering.

PART II

Self

CHAPTER 5

Mattering through Mastery

James Black was about to play Brian Li. James is an African American eighth-grader from IS 318 in Brooklyn. The match was for the 2011 title of the National Junior High Chess Championship in Columbus, Ohio. As they were walking to the ballroom for the decisive game, James told his coach:

> "I'm nervous." "You're nervous?" his coach replied. Understanding that James needed a confidence boost, his coach bent down low next to James, a trainer getting his boxer ready for a fight. "You know who's really nervous right now, James? Brian Li. You know why? Because Brian Li, probably about twenty minutes ago, went and looked at the pairings, and he found out he was playing *James Black* on board one in the last round."[1]

In a reassuring tone, the coach reminded James to be confident and to take his time. The person recounting the exchange is Paul Tough, and the excerpt is from his book *How Children Succeed*. The coach working with James at the tournament was our son, Matan Prilleltensky.

James and Brian played for over three hours. At one point James was in a dangerous position and thought of offering a draw, but Brian made an unusual move and James regained the upper hand. On the forty-eighth move Brian resigned. But James was not the only student from IS 318 to win difficult matches in Columbus, and Columbus was not the only tournament IS 318 dominated. The team had won also sixth, seventh, and eighth grade in the most recent scholastic tournament in Orlando in 2010. They also won all grades in 2008 and two out of three grades in 2009. When Tough compared IS 318 to the winners from all other grades in Orlando, from K to 12, he noticed a stark difference. With the exception of IS 318, all the other kids came from elite private or public schools around the country. IS 318 was the only low-income public school on the list. Situated in South Williamsburg, next to the Bedford-Stuyvesant area, IS 318 is a Title I school with 87 percent of students eligible for meal subsidies.

Although some students on the chess team are White and Asian, most players are African American or Hispanic. The best players, though, are Black.[2]

Matan, a graduate student at the time, was thrilled to join Elizabeth Spiegel, the head chess coach of the school, as an assistant coach. Since then, Elizabeth took maternity leave to raise a family but then returned to coach IS 318. Matan finished graduate school and has continued to coach champions, just like Elizabeth. Matan and Elizabeth are still close friends. James Black is now a student at Webster University in St. Louis, part of their very strong chess team. He is also coaching chess now.

Matan and Elizabeth have continued to train young minds and are accomplished chess players on their own right. For them, chess is a magnificent way to add value to self and others and to promote their own personal development and growth in their students. Amidst the coronavirus pandemic, in August 2020, Matan and Elizabeth organized an online chess camp for sixty-five students. Insofar as wellness entails intellectual, occupational, and psychological development, chess is contributing to their own well-being and the well-being of others.

Wellness, of course, is multidimensional. Intellectual enrichment, while essential, is only one of its facets. For us, wellness is a positive state of affairs in six interrelated domains of life: Interpersonal, Communal, Occupational, Psychological, Physical, and Economic. In short, we call these the I COPPE domains. Chess promotes psychological and occupational wellness, but if you make a living coaching chess, the way Matan and Elizabeth do, then it also promotes economic well-being.

James Black is an extraordinarily smart young man. At one point, when he was ten, he played Yuri Lapshun, a Ukrainian-born international master. James was rated 2,068 and Yuri was rated 2,546. In chess terms, this is a galactic distance. Very few chess players ever make it to 2,300, despite years of training and punishing work. To reach 2,500 is just unattainable for the vast majority of great players. Yet when James was only ten he beat Yuri in fifty-nine moves. His rating soared to 2,150 in one day. Despite moments of brilliance, however, his ascendance in the chess world was by no means a straight line. James struggled to reach 2,200, the level required for the title of national master. He moved close to 2,200 a few times in 2011, only to slip back. He struggled mightily to achieve the title of master. He did not lack determination, however. That year he played sixty-five tournaments. In total, he played 301 rated matches. Eventually, on July 17 at the famed Marshall club in New York City he beat an eighteen-year-old from Connecticut and his rating jumped to 2,205.

During a celebration at Fulton Park, Elizabeth Spiegel praised his tenacity. She said that James worked constantly to improve his tactics, analyze games, reflect on his mistakes, and stick with it. As she put it, "he has worked so hard, so patiently, for so long. That is what I respect the most about James."[3]

In this chapter we explore what it takes to achieve competence in various domains of life. We also discuss the interaction between personal factors, such as grit, and environmental dynamics, such as family support and school experience. We start by looking at how people add value to themselves.

Signs

How can we tell that people are adding value? How do they add value to themselves? How do they help others? How do they achieve greatness in domains as varied as chess, music, sport, politics, business, physics, and literature? In Chapter 4 we reviewed several strategies to promote wellness in diverse areas of life. Here we go one step further and explore not just what it takes to do something, like studying chess or exercising regularly, but what it takes to excel. What can we learn from the very best? We want to know the characteristics of mastery.

Excelling at friendship or parenting is part of interpersonal wellness. You want to be the best partner, friend, or parent that you can be. Shining in athletics is part of physical, occupational, and even psychological well-being. Leading social change is part of community wellness; your calling is to improve the social condition. Regardless of your particular focus, there are six investments you have to make. People who get better at anything invest in six things. We call them the six Ts:

1. *Transcendence*: Going beyond the norm to pursue a passion and a purpose
2. *Time*: Dedicating thousands of hours
3. *Thought*: Concentrating and creating mental representations of the subject matter
4. *Training*: Practicing to reach stretch goals and acquire skills with a coach
5. *Tenacity*: Persevering and following through
6. *Trust*: Believing in yourself, your mentors, and the process

Transcendence. People who want to get better at something consistently show a passion for it, be it swimming, spelling, music, or social justice.

They want to *transcend* expectations. They want to make a difference in their capacities and often in the world as well. This is how Angela Duckworth put it in her book *Grit: The Power of Passion and Perseverance*:

> What ripens passion is the conviction that your work matters .... It is therefore imperative that you identify your work as both personally interesting and, at the same time, integrally connected to the well-being of others .... [E]xemplars of grit invariably tell me, "My work is important – both to me and to others."[4]

Social justice advocates often display this kind of transcendence. That was the case with A. Philip Randolph, an African American civil rights leader who was born near Jacksonville, Florida, in 1899. He moved to Harlem in 1911. In New York, Randolph was involved in theater and was a lover of Shakespeare. He had exceptional talent and a commanding presence. Women found him extremely charming and attractive. He could have been a great actor, but his enduring legacy was in the promotion of civil rights for the Black community. He dedicated his life to a cause that required self-discipline. As David Brooks (2015) observed in *The Road to Character,* "most people are the product of their circumstances, but Randolph's parents, his teachers, and he himself created a moral ecology that transcended circumstances."[5] He transcended not only circumstances but also hedonistic pleasures that might have diverted him from his mission of justice.

Randolph was frequently in jail because of his labor organizing, and he was often penniless. He was incorruptible, however, and refused high-paying jobs that would have muffled his denunciation of racism. Like many other people who achieve greatness, "he fought any tendency towards looseness or moral laziness with constant acts of self-mastery, whether small acts of personal conduct or larges acts of renunciation."[6] His work on the nonviolent resistance movement, desegregation, and civil rights demanded great sacrifice. Randolph went beyond what could be expected of any individual, especially one with great talents and opportunities to settle into a comfortable life, but he defied expectations and the system. He could see a better world for Black people and did not desist. Among his major accomplishments, Randolph organized the famous March on Washington for Jobs and Freedom on August 28, 1963. It was during that march that Martin Luther King Jr. gave the memorable "I Have a Dream" speech.

Time. Lofty and transcendent goals motivate people, but it is only after thousands of hours of practice that distinction is achieved. Over time,

Randolph became an extraordinary negotiator. He knew what language to use to gain supporters and prevent deserters. Instead of inflaming rhetoric that criticized capitalism, which alienated some workers, he talked about the fight for dignity. At one point he met with President Roosevelt to demand that Blacks be allowed to work in the defense industry. Roosevelt offered to call some executives and urge them to hire more Blacks. Randolph was not satisfied. Unless the president met his demands, he threatened to bring 100,000 Blacks to a protest march in Washington. The president eventually conceded and issued Executive Order 8802, banning discrimination of Blacks in the defense sector. Randolph clocked more that the customary 10,000 hours required to become an expert.[7]

In some fields, the relationship between hours of practice is more palpable than in politics and conflict resolution. Anders Ericsson, an expert on expertise, showed in definitive terms the impact of practice in his book *Peak: Secrets from the New Science of Expertise.*[8] He proved the common refrain that practice makes perfect. In a study of gifted violinists at the best music academy in Germany, he divided the students into three groups based on performance: good, better, and best. The first group had practiced an average of 3,420 hours by the time they turned eighteen. The second had practiced an average of 5,301, and the third and best group had practiced an average of 7,410 hours. The amount of time spent practicing was the distinguishing factor among all the gifted players who were admitted into the prestigious academy. According to Ericsson, "no matter which area of study – music, dance, sports, competitive games, or anything else with objective measures of performance – you find that the top performers have devoted a tremendous amount of time to developing their abilities."[9]

Thought. Ericsson studied mastery in diverse areas. In one of his famous studies, he wanted to see how people can develop their memory. To do that, he recruited Steve Faloon, an undergraduate psychology student at Carnegie Mellon University who, by all measures, was a prototypical student. The study consisted of daily sessions of memory training. Ericsson would read out loud a series of numbers, and Steve was supposed to recite them back. At first, Steve could remember on average seven digits, which is typical. From time to time during the first week he could remember up to ten digits. But then, on Friday, Steve made a breakthrough. He jumped from seven, to nine, to eleven. From that point onward, Steve made consistent progress. On the sixtieth session, he could reliably reproduce twenty numbers. After about a hundred sessions, he could remember forty digits, which was by far more than anyone had ever recalled. Ericsson worked with Steve for over two years, and by the end of their training Steve could memorize an amazing eighty-two numbers. As impressive as his record was, in subsequent years people astonished the world remembering digits of pi. A Canadian named David Richard Spencer was able to remember pi to 511 decimals in 1973. As we shall later see, other people, like Roger Bannister, were able to break previously unimaginable records, like running a mile in less than four minutes.

There is no doubt that people who achieve greatness in diverse fields stretch their mental capacities through focus and concentration. Chess grandmaster and philosopher Johnathan Rowson discusses at length the topic of concentration in his new book *The Moves that Matter*:

> Concentration is about building an alliance between parts of ourselves for whatever purposes we are caught up in. We succeed in concentrating when we manage to convene the dispositions that matter; for instance our aware-ness, attention, discernment and willpower, and then the assorted emotions that co-arise and come along for the ride, like fear, anger, determination, joy and hope.[10]

Rowson claims that two experiences confer satisfaction to the chess player: competence and concentration. Our own son relishes solitary time in front of a chess board and a book of famous games. Concentration is pretty much essential for progress in any endeavor. At times, concentration can be such an intense experience that it can hurt, and you can't really do it intensely for more than an hour. But it is also part of flow, the feeling of getting lost in blissful engagement with a hobby or a craft.[11] Without concentration there is neither achievement nor flow.

Studies show that mastery derives from practice, focused attention, and mental maps.[12] The way Steve Faloon improved was by creating mental representations of the digits he had to remember. For example, he imagined that the digits were running times that he could encode into five or more digits. The numbers 2, 1, 0, 4, 7 would become in his mind running two miles in ten minutes and forty-seven seconds. Another participant in Ericsson's study used different mnemonics such as days, dates, and times of day. For example, she would recall 4, 7, 7, 8, 2, 4 5 as April 7, 1978, at 2:45. The key is to chunk or cluster the material into a meaningful narrative, such as running times or dates. When chess players observe games they see patterns that Ericsson calls mental representations. These are mental maps that help you organize the information the way Steve Faloon did. In chess, it is a way of seeing the forest instead of the trees. Graphs and maps often help people retain a lot of information easier than strings of words.

Training. The evidence demonstrates that to improve your skills you must set ambitious goals. You must push yourself beyond your comfort zone, and you must work with a coach. The latter is essential because you need to learn from someone who has already mastered the skill you are trying to acquire. To develop your skills, you must get specific feedback on what you are doing right and what you are doing wrong.[13]

The best way to improve is to apply knowledge. You must experiment with a musical instrument, not just listen to a great performance. You must solve thousands of chess problems on the board. You must swim and swim and swim until you develop the best form. Experiential learning is far superior to didactic methods. Nurses and doctors, for example, improve their skills through role-playing and interactive learning, not through lectures.

The best way to train, Ericsson claims, is through deliberate practice. This is a type of training defined by very specific goals that are just beyond your current abilities. It is a methodic approach guided by a coach who can design a detailed plan for improving particular aspects of your perform- ance. Our son Matan employs the Dutch Steps Program to coach his chess students. It is highly structured and builds gradually students' mastery of chess. He is a firm believer in the gradual approach. Once specific object- ives are set, the student must concentrate on that specific outcome and get feedback from a mentor. Students are encouraged to develop mental representations of the skill they need to acquire. If it is a musical note, they are told to mentally hear the note before they play it. If it is a chess move, they are told to visualize several moves ahead before they lift a piece. Mental representations also allow students to self-monitor and make necessary corrections along the way. Ericsson has documented the success of deliberate practice in gymnastics, ballet, music, chess, and real life.[14]

Tenacity. If Anders Ericsson is the ultimate authority on expertise, Angela Duckworth is the best-known expert on grit. As we saw earlier, grit depends on two things: passion and perseverance.[15] Passion is the devotion to one thing you are fascinated by. It is a goal you must conquer. Perseverance is sticking with it over the long haul and following through with your commitments. To demonstrate the power of grit, she studied students who made it through the rigorous training at West Point Military Academy. West Point had been trying to predict for years who would make it and who would drop out, using something called the Whole Candidate Score, which consisted of scores on the SAT, the ACT, physical tests, and leadership potential. It turns out that this was not a reliable predictor of persistence. Duckworth suspected that cadets who made it excelled not on objective measures of physical performance or cognitive tests but rather on passion and persistence – grit. To test her hypothesis she administered a scale of grit to incoming cadets in 2004. The first observation she made was that grit had nothing to do with aptitude. By the last day of the rigorous induction process, seventy-one cadets had given up and dropped out. The best predictor of persistence was not the Whole Candidate Score or any measure of academic skill. Instead, the best predictor was grit. She repeated the study next year, with same results. Duckworth went on to test grit among salespeople, students in the Chicago schools, Green Berets, winners of the Scripps National Spelling Bee, and several other populations. What distinguished successful kids and adults from the rest was their ability to focus on one thing and their ability to stick with it despite obstacles.

Trust. To master a skill, to make a difference in yourself and others, you must have trust in your abilities, in the process, and in your mentors. Two psychology professors at Stanford University, working independently, made major contributions to our understanding of what it means to trust your abilities. The first, Albert Bandura, born in Canada, demonstrated the powerful impact of believing in yourself. He called this trait self-efficacy. Self-efficacy has been shown to affect your physical and mental health, your work, your relationships, educational progress, life satisfaction, conscientiousness, and optimism.[16] Self-efficacy has been applied in schools, industry, government, and media. Bandura revolutionized psychology with insights about how people change through cognitions, or the way they see the world. The more you trust your skill set, the more successful you become.

The second famous Stanford psychologist is Carol Dweck. Through the concept of mindset, she showed that children and adults with a growth mindset approach success and failure much differently from those with a fixed mindset.[17] The former believe that they can develop skills and talents through hard work, help from mentors, training and strategies. The latter, in turn, believe that talent is fixed and innate. The former group approaches failure with a learning attitude; whereas the latter do so with a judgmental attitude. Having a growth mindset is essential for learning because it basically means that learners trust their ability to develop their talents. When children with a fixed mindset fail a test, the story they tells themselves is "I'm not talented enough." When those with a growth mindset fail, they says to themselves that with training and effort they can get better.

Having self-efficacy and a growth mindset leads you to trust the process of learning and recovery from setbacks. If you work with a teacher or coach and you have faith in them and the method they employ, chances are you will remain engaged in the process of improvement. Having trust in yourself, the process, and your mentors is crucial for adding value, and it is essential for a sense of mattering.

We have seen in Matan, our son, many of the attributes that experts display on their way to excellence. Matan is passionate about chess. He pushes himself all the time to be a better player and a better coach. This is no passing fad. He started playing chess when he was eight years old, twenty-five years ago. He has built an amazing library of chess books and has invested thousands of hours studying, working with a coach, playing in tournaments, taking students to tournaments, and building an amazing coaching program that has benefited hundreds of kids, including some champions. He has also won some pretty amazing competitions himself. A hobby turned into a passion, which turned into an occupation, a calling, and a way of personal development.

In summary, people who devote themselves to mattering through self-improvement and devotion to a cause display some common traits. They push beyond the limits of their present abilities. They wish to transcend expectations for what is the best possible state of affairs, for themselves or others. They invest thousands of hours in training, focus on their goals, engage in deliberate practice, show tenacity, and trust themselves and the process.

Significance

The good news is that deliberate practice, grit, self-efficacy, and mindset can be taught and learned. In one of our own studies, as noted earlier, increasing self-efficacy in all the I COPPE domains of life (interpersonal, community, occupational, physical, psychological, and economic) improved well-being in all these areas.[18] Teaching growth mindset results in improved academic achievements and work-related productivity.[19] Deliberate practice can result in no less than growth in certain parts of the brain. This was discovered in a landmark study of London taxi drivers. To obtain a license as a taxi driver in London, you must pass a series of examinations testing your knowledge of the location of thousands of places within a six mile radius of Charing Cross. That area contains approximately 25,000 streets. The first obstacle is to memorize 320 runs – no navigation system allowed! The point is not just to get to a destination but to do so in the most time-efficient way.

Taxi drivers go through these routes thousands of times to memorize the best ways. The test is almost unpassable, and many prospective cabbies drop out of the race. London taxi drivers develop their spatial and navigational skills to such an extent that a particular part of their brain – the posterior hippocampus – is considerably larger than in a population of non-taxi drivers. It is not the case that their posterior hippocampus was already larger when they started the training. The opposite was the case: their brain grew as a result of the training.[20]

Students with a developed sense of grit graduate not only from military training more successfully but also from regular college. Grit, however, predicts success not only in work and school but also in life. In a longitudinal study of healthy men at Harvard, started in 1940, 130 sophomores were asked to run on a treadmill.[21] The test lasted only five minutes, but the treadmill was positioned at a steep angle and set at a very high speed. The Treadmill Test was designed to be very challenging. The average participant lasted four minutes. Some quit after a minute. The researchers knew that running was not just a test of physical endurance but also of psychological tenacity. For decades, the men in the study had been followed up with every two years to learn more about their income, careers, social life, satisfaction with work and family, and overall physical and mental health. When they were in their sixties, George Vaillant, a psychiatrist at Harvard, contacted them again. He discovered that how long they ran in the Treadmill Test decades earlier was a reliable predictor of psychological adjustment later in adulthood. As the authors noted, "college running time predicted future mental – but not physical – health."[22]

What grit, growth mindset, self-efficacy, and resilience have in common is self-regulation or self-control.[23] This means the ability to regulate your emotions and your behaviors. It is the ability to pause before you act and the capacity to delay immediate gratification for a bigger prize later on. Kids with better self-control do much better in life than those with poor self-regulation. In a longitudinal study, researchers in New Zealand followed a cohort of 1,000 children from birth to the age of thirty-two. The study showed that "childhood self-control predicts physical health, substance dependence, personal finances, and criminal offending outcomes."[24] The more self-control children experienced, the better the outcomes. Studying a second cohort of 500 sibling-pairs in the United Kingdom, the research team discovered that the sibling with lower levels of self-regulation had poorer outcomes, despite the fact that they grew up in similar environments. Based on these and other studies, there is no question that self-control is good for you. But the authors also discovered, significantly, that self-control was related to socioeconomic status (SES).

The kids from low SES backgrounds displayed less self-control than their most advantaged peers. Why is this finding important? Because it shows that there are conditions that predispose kids to be more or less prone to regulate their behaviors. Indeed, there are systemic factors that either promote or inhibit the ability of children to develop self-control and grit.

Sources

Nurturing environments foster self-regulation.[25] Kids who internalize the love of their caregivers learn to trust the world. In times of distress, they know that help is on the way. As kids grow, wise parents expect more autonomy and self-reliance. Gradually, they teach their children to delay gratification. Instead of demanding immediate attention, children learn to wait and regulate their needs. But for them to accomplish this feat, they need to have been exposed to repeated instances of responsiveness on the part of caregivers. This is a very gradual process. At first, because of their helplessness, newborns cannot delay gratification. With time, and nurturance, they learn to regulate their emotions.

In research conducted at McGill University, nurturing maternal behavior on the part of rats (such as licking their pups) has been shown to have a profound and positive effect on the genes that control the stress-response of the young.[26] The same research team discovered the negative effects of parental neglect and abuse on the brain. According to them, child abuse results in epigenetic markings in the brain. These markings affect the hypothalamic-pituitary-adrenal (HPA) function, which is a stress-response that enhances the risk of suicide. They discovered this in a study of thirty-six brains: twelve from suicide victims who were abused; twelve from suicide victims who were not abused; and twelve from a control group.[27] As Dr. Meaney, one of the lead researchers, observed, "the interaction between the environment and the DNA plays a crucial role in determining our resistance to stress thus the risk of suicide. Epigenetic marks are the product of this interaction."[28]

In some cases, parents are too stressed to engage with their kids in "serve and return" interactions: back-and-forth exchanges between parents and infants in which the adults show attention, care, and affection.[29] The baby vocalizes something, and the parent follows with joy. The baby points to a toy, and the parent says, "Yes, that's a red train. You like your train, don't you?" The baby is hungry, and daddy knows it's time for a bottle. Infant starts walking, and mommy rejoices at these first steps. Affective responsiveness and cognitive stimulation literally shape the functioning of the brain. The more parents encourage exploration, and the more secure the attachment they form with their infants, the higher the chances that the child will develop self-regulation and respond to stress in appropriate ways.

While some parents are too stressed to engage in "serve and return," others are insufficiently informed about the importance of these inter-actions. In either case, the result is a tremendous missed opportunity to grow self-control that may never come back.

In other cases, parents are not only misinformed but also unstable. Because of their own lack of wellness – addictions, physical ailments, isolation, poverty, racism, abusive partners, and inconsiderate bosses – parents behave in unpredictable ways.[30] They don't respond to the baby when he or she is hungry, and they often neglect the child or use physical punishment. Babies respond to the external stress in ways that predispose them to act impulsively. It is as if they are always ready to defend against a possible attack. They are jumpy and edgy. They are constantly on high alert. This excessive use of the fight or flight response and the correspond-ing release of cortisol results in diminished self-control in the long run. Since they cannot rely on others to soothe their pain or worry, they try to protect themselves the best way they know how: usually by displaying aggression. Instead of internalizing a calming message that the world is safe and the adults are here to care for them, many kids get the message that the world is a menacing place and there is nobody to protect them. In such situations, kids often respond to perceived threats with anger. Instead of building trust in the world through repeated interactions of responsiveness, they grow suspicious of others and the world around them.

The lack of optimal parenting is often magnified by schools that shortchange kids from disadvantaged backgrounds. That was the case with James Black. James was obviously very smart, but his schooling left much to be desired. By the time he entered IS 318 he was already missing basic academic skills.

Why would such a talented young man miss some fundamental skills? James does not have a learning disability, nor does he lack family support. He grew up in a loving family, and his parents invested in his growth and development. But like many other kids from poor neighborhoods, his education was inadequate. Had it not been for the extraordinary experi-ence that Elizabeth provided, the support of his father, and his own resolve, his educational future might have been uncertain.

At this point in the story we can focus on the heroic efforts by James, his father, and Elizabeth and forget about the injustice that many kids like James face. We can choose to pay attention to his diligence, perseverance, and dogged determination, which he displayed in spades. We can also shine a light on Elizabeth's brilliance as a teacher and forget about the kids who had neither such a marvelous mentor nor a passion for chess. Indeed, there are many lessons to be derived from the study of chess for all manners of competence – the role of concentration, deliberate practice, stretch goals, good coaches, interest, hope, self-efficacy and mindset – as we just saw. But if we were to concentrate only on grit, perseverance, passion, motivation, and resilience, we would be missing an important part of the story. It is inspiring to focus on how extraordinary kids and teachers beat the odds; how athletes break records; how musicians achieve greatness. It is more challenging, however, to focus on the root causes that prevent many kids from getting to college in the first place. There are many stories about how to beat the odds, but fewer on how to change the odds. It is easier to focus on the wellness of the one rather than on the lack of fairness for the many.

We are attracted to success stories because we think that with hard work and perseverance we can all attain fame and prosperity. But the reality for millions of kids does not match the illusion.[31] The achievement gap between Whites and Blacks remains very high and nearly unmoved since 1965.[32] At the current pace the math gap is not expected to close for another 250 years. Social mobility in the United States is among the lowest in the industrialized world.[33]

To close the achievement gap, improve social mobility, and level the playing field, we must work not just on grit and wellness but also on fairness. Fairness is about making sure that everyone, regardless of luck or zip code, has an opportunity to develop their capacities.

When it comes to mattering, we must develop bifocal vision.[34] We must focus on the people close to us and what they can do to improve their lot in life, but we must also see the structural conditions that foster or inhibit their human development. Both are equally important. We must learn how to coach James in the most effective ways, and we must also understand how to change systemic conditions that fail so many Black kids in the first place. However, systemic conditions often remain hidden. It is much simpler to focus on deficient parenting or teaching rather than on structures of inequality and injustice.[35]

Amartya Sen, the Nobel Prize-winning economist, and Martha Nussbaum, the renowned philosopher, articulate clearly the connection between justice and quality of life in their "capability approach."[36] According to them, social justice constitutes the *opportunities* to develop one's capabilities, such as the ability to learn, to play, to work, and to belong. Conditions of injustice, Nussbaum claims, can hurt the child by "stunting the development of internal capabilities or warping their development."[37] External conditions of justice are crucial for affording all children adequate education, health care, nutrition, and protection of their rights. These are the necessary conditions for children to develop their internal capabilities, such as mastering chess, math, or the violin.

The capability approach argues that governments should provide all people opportunities and conditions to sustain ten central capabilities. According to Nussbaum, these are:

1. *Life*: Being able to live a life of normal length, without dying prematurely
2. *Bodily health*: Enjoying physical health through proper nutrition and shelter.
3. *Bodily integrity*: Feeling secure and having choice in matters involving one's body
4. *Senses, imagination, and thought*: Being able to think and reason, to be creative and productive, through proper education
5. *Emotions*: Being able to love and to experience a full range of emotions. Living without fear or abuse.
6. *Practical reason*: Being able to formulate conceptions of the good life and pathways to achieve it
7. *Affiliation*: Being able to belong and be treated with dignity
8. *Other species*: Being able to co-exist with and have concern for animals and nature
9. *Play*: Being able to play and laugh
10. *Control over one's environment*: Being able to participate in political processes, hold property, and seek employment

Nussbaum explains the role of social justice in the provision of these capabilities as follows: "The basic claim of my account of social justice is this: respect for human dignity requires that citizens be placed above an ample (specified) threshold of capability, in all ten areas."[38] According to her, once individuals are afforded these opportunities, it is up to them to actualize them. People can exercise freedom of choice in how they combine these capabilities to chart a specific course for their lives. For people to potentiate their talent, however, everyone must be above a threshold in all categories. Without good health, it is hard to become a great athlete. Without proper nutrition, it is hard to become a great chess player.

In their book *Scarcity*, Sendhil Mullainathan and Eldar Shafir[39] demonstrate what happens when individuals are below a certain threshold in a particular domain of life. For example, if income is insufficient, many other areas of life, such as nutrition and shelter, let alone play, suffer. Deficiencies in some areas often cause disruption in others, whereas abundance in some capabilities can compensate for shortages in others. Owing to their intellectual prowess, some children are able to overcome poverty and chaotic family lives and excel at school. Some even make it to elite colleges. But these youth are a very small minority. The vast majority of kids who find themselves below the threshold succumb to environmental stressors.[40]

Many books and movies have been made about kids who overcome adversity through great effort and talent. While inspirational, they are often shown as proof that *everyone* can overcome adversity. We should remember that *not everyone* overcomes hardship. There is nothing wrong admiring those who do. The problem is in forgetting those who don't.

To guarantee that everyone is above the threshold of needs, policies must change. To provide high-quality health care for everyone, taxes must be collected and health insurance companies fought. To provide minimum wage for everyone, businesses must incur some costs. To make sure that the public is protected, regulations must be passed. Not everyone is happy to pay more taxes or higher wages. Corporations often oppose legislation that will cut into their profits. It is easier to create narratives of success in the current system than to make actual changes to the system. Entire ideologies are built to protect the system. Legends are created, such as the Horatio Alger Myth. Some groups use these mythologies to suppress dissent.

Because I, Isaac, spent a good part of my youth under military dictatorship in Argentina, I grew very suspect of societal institutions that blamed victims for their oppression and misfortune. My understanding of this ideology was crystalized when I read *How to Read Donald Duck*.[41] The book, originally published in Spanish in 1971, had a big impact on me. Subtitled *Imperialist Ideology in the Disney Comic*, the book became an instant classic in my youth movement.

How to Read Donald Duck was a critical analysis of how cultural discourses hide injustice, reproduce structures of power, and sustain the societal status quo. The text was part of our preparation as critical thinkers in the youth movement. The book taught us to challenge assumptions that many took for granted: for instance, that the reigning social system is the best and only possible one; that the poor deserve their fate because they are either lazy or crazy; that success had nothing to do with privilege. We became suspect of official discourse that blamed victims for their fate, that justified the societal status quo, and most of all, that suppressed dissent.

During my undergraduate and master's degrees, I grew very uncomfortable with the way psychology was being used to justify social injustice – the role of social context was all but neglected. Human problems were strictly defined as intra-psychic, as if a person's environment had no role in them whatsoever. It was at that time that I started developing a critique of the "Me Culture," a culture in which success and failure are attributed mainly to individual capacities or deficits. Power dynamics, injustice, discrimination, and exploitation were all but forgotten from the psychology curriculum.[42] It was all about the person and the family and very little about the environment. That bothered me because, as a student doing field work, I could already see the impact of power, inequality, poverty, and injustice on the kids I was working with. As a school psychologist in Canada, my discomfort grew further, especially when I saw the consequences of discrimination on the mental health of Aboriginal children.

My unease with psychology led me to propose a doctoral dissertation that would examine how psychological theories and practices might lend support to the societal status quo. Against conventional wisdom, I was claiming that psychology was a conservative force in society. My initial insight was that, if all human problems can be defined as intra-psychic malaise, there would never be a need to question the social system. That simple hypothesis got me into a lot of trouble.

First, nobody in the history of the Department of Psychology at the University of Manitoba had ever written a theoretical, as opposed to an empirical, dissertation. And second, nobody had dared frame the discipline as anything less than progressive and enlightened. I was naïve. The department did not like the idea of a doctoral student writing a philosophical dissertation, let alone one that would critique the foundations of the discipline. The norm was that every student would write an empirical dissertation based on data to be analyzed with the latest statistical methods. My topic, they thought, did not lend itself to empirical analysis and, therefore, had to be abandoned.

I have to thank my advisor, the late Freddy Marcuse, for sticking with me and fighting to get the dissertation proposal approved. After many trials and tribulations, the department gave the green light, but not before they appointed to my dissertation committee four psychology professors, a philosopher, and an English professor with expertise in discourse analysis. They wanted to be sure that I would be supervised properly. I had to satisfy not three or four professors, which is usually the norm, but six full professors, plus an external examiner. I had to convince them that I had something meaningful to say.

I worked very hard for a couple of years on my dissertation, but I have to admit that before my defense I was pretty anxious. What if they reject it at the last minute? What if they ask me a question I'm not prepared for? What if the external examiner doesn't like it? I knew that the dissertation was sent to an external examiner for review, but I did not know who it was, nor was I aware of the ultimate judgment. The process was very secretive – so secretive, in fact, that during the proposal stage the head of the department assigned a "shadow" reviewer, outside of my committee, to evaluate my research plan. The "shadow," a professor in the department, had veto power, which he exercised. He claimed that my proposal was not of sufficient merit. Freddy and I challenged the judgment and eventually won the battle; I was allowed to pursue the topic I suggested.

We had given the department three names of distinguished psychologists as possible external reviewers: George Albee, former president of the American Psychological Association; Seymour Sarason, an eminent psychologist from Yale University; and Ed Sampson, who had published earlier critiques of psychology in prestigious journals. These were towering figures in psychology. A negative word from them could mean the end of my doctoral program.

Since my doctoral work had been so controversial in the department, I decided to take preventive action. I knew that the ultimate standard for a dissertation was to be publishable in a well-respected journal. To fend off any potential complications at the defense stage, I decided to write a summary of the dissertation and submit it to the prestigious *American Psychologist*. I figured that if a summary of my dissertation gets published in the *American Psychologist* that it would placate the opposition. I wrote a summary, sent the paper (via regular mail, since email submissions were not available yet), and waited. And then I waited some more. Months went by before I got an answer, which came via regular mail. The paper had been accepted, with virtually no changes, which is pretty unheard of in prestigious journals.[43]

A few more months went by, and I eventually was able to get a copy of the prepublication. Since I was living in Winnipeg at the time, and the paper came from the main office of the American Psychological Association in Washington DC, the paper had to be released from customs, at the Winnipeg airport. Today, in the age of electronic communication, the whole process seems incomprehensible, but there was something exciting about getting a paper copy of my first-ever article in the *American Psychologist*. The paper, "Psychology and the Status Quo," was eventually published in the summer of 1989, just before my dissertation defense. Freddy, my advisor, walked into the defense like a proud father with paper in hand, waving it in front of the committee. That was very reassuring.

My confidence was bolstered even more by the review of the external examiner, which Freddy was allowed to share with me minutes before we walked into the defense. George Albee, the former president of APA, had written a glorious evaluation. My dissertation was eventually published as a book in 1994: *The Morals and Politics of Psychology: Psychological Discourse and the Status Quo.*[44]

The story of my dissertation proves three points. First, that my passion and perseverance sustained my interest in the face of obstacles; second, that power concedes nothing without a demand; and third, that society uses psychological language to prevent social change. With regards to the barrier I encountered, the psychological establishment in my department would not allow me to pursue a study that did not conform to their narrow standards of acceptable scholarship. Had Freddy and I not contested their intransigence, the paper and the book would never have seen the light of day. With regard to the actual findings of the study, I was able to identify several ways in which psychological knowledge was used and abused to deflect attention from structures of injustice and inequality. My historical analysis demonstrated that psychology served to justify the existing social order through six distinct stratagems:

1. *It's all in your head*: By explaining behavior strictly in terms of individual factors such as genetic or psychological constitution, and neglecting the role of social, economic, and political causes in human suffering
2. *Blame the Victim:* Through a propensity to understand social problems in terms of psychological maladjustment, as opposed to a reaction to systems of oppression and discrimination
3. *Technophilia*: By embracing technical solutions and innovations that give the appearance of breakthroughs while neglecting systemic, economic, and political problems
4. *Deflection through innovation*: Through the introduction of new treatments or services that attenuate social critique and by creating the impression that something is being done to ameliorate suffering
5. *Unquestionable truths*: Through the promotion of conformist messages that psychology was "value-neutral" and a reflection of an "objective-truth" and, therefore, its prescriptions were never to be questioned
6. *What's good for the elite is good for everyone:* By portraying values that benefit the elite as benefiting the entire society

For over a century now, these ideological messages had become axiomatic truths with two consequential outcomes. First, most people remain unaware of the impact of social conditions on their levels of happiness or misery; and second, few people see the need to engage in social transformation. The only transformation required to achieve success was the transformation of the self – no need to tinker with the social order. And thus, psychology became handmaiden to society.[45]

Amy Cuddy knows all about these discursive strategies. She is featured extensively in Anand Giridharadas's book *Winners Take All: The Elite Charade of Changing the World*.[46] Cuddy, a social psychologist at Harvard Business School, studied racism, sexism, and power dynamics. In October 2011 Cuddy was invited to PopTech, a conference of the corporate elite, to talk about her research. Her guide was the curator for the conference, Andrew Zolli, who had written a book about resilience. Zolli's message was very congenial to the elite: If you want to change the world, do not rock the boat, do not focus on how to eradicate poverty and climate change; instead, focus on how to live with them. He offered changes that essentially protected the status quo. It is very telling that Cuddy chose to talk to the audience about the ultimate ameliorative technique, power poses, as opposed to the causes of sexism.

She came to the stage and assumed her preferred power pose: hands on her hips, feet planted firmly on the ground, perpendicular to her shoulders, wearing brown cowboy boots. That would become her signature power pose. The screen behind her projected an image of Wonder Woman. Cuddy went on to talk about how poses like hers enhanced women's confidence in a male-dominated society. Although she knew a great deal about the power dynamics that perpetuated sexism in society, she chose to talk about coping poses instead. Cuddy provides but one example of how ameliorative discourse prevails in society. Giridharadas offers many more instances in which social thinkers round the edges of their critique so their message is more palatable to wider audiences.

In *The Morals and Politics of Psychology*, I offered extensive evidence for the presence and impact of the six conformist messages. Almost every aspect of human activity, from work to relationships to health care to politics, absorbed these axioms. Entire generations were reared believing that these were self-evident truths, as opposed to socially constructed ideologies. No wonder that we ended up with a "Me Culture" in which the individual is the hero and the context is absent. To repeat, the spirit of the "Me Culture" is *I have the right to feel valued by others so that I may be happy*. In contrast, the "We Culture" envisions a future in which *we* all *have the right and responsibility to feel valued and add value, to our self and others, so that we may* all *experience wellness and fairness. All* means that mattering should not remain the sole province of the powerful and privileged. *All* means the democratization of happiness and well-being.

We live in the reign of the self. Although there are signs that some people want to move from a "Me" to a "We Culture," the transition is partial at best. Many commentators acknowledge that we must move from "I matter" to "We matter," that we must embrace rights and responsibilities, that we should care about the self and others, but they stop there.[47]. When it comes to strategies and outcomes, they stay at the level of wellness and ignore the need for fairness.

To make a meaningful contribution to society, we must make the move from "Me" to "We" complete; we must uphold fairness in relationships, at home, at work, in the community, and in social policies. Without fairness, millions of people will not experience mattering to the fullest extent.[48] If we want to matter in the community as agents of change, we must embrace the full spectrum and implications of a "We Culture." We have had decades of the "Me" approach, and it has not helped us. It is insufficient and inadequate. It has resulted in unprecedented levels of narcissism, racism, inequality, isolation, injustice, and depression.[49]

Lack of fairness is not just a philosophical construct. It has a face and feelings. It lives in people who suffer from exclusion, discrimination, and violence. It resides in Linda Tirado, who was subjected to humiliation because she was poor.[50] It lives in Kenji Yoshino and many others in the LGBTQ community who had to hide their real identity.[51] It lives in Ijeoma Oluo,[52] who was subjected to daily indignities because she is Black. It is part of the lives of people with disabilities who are subjected to stereotype threat.[53] It lived in Black slaves like Frederick Douglass and it lives today in African American parents who lose their kids to unprovoked attacks.[54] It resides in men who were abused by priests they trusted. It is part of women's bodies who were assaulted by men. Wellness is not enough, neither as a strategy nor as an outcome. For all of us to flourish, we also need fairness.

Many wellness experts decry the mind–body dualism but are oblivious to the inner–outer split.[55] They persuasively argue that body and mind are one, while ignoring the impact of lack of fairness on wellness. They delimit the wellness world to what happens within your skin and your head. Mattering does not just happen in our minds. It happens in interactions at work and in the community. There is plenty of evidence that unfair treatment leads to stress, disease, aggression, and disaffection.[56] Fair regard, on the other hand, leads to well-being, happiness, and health.[57]

The main mechanism through which fairness results in wellness is that fair processes protect one's standing in a group.[58] People's dignity is upheld, and threats of shame and humiliation dissipate. The route to mattering must involve internal and external work – psychological and political changes.[59] We must engage in both wellness and fairness.

If you look at your own life, you can easily discern the role of fairness in wellness. Look no further than your own job. Are all your problems at work related to inner conflicts that you might have, or are some of them associated with abuses of power and lack of fairness? Doesn't fairness make a difference in how you feel at work? Of course it does. So much so that people who report higher levels of respect and fairness at work are physically healthier than those who suffer from unfair treatment.[60]

When women are made to feel inferior by abusive husbands, is it their fault? Of course not. They don't suffer from ineptitude – they suffer from injustice. The focus on ourself, rights, and personal wellness has the paradoxical effect of widening the fairness gap because no one is looking into injustice. Instead, we all look at how to improve our wellness, habits, grit, resilience, and motivation. This is how the wellness trap widens the fairness gap.

In low-income communities, children attend schools that teach memorization as opposed to problem-solving. Teachers are told to follow a rigid curriculum guide that prevents creativity and innovation in the classroom. Deep-learning methods, such as project-based, small-group discussions, and experiential education remain the province of well-to-do schools.[61] While deep learning pedagogies motivate kids to participate in the learning process, memorization engenders boredom and disengagement. Instead of fostering competence, many schools promote alienation.

If you feel devalued or incompetent, it is crucial to understand the role of fairness in success and satisfaction, lest you end up blaming yourself for your misfortune. If you attribute your dissatisfaction exclusively to internal failings, you will become despondent and depressed. If you learn to identify how power dynamics affect your sense of mattering, you are less likely to blame yourself and more likely to engage in effective action. In a culture of individualism, it is very common to engage in self-deprecation. The solution, however, is not to blame others either but rather to look at the sources of injustice and to master competencies for personal wellness and social fairness.

Strategies

Adding value is an essential part of mattering. As Angela Duckworth observed, to feel good about ourselves, we must make a contribution to our own growth, and the well-being of others. We must use our competencies for personal and collective good. Since wellness is so tied to fairness, we focus on competencies to improve both.

Competencies for Personal and Collective Wellness

There are two levers of change that are very useful to promote our personal and collective wellness. The first one is *behaviors*, and the second one is *thoughts*. To start an exercise routine, to get better at chess, to finish projects on time, you need to set specific goals and create some positive habits. You need to embrace all the Ts: transcendence, thought, time, trust, training, and tenacity.

As you would recall from Chapter 4, it is important to set SMART goals: *S*pecific, *M*easurable, *A*ttainable, *R*elevant, and *T*ime-Bound. Matan is no stranger to goal attainment. He has been playing chess since he was eight years old, and he has set for himself numerous goals related to his passion: become a master, become a coach, and train champions. Recently, he wanted to work on his physical well-being. He got an app with very specific instructions on how to start a running routine. The program tells him how many minutes to run, how many minutes to walk, and how many times per week to do it. The program is very specific, measureable, attainable, and very relevant to his goal. It is also time-bound. It tells you exactly how long it will take you to achieve certain goals. Matan adhered to the program, and in a few weeks he has been able to run 13K.

A couple of years ago, Ora wanted to get serious about a meditation routine. She set aside specific times during the day in which she would meditate for X number of minutes. The length of time grew gradually until she reached the desired twenty minutes per day, and now it has become a lifestyle that she enjoys.

To matter more, to ourselves and others, we can also cultivate positive habits. Small acts of kindness and fairness will go a long way. Small investments in learning new skills will make you feel more competent. These are all behaviors that can be quantified and measured. For instance, take ten minutes of uninterrupted quality time with your partner to ask open-ended questions after dinner. You ask questions and listen nonjudgmentally. Don't wait for the special date to have a good conversation. Start today, and make it a routine part of your day. The more you make others feel valued, the more they will make you feel valued.

Stories we hear, and stories we tell, shape the stories we create about ourselves and others. Furthermore, they predict our behavior and performance. This is why thoughts are a principal component of the BET I CAN model. When it comes to adding value, thoughts can be our best allies or our worst adversaries. If we think that certain groups are deficient in certain skills, we create stereotypical narratives that will invariably affect their performance. When we think in stereotypes, we traffic in stigmas. Upon encountering members of that group, we project our stigmas in ways that are bound to affect their self-perceptions and performance.[62]

This is an insidious and barely perceptible process. As social psychologist Claude Steele put it, when there is a threat in the air, stereotypes will inevitably shape intellectual identity and performance.[63] When women are subtly reminded of gender differences in math and science, they perform worse than men. But when these cues are eliminated, the gap in performance disappears. The same happens with African Americans. When they are primed to think about race before a test, African Americans perform worse than Whites. But when no such allusions take place, there is no difference in the performance of both groups.

What Steele demonstrated is that even a very subtle reminder of negative stereotypes can affect the performance of the stigmatized group. Steele calls this phenomenon *stereotype threat*. This is a "situational threat – a threat in the air – that, in general form, can affect the members of any group about whom a negative stereotype exists . . . . The threat of these stereotypes can be sharply felt and, in several ways, hampers their achievement."[64] In one study, Steele told a group of women that a math test they were about to take showed gender differences. This condition invoked stereotypical thinking about women's lower abilities in math, thus eliciting stereotype threat. A second group was told that the math test showed no gender differences. The results showed that women performed worse than men when they were told that this type of test is indicative of gender differences. The moment a stereotype is in the air, women's performance suffers because their cognitive process experiences interference from social pressures, anxiety, and evaluative apprehension.

In another study with African Americans in a highly selective university, one group was told that they were about to take a test that was related to intellectual ability. The second group was told that the test was not related to intellectual ability. The first group experienced stereotype threat because they were primed to think about social stereotypes that Blacks may not be as talented as Whites. The second group did not experience stereotype threat because they were told that this was just a problem-solving exercise unrelated to intellectual ability. As in the case of women with the math test, Blacks in the stereotype threat condition performed worse than Whites but did just as well as Whites in the non-stereotype condition. In another study, the mere fact of asking students their race on a demographic questionnaire affected performance. As Steele concludes, "salience of the racial stereotype alone was enough to depress the performance of identified Black students."[65]

Women, Blacks, people with disabilities, and other disadvantaged groups encounter "threats in the air" all the time. These threats ignite performance anxiety that hampers their efforts. The story that these groups are not as competent as others has had the perverse effect of depressing performance. Stress and distractions diminish focus and attention. When stereotypes are eliminated, however, the achievement gap evaporates.

Groups subjected to stigmas carry a heavy burden. Not only do they have to contend with societal barriers, structural inequalities, and histories of marginalization, but they also have to cope with stereotypical thinking about their abilities. To help students and colleagues from all groups add value, we must challenge negative assumptions about their competence, and we must create a new story about their potential. These strategies must never replace the need to change discriminatory policies, but we must remind ourselves that changing laws is rarely enough to change minds. Societal and psychological changes are required. Both are essential – and very much needed. "The effectiveness of these strategies," argues Steele, "is not an argument for neglecting structural and other changes that would help unwind the disadvantages attached to racial, gender, class, and other identities in our society. Such changes have to remain an important focus. But we can make a good deal of progress by addressing identity threat in our lives. And doing so is a big part of unwinding the disadvantages of identity."[66] Steele's research gave rise to a number of successful interventions to minimize the negative repercussions of stereotype threat. His work can be credited with a push to transform negative narratives about the ability of minorities.

When I, Isaac, was a freshman at Bar Ilan University in Israel, I harbored serious doubts about my ability to finish college. I had been in the country for only eighteen months, and my Hebrew was not great. I was disadvantaged in not only one language but two, since most reading materials were in English, and my English was poorer than my Hebrew. I had recently migrated from Argentina where the study of foreign languages could not compete with my devotion to soccer and politics. Thus, I had a lot of academic catch-up to do in Israel. My beginner level in English and Hebrew posed serious challenges to my ability to succeed in college.

Ready to quit, I jumped on a bus to Beer Sheba to share the news with my older cousin Oscar. When my parents died in a car accident when I was eight years old, my two siblings and I went to live with Oscar, his two siblings, my aunt, and my grandmother. Oscar was always the wise older cousin, and I always held him in high regard, which I still do. Oscar and his wife Sylvia, both physicians, always welcomed me to their home. That time in Beer Sheba was no different.

When I shared with Oscar my academic struggles he did what has come to be known as a "lay theory intervention." He told me that struggling in college, especially for a newcomer like me, was not uncommon, and in all likelihood I would do better next year. He told me that my struggles should not be interpreted as lack of ability or potential. He reassured me that "I belonged" in a university setting. Little did he know that his reassuring, normalizing approach to my woes would be the subject of double-bind experiments years later. Lay theory intervention has been used to keep minorities from choosing to drop out of college, closing the achievement gap.

As noted in a recent paper, "in the United States, students from racial/ethnic minorities groups and those who would be the first in their families to earn a college degree (i.e., first-generation students) can face negative stereotypes about their intellectual ability, numeric underrepresentation, and other group-based threats on campus."[67] Since achievement in college is predictive of future health, earning, and occupational opportunities, successful preventive programs using lay theory are crucial. Negative experiences early in college lead many, like I did, to think that "I don't belong here."

In a series of studies involving over 9,500 students from disadvantaged backgrounds in three colleges, participants attended a single online session on lay theory.[68] The session taught students that many feel they don't belong at first, but with time they come to feel valued in the community. Although the students were from varied minority identities, all shared common threats: worries about belonging, intellectual capacity, and cultural fit. There were many positive results from the studies. In the first experiment, students exposed to the lay theory on social belonging – stating that it tends to improve over time – were more likely to use academic support services, join extracurricular activities, and choose to live on campus.

In the second experiment, exposure to lay theory prior to matriculation reduced inequality in first-year completion by 40 percent. Among disadvantaged students who did not get the single session intervention,

13 percent were identified as risk of dropping out due to social and academic difficulties, whereas among those who did get the intervention the proportion at risk was only 7 percent.

In a third experiment in a selective private university, minority students exposed to the normalizing message of the intervention obtained a higher GPA than disadvantaged students who were not exposed to the lay theory intervention. In addition to higher GPA, eleven months after the intervention, treated students reported greater social and academic integration at school. Taken together, the first two experiments reduced the achievement gap by between 31 and 40 percent.

Since social mobility hinges so much on educational attainment, these results are very significant. The ability to retain and promote minority students by reducing stereotype threat and increasing confidence in their potential is critical. Minority students can interpret challenges in college in two ways. The typical thinking is "people like me can't succeed in college." The typical behavior is to withdraw from the social and academic environment, and the typical outcome is poor persistence and lower rates of graduation. With a lay theory prior to matriculation, the thinking changes to "it's common to experience these challenges and overcome them." Accordingly, they stay engaged, socially and academically, and end up graduating.

In another study meant to frame social adversity as common and transient among Black freshman, a three-year follow-up revealed higher GPA and self-reported health and well-being relative to groups not exposed to the intervention.[69] In a similar vein, women entering a selective engineering university program were exposed to lay theory interventions aimed at increasing their confidence and normalizing challenges.[70] Compared to the control group, women exposed to the program had higher GPAs and were better able to integrate into the male-dominated profession.

In essence, these students challenge negative assumptions about themselves and tell themselves a new story. As a result, their performance improves. This is the power of leveraging thoughts. Leaders and managers must help others by challenging negative assumptions, in themselves and others, about the inferior capacity of women, minorities, and people with disabilities. They must help workers from disadvantaged backgrounds – and the workforce as a whole – create a new story: "we all possess the capacity to excel." But as Steele and other researchers caution, it would be a mistake to focus exclusively on the victim of prejudice and leave the system of injustice intact.

If we want to help others improve their performance and enhance their sense of mattering, something must be done to improve not just their wellness but also their fairness. Institutionalized injustice is often entrenched. This is why we must not only zoom in on the psychology of the victim but also zoom out on the sociology of the system.

Although all these experiments were very successful, some of the authors include a note of caution, like Steele did:

> A critical misinterpretation of our research would be to conclude that psychological disadvantage is simply in the head. To the contrary, worries about belonging and potential are pernicious precisely because they arise from awareness of real social disadvantage before and during college, including biased treatment, university policies and practices that inadvertently advantage some groups of students over others, and awareness of negative stereotypes and numeric underrepresentation.[71]

Competencies for Personal and Collective Fairness

To fight lack of fairness we must develop good radars because some cues are subtle and nuanced. Somebody "forgot" to invite you to a meeting or "just made a joke" about your ethnic group. A teacher fails to call on the minority student. A professor always turns to the same person for answers. Implicit bias is the unconscious tendency to favor people from certain groups over others. It happens in job interviews and in promotion decisions. These behaviors tell us how valued or devalued we are in certain circumstances. When we perceive, consciously or unconsciously, that our contributions don't really matter, our performance and well-being deteriorate. We must have good radars for subtle or blatant cues.

From time to time, it is best to change the cues altogether. Some children do not have a choice but to live with parents who often make them feel invisible or worthless. Kids cannot easily escape neglectful or abusive environments, but adults have more freedom. If you are engaged in a bad relationship, with your boss, your partner, or your father, sometimes the best thing to do is to remove yourself from the situation and avoid the negative cues altogether. We are aware that sometimes it is not easy to leave a job because there may not be another one just waiting for you. Moving on is a privilege not everyone can afford.

Nowadays you also have to worry about your online connections. Corrosive relationships do not have to rise to the level of cyberbullying to exert a negative impact on you. Constant social comparisons with online friends can be toxic since they result in either envy or scorn.[72]

The ability to identify the external source of suffering is essential. This is what we call *knowing the issue*. If you define social problems in intrapsychic terms, you will never get to the root cause of the problem. Confronting bullies and injustice is not easy or pretty, but, as we noted earlier, *qui tacet consentit* – whoever keeps silent consents. It is very important to call issues for what they are: abuse, discrimination, racism, heterosexism, ableism, and other forms of injustice. Lack of mattering does not derive just from unresolved personal conflicts. It also emanates from oppression at home, at work, and in the community.

CHAPTER 6

Mattering through Self-Regard

When we were raising our now 33-year-old son, we tried our best to do what all good parents try to do. We gave Matan a consistent message that we love him and always will; that we approve of him as a person even when we disapprove of certain behaviors; and that his worth as a human being is not based on good grades, athletic achievements, or popularity. I (Ora) remember one particularly sweet exchange with Matan as a four-year-old. It was after I needed to discipline him with a time-out for some misbehavior, and he was not happy with me. Since I realized that my irritation with him was palpable, I told him that I always love him, even when I'm upset with him. Matan pondered this for a second before he responded: "Really, mommy? When I'm mad at you I don't love you."

This was a classic "from the mouths of babes" moment. At some level, Matan was right. Love is not the predominant emotion when we interact with someone whose behavior has upset, disappointed, or frustrated us. Nonetheless, most parents understand the importance of unconditional positive regard and its relationship to self-acceptance and self-esteem. Unconditional positive regard by parents paves the way to unconditional self-regard, a felt sense that one is worthy and acceptable even when he or she makes mistakes, experiences failure, or behaves in less than desirable ways.[1] People with high self-esteem perceive themselves favorably. They generally like themselves and believe they are competent and capable of handling life's challenges. Conversely, those with low self-esteem regard themselves as incapable, unlikable, or even unworthy.[2] As Morris Rosenberg, the author of the famous self-esteem scale, observed, low self-esteem is related to depression and a number of psychosomatic ailments such as loss of appetite, insomnia, nervousness, and headaches. He argued also that there is a clear "relationship between self-esteem and psychosomatic symptoms of anxiety."[3]

On the whole, people with low self-esteem do not feel valued by themselves or by others and doubt their ability to add value. Self-acceptance and self-esteem are thus critical for mattering. We first describe the signs and manifestations of high and low self-esteem and related constructs. Next, we draw on research that demonstrates their significance to well-being and thriving, followed by a review of their sources and root causes. Finally, we provide strategies for promoting self-acceptance and healthy self-regard at various stages of life.

Signs

Sheila was born with a rare neuromuscular disorder, the second child to working-class parents. She was born in an era when children with disabilities were more likely to be raised in an institution than as part of their family and community. They spent most of their childhood segregated from nondisabled siblings and peers and were transferred to nursing homes when they turned eighteen. Sheila's parents loved their curious and precocious infant. They wanted to raise her at home even as they learned that she would never walk and would require assistance with all aspects of physical care. However, they had no way to pay for the equipment she required or for her care. In their case, the decision to place her in an institution for children with physical disabilities was a way to ensure that her needs would be met. With a heavy heart, they made the decision to institutionalize their six-year-old daughter.

Sheila's parents visited her regularly and remained a consistent and supportive presence in her life. But this was in the 1960s and parents in this position didn't have much of a say. From the day she entered the institution at the age of six until she left for good at eighteen, Sheila's life was largely dictated by institutional routines and revolving staff. Even when she attended regular public school at the age of twelve, she was bused back to the institution when school let out each day.

This is what Sheila said in her mid-thirties, as she described her childhood in the institution:

> You had no say in anything . . . . You didn't have a say about what you ate or when you ate it. You didn't have a say about when you got up or when you went to bed. You didn't have a say about what times you could play or have free time. Even what you were wearing . . . they were going to open the closet door and pick item a or item b . . . . It was a power issue . . . . They were in charge.[4]

The lack of choice and self-determination also applied to critical decisions about where one would live beyond childhood.

> You had to leave when you were 18 and they would just dump people wherever there was a spot. I mean they didn't really care. They would place you out to a nursing home or some convent ... it didn't matter, wherever there was an opening.[5]

Under such circumstances, a child might conclude that where she spends the rest of her life doesn't really matter because *she* doesn't really matter. Such pervasive and consistent messages can lead to low self-worth and self-esteem. But Sheila was a feisty and determined child with a healthy and positive self-regard. She excelled in school and became a leader among her peers. She boldly stood up to staff and resisted unfair and oppressive practices. Even though she was frequently in trouble for talking and pushing back, she was unrelenting in her fight for self-determination.

> I knew there'd be a backlash but I didn't care – it was more important to name the score. I also knew that I would let the other kids down if I didn't fight back because they would expect me to fight back about it. In a way I think they were vicariously fighting some of their fights through me.[6]

Sheila also fought "tooth and nail" for a quiet study spot where she could complete her homework. Since some children passed away and the others were not expected to live as self-sufficient adults, little attention was paid to the quality of their education. Nonetheless, Sheila attained the sought-after study space. She attended high school in the community and was a strong and high-performing student. She knew that she and the other children in the institution were just as worthy and deserving as her nondisabled peers. In her last year of high school, Sheila was actively planning the next stage of her life. In addition to applying to college, she knew she must find an alternative to the standard nursing home placement. As she researched her options and learned her rights, she discovered consumer-directed attendant services – a nascent policy culminating from the advocacy of parents and disability activists. When her application was accepted, this was her ticket to living life on her own terms, free to find out who she could become.

Sheila (not her real name) was a research participant in Ora's doctoral research study on women with disabilities and motherhood twenty-five years ago. In her mid-thirties when the study was conducted, Sheila was married with two young children. She graduated from university and worked in a management position with a lot of responsibility. She was a well-respected manager at work, a busy mom at home, and a disability rights advocate in the community. She was very capable, highly articulate, and self-assured.

Sheila clearly fits our description of someone who matters. She exemplifies a person who matters and adds value – to herself, her family, her work, and her community. Even as a child, she advocated for the rights of other children as well as her own rights. When her first child was born, Sheila lobbied for a funded assistant – someone who would enable her to physically care for her infant. She used her sharp intellect and strong communication skills to make a strong case for this type of assistance. Her request was ultimately granted and the necessary funding was secured. But in addition to lobbying for and benefiting from this assistance herself, Sheila worked to extend it to other families in a similar situation.

Undoubtedly, Sheila's ability to add value was predicated on feeling valued by others and by herself. Someone who feels worthy and believes that he or she is a valuable person is considered to have high self-esteem. It is one of the oldest, most heavily researched, and widely debated constructs in psychology.[7] If you like yourself for who you are and consider yourself efficacious and capable, you have high self-esteem. Your *trait* self-esteem is your global evaluation of yourself. It is a stable trait that does not change appreciably from one stage of adult life to another.[8] On the other hand, *state* self-esteem is how we feel about ourselves in response to daily occurrences.

But self-esteem is not merely an internal experience that resides between our ears and exists exclusively in our thoughts and feelings. People with high self-esteem behave differently from their low self-esteem counterparts.[9] Because they feel good about themselves, they have an *approach* rather than an *avoidance* orientation to challenges. They trust their own judgment, speak their minds, and take initiative. They work to solve problems and expend efforts in order to achieve their goals. Setbacks are disappointing but not devastating or soul-crushing as their self-worth does not stand in the balance. Perceiving themselves as competent and efficacious, those with healthy self-esteem are motivated to try harder when they fail. They are able to take advantage of opportunities for growth and advancement even when there is no guarantee of success.[10]

Those with low self-esteem are a lot less likely to take such chances. They are desperate to avoid making mistakes and shy away from situations where success is not guaranteed.[11] In an experiment where participants received bogus negative feedback about their performance, those with low self-esteem felt worse about themselves than their higher self-esteem counterparts.[12] This pattern persisted when the feedback was social rather than intellectual.

Self-esteem has significant implications for how we relate to others in general and those close to us in particular.[13] Most people thrive on positive feedback and affirming messages about themselves. Those with high self-esteem embrace those messages as they mirror and bolster their own self-evaluation. Conversely, those with low self-esteem tend to resist or even disparage such feedback as it is inconsistent with how they view themselves. Thus, they undermine positive feedback that can potentially bolster their self-esteem and enhance their well-being.

In one study participants were presented with the following scenario:

> Imagine that you have just received a high mark on a midterm in one of your classes. You had studied a lot for this midterm, but found it very difficult and so you weren't sure you did that well. Your mark is much higher than you expected and so you are very pleased with it. When you tell your romantic partner about this test mark, he [or she] says "That's awesome! I'm proud of you. You are really intelligent and hard-working!"[14]

Compared to those with high self-esteem, low self-esteem participants perceived this feedback as less sincere, less meaningful, and less likely to be repeated by their partner. They further reported that such a compliment would make them feel worse about themselves and less secure in the relationship. Apparently, what they could not believe about themselves they could not easily accept from their romantic partners either. Other studies found that those with low self-esteem tend to evaluate negatively their intimate partner and the relationship as a whole.[15] When difficulties arise, they are more likely to distance themselves rather than confront the problem and act to mend the rift.

Self-esteem also manifests in parenting behavior.[16] According to a recent literature review, parents with high self-esteem display more positive behaviors as they interact with their children, are more satisfied with them, and report a more satisfying and rewarding relationship overall. Conversely, low parental self-esteem is positively associated with child maltreatment and neglect.

Significance

Self-esteem has important implications for a host of life domains. Those high in self-esteem experience more positive emotions and are significantly happier than those with low self-esteem. In fact, high self-esteem is considered one of the most dominant predictors of happiness.[17] In the last few decades, a vast amount of research has attested to the benefits that accrue from happiness – for individuals, those they associate with, their work environments, and their communities. Research by Martin Seligman, Barbara Fredrickson, Sonia Lyubomirsky, and others has demonstrated the benefits that happiness confers.[18] Positive emotions facilitate creative thinking, problem-solving, and ingenuity. Happier people are also kinder and more compassionate toward others. They act in ways that strengthen relational bonds, which further contributes to their happiness. And since emotions in general and positive ones in particular are infectious, those who associate with happy people can also benefit.[19]

Just as greater happiness is positively correlated with higher self-esteem, depression and self-esteem are inversely correlated. Multiple studies have found that feeling worthless and inadequate is a significant risk factor for depression. But is low self-esteem the cause of depression, or merely its consequence? By utilizing statistical techniques that demonstrate the prospective effect of one variable on another, researchers have concluded that self-esteem is a predictor for depression, rather than the other way around.[20] Depression also contributes to low self-esteem, but the impact of low self-esteem on depression is twice as large. Other forms of psychopathology associated with low self-esteem include anxiety, anorexia, bulimia, social phobia, and alcohol abuse, among others.[21] In fact, "people with lower self-esteem experience virtually every aversive emotion more frequently than those with higher self-esteem."[22] Cardiovascular problems and higher body mass are also associated with low self-esteem, as are smoking and alcohol consumption.

But the field of self-esteem has had its critics and skeptics. For one, the research literature has yielded some mixed results regarding the influence of self-esteem on future success in economic, academic, and social spheres. Critics have rightfully cautioned against a trend, which gained force in the 1980s, that vehemently promoted sweeping and wide-ranging efforts to raise self-esteem in schools across the nation. It was based on a collective belief that high self-esteem is a fundamental source of desirable behaviors and outcomes that would help individuals and society. Conversely, many believed that low self-esteem is an epidemic which accounts for most individual and social ills. Meanwhile, psychological research showed that most people report fairly high self-esteem and believe that they are above average. As a nation, we were not suffering from a low self-esteem epidemic.[23]

The California legislature created a special task force in 1986 with a mission to cultivate and boost self-esteem.[24] It was named "Task Force on Self-Esteem and Personal and Social Responsibility" and was awarded a hefty yearly budget for several years. Many California counties created self-esteem committees designed to eradicate low self-esteem and ensure that children feel good about themselves. Children's books and curricula taught them to see themselves as special, unique, and successful. In some cases, great caution was taken with critical feedback lest it present a barrier to high self-esteem. Often times, this approach to children, and the programs and initiatives that it propelled, were not based on sound research, nor was it necessarily conducive to their growth and development.[25]

As the self-esteem movement was at its peak, a more nuanced and tempered story was emerging from the scientific community. The Association for Psychological Science assembled a group of experts led by Roy Baumeister, an eminent social psychologist, to conduct a comprehensive review of the research on self-esteem.[26] Baumeister and his colleagues published the results of their review in 2003 in an article that continues to be widely read and cited. They cautioned that the benefits of high self-esteem are not as clear-cut as the lay public believes them to be.[27]

For one, the methodology used in some studies did not lend itself to firm conclusions. The fact that high-achieving students report high self-esteem does not mean that high self-esteem leads to high achievement. High self-esteem can be the consequence of high achievement, or the two variables can be explained by a third factor such as privileged upbringing. Furthermore, many studies are based on self-reports and lack any objective verification. Those who report high self-esteem may also be inclined to inflate their success in other domains. Baumeister and his colleagues concurred that high self-esteem leads to greater happiness, lower risk for depression, and more initiative and risk-taking. They were less optimistic about its impact on academic achievement, career advancement, and other desirable outcomes.

Since the publication of that article, other studies and reviews have highlighted the potential benefit of high self-esteem – and the corrosive impact of its opposite.[28] Is low self-esteem a risk factor for important life outcomes? A group of researchers conducted a rigorous, multimethod longitudinal study in order to address this question. They followed up 1,037 New Zealanders born in 1972 and 1973, assessing them every two years from age three to twenty-six. This study is particularly significant as it did not rely exclusively on self-reports. Participants allowed the research team to gather data on their mental health and substance use from people who know them well. They let health professionals take their blood pressure and measure their cardiorespiratory fitness. They gave consent for their education and employment records to be examined and criminal conviction history to be externally verified by the courts. Those found to have low self-esteem as adolescents were more likely to develop depression, anxiety disorders, physical health problems, and tobacco addiction, in line with the predictions by Rosenberg in the 1960s.[29] The results were even more compelling for those who had a number of problem behaviors as adults:

> Only 17% of adolescents with low self-esteem were free from problems as adults, whereas 56% had multiple problems as adults. In contrast, 51% of adolescents with high self-esteem were free from problems as adults, whereas only 17% had multiple problems.[30]

Adolescents with low self-esteem were twice as likely to leave school early. They had fewer economic prospects, poorer cardiorespiratory health, and more criminal convictions than those with high self-esteem. The results held even as researchers controlled for the increased risk of low self-esteem due to gender, socioeconomic status, and IQ. Finally, in a more recently published longitudinal multigenerational study, researchers concluded that "regardless of whether one was born in the early 1900s or in the 1980s, self-esteem had significant benefits for people's experiences of love, work, and health, supporting hypotheses about the beneficial conse-quences of high self-esteem."[31]

The Rosenberg self-esteem inventory, developed in 1965, continues to be the most widely used inventory in research on the subject. It is thus interesting to see how high self-esteem was conceptualized by Rosenberg himself:

> When we speak of high self-esteem, then, we shall simply mean that the individual respects himself [sic], considers himself worthy; he does not necessarily consider himself better than others, but he definitely does not consider himself worse; he does not feel that he is the ultimate in perfection but, on the contrary, recognizes his limitations and expects to grow and improve.[32]

This is a description of someone with healthy positive self-regard. It is certainly a befitting description for Sheila and for many other people who are undoubtedly happier and better adjusted than those who experience "self-rejection, self-dissatisfaction, self-contempt."[33] Nonetheless, knowing a person's level of self-esteem tells an incomplete story.

More current research points to the need to attend to the specific quality of self-esteem and not merely its level. While Rosenberg's description is befitting for those with a healthy self-esteem, who appreciate themselves without depreciating others and recognize their strengths as well as their limitations, high self-esteem can have a dark side as well.[34] For one, it "may refer to an accurate, justified and balanced appreciation of one's worth as a person and one's successes and competencies, but it can also refer to an inflated, arrogant, grandiose, unwarranted sense of conceited superiority over others."[35] The Rosenberg self-esteem inventory, like many others, does not distinguish the former from the latter.

Narcissists, as we noted in Chapter 2, think very highly of themselves. But narcissists clearly don't fit Rosenberg's description of high self-esteem. They *do* see themselves as superior to others and deserving of more admiration and esteem. They believe they are more talented, make better leaders, and are entitled to the best. They are boastful, self-centered, and unconcerned with the welfare of others. They use others as a tool for their own self-aggrandizement. They have an inflated sense of worth and are only interested in feedback that confirms their pompous self-views. They see life as a zero-sum game of losers and winners and actively pursue their own winning positions at others' expense. They choose competition over communion, getting ahead versus getting along. Compared to non-narcissists, they are more likely to become hostile and aggressive when others challenge or cast doubt on their inflated self-worth.[36]

Another important distinction is between *secure* and *fragile* high self-esteem.[37] Secure high self-esteem is relatively consistent across situations and not easily challenged by a disappointing achievement or an interpersonal rebuff. It is anchored in *realistic* rather than *inflated* self-appraisal. It is also not conditional upon looks, feats, or outstanding accomplishments, nor does it require constant validation from others. "In contrast, fragile high self-esteem is conceptualized as feelings of self-worth that are unrealistic, vulnerable to threat, and require constant validation."[38]

Fragile self-esteem is also unstable. We are all happier when we experience success than when we fail. However, those with fragile self-esteem are particularly prone to a fluctuating self-regard in response to such experiences. Those with a secure and noncontingent self-esteem are not easily shattered by negative feedback or a disappointing achievement. They feel bad but not unworthy. In contrast, those with contingent self-esteem stake their self-worth on certain standards and can enjoy positive self-regard only if and when these standards are met.[39] If their self-worth is conditional on academic achievement they are at the mercy of their grades. If it is athletic excellence they pine for, it's at the mercy of their wins and losses.

Failure is particularly devastating for people who possess a low general self-regard. If they stake their self-worth on academic achievement, they are likely to become disengaged learners following negative feedback on their performance. Their urge is to protect an already poor self-regard from plummeting even further. Those with a high but contingent self-esteem tend to become defensive and attribute their failure to others or to external circumstances. They may become angry and hostile in response to evaluative feedback as they attempt to maintain their high self-esteem.

In a particularly memorable encounter I (Ora) had as a professor, a visibly angry student approached me at the end of class after I handed back graded term papers. The paper guidelines were very clear, and I had provided detailed written feedback along with the grade. "Do you realize this is a really bad grade?" she asked loudly and accusingly, pointing to the B at the top of her paper. The student was not interested in reading the feedback or learning how she can improve her research and writing skills. She was fully focused on the B grade, as though it marked her as a second-class citizen. *How dare I*, was her implicit message.

Like this student, those who base their self-worth on academic achievement are preoccupied with performing well at the expense of learning well.[40] They are more focused on *proving* rather than *improving* themselves; they are less likely to pursue challenging goals where success is not guaranteed. This often comes with a heavy price tag: avoiding or disengaging from personally meaningful pursuits that can promote wellness and happiness. In a similar vein, critical interpersonal feedback is particularly corrosive for those who stake their self-worth on ubiquitous social approval. They are more likely to pursue goals that will gain them the approval they crave than those that are driven by their values, passions, and interests.

Can low self-esteem impede well-being? The answer is absolutely yes. Will efforts to boost self-esteem across the board solve all personal, interpersonal, and social ills plaguing our society? The answer is absolutely no. Consider the name of California's "Task Force on Self-Esteem and Personal and Social Responsibility." Self-esteem is a lot more about feeling valued than about adding value, especially to people and causes beyond oneself. If the goal is to also promote social responsibility, we need to promote social responsibility rather than expect that it will be the natural outgrowth of high self-esteem. Narcissists who already feel overvalued are interested in adding value only to themselves.

Low self-esteem is far from optimal to well-being in general and to mattering in particular. It's logical to conclude that those who perceive themselves as unworthy and incompetent are not in a good position to add value to the self and others. But neither are narcissists or those whose self-worth is perpetually on the line and requires the validation of good grades, professional promotions, Idealized body shapes, or constant social approval. The latter reflects an introjection of externally imposed conditions of worth and can result in a preoccupation with the pursuit of self-esteem.[41] Actions are guided by what will garner approval or admiration, rather than what can advance core needs, values, and interests.

Those who stake their self-worth on external factors (achievements, wins, looks, approval) are more susceptible to poor outcomes than those who base their self-worth on communal, virtuous, or spiritual benchmarks.[42] And whereas having a high self-esteem is preferable to a low one, pursuing self-esteem can backfire.

For Albert Ellis (1913–2007), one of the most influential psychotherapists of the twentieth century and the creator of Rational Emotive Behavior Therapy, self-esteem is "the greatest sickness known to man or woman because it's conditional."[43] Ellis contended that it is irrational for people to rate their self-worth by giving themselves a global report card. He advocated for evaluating our traits and behaviors but not our self-worth.[44] Since human beings are dynamic and always in progress, it is irrational to label ourselves and judge our worth. Others have followed in Ellis's footsteps and argued for pursuing *self-acceptance in lieu of self-esteem.*[45]

Psychologist Kristin Neff has dedicated her career to the study of self-compassion, which is strongly aligned with self-acceptance.[46] Although self-esteem and self-compassion are related constructs, they are not the same. Self-compassion refers to treating oneself kindly in the face of pain and suffering. It is about extending to ourselves the compassion we feel for others in their difficult moments and our desire to alleviate their pain. Since pain and suffering is something that everyone experiences, self-compassion is an invitation to perceive our distress as part of the shared human experience, one that connects rather than separates us from others.[47]

The capacity to accept our suffering nonjudgmentally and relate to ourselves with kindness and compassion as we would relate to a friend in distress is an important protective factor that can enhance personal and relational well-being. When self-esteem is contingent, it is a fair-weather friend who is only available when the contingency is met.[48] Conversely, self-compassion is available in the most vulnerable of moments. The reality is that a purely noncontingent self-esteem is instinctively appealing but not so easy to achieve. We may care little about our physical appearance but a lot about our athletic ability. We may yearn for high grades and professional attainment but be relatively unconcerned with our popularity. In one study only a small percentage of college freshmen were found to have self-esteem that is truly noncontingent.[49]

Feeling disappointed, deflated, and not so good about ourselves are common reactions to failure in a valued domain. But when such feelings are not mild and transient but rather sticky, unrelenting, and lead to diminished self-worth, the need to protect self-esteem can be an all-encompassing preoccupation. The tools of self-compassion, which we will later discuss, can be there for us when we need them the most.

Sources

> Stefani was very unique and that wasn't always appreciated by her peers and, as a result, she went through a lot of difficult times. Humiliated, taunted, isolated. When you're a young woman, this really severely impacts you . . . It was in middle school when I saw that turn happen – when she went from a very happy and aspirational young girl to somebody that started to question her self-worth, to have doubts about herself and that is when we actually saw the turn.

In this excerpt from a recent television interview, Cynthia Germanota shared her daughter's painful middle school days and the impact it had on her life.[50] It would seem unremarkable, if it weren't for the fact that Cynthia Germanota is the mother of Lady Gaga – famed singer, musician, and performer. These days, Lady Gaga is using her fame to promote an atmosphere where teens and young adults with mental health issues feel comfortable to reach out for help. Her mother Cynthia has joined her in these efforts.

Where do self-views come from and how do they manifest at different stages of development? How do some children come to like themselves and feel competent and worthy while others are plagued by self-doubts and poor self-regard? Why are some preoccupied with living up to conditions of worth, while others feel free to pursue intrinsically appealing interests and aspirations? And how do other children come to see themselves as more special and deserving than the rest?

To begin with, early childhood is when self-esteem is generally high but unstable.[51] Very young children are unable to distinguish between their ideal self and real self, between what they want to do and what they can do. They overestimate their abilities and performance, and their self-evaluations are unrealistically positive. Their capacity to see themselves through the eyes of others and to measure their skills in relation to those of their peers increases gradually as children move from early to middle childhood and beyond. Self-esteem generally declines as children transition to adolescence, for girls more so than for boys.[52] It increases in young and middle adulthood and is generally stable until the seventh decade of life when it tends to decline. The gender difference which first appears in adolescence is maintained throughout the lifespan, with self-esteem of males being slightly higher than that of females.

Like many other psychological traits, self-esteem has a genetic component but is largely determined by our social environment.[53] In fact, self-evaluations are formed through interactions with significant others, beginning with our primary caregivers. The quality of early attachments, which we covered in Chapter 2, lays the foundations for how we come to view the world, other people, and ourselves. Babies who receive sensitive caregiving develop a working model that can serve them well as they continue to grow and mature.[54] The world, according to this working model, is a safe place. Others, especially close others, are supportive and trustworthy. And since others love me and respond to my needs, I am lovable, capable, and worthy of care and support. The rudimentary foundations of high self-esteem is thus instilled.

But babies are born with different temperaments, and some are easier to care for than others.[55] All parents find it easier and more rewarding to interact with a mild-tempered and smiley baby, one who is generally content and easy to pacify. An irritable one who is difficult to soothe is more of a challenge for sleep-deprived parents who are struggling to understand their infant's needs. This is how temperament interacts with early attachments. Parents who are stable, mature, and sufficiently resourced have a wider repertoire for responding to infants with more challenging temperaments. They study their infants, learn to read their signals, and use it to guide their interactions with them. They get better at telling the difference between a baby in need of stimulation and play and one in need of soothing and rest.

Furthermore, infancy and early attachments are only the beginning. Babies grow into toddlers who display preferences, express wishes, and want to make choices and do things for themselves. They say no, want their own way, and test parental limits. Child-centered parents respond with the child's shifting developmental needs in mind.[56] They are warm and supportive but also set limits to ensure safety and cultivate self-control. They provide reasons for the rules they set in a way their child can understand, but they also encourage the expression of feelings, opinions, and preferences. They understand their preschooler's growing need for autonomy and allow him or her to make age-appropriate choices. Will it be the red pajamas tonight or the blue one? They plan sufficient time in the morning so they can honor the child's wish to dress him- or herself.

But parenting does not happen in a vacuum, and it is affected by a host of proximal and distal factors. Compared to their high-school educated peers, college-educated parents are more likely to raise their children in a financially stable, two-parent household.[57] They interact with their children using larger vocabulary and more complex syntax. They provide more encouragement, spend more time reading and playing, and focus more on skill building than on achieving compliance. Harvard political scientist Robert Putnam refers to this as the hug/spank ratio.[58]

More educated parents also have more *Goodnight Moon* time with their children compared to more "diaper time" in less educated households.[59] The latter use more coercive discipline and give less elaborate explanations of the reasoning behind their disciplinary practices. They are more likely to raise their children in single-parent, financially strained households that are located in impoverished and unsafe neighborhoods. Not only are these parents likely to experience chronic stress themselves, they also need to worry about keeping their children safe in the neighborhood and the community. For all those reasons, children growing up in more affluent and educated households have a distinct advantage that is also relevant to how they view themselves.

As children mature, so does their capacity to compare their skills and abilities to those of their peers.[60] They receive messages about their likability and capability and begin to see themselves through others' reflected appraisals. Increasingly, their global self-esteem is affected by their level of competence in valued domains, a process which will continue as they transition to adolescence and beyond. School is an arena where children can experience mastery and self-efficacy but can also encounter disappointment and failure. The reactions of the important adults in their lives will have a substantial effect on the conclusions they form about learning and about themselves.

Children's social world expands once they start to go to school and parents cease to be their preferred playmates. The attachment system and parenting practices continue to play a critical yet changing role.[61] Those securely attached as infants, whose parents balance affection and support with expectations and rules, fare the best. For parents, this requires an ability to adapt their parenting to their child's unfolding development. A nine-year-old girl, for instance, does not need the intensive monitoring of a three-year-old girl; but she does need parents who can impart skills and scaffold her ability to solve problems and make good decisions. She is no longer the baby who protested separation from mom and dad, but she still turns to them when upset and in need of comfort. As her world expands and she becomes more independent, she is comfortable to venture out knowing that her parents are there for her.

Thus, the three main functions of the attachment system are proximity maintenance, safe haven, and secure base.[62] It is their parents' availability, rather than their constant presence, that children at this stage of development really need. In fact, studies confirm that, when sad or distressed, even eleven- and twelve-year-olds turn to their parents more so than to peers.[63]

Whereas early childhood is the stage of life where self-esteem is generally at its highest point, adolescence marks its lowest point. It is at this stage of development that we are most concerned with being liked and accepted by our peers and their opinion of us looms particularly large. For teenagers like Lady Gaga who struggle with peer rejection or disregard, adolescence is a particularly trying stage of development.

Furthermore, as teens strive for mastery and competence in important domains, some gaps between one's real self and ideal self are bound to occur.[64] Invariably, some teenagers excel academically whereas others do not, and some demonstrate greater athletic prowess than their peers. Adolescents receive evaluative feedback on their school performance, athletic competence, popularity, and looks. Their self-concept will be affected by how they perceive such feedback and the meaning they make of it.

On a personal note, I (Ora) can recount the early adolescent sting of not measuring up to my peers in athletic ability. As much as I tried to keep up in gym class, my performance always fell short. I was always the last to be "chosen" by the captains when we were divided into teams for basketball or baseball. Unbeknownst to me at the time, these were early signs of the muscular dystrophy with which I was diagnosed at age eighteen. As an eighth or ninth grader in gym class, it simply made me feel like a loser. Athletic ability was something that was highly regarded by my peers and that I clearly didn't have.

My painful experience as an adolescent is best explained by the sociometer theory. Self-esteem, according to this theory, is really a gauge of our relational value and a way of alerting us that we are at risk of social exclusion and rejection. The need to belong and be valued by others is a fundamental human need. When this need is threatened, we are motivated to take action that would increase our relational value in the eyes of others. Like my experience in gym classes, "events that connote social exclusion set off the bells in the sociometer's warning system."[65] I could not "escape" gym until it was an elective course in grade ten. However, I developed an interest in acting and joined the drama club, where I was accepted with open arms.

Whereas adolescents' self-esteem is highly affected by their peer group, parents continue to play a pivotal role. Teenagers yearn to form their own identity and establish emotional self-sufficiency apart from their parents. As they form emotional bonds with friends and later with romantic partners, their relationship with parents undergoes a change. The need for intimacy and support is increasingly shifted to peers and romantic partners, paving the way for future adult relationships. Nonetheless, parents continue to serve an important function, especially in times of danger or significant distress. A healthy self-regard is bolstered by parents who facilitate autonomous thinking and responsible decision-making while continuing to be a reliable source of guidance and emotional support.[66]

Carl Rogers (1902–1987) was a humanistic psychologist and the founder of Person-Centered Therapy. Rogers highlighted the importance of providing children with unconditional positive regard, which ultimately leads to unconditional positive self-regard.[67] Human beings, according to Rogers, are naturally driven to self-actualization. When parents' love and support is provided unconditionally, children are free to pursue authentic and freely chosen goals. Conversely, parental love that is conditional on certain standards of performance or behavior leads to the type of fragile and contingent self-esteem we described earlier.

In my years as a college mental health counselor and later as a professor, I (Ora) encountered a number of students who struggled to measure up to parental expectations. One case involved a student athlete whose father also worked in athletics. The student described the agony he felt whenever his athletic performance wasn't up to par. The thought that he was a disappointment to his father was incredibly painful.

In another memorable case, a freshman was devastated when he was rejected from the fraternity of his choice. His counselor, a graduate student, tried to understand why this was such a blow to the student, who had even considered transferring to another university. What she was told was that the student's father and two older brothers belonged to the same fraternity. In fact, all the men in his extended family were alums. Not receiving a "bid" and becoming a "pledge" made him feel like he didn't matter, didn't belong, wasn't worthy – and not just with respect to this fraternity.

These two examples stand out due to the criteria on which self-esteem was wagered: athleticism in one case and "fraternalism" in the other. Nonetheless, these were not the only students I encountered who seemed to stake their self-worth on some external measure of success. A more common encounter was with students who felt compelled to excel academically in order to feel good about themselves. Getting rejected from a graduate program or receiving a poor grade despite your efforts is understandingly deflating and disappointing. But when success is internalized as a marker of worth, lack thereof is particularly devastating and demoralizing.

Those of us who are parents like to believe that we always give our children the message that our love for them is unconditional. Nonetheless, there is no denying that caring and well-intentioned parents can get swept up by the pressures of meritocracy. It's a competitive world out there, they reason, and excelling in school will give children a leg up. More often than not, such children are schooled alongside other high-achieving peers whose parents have similar beliefs. But among this already highly privileged and selective group of students, not everyone has the aptitude or grit required for rising to the top. "When parents, teachers, or other significant figures are invested in specific outcomes they often wittingly or unwittingly convey that their love, regard, or support is contingent on the child attaining that outcome."[68] Indeed, studies have found that such parental academic conditional positive regard – the provision of more affection and attention as a way of promoting academic achievement – can have untoward consequences.

In one such study, the perception of adolescents that their parents use conditional positive regard in order to promote academic achievement was associated with maladaptive thoughts, feelings, and behaviors.[69] Consistent with fragile self-esteem, these youngsters were elated following academic success but experienced great shame and self-denigration following failure. In another study, students' perception of parental academic positive regard was associated with independent teacher evaluation that those students are more focused on achieving high grades than on the learning process.[70] In a study of sixth and seventh graders, parents who were affectionate and supportive on the one hand but also set clear rules and monitored their children's behavior were more likely to have children with high global self-esteem. On the other hand, parents who manipulate their children by making affection and attention conditional on accomplishments – a form of psychological control – were more likely to foster contingent self-esteem.[71]

Not surprisingly perhaps, parents who use such conditional positive regard are more likely themselves to have contingent self-esteem and to report that their own parents were achievement-promoting parents who used similar practices.[72] It is also undeniable that in this day and age of highly invested parenting, some parents run the risk of staking their own self-worth on their children's accomplishments – dubbed "parental child-invested contingent self-esteem." And indeed, parents of ten-year-olds whose self-esteem was invested on their offspring's accomplishments were more likely to use conditional positive regard as a way of promoting high academic achievement.[73] In effect, such parental practices set the stage for contingent self-esteem which is associated with a host of emotional and behavioral difficulties.

We are not suggesting that most parents make positive regard conditional on academic excellence or that most kids have an insecure form of self-esteem. Nonetheless, studies such as these warrant our attention. In a recent survey, some 80 percent of high school students reported that being successful is more valued by their parents than being kind.[74] Driving around in Miami, we've seen cars with "my child is an honor student in school XYZ" stickers on the back. We have yet to see a corresponding placard stating "my child is kind," "my child shares his toys," or "my child treats others with respect." Kids learn which attributes and behaviors are most valued by the important adults in their lives.

Furthermore, the role of parents is not only to provide the care, structure, and unconditional support that is foundational for positive self-regard. Children need to be confident about their own self-worth, but they also need to value the worth of others. Interactions with parents is a fertile ground for nurturing prosocial values and behaviors that are foundational to mattering. Raising children who not only feel valued but also care about and value others requires the nurturing of our hardwired prosocial tendencies.[75] This begins from a very young age with daily interactions with parents and siblings.

In a supportive and predictable home environment that values the worth of all human beings, children gain important skills about their own and others' emotional world. They become increasingly adept at regulating difficult emotions and balancing their own needs and wishes with those of others. They grow more empathic and compassionate the more they understand how their behavior can contribute to others' happiness – or distress, as the case may be.

Earlier, in Chapter 2, we discussed the important difference between healthy versus inflated self-regard and the overvaluing of oneself that is endemic to narcissists. Like adults, some children overvalue themselves and even exhibit narcissistic tendencies. Compared to those with a healthy self-regard, narcissistic children perceive themselves as superior, more special, and more entitled than others. They relish external validation that they are outstanding and special, and they are on top of the world when it's forthcoming. They also experience minor slights as humiliating, which may trigger a disproportionate response. Narcissism, like many other psychological traits, has a constitutional and temperamental component. Nonetheless, it is shaped by early socialization and specific parental practices. This is the conclusion of Dutch psychologist Eddie Brummelman, who has published a series of studies on overvalued children.[76]

Not surprisingly, overvalued children have overvaluing parents. When it comes to one's children, the term "overvaluing" is perhaps misleading. There is no limit to the extent to which the two of us, Isaac and Ora, love and value our now 33-year-old son. We named him Matan – the Hebrew word for gift – because that is what he is to us. But thinking of our child as our gift is not the same as believing that "my child is God's gift to humanity" – the title of an article by Brummelman and his colleagues. They define parental overvaluation as "parents' belief that their own child is more special and more entitled than other children."[77] Their study of 465 seven- to eleven-year-olds and their parents sheds light on how this parental belief is manifested: "Overvaluing parents over-claim their child's knowledge, overestimate the child's IQ, and overpraise the child's performances."[78] They also cause the child to stand out by giving him or her an unusual first name.

Consistent parental messages that one is head and shoulders above the rest – smarter, more knowledgeable, and thus more deserving – can lead to narcissistic tendencies in children. Importantly, narcissism and high self-esteem have different underpinnings and emanate from dissimilar socialization processes. Whereas parental overvaluation preludes the former, parental affection and support underpins the latter.[79] Spending quality time with your child, showing interest in his or her activities, and demonstrating your love and affection cultivate positive self-regard. It reinforces the child's self-view as one who is worthy and matters, rather than one who is superior and matters more. And when the importance of treating others with respect and compassion is both imparted as a family value and modeled by parents, the seeds of mattering are spread even further.

Strategies

Now that you know the signs of healthy self-regard, its importance to well-being and mattering, and its developmental trajectory, it is time to consider specific applications for seeding more of it in your life.

Invariably, some of you who are reading this book already possess high and stable self-esteem that is not easily threatened by relational, professional, or financial setbacks. You are driven to pursue goals that are concordant with your values, interests, and aspirations, rather than those that will gain you social approval. Furthermore, you don't tend to judge yourself harshly when you make mistakes or fail to live up to your own standards. You feel bad and take steps to improve or correct your ways but understand that you are not perfect and neither is anyone else. You also recognize that there are multiple ways of adding value and mattering to yourself and others; it doesn't require you to take outstanding action or change the world all by yourself.

This section is particularly relevant to those of us who experience challenges with self-esteem, self-acceptance, or self-compassion. This may be due to some combination of genes, early family life, relationships with caregivers and teachers, peer relations, and other formative life events.

Challenge Negative Assumptions

Awareness is the first and most important lever of change for healthy self-regard. We can cultivate greater awareness of and insight into the multiple factors that have impacted our lives and may continue to play a role in the beliefs we hold about ourselves. For example, experiences of abandonment, rejection, or even ongoing teasing and criticism that pose a threat to one's sense of security and acceptance can lead to entrenched beliefs that one needs to be a certain way or do certain things in order to be worthy.[80] Such beliefs can be sticky, but they're not immutable: cognitive-behavior therapy has helped scores of people evaluate and modify self-defeating thoughts and beliefs that can get in the way of mattering.

You can learn to identify situations that trigger harsh self-criticism, self-judgment, or poor self-regard. What are you saying to yourself at such times? Are these thoughts really accurate? We tend to believe our own thoughts as if they are verified truths, but this is often not the case. In fact, self-defeating thoughts are often distorted.[81] Being passed over for a coveted promotion is understandably disappointing, even painful. But it is particularly punishing if it's interpreted as "I just don't have what it takes to get ahead," "no one appreciates me," or "there's no point in ever trying again." Rather than torturing yourself with these thoughts, you can examine their accuracy. You can probably come up with a list of people who clearly appreciate you; of situations where you worked hard and got ahead; of what you have learned from this experience that will help you next time.

Remember that *failing at something* does not mean that *you are a failure*. In fact, those who avoid all challenges because they refuse to fail are depriving themselves of various growth opportunities and depriving others of their potential contributions. As our good friend and happiness scholar Tal Ben Shahar says, "learn to fail or fail to learn. You can't have both." Think about what you would say to your child or a good friend in a similar situation. We almost guarantee that it would be kinder and more productive than the harsh statements you are saying to yourself.

We can also develop greater awareness and insight about what motivates us and regulates our behavior. Do you engage in activities and pursuits that are authentically meaningful to you and congruent with your values and interests; or are you preoccupied with enhancing or preserving your self-image? Have you internalized conditions of worth that you feel compelled to meet and which largely drive your behavior? What price are you paying for this?

According to self-determination theory, as noted earlier, human beings have three core psychological needs that act as essential nutrients for our growth and well-being: the needs for autonomy, competence, and relatedness.[82] Just as we need food, water, and oxygen to sustain us physically, we need to fulfill these basic psychological needs to sustain us emotionally.

Our need for autonomy is met when our behavior is congruent with our authentic interests and values, rather than driven by external or internal pressures. Competence relates to the need to master our environment and feel efficacious in important domains of life. Relatedness is about the universal need to be cared for and also care about others and contribute to their lives. It is about the need to be connected to close others and also to make a difference beyond ourselves.

Cultivate Positive Emotions

When behavior is regulated by our need for autonomy, competence, and relatedness, true self-esteem is the natural outgrowth.[83] Thus, we should heed the advice of self-esteem scholars that "the most effective way to cultivate healthy self-esteem may be to worry less about having high self-esteem."[84] Instead, consider ways of adding value to those in your close social circle and in the wider community. What gifts do you have that could make a difference to the lives of others? What are you already doing that you can build on? What do you care about beyond yourself? Rather than just thinking about important values, writing about them can help you transcend concerns about self-esteem.

Get in touch with your true passions and aspirations. What do you love to do for its own sake? Which skills would you like to further develop? For years, learning Spanish is something that I (Ora) wanted to do. I couldn't do it while working full-time, as most of my energy was dedicated to my career. I loved teaching, and living across the street from campus enabled me to go from home to office to class in my wheelchair. When I withdrew from work, I took advantage of the proximity to campus and the ability to audit an undergraduate Spanish course. The class was a lot more challenging and work-intensive than I had envisioned, but I persisted. The students knew that I was a professor, so I felt obliged to come prepared and do all the work. One course ended, followed by another and another. For a while it felt like Spanish was all I was doing. But I was learning and I was loving it. There was a great sense of mastery and competence in learning a new language that enabled me to communicate with Spanish speakers in Miami. I also saw it as a gym for my brain.

For the purpose of full disclosure, I admit that this was quite a while ago, and my Spanish is currently very rusty. But I know what I need to do to refresh my knowledge. I currently do not have the time or motivation for such intensive courses, so I have to create my own structure. I need to set a specific and measurable goal and begin with a small step that will be easy to integrate into my daily routine. For example, I have the Babbel app on my phone, which I used for a while but later stopped. Making a plan to do twenty minutes of Babbel a day for at least four days a week is a specific, measurable, and easily achievable first step. After dinner is the best time for me to me to Babbel as I prefer to use the morning for my work. My goal can thus be: "as soon as I finish brushing and flossing my teeth after dinner I will practice Spanish with Babbel for twenty minutes."

This is how we adopt a new behavior, one small step at a time. We may have setbacks like I've had with Spanish: I feel dispirited and frustrated any time I try to speak and have to contend with how much I have forgotten due to lack of practice. I regret that I let it slide like this and have berated myself for my laziness. But I also know that setbacks are surprisingly common. In fact, most people experience a setback when they try to adopt a new behavior.[85] Rather than berating myself I can treat myself with kindness for this disappointment and take active steps to brush up on my skills. Of course, this is easier said than done, especially for those of us with an overdeveloped inner critic. Trust me – I know this one well.

Manage Negative Emotions

How do you relate to yourself when you fail to achieve something you wanted, regret a mistake you made, or encounter a weakness or something undesirable about yourself?

- Are you able to accept that it makes you feel bad but that it's not the end of the world; or do you ruminate about it and end up feeling even worse?
- Do you remind yourself that no one is perfect and everyone makes mistakes; or do you feel separate from and less worthy than others?
- Are you kind to yourself and do you try to soften your painful experience; or is your internal dialogue punishing and judgmental?

These are the three core components of self-compassion, according to psychologist Kristin Neff, the leading expert in the field.[86] Each component can be considered in relation to its polar opposite: mindfulness versus overidentification; common humanity versus isolation; and self-kindness versus self-judgment.

Mindfulness involves an open awareness and acceptance of our full range of emotions, including painful ones we would rather not have. Many bad habits like drinking and eating junk food are used to blunt emotional pain.[87] They provide momentary relief at the cost of long-term health. Some people also avoid certain interactions or situations because they worry that they will fail or others will judge them. They bypass opportunities for growth or meaningful engagement because they are anxious about not measuring up or somehow feeling out of place.

The ability to make room for emotional struggles is thus an important psychological resource that is worth developing.[88] If you are aware of your internal struggle and are willing to accept it, you don't have to avoid situations you may enjoy or benefit from as a way of protecting yourself from emotional pain. Neither do you need to blunt your suffering by ingesting unhealthy foods or substances that will not serve you well in the long run.

Mindfulness can also help you keep things in perspective. It's easy to get lost in the storyline when something is going wrong in our life, whether it's due to our own behavior or something that is outside of our control. We can become so absorbed in the drama that it's difficult to see past it or hold it in perspective. Developing a mindful presence is like metaphorically stepping back from your predicament rather than overidentifying with it. Stepping back can lessen the hold that this has on your life and allow you to observe your predicament in a more balanced fashion.

Envision your suffering as a dark cloud. When you overidentify with suffering, all you can see is the world through this dark cloud. A mindful state enables you to make room for the cloud without losing sight of the vast sky that contains it. You don't deny the situation or the pain it causes you, but you also realize that it does not need to define you; it is one passing dark cloud in a vast and open sky. Acknowledging and accepting your negative internal experience also means that it does not need to dictate your actions. Your actions can be guided by what you truly value and believe in rather than what will make the pain go away.[89] This is where common humanity comes in – the second component of self-compassion. Common humanity is a reminder that suffering and emotional struggles are simply a part of life.[90] Everyone has their dark clouds; it is a universal human experience. Despite how happy everybody seems in their social media posts, they have their mishaps, setbacks, and disappointments. More importantly perhaps, we all make mistakes, have weaknesses, and experience failure. None of us are perfect. We all know this in theory but may struggle with it in practice. Failure, disappointment, misfortune, and suffering can feel like we are set apart from others. This sense of isolation further exacerbates our pain. Reminding ourselves of our common humanity can combat this isolation and connect us with others.

Self-kindness is the third and most important component of self-compassion. While mindfulness is an awareness and acceptance of suffering, self-kindness is about tending to ourselves as we struggle. This is particularly important when we are disappointed with ourselves – our behavior, our accomplishments, a flaw, or a weakness. Often times, rather than holding ourselves in compassion for our struggle, we turn on ourselves in harsh judgment. Our self-talk can be disapproving, disparaging, even nasty.

Many years ago, I (Ora) led a depression management group for women in a mental health center. I asked the participants to make a list of some of the things they typically say to themselves when they screw up. Then working in pairs, I asked each one to read her sentences to her partner as though they were directed at her. "I'll never learn this!" became "you'll never learn this!"; "I'm a terrible mother!" was replaced with "you're terrible mother!" Just imagine how difficult it was for these women to look one another in the eye and do this. Some of them simply refused, yet they were constantly indoctrinating themselves with this toxic self-talk.

So why do we do this to ourselves? You can think of your inner self-critic as the reptilian part of your brain whose job is to warn you of impending danger.[91] It releases hormones that prepare you to fight off an intruder or flee a dangerous situation. The problem is that it responds in a similar fashion to a perceived danger to your self-esteem. In other words, your punishing inner critic is trying to protect you the best it knows how. Nonetheless, this is definitely not helping. Disparaging yourself is not the path to self-improvement any more than shaming your partner for being passed over for a promotion will motivate him or her to try harder.

What your partner needs in this situation is the gift of your unconditional love and support made possible by the mammalian part of your brain. Feeling your compassion and desire for their happiness means the world. And this is the gift you need to give yourself when you are struggling. The compassion you feel for the plight of another and your wish to alleviate their pain can be turned inward. Self-compassion does not require a whole new set of skills; it's more of a repurposing of skills most of us already have.[92]

- Think about someone who cares for you and knows you well, warts and all. What would this person say to you if they knew you were having a difficult time? What would they say if they knew you were suffering due to your own self-criticism?
- Write a letter to yourself as though it was written by this person. Alternatively, write yourself a letter from an imaginary friend who knows you well and cares about you deeply.
- Think about something you are currently struggling with that is not your most difficult struggle. Allow yourself to feel compassion for the pain that it is causing you. If you feel that pain in your heart, put your hand or two hands over your heart in a soothing and comforting way. Wish yourself well and ask yourself what you need in order to take care of yourself.
- Use the three core elements of self-compassion next time you encounter a difficult or painful situation:
  - Acknowledge your pain by saying to yourself: "this is a moment of suffering" or "I'm struggling now" or "this is really hard." Alternatively, come up with another phrase that works for you.
  - Remind yourself that this is a universal experience you share with others. Say to yourself: "Suffering is a part of life." "Everyone struggles now and then." "No one is perfect and we all make mistakes." Or come up with different words that would connect you with the experience of others.
  - Bring kindness to yourself for the difficulty you are experiencing. Say to yourself: "May I be kind to myself; may I accept myself; may I give myself what I need." Think about what else you can say to yourself to express kindness and caring.

The Center for Mindful Self-Compassion (www.centerformsc.org) has a host of exercises, meditations, and resources to get you started. Self-compassion has many of the benefits of high self-esteem: less stress, anxiety, depression, self-criticism; greater motivation, optimism, life satisfaction, and self-care.[93] Because it emphasizes our similarity rather than our differences, it is not based on standing out and does not engender social comparisons.[94] It is a more stable and less conditional form of self-regard that is not associated with narcissism and self-aggrandizement. Those with higher self-compassion are also rated by their partners as more emotionally available and compassionate.[95] The ability to care for ourselves and give ourselves what we need places us in a better position to be there for others in caring and supportive ways. Thus, self-compassion is well aligned with mattering. When self-acceptance and self-valuing are given, we have more time and energy to pursue intrinsically meaningful goals and add value to ourselves and others, which lead us to mattering in relationships.

PART III

Relationships

CHAPTER 7

Mattering in the Inner Circle

To matter in relationships is to feel valued and to add value. Strong bonds enable us to feel loved, appreciated, recognized, and affirmed. This is the first part of the equation. The second part is helping one another add value to the relationship and the world.[1]

In this chapter, we focus on the bonds we have with people close to us: family, friends, and fellow workers. In Chapter 10, we deal with mattering in the community. Even though we don't interact frequently and personally with many people in the community, they exert a powerful influence on us nonetheless. But first, what does mattering look like in the inner circle?

Signs

Since our relationship is our Petri dish, this is what we see. Isaac loves to tell Ora that she is one of the most perceptive psychological observers he knows. He also tells her that she is very supportive, especially when Isaac goes through some existential crises. He also admires her ability to teach him how to deal with conflict. Isaac also praises her cooking, which is healthy and absolutely delicious, especially her vegan banana bread and black bean soup. Isaac also loves Ora's writing and thinking about psychological issues. Isaac is in awe of what a great mom, spouse, sister, and aunt Ora is. She is a great listener to family and friends. Isaac tells Ora that she is one of the most mature people he knows. Isaac also thanks Ora for going along for the ride when we move continents, which is not always easy. He also appreciates how they contemplate life's choices together and how she helps him deal with his psychological hang-ups.

Ora, in turn, appreciates Isaac's humor and funny faces, as well as his made-up songs, in multiple languages, some of which he actually speaks. She also appreciates his writing. Ora values his discipline, responsibility, neatness, and organizational skills. Living with a serious and progressive disability, Ora is keenly aware and appreciative of the multiple ways in which Isaac provides her with tangible help and the loving and respectful way in which he does so. She loves to tell Isaac how happy he has made her in his multiple roles as husband, lover, best friend, confidant, co-parent, co-author, and entertainer-in-chief for nearly four decades.

In short, we tell each other how we appreciate one another. But of course, it was not always like that. We learned the value of expressing appreciation. And, lest you get the impression that we live in relational nirvana, let us assure you that this is not the case. We are each strong people with unique needs and personalities that are not always in sync, but we have learned to talk in ways that are respectful and that promote growth. We have learned to trust the process of coming to decisions together.

These are all examples of verbal expressions of appreciation. There is compelling evidence that telling your partner how much you appreciate him or her makes a real difference in the health of the relationship.[2] You can tell that partners value one another when they say things like:

- Thank you for inviting my mom to come for dinner on Sunday
- I appreciate how you talked to our daughter about her disappointment
- I noticed that you did the laundry last night
- It means a lot to me that you are willing to move so that I can take this new job
- You were such a good listener to your sister last night
- You helped me so much with that project
- I admire how you handled that conflict at work
- You were there for me when I needed you
- Thank you for being such a great partner
- It is so much fun to laugh with you
- You spend a lot of time cooking healthy and delicious meals for us
- Thank you for listening
- You are very wise and caring
- You deal with difficult situations so well
- Thanks for handling all the bills
- I love spending time with you – it is the most fun thing to do
- The way you analyzed the situation made a lot of sense to me

These are all verbal expressions that make your partner feel valued. If you want to experience mattering in a relationship it is essential to say, and not just think, these things. We can learn from a couple in which the wife complained that her husband hasn't told her that he loves her in a long time, to which the husband replied: "I told you that I love you when we got married forty years ago. If anything changes I will let you know." Don't just think it, say it!

There are, of course, many nonverbal ways to show affection as well. Couples kiss, touch, hug, and have sexual relations. They walk hand in hand and look at each other romantically. Friends embrace and pat each other on the back. Each one of these verbal and nonverbal expressions of love are deposits into your emotional bank account. You can think of these affirmations as relational capital. This type of psychological capital serves two functions. One, it makes you healthier and happier. Two, it buffers against emotional withdrawals. Every time you have a negative interaction with your partner or friend it is like taking relational capital out of your emotional bank account. You have to accumulate enough positive experiences to compensate for the occurrence of negative ones. Since you are bound to have conflict, it is essential to have gathered enough positive experiences to buffer against the impact of negative interactions.

If you want to matter in the inner circle, you don't have to avoid conflict – you just have to know how to handle it. Healthy relationships are characterized by effective management of conflict, not by the avoidance of it, which is all but inevitable. Many people stay away from conflict because they think that it is the end of the world. Maybe they learned in their family of origin that when people argue all hell breaks loose. Perhaps they are afraid that if they voice disagreement, address a conflict of interest, or display hurt or anger, it will be the end of the relationship. They close up, shut down, and avoid addressing the conflict, leaving neither party satisfied. But well-managed conflict can lead to intrapersonal and interpersonal growth and to a stronger relational bond.

There are rules for fighting fair.[3] First, healthy couples learn to express how they feel without blaming the other person. Using "I" statements does wonders. Instead of saying "you ruined my day," partners in healthy relationships say: "I am upset with the conversation we had." Second, they ask open-ended questions to try to understand where the other person is coming from. Some examples include:

- Tell me how you are feeling
- Please share with me what is going through your mind right now
- Your needs are important to me
- Is there anything I can do that will help us move forward?
- I'd like to understand what I am doing that is causing pain

Third, they are not defensive. Instead of trying to rationalize or argue the righteousness of their position, they listen without judgment. Fourth, they take responsibility. When one of the parties understands that they've hurt the other, they say, "I am sorry that I hurt your feelings. I will be more sensitive next time." When one partner realizes that they have ignored the other's needs, they own up and resolve to do better. The goal of conflict management is not victory but reciprocity. None of this is easy, but a commitment to grow in the relationship puts these principles front and center. My own need to be treated with respect, to be cared for, and to accomplish valued personal goals must be balanced with those of my partner. Given the interdependent nature of close relationships, those needs will collide at times. How we manage them is key.

Many couples deposit relational capital in their emotional bank account spontaneously, but others create daily, weekly, or monthly rituals. We are more of the spontaneous type, but others have dates and special dinners where they discuss relational issues. In fact, John Gottman, a world-renown relationship expert, sends couples on dates to discuss important issues such as trust, sex, and work–life balance.[4]

Verbal and nonverbal exchanges can signal that partners value one another and that they can add value to one another. Through words and actions, family and friends can enrich their lives. Studying is one way to add value to your personal life. Ora was very supportive of Isaac when they had a newborn and he was still working on his dissertation. A few years later Isaac returned the favor when he encouraged Ora to pursue her doctorate in counseling psychology. Ora supported Isaac when the family left Melbourne, Australia, which we loved, to get a better position at Vanderbilt University. Isaac encouraged Ora to publish her dissertation as a book, and Ora gradually persuaded Isaac to start meditating. We have done many things for each other that are typical of mattering in relation-ships. We find meaning and love in making small sacrifices for the other person. We also celebrate each other's small triumphs. We rarely miss an opportunity to congratulate each other on a job well done. This is neither easy nor inauthentic. We don't just parrot platitudes such as "great job." It takes focus to be in the moment with your partner and identify how he or she is feeling and what the most helpful thing is that you can say right now. We try to be as specific as possible.

Of the two of us, Isaac credits Ora with being more relational. Isaac learned a great deal from Ora about how to handle charged situations and how to make good decisions together. At one point we considered leaving Miami so that Isaac could take another job. The anatomy of decision-making is very complex. Meaning, mattering, finances, diverging needs, distance from our son, time away from home, accessible housing, and

weather (wheelchairs don't like snow very much) were some of the considerations. It was quite a list of considerations, and the risk of making
a mistake was high. Yet Ora was able to engage in a process of exploration
that calmed Isaac's anxieties. We pondered the best ways to add value to
ourselves, each other, and the family unit as well.

Decision-making requires quite a bit of self-disclosure and vulnerability.[5]
To make a sound decision, you have to put all the cards on the table and be
willing to share your fears and fantasies. It requires a great deal of trust and
courage to reveal your innermost worries and aspirations. Empathic and
supportive partners don't judge your wishes. Yet taking into account everybody's needs is a complicated affair. To reach a mutually satisfying outcome,
psychologically mature couples try to be fair to all parties.

To be sure, putting all the cards on the table can feel risky – even in the
closest of relationships such as ours. Isaac struggled with how to express his
desire to hike in the mountains – something that Ora obviously cannot do.
But it was courageous and important for him to express this wish and
critical for Ora to hear it. It made for an emotionally painful but nonetheless deep conversation that has helped shape our plans and decisions.

It has made it easier to acknowledge at times diverging priorities and
seek integrative solutions that will work for both of us. Since Ora needs
physical assistance and cannot stay on her own, she now plans retreats with
women she loves who have come to stay when Isaac traveled to give talks in
Chile, South Africa, and Japan, among other places. Our son Matan joined
his father on the trip to Japan, while our niece and sister-in-law, the two
women Ora is closest to in the world, came from Israel for memorable
visits. They have held these retreats on three different occasions so far and
have achieved a level of closeness that would not have been possible
without them.

Fair decisions are a balancing act between what each party needs and
what they deserve. Fairness in the inner circle consists of making sure that
everyone affected by a decision get their fair share of need satisfaction,
opportunities, time, space, and resources. It is helpful to think of fairness in
terms of outcomes and processes.[6] Outcomes refer to *what* piece of the pie
you get – distributive justice. Procedural justice, in turn, refers to *how* the
decision was made. Human beings are exquisitely sensitive to fairness
transgressions. In relationships, it is important not only *what* decision is
made, and *what* piece of the pie each person gets, but also *how* the decision
was made. Did both parties have a say? Does one person control most
decisions in the home? Ultimately, fairness is about control in decision-
making. To matter in the inner circle, both parties must have equal control

and an equal say. If one person feels chronically deprived of control, as we shall later see, the prospects for the relationship are grim.

In addition to our investments in intimate relationships, many people derive a great deal of mattering and joy from relationships with their parents, siblings, and children. While the depth and complexity of the connections vary a great deal, many of the principles discussed in the context of romantic love apply also to family bonds. We want to make our kids feel valued and promote their self-efficacy. In fact, crucial outcomes depend on our success in these two tasks. The more valued our kids feel, the more secure they are in exploring the world around them.

Over time, our relationship with our kids morphes from one of caring for them into one of being cared for by them. With our parents, the opposite takes place. We go from being cared for by them to caring for them. But in all instances, across the lifespan, we seek to feel valued and add value in our relationships with family members. The same applies to close friends and fellow workers. The success of our relationships with them will hinge on our ability to nurture the two foundational elements of mattering: feeling valued and adding value.

Significance

Music legend Johnny Cash passed away only a few months after his wife June died. We were living in Nashville at the time, and the news were received with much dismay. Indeed, it is not uncommon for men to develop emotional and health issues after they lose their wives. Data show that, compared to men who have not been recently widowed, grieving husbands are more likely to develop serious physical and psychological problems.[7]

It is a well-established fact that what happens in the inner circle matters a great deal to our psychological and physical well-being.[8] When the inner circle is supportive, people within it are more resilient and report lower levels of stress. When the inner circle is absent or neglectful, we suffer emotionally and physiologically. It will not surprise you to learn that people report higher levels of happiness when they interact with others. This is true for extroverts as well as introverts.[9]

We spend many of our waking hours interacting with other people, and, not surprisingly, our well-being is highly correlated with the quality of these experiences. When either the quality or quantity of our interactions do not satisfy our longing for connection, we feel distressed and lonely. Isolation is so pernicious that it has been deemed more dangerous to our health than obesity and smoking.[10] We do not need just any kind of relationship but ones that boost our sense of mattering.

Love is the ultimate expression of mattering in the inner circle. According to Barbara Fredrickson, the author of *Love 2.0*, "love is the essential nutrient that your cells crave: true positivity-charged connection with other living beings." She goes on to say that love "nourishes your body the way the right balance of sunlight, nutrient-rich soil, and water nourishes plants and allows them to flourish. The more you experience it, the more you open up and grow, becoming wiser and more attuned, more resilient and effective, happier and healthier."[11]

According to the research, men who reported being most satisfied with their relationships at age fifty were the healthiest at age eighty.[12] In the same study, it was found that involvement in civic affairs and supportive relationship are associated with lower rates of dementia among the elderly. In fact, some doctors believe that volunteering should be recommended along with proper nutrition and physical activity.[13]

So powerful are the effects of friendship that the benefits of these bonds is equivalent to an increase in income of $100,000 a year.[14] In general, loving relationships are associated with lower morbidity, a stronger immune system, and better cardiovascular health.[15] For nurses diagnosed with invasive breast cancer, a robust network was associated with a four-fold increase in the chances of survival.[16] As Christopher Peterson, one of the founders of positive psychology used to say, *other people matter*. Do they ever![17]

I, Ora, witnessed the power of social support when my friend Sara was diagnosed with breast cancer. Sara and I met as doctoral students over twenty-five years ago. We have been friends ever since. Soon after her diagnosis, Sara began sending email updates about her condition to close friends and colleagues. She created an impressive network of digital and face-to-face support. Sara did not spare her friends the pain and agony of the treatment, but she did not despair either. Her updates were often funny, touching, and warm. Sara received a lot of informational, instrumental, and emotional support from family and friends. But Sara did not just receive help – she also gave her friends a present, the opportunity to be useful. She helped others be helpful, which is a wonderful gift. Five years later, Sara is doing very well.

Fredrickson makes a compelling case for the relationship between love and health: "Love – like taking a deep breath or eating an orange when you're depleted and thirsty – not only feels great but is also life-giving, an indispensable source of energy, sustenance, and health."[18] Love seems to be working very well for Sara, who is surrounded by a loving husband, caring daughters, and supportive friends.

On a recent Sunday afternoon, I received the following email from a good friend:

> Hi Dear Friends,
>
> How are you holding up? I think you know I rarely complain and have a hard time asking for help and what I need. I'm taking my hero Brené Brown's advice to share with you how hard it's been for me lately. And what I need. This is not easy for me, but here goes . . .

She went on to share that a good friend of hers had recently passed away from COVID-19 and that she herself had had a health setback. Her chronic health condition has forced her to work from home, missing out on the face-to-face interaction with colleagues and team members which she enjoys. Importantly, she also specified the kinds of gestures that would help her feel more supported.

My friend, who allowed me to share this story, is a smart, stable, and generous person who others often turn to for support. She has certainly been there for me when I needed her. Her ability to reach out is a testament to her emotional maturity and authenticity. She embodied Brené Brown's core message that expressing vulnerability takes strength and courage and can lead to personal and relational growth.[19] I certainly admired and appreciated her courage to tell us where she's at and what she needs. Such role models are much needed and in short supply.

Sources

We are biologically wired to connect with others.[20] Our brain lights up when we experience closeness and warmth. Oxytocin, the "happy hormone," courses through our body when we make love. Our nervous system becomes more adaptive when we connect intimately with another person. Our organism both nourishes and is nourished by feeling valued and adding value in close relationships.

The feeling of mattering in the inner circle evolves over time. From the moment our babies are born we begin the process of cultivating their sense of mattering. That experience is crucial for their intellectual, emotional, social, and physical development. As noted in Chapter 2, infants feel valued and have the confidence to add value in proportion to their secure attachment. Responsive parents build a secure base for their babies, whereas those who are unresponsive lay the groundwork for anxious, ambivalent, or avoidant attachment styles. The attachment studies clearly demonstrate that our ability to add value, to ourselves and others, depends on the extent to which we are made to feel valued and secure. The more we trust those who take care of us, the more confident we are in our ability to venture into the world without apprehension.

A secure attachment is the best insurance policy against stressors later in life, especially when we seek romantic relationships.[21] Insecure attachment, in turn, will tend to be replicated in adulthood, leading to ambivalence and lack of trust. For some, the lessons of insecure attachment will be expressed in anxious behavior, while for others it will be manifested in avoidance. While the former are clingy and seek constant reassurance, the latter are removed and aloof. Avoidant types are guided by the fear that if they get too close to someone, and things go wrong, they will be very badly hurt, the way they were with their parents. As a result, they prefer to keep their distance and assume a defensive posture. There is a certain logic to this attitude, but it is ultimately harmful. In an effort to prevent pain, they also prevent intimacy.

Responsive parents not only make their kids feel valued, but they also cultivate self-efficacy and a sense of mastery. These parents afford their kids an opportunity to exercise control over their surroundings, a key precursor of the confidence required to add value to themselves and the world. Wise parents create opportunities for their children to experience mastery and success in diverse areas of life. If the kids encounter barriers in one domain, they can turn to other areas in which they feel competent. If academics is not their thing, they may gain self-confidence through their musical or athletic prowess. Wise parents indeed create opportunities, but they also refrain from overwhelming their kids with so many activities that it takes the pleasure out of them.

In addition, parents and friends know how to ask for and receive help. This is essential if we are to move from a "Me Culture" to a "We Culture." We must have expectations of our kids and friends not only to get help from us but also to help us when we are in need. We must cultivate responsibility to help others in need. It turns out that there are tangible benefits not just for the receiver but also for the provider of kindness. In experiments that instructed some participants to do three enjoyable things a day and others to perform three acts of kindness per day, the latter group derived more benefits.[22] Behaving compassionately confers many physical, psychological, and spiritual benefits to the giver.

Indeed, there are many things parents and partners can do to make their kids, lovers, and friends feel like they matter. They make them feel valued through affection, recognition, and celebration, and they help them add value through opportunities to build on their strengths. They also let their grown children and relatives help them when they are themselves in need. These are some of the things we should do to foster mattering in the inner circle. But there are also many things we should not do.

In the context of romantic couples, John Gottman and his associates discovered four patterns of conflict management that destroy love.[23] The four negative patterns of interaction are stonewalling, criticism, contempt, and defensiveness. Stonewalling describes avoidant behavior on the part of the spouse. She removes herself from the situation, pretends you are not there, stays silent, and just ignores you. She gives you the cold shoulder. This demeanor, which makes you feel invisible, is a strong predictor of divorce. Criticism is characterized by attacking the person as opposed to the issue. This is sometimes called character assassination. You stigmatize the person and tell her that she is selfish, inconsiderate, and irresponsible. Instead of making "I" statements, such as "I wish that we had more time to spend together," the attacker says, "You are so selfish – you never think about my needs." Related to criticism is defensiveness. Instead of listening to the needs, thoughts, or beliefs of the other person you shift responsibility to the other party. As opposed to saying "I'm sorry you feel overwhelmed with all the chores at home," the defensive responder says, "You knew that my job was very demanding when we decided to have kids."

When trying to deal with conflict, contempt is particularly toxic because it is disrespectful and dismissive. Contemptuous behavior makes the other person feel inferior through put-downs, sarcastic comments, and hostility. You are basically diminishing the other person's dignity.

While these four negative patterns of interaction were studied in the context of romantic relationships, they apply all the same to others in the inner circle of family, friends, and fellow workers. It is not unusual to hear parents berating their children and bosses stonewalling their employees.

Strategies

As we noted in Chapter 4, there are two main strategies to cultivate positive interactions: connect and communicate. The two, of course, are interdependent, since you cannot connect without communicating. To matter in the inner circle, you need to cultivate positive exchanges that are rewarding and satisfying to both parties. These experiences must be nurtured and planned. They do not happen automatically. What often does happen automatically, though, are the kinds of routine chores that are not the most inspiring and elevating moments in family life. We make breakfast for our kids, rush to get them ready for school, worry that they will miss the bus, and fret all morning. It is very easy to be on automatic pilot because the laundry must be done and the dishes washed. When we are on autopilot, though, we forget to cultivate moments of fun and intimacy. The next sections start with the importance of connecting, followed by some tips on effective communication.

How to Connect

In Chapter 5, we explored the six Ts of mastering a skill: *transcendence, time, thought, trust, tenacity,* and *training*. Since building positive relationships is probably the best investment you can make to increase your health and happiness, we suggest you master the skill of connecting the way experts develop their crafts.

Earlier we defined *transcendence* as going beyond the norm to pursue a passion and a purpose. Relationship scholars often define love as going beyond oneself to promote the goodness and well-being of another person.[24] In many ways, love is the quintessential experience of mattering in the "We Culture" since it requires that we add value not just to ourselves but to others as well. Lovers make the well-being of their partners a passion and a purpose. When you think about it, people spend inordinate amounts of time thinking and doing things to start, build, maintain, and repair romantic relationships. We see *transcendence*, then, as a necessary condition for connections. It is an attitude of caring and concern that calls for a great investment of *time* and *thought*. Just like chess players devote thousands of hours to become grand masters, relationship masters invest days, weeks, months, and years to get the connection right. In our case, we have been at it for nearly forty years and are still purposefully and deliberately creating opportunities to connect in meaningful ways.

We use deliberate practice to connect in ways that build on our strengths and increase positive emotions. We make time to create moments of connection. We start our day by cuddling in bed before we get up. We spend time having a leisurely breakfast together. We watch movies we like and often read the same books. We love watching series together. We've spent a lot of time together lately watching *Downton Abbey, Shtisel, The Kominsky Method, Modern Love, Offspring, A Place to Call Home,* and *The Marvelous Mrs. Maisel*. We laugh a lot, sometimes with a reason and sometimes without.

We love going for strolls around our beautiful neighborhood in Miami next to the water. We savor our moments together. We take time to observe nature and comment on it. Ora is fascinated by the pelicans, manatees, and dolphins that grace the bay near our place. We also savor our food. Ora is an excellent vegan cook and Isaac absolutely loves her soups and healthy dishes. We also talk shop a lot. This is not a burden, though. On the contrary, it is something that builds on our strengths. We talk to each other about our writing and share interesting readings.

As in deliberate practice, we also challenge ourselves. The task of co-authoring a book is challenging indeed. Ora is quite a perfectionistic; Isaac less so. Ora feels the need to read 200 scientific studies before she starts writing a chapter. Isaac is ok reading twenty sources. Ora revises her chapters multiple times. Isaac wants to get it done already! In light of these differences, it may be easier just to let go and not work together on projects, but we challenge ourselves because the process is very enriching for each of us individually and for the relationship. We also think that people who read our work and take our classes derive some benefit that neither of us could have produced alone. We taught an undergraduate course together for a number of years where we sometimes laughed at ourselves but also poked fun at each other and occasionally challenged one another's ideas. Students responded well to this and some even commented on it in course evaluations.

We also challenge ourselves to get outside our comfort zone. Traveling with a serious physical disability is very complicated. Airlines are not always familiar with oxygen concentrators, sometimes mishandle wheelchairs, and cannot possibly understand the meaning of pre-boarding. They think that forty-five seconds is enough for a person with a disability to get to her seat before the masses gallop down the ramp in a mad dash, rushing to get stuck in a metal tube for hours. Booking accessible accommodations is never easy, and, depending on where you go, finding accessible taxis can be even more frustrating. Yet, despite the ordeal, we like traveling together because we like new places and visiting with family and friends. Working and going places together requires a lot of thought and planning. Yes, it is work, but it is gratifying. Remember that relationships are the most important investment you will ever make, so it's worth the time and effort. Plan outings together and opportunities to create moments of connection and intimacy.

Making sure each partner feels valued and has an opportunity to add value requires learning and training. How does your partner thrive? What is he or she good at? How can you facilitate growth? How can we get better at enabling the other person to do what he or she does best? How can I improve my listening? We will answer some of these questions in the next section on communication, but here we want to make the point that we need to learn from experience and dedicate time to get better at it. Lasting relationships are marathons, not sprints. They require *training*. You need to learn how make them last and how to get better at it. In our case, we do a lot of reading and studying. We also give feedback to each other.

Tenacity refers to perseverance in the face of obstacles. Many people quit relationships at the first sign of adversity. This often happens when love is expected to be blissful and magical – when people think that passion and infatuation will carry the day. What people fail to see is that relationships require work and the willingness to question yourself. They often entail the willingness to say "I am sorry, I was wrong" and the ability to compromise. If we just expect magic attunement, we are in for a big surprise. Instead of giving up without trying, we suggest learning ways to make each other feel valued and helping one another add value to themselves, the relationship, and the world.

Finally, we must develop *trust*. We must be able to feel safe in the relationship and know that our confidence will not be betrayed. Also, we must be able to rely on one another to come through on promises and plans. Trustworthy partners are reliable, empathic, and understanding. They are willing to negotiate how to share time, space, and resources in the fairest possible way.

In short, we connect by investing time and thought in experiences that are enjoyable to both parties. This is how we create memories. We learn from experience and study what we can do to maximize pleasure and purpose. We take time to savor moments of intimacy by being conscious and mindful in the present. We build trust by being reliable and empathic. We transcend the boundaries of our personal interests to nurture the development of our partners.

Many of these lessons apply to other relationships in the inner circle. We expect friends to be trustworthy, and we invest time and thought in making our friends feel valued and helping them add value. With kids, however, it is different. We definitely invest time, thought, and training as parents, and we surely need tenacity to stick with all the tasks associated with raising children, but we cannot expect reciprocity for quite some time. Yet, in all cases, investing in getting better as a partner or parent will produce dividends that will last a lifetime. And getting better requires that we learn some communication skills.

How to Communicate

To build lasting relationships we have to master the arts of listening and expressing ourselves. We start with listening because it is often a neglected art. Many people attend public speaking courses, enroll in organizations like Toastmasters International, or join debate teams, but very few go to listening classes. This is a shame, because without good listening relationships often go off the rails.

Listening for meaning. Listening is about adding value to the other person by making him or her feel valued. Being a good listener is in many ways like being a good detective. We are trying to discover the meaning of communication. Often, our partners are trying to tell us something related to a *need*, a *feeling*, or a *belief*, and it is our job to detect which one is at play and how to respond empathically.[25] Consider the following statements:

- I completed the proposal you requested
- It's your turn to buy groceries
- Cruises to the Caribbean islands are on sale

The first sentence quite likely represents a feeling of pride. The second statement is about a need, and the third one is about a belief that we need a vacation. When we ascertain the subject of the communication we can respond accordingly. Although there is often a need, a feeling, or a belief embedded in the communication, people not always come out and say it. After all, your employee is not going to come to you and say, "I finished the job – where is my cookie?" Still, he or she is probably expecting a good word from you. At this point you can say something like "Ok," or "I'm so glad you finished the proposal on time. I'm looking forward to reading it. Thank you."

If your partner is telling you that it is your turn to buy groceries, it may be just a matter-of-fact statement, but it may also be a desire for a break from daily chores. Similarly, if your partner says that cruises are on sale, it may be intended as a reminder that you promised to go on a cruise three years ago and there hasn't been any movement on the matter since. There may be other hidden meanings in it as well, such as "you work too much and I feel neglected" or "we have not had a vacation in four years." Talking about the cruise sale may be interpreted as a need (we need a break), a belief (normal people take breaks once in a while), or a feeling (I'm sick and tired of you having to spend the weekends working for a boss that is inconsiderate).

As a good detective, try to identify the hidden message of verbal expressions. Your employee may be fishing for a compliment and your partner may be expressing frustration. Needless to say, some statements just reflect a fact, and there is nothing to interpret. As Freud, the master of interpretations famously said, a cigar is sometimes just a cigar. But often there is more than meets the eye. If you really want to communicate with people in your inner circle, try to sensitize yourself to the needs, feelings, or beliefs expressed in their statements. The more perceptive you become, the deeper the conversation will be and the stronger the bond between the two of you will become. When you hit it on the nail, the other person will often say, "Yeah, that's exactly how I feel." Bingo!

In addition to listening for hidden meanings, there are a few other important tasks. You also have to control what you think and what you say. If instead of focusing on the experience of the other person you are thinking about dinner, a deadline, or a debt, there is no way you are going to connect with the other person. In fact, there are many interferences with our ability to listen intently.[26] We don't listen well when we

- Rehearse our response in our heads
- Are distracted by hunger or lack of sleep
- Have preconceived notions about the speaker based on ethnicity, looks, gender, education, or language
- Are busy judging the speaker
- Are doing all the talking!

Listening is an exercise in mindfulness. We must concentrate on the speaker and demonstrate with our words and actions that we are fully present. To show our attention we can establish eye contact, face the speaker, and assume an engaged posture, like leaning forward. To convey your interest in the other person, these are some things you can do:

- Ask questions to make sure you understand what the speaker is saying
- Allow the other person to talk without interruptions
- Refrain from hijacking the conversation and redirecting it toward yourself
- Show understanding with nonverbal behaviors like nodding
- Refrain from giving unsolicited advice

It is also crucial that you monitor your speech. Remember to press the "pause" button before you utter the first thing that comes to mind, such as:

- That's not a big deal
- I'm sure you will feel better tomorrow
- You should not have done that
- It's your fault
- Yeah, that also happened to me last year when I was going out with Rachel and she told me . . .
- It's so hot outside

Better to park these intrusive thoughts and statements than letting them ruin your conversation.

If these are examples of what *not* to say, what is it that you *can* say? To start, begin by reflecting back to the speaker what you heard. To the spouse in need of a vacation, you might say: "I'm sorry I have been working a lot lately. I can see you are frustrated by my schedule. It is time we had a vacation. I agree." To a conscientious employee who usually delivers high-quality work, you might say: "You deserve to be congratulated for your work. I always appreciate the work you do. It is detailed and comprehensive. You usually try to anticipate key issues. Thank you for doing such a great job in such a short period of time."

Remember, though, that it takes time and training to ascertain how the other person is feeling right now. So it is best to be cautious and humble about your interpretations. You do not want to come across as a know-it-all. It is best to offer a tentative reading of the situation, such as "It seems to me that you are frustrated by my work schedule lately. Am I right?" Do not pretend to know for certain what the other person is experiencing or feeling. You have to adopt a curious attitude, not an imposing approach.

When you are uncertain about your understanding of events or emotions, you can ask open-ended questions that invite the speaker to clarify further his or her feelings. For example, you can say, "I'm not sure I understand how that made you feel. Do you mind telling me more?" Other useful open-ended questions include: "How did you feel when Mark shared the news with you?" or "What went through your mind when that happened?"

If there is one thing you should avoid at all costs it is being judgmental. A curious attitude beats a judgmental one every time. This does not mean that you have to agree with the person's actions, but if you are trying to build a trusting relationship, you should first try to establish a safe space where people can speak without fear of being judged. You don't want to win the argument and lose the relationship. Remember, you want reciprocity, not victory.

How we respond to good news is as important as how we respond to bad ones. If our partner, child, or friend is sharing with us an uplifting moment, we should not miss the opportunity to celebrate with them and cheer them on. While most of us are familiar with the need to respond empathetically to a colleague or friend when something goes wrong, few of us realize the need to respond enthusiastically when things go right. In a series of studies, Shelly Gable, a professor of psychology at

UCLA, demonstrated the positive effects of sharing good news with friends and relatives, a phenomenon called capitalization.[27] It turns out that when people share good news, such as a promotion, responses from others can be passive or active, constructive or destructive. Imagine sharing with close friends that your promotion requires you to relocate to another city. Your friends' responses may fall into one of the following categories:

1. *Active-Constructive*: Wow! That's incredible. How exciting. I'm so pleased for you. I want to know the details. I'll miss having you close, but I know this is what you wanted.
2. *Passive-Constructive*: Cool, congrats
3. *Active-Destructive*: We probably won't be able to keep in touch; it's just too hard to keep a friendship long distance
4. *Passive-Destructive*: It's late, I have to prepare dinner for Joe and Susie

Gable found that the benefits of capitalization attempts are further enhanced by responses perceived to be active and constructive. In close relationships, when partners typically respond enthusiastically, intimacy, marital satisfaction, and relational well-being increase. In another study she found that responses to positive events were better predictors of relational well-being than were responses to negative events. Overall, her studies demonstrate that how we respond to good news is crucial for intrapersonal and interpersonal well-being.

To summarize, you can improve your listening by practicing the following six skills:

1. Control intrusive thoughts and behaviors
2. Identify hidden feelings, beliefs, and needs
3. Share, humbly, what you think the other person is needing, feeling, or believing
4. Formulate open-ended questions
5. Refrain from judgement
6. Celebrate others when things go well

Expressing ourselves. In close relationships, we often express ourselves to be understood, affirmed, valued, or all of the above. If listening is about helping others feel valued and heard, expressing ourselves is about being heard ourselves. To be heard, first we need to identify the *needs, feelings*, or *beliefs* that we want to convey. Am I feeling forgotten or neglected in the relationship? Do I wish she paid more attention to me? Do I believe he is not fair toward me?

Second, we have to express our needs, feelings, or beliefs in ways that build the relationship. If we want to open up a channel of communication, we suggest the use of "I" statements. Instead of saying "you never pay attention to my needs," we suggest "I need you to pay more attention to my needs." The former shuts down conversation; the latter invites dialogue. By using "I" statements you are making yourself vulnerable. This type of self-disclosure brings you closer to your partner. By using blaming terms such as "you never think about me" you are forcing the other person to erect walls of protection. You are pretty much cornering the other person and are bound to elicit defensive reactions.

Third, when expressing yourself, take into consideration the other person's state of mind. You may wish to share many details about an event of personal significance, but others may not be so interested in the minutiae of the situation. Unless you are careful, you may bore the other person to death. Keep the listener in mind. If you are trying to teach something, consider what the listener already knows. Otherwise, you run the risk of boring the expert or overwhelming the novice.

Fourth, when you have to give some critical feedback to a partner, child, friend, or colleague, it helps to follow a few simple rules. Sometimes it helps to ask the other person if he or she would like to hear something you have to say. If the other person is unwilling to engage in reciprocal feedback, there may not be a point to the conversation to begin with. However, sometimes you don't have a choice and must provide feedback to a partner or employee. If that is the case, make sure to select a time that works for you and the other person. Do this in a private place. Make sure the other person feels safe and respected. If possible, start by acknowledging what the other person does well and how he or she adds value to you, the family, the relationship, or work. Make it clear that your goal is to resolve a conflict or improve a situation, not just to criticize.

It helps to be as specific as possible about the behavior or situation that is bothering you. Refrain from rehashing the past and stay in the present. Avoid generalizations like "you always . . . ."

Invite the other person to share his or her views about the subject at hand. This gives the message that you are open to alternative interpretations. When the other person shares these views, do not act defensively. After you listen to the other side, express your wish to resolve the situation and offer alternatives. Show gratitude to the other person for being willing to engage in a difficult conversation.[28]

In short, we can strengthen relationships by expressing ourselves in the following ways:

1. Identify the need, feeling, or belief you wish to express
2. Make "I" statements
3. Pay attention to the needs and interests of the listener
4. If you have to provide critical feedback, first acknowledge how the other person adds value to your life
5. Show gratitude to the other person for being willing to listen to you

PART IV

Work

CHAPTER 8

Mattering in Teams

Teaming is about creating the conditions that will enable people to feel valued at work. Teaming encompasses our behaviors, emotions, thoughts, and interactions. These four elements of teaming create a particular context. What we do, feel, and think can foster a culture of inclusion or exclusion, safety or fear. The consequences of our actions, feelings, and exchanges have short- and long-term repercussions for the health of employees and the organization as a whole. This chapter deals with the signs, significance, sources, and strategies related to feeling valued at work.

Signs

Meet Jim Churchman. Jim was a teacher and later a school principal. He is featured in the book *Gig: Americans Talk about Their Jobs*.[1] He taught school in Missouri and Illinois for many years. He liked teaching fifth and sixth grades the best. He obtained a master's and eventually a doctorate in education. Upon retirement he played a lot of golf, but, in his own words: "Got tired of that pretty quick. I didn't feel like I had much self-worth."[2] Like many retirees, Jim was still looking for ways to be relevant and to feel valued, so he looked for a part-time job, which he found in a big box store. There, he works as a greeter. But more important than the job itself, he found a community.

Since his wife was diagnosed with cancer, everyone has been very supportive at work. "We're a big family. We all work and help each other and socialize with each other. Some of my co-workers come over to my house and we play our guitars. They're real nice."[3] Jim is part of a team, which makes him feel valued, and to which he adds value. But he gets satisfaction not only from peers but also from customers: "I had a lady come in here the other day and I opened the door for her and I called her ma'am. She looked at my name tag and said . . . 'Can I take you home with me?'"[4] Jim is appreciated by his peers and valued by his customers. He is gratified.

Nayan Busa is a software engineer featured in the book *An everyone Culture: Becoming a Deliberately Developmental Organization.*[5] He works at Next Jump, an e-commerce business. To thrive in the company, Nayan had to overcome insecurities and anxieties. But he was not expected to do this by himself. His colleagues and bosses were there to help. During a recruitment event, he shared with newcomers his trajectory: "I have been here since 2010 . . . . When I first started, I lacked confidence. I was insecure. I was scared about how I was portrayed by my peers. This has not been easy to overcome . . . . And I still have a long way to go." Nayan got a lot of support from peers and from the CEO, who asked him to address the board. Reflecting on his experience with the board, Nayan shares his appreciation for the opportunity: "I was like, 'Shit! Which company allows such a young engineer to be sitting in front of the board talking about strategy?"[6] Next Jump is a deliberately developmental organization that makes people feel part of the team. In fact, its motto is "Better Me + Better You = Better Us." In our words, the company practices a "We Culture."

Although they are in vastly different industries, Jim and Nayan thrive because they feel part of a supportive team – they feel valued. They feel like they matter at work. Jim feels valued by peers and customers. Nayan is respected by his boss. The CEO trusts him enough to ask him to partici-pate in board meetings. The satisfaction that Jim and Nayan experience derives from teaming, working with people who collaborate with you and who make you feel part of the group. To quote our dear friend and scholar David Blustein, work is, after all, a highly relational endeavor. According to Harvard Business School Professor Amy Edmondson,

> Teaming blends relating to people, listening to other points of view, coordinating actions, and making shared decisions. Effective teaming requires everyone to remain vigilantly aware of others' needs, roles, and perspectives . . . . Therefore, teaming calls for developing both affective (feeling) and cognitive (thinking) skills.[7]

Teaming, then, is the practice of moving from a "Me Culture" to a "We Culture." It is about creating a psychological climate of safety and accept-ance where people can be honest and human. These conditions are propi-tious for creativity, productivity, and well-being.[8] Teaming meets the needs for belonging, dignity, and growth, and it requires effort on every-one's part: boss, employee, peers. It is a collective responsibility. In high-performing teams, members add value and pay attention to the needs of their peers. They create a climate of fairness where everyone can make a contribution and where nobody is a free rider.

Working for Next Jump is rewarding, but it's not easy. Teaming is not the equivalent of coddling. People are respected but also expected to do the hard work required to improve and contribute, to themselves and others. To build such a culture, as Edmondson notes, requires affective and cognitive skills.[9] Affective skills entail deep listening, empathy, collaboration, conflict management, reciprocity, and compassion. Cognitive skills include strategic planning, problem solving, and technical knowledge.

Teams usually succeed or fail on the basis of their *affective, not cognitive* acumen. Yet ironically, most leaders focus on the latter and neglect the former. They think, erroneously, that people should be able to check their emotions at the door and focus on the task at hand. Nothing could be further from the truth. We carry our emotional brain wherever we go, and especially to places where we might feel slightly threatened.

Jim and Nayan are fortunate. They experience teaming and appreciation, but not everyone shares their luck. To understand the experience of feeling valued or devalued at work, Jane Dutton, Gelaye Debebe, and Amy Wrzesniewski conducted two focus groups and twenty-nine interviews with members of the cleaning staff of a hospital.[10] At the time of the study, the hospital had 850 beds, over 800 doctors, 640 residents, and 1,500 registered nurses. The hospital handled approximately 34,000 admissions per year. In addition, there were 714,000 outpatient visits annually. In short, there was a lot of cleaning to do. Despite cleaners making an essential contribution to the hospital, there were clear signs they were being devalued.

For the most part, cleaners felt completely ignored. They felt invisible, especially to the doctors. At times the physicians behaved as if the cleaners did not exist. Harry, a participant in the study, shares his frustration as follows: "And the doctors stand in the way. And what I mean by doctors stand in the way, I mean literally . . . . They have no regard for whatever anyone else is doing in the hallway."[11] Bertie talked about feeling devalued: "I don't think they (doctors and nurses) value our jobs . . . . They take advantage of, you know, our jobs as being housekeepers and pick up after them. I've sat there and watched doctors and nurses throw something on the floor and just, you know, look at it, like 'She'll pick that up.'"[12]

The cleaning staff felt insulted, diminished, and disrespected. As a rule, cleaners got the message that they were not worthy of acknowledgment, and, if they were, they were dismissed and disrespected.

Signs of devaluation come in two forms: omission or commission. Ignoring is an error of omission: failing to do something. Errors of commission consist of active disrespect, like a dismissive look or ordering you around. We can understand these errors by contrasting them with instances in which cleaners did feel valued. Acknowledging a cleaner's presence, saying hi, being polite, and holding a door were manifestations of respect. Treating the cleaning staff as part of the team was also viewed favorably. Some nurses would invite them for coffee, lunch, or celebrations. Another sign of valuing was making the cleaner's job easier, as in picking up lunch leftovers and moving out of the way. Words of appreciation and gratitude went a long way to making them feel part of the team.

The researchers argue that we build our sense of mattering through interactions with others at work. Every interaction is an opportunity to make you feel valued or devalued. The message you get from colleagues and bosses, they claim, can build you up or put you down. "Valuing interactions are associated with positive emotions such as pleasure, gratitude, and appreciation. Devaluing interactions are associated with hurt, anger, frustration, and sadness. Thus, social valuing emphasizes that interaction at work creates powerful feelings for individuals that contribute to a sense of felt worth."[13]

People signal mattering at work through their behaviors. Verbal and nonverbal behaviors convey messages of inclusion or exclusion. They take the form of a smile, a hug, a question, or rolling of the eyes. Talk can be supportive or sarcastic. Jokes can be uplifting or demeaning. A gaze can be compassionate or critical. A great deal of empirical evidence shows that a climate of respect, enacted through affective skills, results in satisfaction and high team performance.[14] Teaming is a process consisting of all these inviting behaviors and interpersonal skills. When properly deployed, these skills and behaviors result in trust. In a climate of trust, it is easier to give and get feedback and to get better.

The climate is created by the players in the room, and while skills no doubt play a role, so do personality traits. The more cooperative, conscientious, agreeable, and emotionally stable team members are, the easier it will be to create a high-performing team.[15] This is why personality and knowledge must be considered in nurturing mattering at work. It is a question of recruiting the right people, training them in the art of mattering, and getting rid of those who refuse to build a healthy culture. A manager can create a lot of good or a lot of damage.

William Rosario was a full-time driver for a delivery company. This is a job he had had for ten years. Unlike Jim, who felt valued by managers and peers, William resented the treatment he got from his boss. "Every day there's a meeting in the morning to tell you what you did wrong the day before. Every day . . . . You're never told what you did well."[16]

The type of treatment William was subjected to by his bosses has serious consequences. The evidence shows that constant devaluing lowers not only morale but also productivity.[17] Warmth and friendliness, on the other hand, can elevate everyone's game. This was precisely what Dacher Keltner from Berkeley set out to study.[18] Can friendly touch by basketball players elevate everyone's game? Can supportive touch improve team collaboration and performance? His participants were none other than National Basketball Association players. At the beginning of the 2008 season, researchers coded all the observed touches during entire games. For seven months, they catalogued twenty-five different types of touch. They included high-fives, bear hugs, and fist bumps. They discovered that, on average, players touched teammates for a short period of time during a game. But the surprising thing was that these brief touches made a real difference. Based on scientific statistical analyses, Keltner found that the more players touched one another in a supportive way at the beginning of the season, the better they performed at the end of the season. Some of the positive behaviors observed included more efficient possession on offense, helping one another more on defense, and hustling more for loose balls. Most importantly, teams classified as high-touch won more games during the season.

Some players touched their teammates more than others. They did so to affirm, encourage, celebrate, and appreciate them. In 2008, Kevin Garnett from the Boston Celtics won the "Keltner award" for most valuable toucher. The impact of Garnett's touching was noticeable. He made his team play better.

Keltner loves basketball teams, but he is making a bigger point about group performance in general. Affirmative interactions build teams. According to him, "the empowering qualities of touch illustrate a broader power principle: that in providing rewards to others, we find enduring power . . . through sharing, encouraging, sacrificing, affirming, valuing, giving responsibilities, and performing the seemingly incidental touches that make up our social lives."[19] Keltner is talking about adding value as a way of creating a "We Culture."

Valuing and devaluing interactions, verbal and nonverbal, make a big difference. From the hospital floor to the basketball court, from the big box store to the e-commerce shop, the quality of interactions matter. They matter for the well-being of employees and the overall health of the company.

Significance

Leaders, researchers, and organizations are paying more attention to mattering at work. They are concerned with the consequences of feeling valued or devalued. And for good reason. Summarizing the state of the art on psychologically healthy workplaces, David Ballard and Matthew Grawitch argue that "feeling valued at work is critical to employee well-being and performance, as workers who feel valued by their employer are more likely to be engaged in their work. Employees who feel valued are significantly more likely to report having high levels of energy, being strongly involved in their work, and feeling happily engrossed in what they do."[20]

Earlier work by Pierce and colleagues, published in 1989 in the *Academy of Management Journal,* showed that being important to the organization was highly associated with positive citizenship behavior, commitment to the workplace, intrinsic motivation to do well, job performance and job satisfaction.[21] A 2017 study on mattering at work confirmed that it is significantly associated with work meaning, job satisfaction, life satisfaction, commitment to the organization, and positive affect.[22] Furthermore, the more workers felt that they mattered, the less they thought about quitting. The most recent review of mattering in the workplace, conducted by Flett in 2018, shows that feeling valued at work is related to a number of positive outcomes, including low absenteeism; better employee–manager relationships, higher engagement in goal settings, greater resilience and perceived social support, and higher levels of health and well-being.[23]

The association between feeling valued and well-being is highly significant, for the latter predicts health-care costs, productivity, and retention.[24] A large-scale study makes this point convincingly. In the summer of 2010, 11,775 employees of a large Fortune 100 finance and insurance company completed a well-being questionnaire. A year later, 6,170 of those employees completed the well-being assessment for a second time. This design allowed researchers to see whether changes in overall well-being had any impact on important outcomes. The study found that the level of overall well-being was predictive of important outcomes. Employees who scored high on well-being spent less money on pharmacy and doctor visits and had fewer hospital and emergency room admissions. In addition, those high in well-being were more productive. They had higher job performance ratings and fewer unscheduled absences and short-term disability leave. Finally, a high level of well-being was associated with better retention rates. The study demonstrated that employees with low levels of well-being are less likely to stay with the company, whether due to voluntary or involuntary withdrawal.

Another study with 2,245 members of a health plan discovered an inverse relationship between well-being scores and emergency room visits, hospital admissions, and medical and prescription expenditures.[25] Compared to participants with high well-being scores, those with low scores incurred 2.7 times more expenses ($5,172 as opposed to $1,885).

Isaac's Office of Institutional Culture conducted a similar study with close to 4,800 faculty and staff at the University of Miami. We wanted to see whether organizational culture had an effect on a number of outcomes. We created and validated a Culture Index consisting of items measuring the extent to which employees felt valued and had opportunities to add value at the university. The Culture Index assessed whether faculty and staff had a sense of mattering at work.[26] What we found was that increases in the sense of mattering led to increases in engagement and feelings of inclusion, which, in turn, were highly predictive of overall, social, community, physical, and financial well-being.[27]

If feeling valued is highly associated with well-being, and if well-being is highly predictive of important corporate outcomes, there is a strong business case to be made for making people feel valued at work. Further evidence comes from recent studies on compassion in the workplace. Monica Worline and Jane Dutton show in their work that compassionate workplaces have positive effects on financial performance, innovation, service quality, collaboration, customer retention, employee retention, and adaptability to change.[28] If treating you compassionately and with respect is important, it is no surprise that treating you fairly will also impact satisfaction and performance. Indeed, when employees are treated fairly, they report more commitment, willingness to help, and trust in the organization. In addition, they perform better. Fair treatment is also associated with a sense of belonging and pride at work. Fairness enhances identification with the company, which, in turn, leads to stronger engagement at work.[29]

Just as kindness, respect, and fairness make you feel valued at work, ostracism, exclusion, and rejection make you feel devalued. And just as feeling valued improves satisfaction and efficiency, feeling devalued lowers commitment, engagement, performance, and well-being. Ostracism in particular has been shown to have negative effects on turnover, performance, sleep, well-being, and workplace attitudes.[30]

Feeling devalued is a primary stressor at work. Stressors like this have deleterious long-term consequences. In a recent comprehensive review, it was found that job stressors lead to emotional exhaustion, psychological distress, fatigue, irritation, anxiety, and tension. The same review noted that aggressive interactions are linked to poor mental health and that social undermining predicts deterioration in well-being over time. The negative effects are especially profound when the aggressor happens to be a manager.[31]

One of the consequences of feeling devalued is that people are afraid to speak up.[32] In a study with 260 employees from 22 companies across diverse industries, 70 percent of interviewees reported being afraid to speak up about issues or problems at work. In another study, with 40 young professionals, 85 percent reported that they felt, at least once, unable to bring up an issue at work. In the same study, only 51 percent claimed that they were comfortable talking to their boss about concerns. The other 49 percent prefer to keep quiet. This is most unfortunate, since teams and companies perform much better when workers share ideas and concerns. When silence prevails, performance deteriorates.

Negative treatment of colleagues exists along a continuum, the end of which is bullying. Bullying is defined as "a deliberate, repeated, health-endangering mistreatment of an employee by a supervisor or coworker."[33] Bullying can take many forms, including direct and indirect attacks. Direct attacks consist of yelling, verbal humiliation, silence, ostracism, exclusion, and hostile looks. Indirect forms of bullying include spreading rumors, sabotage, or the imposition of unrealistic targets or deadlines. A national study revealed that 35 percent of American adults have experienced bullying at work.[34] Another 15 percent stated that they witnessed others being bullied. According to the Workplace Bullying Institute survey, 53 percent reported verbal abuse in the form of swearing, name calling, shouting, and sarcasm. Also 53 percent mentioned being the subject of cruel behaviors such as threatening, intimidating, humiliating, and offensive acts. Another 45 percent reported interference with work, sabotage, and ensuring failure. Finally, 47 percent reported being mistreated by managers. This included stealing credit, denial of career advancement, and unsafe assignments. Judging by these numbers, bullying is nothing less than an epidemic.

Bullying lowers morale and productivity and increases absenteeism and turnover, not to mention the psychological pain and agony. Bullied workers suffer from a number of health conditions, including depression and anxiety disorders. Take the case of Sandra White.

Sandra got a great job at Credit Commercial de France in New York City when she was twenty-six. She worked there for seven years, and then, all of a sudden, she was laid off – the result of downsizing. She had no choice but to go on welfare. To receive benefits Sandra had to join the Work Experience Program, also known as workfare. The first two weeks were fine. She was part of a training program aimed at improving interview and job application skills. If you don't get a job at the end of the training program, you are put to work for the state, which in her case meant cleaning the streets of New York. This is when her nightmare began. Sandra was more than willing to work for her welfare check, but she did not expect to be treated the way she was. Her days were miserable. She cried because she was treated with disdain. If it rained, she was not allowed to look for shelter. "They want you working – without any gear, no gloves, no rain garments at all. They want you drenching wet . . . . We're treated so poorly . . . . I was told by my supervisor that workfare was created to humiliate you."[35]

We may be tempted to blame Sandra's problems on a few rotten apples – her callous managers. But while there's no doubt rotten apples exist, they are part of an orchard, an ecosystem that is conducive to health or disease, growth or putrefaction. Organizational ecosystems work like orchards, sometimes promoting valuing behaviors and sometimes condoning demeaning acts.

As Terence Mitchell, a leading academic in the field of organizational behavior recently put it, cultures of ostracism and incivility "have disastrous effects on the target in terms of affect; psychological functioning; and organizational outcomes such as performance, satisfaction, and turnover."[36] To get to the root cause of these behaviors and prevent them, we need to explore organizational culture.

Sources

Gary Namie is a pioneer. He is a leading figure in the movement to eradicate bullying from the workplace. He has researched the topic in depth, written about it, advocated on behalf of workers, built coalitions to tackle the problem, and created the Workplace Bullying Institute. He knows a few rotten apples. But he also knows a few rotten orchards. Reflecting on the culture that enables bullying and mobbing (bullying by a group), he recently wrote that, while other forms of abuse such as child abuse and domestic violence have become taboo, "bullying and mobbing at work remain widespread, acceptable, and even promoted."[37] He goes on to say that "executives and administrators all too often ignore clear reports of bullying and mobbing, sometimes preferring to rationalize aggressive acts as natural and indispensable parts of a successful workplace climate."[38]

There is something about the culture of individualism that ascribes success and failure to individuals, neglecting evidence that our victories and defeats are the result of an interaction between us and our environments. There is no denying that some people work hard to succeed, and some others engage in self-defeating behavior, but there is also no denying that the culture we are exposed to can inhibit or facilitate success as well as abuse.

We live in a culture that blames people for their misfortune. Just like we blame the poor for their lot in life, we ignore the plight of the mistreated worker. We face a culture of silence and complicity. Nobody wants to rock the boat. If you out aggressors you can get into serious trouble. Witness the case of Harvey Weinstein that gave rise to the #MeToo movement.[39] Scores of people knew that he was sexually abusing women, but no one came forward for years. Many people in the film industry declared mea culpa for knowing and not doing anything about it. The culture is stronger than the individual. There are a thousand ways to rationalize why we tolerate abuse. These excuses make up the fabric of institutional culture.

Raj Sisodia, a business professor who has been advocating for compassionate and caring workplaces, recently wrote: "Business has become dehumanized and impersonal. Human beings are treated as functions or objects, interchangeable and disposable as machine parts . . . . The vast majority of people are dispirited and uninspired at work. They feel disrespected, not listened to, and devalued."[40] When the predominant narrative of business is *treat people as means to ends, as opposed to end in themselves*, safety disappears, creativity shuts down, engagement evaporates, and customer satisfaction declines. Sisodia claims that "we must create environments in which people are inspired, feel safe, are cared for, and receive recognition and celebration for who they are and what they do."[41] The extent to which we feel valued or devalued at work depends on the culture of the workplace. A healthy, vibrant, safe, and productive culture can be characterized as Supportive, Effective, and Reflective.[42] These three words form the acronym SER, which in Spanish means "to be." The way an organization is, or should be, can be gauged by their efforts to become a SER organization. This is a three-legged stool. All aspects of SER are important.

By supportive we mean a culture that affirms, values, and appreciates people.[43] This is a place where people feel like they matter. When they succeed they are celebrated. When they struggle they are supported. When they experiment with new ways of doing things, they are not scolded for trying, even when they fail. This type of organization fosters psychological safety and recognition. Furthermore, it focuses on the rights and responsibilities of employees and managers, and it fosters fairness as much as wellness. In short, being a supportive organization is essential for a "We Culture."

But employees aspire to more than feeling valued. They want to add value. This is why a healthy organization is an effective organization. To accomplish goals we must have clear objectives, make a plan, take initiative, coordinate effort, communicate clearly, respond to requests in a timely fashion, offer feedback, engage in corrective action, and monitor progress. These are the basic ingredients of effectiveness. This second leg of the stool is aligned with the human need for competence and meaning.

The third and last leg builds on our need for learning, innovation, and growth.[44] We call it reflectiveness. To keep us motivated, organizations must provide opportunities for career growth and development. Workers need to feel a sense of personal progress and must satisfy their curiosity. This can only happen when the culture fosters a climate of personal and collective development. Such efforts must be structured. Time and place must be designated for these activities. Furthermore, managers should reward the desire to learn and question the old ways of doing things. We are at our best when we refresh our practices. A reflective organization seeks opportunities to evaluate the usefulness of established habits and the potential of new ones.

Organizations that embrace a "We Culture" make sure that their people feel supported, stimulated, and effective. They find ways to make them feel valued and to give them opportunities to add value, to themselves and to the entire enterprise. Managers feel responsible not just for the corporation but for the individual employees under their tutelage as well.

To define a "We Culture" is one thing, but to shape it is quite another. Isaac is on the seventh year of a massive effort to improve the culture in an institution inhabited by highly accomplished skeptics. Universities are notorious for having opinionated people who have been trained in the art of critique. As academics, we undergo rigorous training in dissecting the work of our colleagues and finding flaws. This is how science gets better and how scholarship progresses. No complaints there. But trying to engage thousands of people with PhDs and MDs in culture transformation is rather humbling. If you want to try it, be prepared to get a lecture or two by your colleagues. For good or ill, Isaac tried it.

Around 2013, the University of Miami embarked on an ambitious project to improve its culture. Isaac was part of a small culture leadership team created to oversee the process. The group, appointed by former University

President Donna Shalala, formulated a comprehensive plan that would improve our support to employees, our effectiveness, and our reflectiveness. This process culminated in the creation of an Office of Institutional Culture, which Isaac currently leads. Our aim is to foster a culture of belonging where everyone feels valued and everyone has an opportunity to add value.

Since the beginning in 2013, the process has entailed the creation of task forces, assessments of our culture, the formulation of a new common purpose, and the establishment of common values as well as new leadership expectations and service standards. Thousands of hours and significant financial resources have been invested in this project. Our former provost, Tom LeBlanc, now president of The George Washington University, attended every single meeting of the culture leadership team.

Caution: Culture transformation is not for the faint of heart. You have to be willing to challenge old assumptions, challenge colleagues, and challenge yourself. This is a threefold increase in the number of challenges most leaders are willing to undertake on any given day. But to do it right, you can't escape them.

This labor-intensive project resulted in a new common purpose: "At the University of Miami, we transform lives through excellence in teaching, innovation, research, and service."[45] This seemingly simple statement took hours and hours to craft. We also articulated a set of values captured in the acronym DIRECCT: Diversity, Integrity, Responsibility, Excellence, Compassion, Creativity, and Teamwork. These values were formulated in consultation with vast numbers of employees in focus groups and workshops. The list of our defining values went through over twenty drafts. In the end, most people could live with it, even some of the skeptics. To make sure these were not just pretty words on a poster, we also defined in behavioral terms how each of the DIRECCT values would be manifested in our work.

Managers were not off the hook. We also produced, in collaboration with a representative task force, leadership expectations. Among others, these included nurturing trust, developing employees, serving others, and acting with courage. To make sure we provided the highest quality of service to our students, patients, and colleagues, we formulated four service standards: safety, caring, responsiveness, and professionalism. The new values, leadership expectations, and service standards are now part of the formal employee evaluation process. We are all evaluated against our belief system.

What began as a culture transformation project evolved into a clearly articulated vision for a *Culture of Belonging*. Once we established the pillars of our culture, we set out to train thousands of employees. Over 9,000 faculty and staff participated in educational workshops. We also reinvented our orientation program, created leadership programs, started a culture ambassador project, rolled out online recognition tools, provided extensive consultation to many units, and embarked on a massive education campaign. After about four years of hard labor, our efforts were recognized by *Forbes*, which in 2017 listed the University of Miami as the best employer in the country in the education sector.[46]

Since a "We Culture" is a journey and not a destination, the effort at the University of Miami continues. But it is worth reflecting on what is it that we did that earned us high rankings. In terms of mattering, the Culture of Belonging campaign had a clear message to all employees: we value your work, and we will create opportunities for you to add value. *Feeling valued* and *adding value* became a call to action. We established a robust culture ambassador program in which people were able to spread the DIRECCT values among their colleagues. We held workshops and summits in which employees reflected on how they embodied diversity, integrity, responsibility, excellence, compassion, creativity, and teamwork. We sent a signal to employees that they were valued and that they were expected to add value.

The balance of rights with responsibilities is reflected in the composite set of values we adopted. Diversity and compassion support the right to feel valued, but responsibility, excellence, and creativity remind us that we must add value. Our belief in teamwork and integrity emphasize fairness in dealing with colleagues. The set of values balances respect with accountability, focus on self with focus on others, and attention to fairness and not just to wellness. We are building a "We Culture."

The fact that thousands of people participated in the process, and hundreds still volunteer to train and mentor others is fundamental to success. This entire process has given voice to many people who did not have opportunities to be heard before. Many people with leadership potential saw a real opportunity to make a contribution. All of a sudden, many people had an important role to play, a role that went above and beyond their daily duties. They felt promoted to agents of change, not agents of tasks.

We created a climate of safety in which people can express varied opinions, including a critique of the process itself. People saw a serious and concerted effort on the part of senior administrators to reflect on our practices and create a more effective and supportive institution. Seven years in, challenges remain, but there is commitment on the part of our senior leaders to shape a SER culture, a place in which all of us matter.

Strategies

Feeling valued at work depends on teaming, which, in turn, depends on skillful exchanges among group members. Our job here is to present proven methods of teaming, and yours is to select the ones that apply to your situation. The methods can be derived from the seven BET I CAN principles of action we introduced in Chapter 4. To refresh your memory, this is what they stand for:

- Behaviors
- Emotions
- Thoughts
- Interactions
- Context
- Awareness
- Next Steps

Each one of the BET I CAN drivers of change can be used to feel valued at work. You can use them to answer two basic questions:

- What can I do to feel valued at work?
- What can I do to help others feel valued at work?

What Can I Do to Feel Valued at Work?

Two drivers of change are especially relevant to answering this question: Awareness and Behaviors. Awareness is about *knowing yourself* and *knowing the issue at hand*. In this case, knowing yourself requires that you answer the following question: *Do I feel valued or undervalued at work?* If you feel valued, you may not need to change much but rather to reinforce and maintain what is going well. On the other hand, if you feel undervalued, you need to gear up for action.

Knowing yourself requires honesty. Are you not feeling valued because of something you do, or because the workplace is unsupportive? Do you behave in ways that antagonize others? Are you doing something that rubs people the wrong way? Do you interrupt too often in meetings? Do you put other people down? We know many people who behave in disrespectful ways, but they are totally clueless about what they are doing. Others, in turn, just feel entitled to behave this way because they think that they own the truth and they deserve to behave in whichever way they darn please. In either case, the result is that such individual will not get much love from others in return. Even assuming that you will never engage in such entitled or clueless behavior, it never hurts to engage in a little bit of reflection. Is it possible that you may alienate colleagues unknowingly?

You can't build a reflective organization if you don't engage in a little reflection yourself. If you're not sure how you come across, just ask a trusted colleague. There is no avoiding this moment of truth when you are willing to confront yourself in the mirror. This is all part of knowing yourself and being true to your values. We often behave in ways that betray our values. We feel defensive and react offensively. We are perturbed by internal worries and rumination about our own worth. Instead of looking at the source of our frustration, we act it out. This is where psychological flexibility can help.[47] This is the ability to act according to your values and not according to your impulses or fears. But you can't act according to your values if you don't know what these are. Once you know what they are you can judge your actions against your principles and correct course as needed.

Knowing your values is essential for mattering and well-being. How do you want to behave toward others? What ethical guidelines should guide your life? What principles should inform your behavior toward yourself and others? To practice value-awareness, list just the top three that guide your life.

1. _____
2. _____
3. _____

Let's say that you listed the value of respect as one of yours. How would respect look in actual practice? What words and actions reflect respect in the workplace? Is your behavior consistent with this value? Once you have clarified for yourself what values you stand for and how they are manifested in your actions, you can commit to behaving in corresponding ways. You now have an anchor and a compass to guide your teaming efforts. Once you are aware of the value you want to enact – respect, in this instance – you can challenge your impulses, fears, and intruding thoughts with the following metaphorical question: *Dear thought, are you pushing me to behave in respectful or disrespectful ways?*

But awareness of your values is only the first step in nurturing psychological flexibility. The second step consists of observing your internal thoughts, worries, and frustrations in a nonjudgmental way.[48] Instead of fighting these negative thoughts, or acting according to them, we can learn to accept them, label them, and effectively neutralize their toxic effects.

This type of mindfulness fosters psychological flexibility. Instead of trying to control, eliminate or otherwise suppress these disturbing psychological events, we learn to accept them.

The third step in this process is to behave according to your values. You can say to your negative thoughts that you accept them but you're not going to behave according to their dictates. Instead you are going to engage in value-based actions. We can call the three steps value clarification, acceptance, and commitment. You accept that there are going to be disruptive psychological events from time to time, but, instead of futile attempts to wish them away, you are going to practice mindful and nonjudgmental observation of these thoughts and feelings. This doesn't mean that you are going to act according to their whims. Instead you are going to follow the values that you committed to. These are the essential components of ACT, or acceptance and commitment therapy.[49]

Awareness of your values and internal events can help you behave in respectful ways, not just toward others but also toward yourself. Respect, after all, is something we bestow not just upon others but also upon ourselves.

Is it possible that you don't feel valued at work even though your colleagues and your boss respect you and show appreciation? It is definitely possible, and when this happens it is usually the result of negative internal talk. If you don't believe that you deserve to be valued, you are likely to ignore signs of compassion. If you are not happy with yourself, you are likely to dismiss expressions of appreciation (as we saw earlier in our discussion of self-esteem). Unlike the entitled employee, who berates others, the despondent employee berates him- or herself. Self-deprecating thoughts flood the system.

The internal talk of these two people is different, but both are just that – internal chatter. Neither type can force you to behave or do things you don't want. In fact, according to ACT, you are better off investing time in behaving in value-concordant ways than in fighting mental events. Mindfulness can help you observe and accept these thoughts as momentary occurrences. As you contemplate them, you can press the pause button and interrupt a vicious cycle of rumination, where past or future concerns about adequacy and status dominate the present. After you press the pause button on negative mental events, you can press the play button on value-congruent behaviors.

In short, psychological flexibility can help you neutralize depressive or aggressive thoughts that can lead to abrasive or dysphoric behavior. Moreover, it can help you commit to acting in accordance to principles of meaning and mattering. These practices have proven effective in the workplace.[50] They have been shown to improve mental health, performance, learning at work, job satisfaction, goal-oriented behavior, collaboration, and retention. In addition, they reduce stress, emotional exhaustion, absenteeism, and burnout.

So far we have dealt with the first part of awareness: *know yourself*. But it is also important to *know the issue*. In this case, the issue may very well be that your boss does not show respect or appreciation. If your boss is like many others, chances are he or she is not paying much attention to the mattering needs of employees.

Research shows that many leaders are oblivious to workers' need to feel valued and respected. In a study of over 20,000 employees by Christine Porath, a professor of management at Georgetown University, 54 percent of participants claimed that they do not get respect from their leaders.[51] Yet the study found that respect from your leader was the most important predictor of work-related outcomes. Getting respect was even more important than recognition efforts, an inspiring vision, getting feedback, and opportunities for development. Participants who got respect from their superiors reported 56 percent better health and well-being, 89 percent greater satisfaction and enjoyment at work, 92 percent more focus and concentration, and 1.26 times more purpose and meaning at work. In addition, workers who reported being treated with respect by their bosses were 55 percent more engaged at work. In a separate study, Porath asked why leaders neglect to show respect. She found that most leaders are simply clueless and have no self-awareness of their behavior whatsoever.

Since the boss sets the tone and incivility is contagious, you may be working in an unsupportive environment. If this is the case, it is not you who needs to change but rather the culture of the place. Once you have determined that the environment is not supportive – or is outright toxic – you have a few options. In some cases, you can play a role in improving the climate, but in others the best you can do is to get out of there. If you have sufficient gravitas in the workplace and the other players are amenable, you may start a process of culture change. That would be ideal. You wear your agent-of-change cape, and off you go. But if your assessment determines that nothing short of a miracle will make your workplace supportive, you may need to start polishing your résumé.

Leaving a job is never easy, especially when new ones are hard to come by. Challenging your boss is not easy either. But you need to be aware of the negative consequences that might result from prolonged exposure to devaluing environments: stress, burnout, and depression.[52] Just like a divorce is never easy, for some people it is healthier to get out of a sick relationship than to stay and hope for the best.

Practicing mindfulness to achieve psychological flexibility requires effort. The same goes for changing the culture at work. But there are ways to move forward that can make these tasks manageable. Earlier we saw that setting goals and creating positive habits can lead to desirable behavioral outcomes. You can focus on a behavior that can align your values with your actions.

If you feel that you are not getting the respect that you deserve from others, you can experiment with GREASE goals:

- **Gradual:** If you feel that your voice is not heard in meetings, for example, you can rehearse an "I" statement next time this happens. When you encounter the situation you might say something like: "I feel I haven't been heard. I'd like to come back for a minute to the point I made before." This is not a dramatic statement accusing anyone but rather a gradual way to say to your boss or peers that you would appreciate being heard. Keep track of how often you assert yourself.
- **Rewarded:** Take time to congratulate yourself on taking a small risk to address the issue.
- **Easy:** If you rehearse the statement it won't be too hard to express it. Furthermore, you can apply this technique to other instances in which you may feel devalued. You can experiment with other "I" statements such as: "I'm not sure this is what you meant, but what you just said felt sarcastic and didn't make me feel good. I'd appreciate it if you refrained from comments like these."
- **Alternatives:** Instead of feeling devalued or not appreciated, the "I" statement can help you take action.
- **Supported:** Share your new behavior with a supportive colleague and ask for feedback.
- **Educated:** Learn about the benefits of "I" statements and assertive behavior.

If you are trying to transform the culture of your organization, the GREASE principles can also help:

- **Gradual:** Add an item to the agenda of the next team meeting where you can share an article about the importance of a respectful organizational culture (you can bring the article by Christine Porath). From there you can create a reading club on organizational culture.
- **Rewarded:** Take a moment to feel proud about raising an important issue, even if the first attempt does not get you very far.

- Easy: Including an item on the agenda is a pretty safe thing, especially if you share some important information. You are not attacking or confronting anyone.
- Alternatives: If the culture of the place is not very healthy, make sure to role model alternative ways of behaving toward one another. People will notice.
- Supported: Talk to a trusted colleague about the need to improve the culture, and come up with a plan of action. What will you do after you discuss the article on organizational culture? May you suggest the creation of a task force?
- Educated: Read about the process of creating a supportive, effective, and reflective culture.[53]

If you are plagued by self-doubt and often visited by unpleasant thoughts, you may wish to practice mindfulness meditation on a regular basis. Try the following:

- Gradual: Set aside ten minutes twice a week to start a meditation routine. Increase one more session every week.
- Rewarded: Send a congratulatory email to yourself!
- Easy: You can easily download meditations to your phone and find ten minutes here and there to engage in the practice.
- Alternatives: If at first you cannot manage ten minutes, start with three!
- Supported: You may wish to meditate with your spouse. We often do this at home.
- Educated: Learn about the benefits of mindfulness meditation and psychological flexibility.[54]

What Can I Do to Help Others Feel Valued at Work?

If your goal is to be kinder to others, you can set a behavioral goal that also follows the GREASE principles:

- Gradual: Send two notes of appreciation per day for a week to peers who have helped you in some way. Increase gradually every week. During his tenure as CEO of Campbell's Soup, Doug Conant sent over 30,000 individualized thank-you notes to his 20,000 employees. He was credited with transforming the culture of the company.[55]
- Rewarded: Praise yourself for your kinder behavior.
- Easy: You send dozens of emails per day – sending two more per day for a week is not so hard.

- **A**lternatives: Every time you have the urge to make a sarcastic comment, count to three.
- **S**upported: Share your goal with your spouse and talk about progress together.
- **E**ducated: Learn about the benefits of respect in the workplace.[56]

By being kinder to others, wonderful things can happen. They might just reciprocate and make you feel valued too! There is extensive research on the benefits of recognition. In a study of nearly 600 employees, 77.6 percent reported that it was very or extremely important to feel recognized by their boss when they perform well. Unfortunately, in another major study barely more than half (51 percent) of working Americans reported feeling valued at work. In a series of studies from the 1940s to the present day, workers consistently rank involvement and moral support higher than monetary incentives. Employees typically enjoy more "appreciation for work done," "feeling in on things," and engaging in "interesting work."[57]

In a recent volume on the psychologically healthy workplace, Bob Nelson defines employee recognition as "a positive consequence provided to a person for a behavior or result. Recognition can take the form of acknowledgment, approval, or the expression of gratitude. It means appreciating someone for something he or she has done for an individual, a group, or an organization."[58] Nelson claims that there are four major forms of recognition: *interpersonal* recognition, such as thank-you cards; *social* recognition, in the form of a public acknowledgment for a job well done; *tangible* recognition, such as a certificate, for example; and *intangible* recognition, which can take the form of enhanced involvement in decision-making.[59]

Rewards and recognition go a long way toward increasing motivation, engagement, and involvement. To make the most of recognition, Nelson recommends the following seven principles:

1. *Contingency*: Provided closely to expressed and desired behavior
2. *Timing*: Given close to event
3. *Frequency*: Given often
4. *Formality*: Employee recognized in planned events such as awards ceremonies for employees of the month
5. *Setting and context*: The more personalized, and public, the better
6. *Significance of the provider*: Usually varies from person to person, but should be either a manager or a good friend who knows the employee
7. *Value to the recipient*: Recognition is most useful when customized to wishes of the individual; some like work-related tools or educational

opportunities, while others prefer more personal things like a dinner or vacation

Rewards and recognition programs combine behavioral and interaction drivers of change. On the behavioral side, you can set a goal to reward employees who exhibit desirable behaviors, creating a positive habit of recognizing them often. On the interactional side, through a recognition program you connect and communicate with workers and peers in ways that make them feel valued. At the University of Miami we implemented a popular online recognition system called "ThankU." Anyone can recognize a colleague for expressing one of our values: Diversity, Integrity, Responsibility, Excellence, Compassion, Creativity, and Teamwork. The sender can copy the individual's boss, and the receiver can choose to make the electronic ThankU card visible to others or not. Faculty and staff have sent thousands of ThankU cards to colleagues since its inception a couple of years ago.

Behaviors and interactions can help with teaming, but context can help too. Cues in the environment send powerful signals to employees. Owning a mistake in public sends a message to others that responsibility and integrity are highly valued. Such public displays of ownership send a message that we value responsibility and accountability. Furthermore, treating the culprit with compassion sends the message that people are allowed to make mistakes. Exchanges, written communication, memos, and public interactions are cues of culture. The cues convey meaning. The more we convey cues that this is a psychologically safe place, the higher the level of employee engagement, motivation, and well-being.

Amy Edmondson defines psychological safety as "a climate in which people feel free to express relevant thoughts and feelings . . . . Yet, frank conversations and public missteps must occur if teaming is to realize the promise of collaboration across differences."[60] Psychological safety is a precondition for free expression; but, while important, it is not always present. People often refrain from speaking up because they are afraid of being seen as ignorant, incompetent, negative or disruptive. Yet, the benefits of speaking up are many and varied: participation leads to innovation, mitigates failure, enables clarity of thought, supports productive conflict, removes obstacles, and increases accountability. Edmondson has a few suggestions for leaders who wish to foster psychological safety in their teams:

- Be willing to show vulnerability
- Be accessible and approachable

- Acknowledge limits of knowledge on the subject
- Invite participation
- Talk about failures as opportunities for growth
- Hold people accountable for transgressions of culture

In a psychologically safe environment people laugh, respect each other, take collective responsibility, and share mistakes.

To solidify the benefits of recognition and safety, key ingredients in teaming, a leader can institute formal training in team development. This is part of the driver of change we call Next Steps. This driver consists of two strategies: *make a plan*; and *make it stick*. It is important to embed training in team development in all organizations wishing to build a "We Culture." We cannot expect all team members to be naturally skilled in the art of emotional intelligence or mattering. Therefore, we must introduce proven methods of team building. As a leader, you have to plan for it, and you have to make it stick. Luckily, the science of team development has a lot to offer.

There are three types of processes that characterize effective teamwork: *goal setting processes* (define goals and objectives, set course of action, planning); *action processes* (tracking and monitoring progress, coordination of efforts, division of labor); and *interpersonal processes* (affect regulation, building positive relationships, psychological safety, recognition, conflict prevention and management, group morale, trust, motivation). The first two usually refer to *task management*, while the third one refers to *relationship management*.

To succeed in task management, teams must invest in relationship building. Research demonstrates that social support, in the form of mutual recognition and affirmation, can raise the level of performance in teams. The more comfortable team members feel with one another, the more they can help each other with the task at hand, providing information and advice and lending a hand. Task and relationship management can be trained. If you are group leader, you would do well to invest in team development, since, as experts conclude, "team training has been shown to have a positive impact on team performance, enhancing affective, cognitive, process, and performance outcomes."[61]

Most orientation programs tend to focus on tasks, not relationships. This is a serious oversight. To foster teamwork, training must include modules on psychological safety, trust building, cooperation, conflict resolution, giving and getting feedback, and value clarification. In a recent review on the state of team development science, the authors conclude that "in addition to being technically able to perform their assignments, team members must also demonstrate teamwork competencies and leader capabilities, and the team as a whole must engage in effective interpersonal and team processing."[62] The authors make the point that teams must engage in training, for which there is compelling empirical evidence.

Altogether, we have seen that several drivers of change can help with teaming efforts. These include *raising awareness* of internal or external issues affecting your sense of mattering, setting *behavioral goals* to take action, addressing *contextual cues* that convey psychological safety, *interacting* in affirming ways that recognize employees, and thinking of *next steps* in terms of team development and training. Whether you are a leader or you report to a leader, there are many things you can do to improve teaming and to make sure all your members feel valued. Once they feel valued, they will be much more motivated to add value. Remember, everyone is *owed respect*. This is a fundamental right we all have. When we add value, however, we move from owed respect to *earned respect*.[63] This is the type of respect we earn by making meaningful contributions to the team. Let's explore how to add value and move from owed respect to earned respect.

CHAPTER 9

Mattering through Performance

Performing is about adding value to work. You can add value to a paid or unpaid job; to a vocation or avocation; or to both, the way Roger Bannister did.[1] He was a highly respected British neurologist who made significant contributions to medicine. But while pursuing medical education at Oxford, he invested heavily in athletics as well. Bannister, who passed away in 2018, became a sport legend as a runner. In his 2014 autobiography he wrote that "sport and medicine have a vital and expanding role in improving the lives of individuals across the world. These are the twin tracks that have run through my life. I feel very grateful to have been given the chance to make some contributions in both these fields."[2]

When the work you do includes more than yourself, you can make contributions through *productive* or *relational value*. Productive value refers to contributions you make to create a good or a service. You may have insights about how to sell a product to a new market, how to deliver a service more efficiently, or how to perform a dance more graciously. These ideas and actions enhance the productive value of a task. This is all about delivering great goods and services efficiently and accomplishing tasks with the highest quality. Relational value, as we will see, is about fostering mattering in the workplace.

Bannister made meaningful contributions to the practice of neurology (his vocation) and running (his avocation). May 6, 1954, was going to be the day when he would make running history. Although he had been preparing for years, the inauspicious weather threatened to postpone the much-awaited trial. Strong winds could mean the difference between four minutes and three minutes 59.9 seconds. Anything above four minutes would have meant defeat; anything below, history-making jubilation.

Until that day, nobody had ever run a mile in less than four minutes, and Bannister was determined to show the world that this was not an unbreakable barrier. Yet the weather was so unpredictable that he could not make up his mind whether to run or not. He was physically and psychologically ready, but the strong winds could spell disaster. His running mates, Chris Brasher and Chris Chataway, were growing impatient with him. Bannister's indecision created unbearable tension. Then, thirty minutes before the race, he declared: "Right, we'll go for it, we all know what we have to do."[3] For a brief moment, there was a drop in the wind – perfect timing – but there was a false start by Chris Brasher. The gun fired for a second time and Bannister was off, full of energy. His pacers forced him to reserve strength for the last stretch. Although Bannister was ready to push ahead full speed, his mates knew better. His coach, Franz Stampfl, shouted "relax" from the sidelines. Bannister had to run the last lap in 59 seconds. When there were 300 yards left, he accelerated vigorously and the crowd exploded. "Their hope and encouragement gave me greater strength," Bannister recalled. With just five yards to the finish, his body was so depleted that the finish line seemed out of reach. "Those last few seconds seemed an eternity ... The faint line of the finishing tape stood ahead as a haven of peace after the struggle . . . . I leapt at the tape like a man taking his last desperate spring to save himself from a chasm that threatens to engulf him. Then my effort was over and I collapsed almost unconscious."[4] A few moments later the announcer would confirm what Bannister had sensed; he had broken the four-minute mile.

Bannister's life was full of productive value. Not only did he break a physical and psychological barrier in running, but he also directed important health and sport organizations and contributed to the development of recreational exercise. But his contributions were not only in the form of productive value, for he also added a great deal of relational worth to his work. By his own account, he could not have accomplished his athletic feat without the help of Chris Chataway and Chris Brasher, coach Franz Stampfl, or his friends. Bannister cultivated friendships and camaraderie with running mates and opponents alike. He formed life-long friendships that helped him on and off the field. Bannister created a supportive environment among athletes and patients and, while Master of Pembroke College at Oxford, among students and faculty as well.

Relational value is about fostering a climate of support and growth among your peers and employees. You add relational value when you behave compassionately, when you encourage your peers to learn, and when you create a psychologically safe place. The more relational value you create in the workplace, the higher the likelihood to generate productive value. Fear, the opposite of psychological safety, imposes a tax on productivity and most certainly kills creativity.

We matter at work by contributing productive and relational worth. Both are essential. In a "Me Culture" people worry mostly about product- ive value. What can I bring to the table that will make me shine? In a "We Culture," relational is of no less consequence than productive value.

In the next sections, we answer the following four questions: How can we tell that people are adding value? What is the significance of adding value or failing to do so? Where do productive and relational value come from? What strategies can we use to ensure people have an opportunity to add value?

Signs

Roger Bannister was a conscientious student, a dedicated doctor, and a capable administrator. We could tell he was adding productive value because he invested time and thought in all his endeavors. When you add training to time and thought you have a pretty powerful combination. The six Ts (time, thought, training, tenacity, trust, and transcendence) com- bined to help make Bannister a highly successful athlete, neurologist, and leader.

In his bestselling book *Better: A Surgeon's Notes on Performance*, Atul Gawande invokes all the Ts when he talks about diligence.[5] For him, diligence is the unceasing pursuit of improvement and transcendence, something that cannot be done without heavy doses of time, thought, training, tenacity, and trust. Medicine and public health, he argues, could not have made so much progress without the diligence, persistence, and ingenuity of many unsung heroes.

When I, Isaac, joined a clinic as a young school psychologist, there was a supervisor who loved to congratulate himself on all his years of experi- ence. Indeed, he had spent a lot of time at the clinic, but he had not invested much thought in improving his knowledge, nor undergone much training. As a result, he was accustomed to the application of old theories and methods, the validity of which were very much in question by the time I joined the clinic. People often confuse seniority with wisdom, but time by itself does not produce value. My supervisor was not very diligent.

To achieve wisdom, we need time, thought, training, tenacity, trust, and the desire for transcendence. In just about any field, it is impossible to achieve distinction without the six Ts. Of course, one must be motivated to invest in them. Bannister was intrinsically motivated as well as highly rewarded and supported by his family, friends, and fans. He enjoyed the perfect combination of self-directed activity and encouragement. He was the beneficiary of personal motivation and cultural support. And to add value, as Bartleby will show us, we need a measure of both.

Bartleby had been looking for a job in Wall Street, which he eventually obtained, and for which he was grateful. At first, he performed his duties superbly, doing pretty much what his boss, a lawyer, requested from him. Bartleby spent most of his waking hours at his desk, dutifully copying documents the lawyer had prepared. The copying was done at his desk because Bartleby was a scrivener, and his boss did not have a photocopying machine. In 1853, all the copying was done by hand.

Bartleby is the eponymous main character of a short story by Herman Melville.[6] The narrator, a lawyer and Bartleby's boss, is a nice and compassionate man. His transactions and contracts require multiple copies – which Bartleby was happy to produce, for a while. For as long as Bartleby was asked to copy documents, he was very compliant. But, when the boss expected something else of him, such as checking the work that he or others had done, his typical reply was "I would prefer not to." Bartleby was affable and his boss cordial. There was no apparent animosity between the two men. On the contrary, the lawyer seemed quite empathic. However, Bartleby's enigmatic behavior – his refusal to add value in any other way – perplexed his boss.

Today, Bartleby's refusal to do anything he did not want remains a symbol for the challenge managers encounter: How to motivate employees to do things they do not find appealing? Just as Bannister was full of verve, Bartleby was devoid of energy, and no amount of public scolding would move him an inch. By all accounts, Bartleby seemed to have a motivation problem. He invested time, thought, and training, but only in what he wanted to do. Bartleby was missing another T: teaming.

With the exception of very few jobs, it is very hard to succeed without teaming. You can add value to your own piece of the puzzle, but eventually you have to team up to put the entire puzzle together. Your own piece may be beautiful and shiny, but unless if fits with the rest of pieces, it is worthless. This is where relational value comes in.

Bartleby's boss was more than amiable, and his peers were accommodating enough, but when Bartleby refused to cooperate his coworkers, and his boss, naturally lost patience. The lack of relational value on Bartleby's part resulted in the loss of productive value. We see this in the workplace all the time. When people do not invest in relationships, there are a thousand ways to sabotage productivity. This is why, to add value, we require not six but seven Ts: time, thought, training, tenacity, trust, transcendence, and teaming.

Women are particularly good at building teams. Denise Barber, featured in the book *Gig*, knows quite well how to socialize with coworkers. Working at a steel mill, she is surrounded mostly by men. A lot of them pour their hearts out to her. "I've had guys, almost complete strangers, sit down beside me and start talking about their relationships."[7] Women like Denise build teams based on relationships. In fact, groups operate better or worse depending on the proportion of women. This is not just an intuition or experiential observation on our part but an empirical finding. A group of researchers from MIT, Carnegie Mellon, and Union College wanted to know if there is evidence for a collective intelligence factor in the performance of teams.[8] To study this question they devised two investigations. The results were published in *Science* in 2010.

In the first study they randomly assigned 120 people to forty groups, three in each. The groups worked on a variety of simple and complex tasks for up to five hours. The tasks included puzzles, moral dilemmas, and negotiations. The results showed that there is, indeed, a collective intelligence factor that is superior to the average or maximum intelligence of the individual members of the group.

In the second study they used 152 groups. The groups ranged from two to five members. Investigators wanted to ascertain if the same results would hold in groups of different sizes, coping with different challenges. This time some of the tasks included video games and complex architectural designs. The findings were replicated. The collective intelligence of the teams proved superior to the intelligence of individual members of the teams. Having found evidence that collective intelligence exists, researchers asked the obvious question: what causes it? If the performance of a team is better than the performance of the average intelligence of individual members, what accounts for this superiority? Three rather surprising factors explained collective intelligence: *the average social sensitivity of team members*; *equal distribution of conversational turn-taking*; and *the proportion of women in the group*. It was not their technical skills, business experience, or education but rather their teaming acumen that drove greater productivity. The more they were tuned into each other's moods and feelings, the more they invited participation, and the more women were in the group, the higher the performance of the group. This trio was later replicated outside the laboratory. As we shall later see, similar results were observed at Google.

Time, thought, training, tenacity, trust, and teaming are necessary but insufficient conditions for adding value at work. One could embrace these requirements without excelling. This is where the sixth and final T comes in: transcendence. What do we mean by transcendence?[9] We mean deriving satisfaction by going beyond the task, beyond the self, and beyond the present. When we engage in an activity that consumes our focus, builds on our strengths, and motivates us to keep going, we are adding value in extraordinary ways. The magic of engagement is focusing on something challenging but that we are already good at. This has typically being called a state of flow.[10] We are in flow when we are consumed by the task, challenged by it, and unperturbed by the surroundings.

For some, flow derives from doing math; for others, from painting or running. Being engrossed in an activity we love is self-reinforcing. We transcend the need to complete a job. We work not just to get the work done but to enjoy ourselves. The activity has meaning beyond the required job. In an ideal situation, we add value to other people and we contribute to the future. What we do is significant beyond the present task and time. Transcendence is about adding value by excelling at the job, and creating meaning and purpose for self and others. The more we engage our strengths, concentration, and devotion, the more value we add to our work and team members. Meaning and significance, as we report next, are not driven by epiphanies. Rather, these are virtues we cultivate.

Significance

If you want to know if employees are adding value to your organization, look for signs of time, thought, training, tenacity, trust, teaming, and transcendence. Your chances of running an efficient organization increase with investments in every T. They matter for quality, for performance, and for the success of the enterprise. Take the role of task transcendence, or significance. Adam Grant, organizational psychologist and professor at the Wharton Business School, predicted that the more significance employees ascribe to a task, the better they would perform. Paralleling our definition of mattering as feeling valued and adding value, he conjectured that tasks perceived as having social impact (adding value to others) and social worth (feeling valued by others) would improve performance. To test this hypothesis, he devised a series of clever experiments that he published in the *Journal of Applied Psychology*.[11]

In the first experiment, he wanted to see the effect of social impact on college fundraisers. These were folks entrusted with calling alumni and donors to request new pledges for the college. To see whether social impact made a difference in the number of pledges and money raised, Grant divided callers into three groups. The first group, called the task significance group, read two stories about how scholarships raised by the callers had helped two students. One scholarship recipient wrote about how the fundraising efforts had enabled him to study neuroscience and engineering and pursue a variety of extracurricular activities. The second scholarship recipient wrote about how the funds afforded her a chance to attend school out of state and form meaningful bonds with other scholarship recipients.

The second group of callers were primed to think about the personal benefit of being a fundraiser. Instead of reading how fundraising had helped others, this group read stories about how fundraising had helped two previous fundraisers. One wrote about how the experience in fundraising helped him become successful in real estate, while a second wrote about how the job helped her with organizational skills in graduate school. The control group did not read any stories. They just completed a few surveys.

Results? Callers in the first group, the task significance condition, more than doubled the number of pledges and the money raised on behalf of the college. The mere act of reading two stories about how the job impacted the lives of students improved performance significantly. No changes in the number of pledges or money raised were noticed in the personal benefit and control groups.

To see whether the results would extend to another line of work, Grant conducted a similar study with lifeguards. Instead of money raised, Grant wanted to see if job dedication and helping behaviors would improve as a result of reading four stories. To test his theory he recruited thirty-two paid lifeguards from a community recreation center. They were divided into two groups. Those in the task significance condition read four stories about lifesaving rescues that other lifeguards had performed. Those in the personal benefit condition read four stories about how the job had benefited previous lifeguards personally. He collected data from three sources: pool supervisors, the aquatics director, and the lifeguards themselves. Confirming the results previously obtained with fundraisers, lifeguards in the task significance condition improved their helping behaviors and job dedication after they read stories about how lifeguards save lives. Lifeguards who read stories about the personal benefit of the job did not improve in either helping behaviors or job dedication. Moreover, those in the task significance condition showed improvements in their perceived social impact and social worth.

In a final experiment, Grant wanted to know if fundraisers who are high in prosocial values and conscientiousness would also benefit from the task significance manipulation (reading stories about how scholarships benefited students). This was an important question because people's personalities and proclivities are expected to impact their performance as well. One group read stories about how scholarships helped students, and a second group read organizational policies and procedures. As predicted, callers in the task significance condition earned more pledges, but there was an interesting twist to the results. As Grant noted, the findings "suggest that task signifi-cance is more likely to increase performance for employees with strong prosocial values, which can be expressed and fulfilled by task significance."[12]

There are important lessons from these three experiments. First, they show that the more workers are aware of the positive impact of their jobs on others, the higher their performance. Second, they demonstrate that task significance is important across industries; and third, they point to the fact that task significance is more important for some people than others. Overall, we can see that making the social contributions of a job visible and palpable to employees improves performance. In other words, people must be given an opportunity to appreciate the social impact they are having. The value employees add to the lives of others should be highlighted and celebrated.

As Adam Grant and others have demonstrated, as significance increases, people feel more engaged, and as engagement goes up, so too does per-formance. This is a very robust finding that has been corroborated by a series of studies conducted by Gallup. Using their Q12 survey, Gallup has been able to study engagement across time, place, and sectors. The Q12 contains twelve items that deal with either feeling valued or adding value. This widely used instrument has been validated multiple times and is an excellent measure of engagement. In a meta-analysis published in 2002 in the *Journal of Applied Psychology*, Gallup measured the relationship between satisfaction and engagement at work and a series of organizational outcomes, including customer satisfaction, productivity, profit, employee turnover, and accidents.[13]

The study, based on 7,939 business units in thirty-six companies, found that the level of engagement of employees is highly correlated to measures of performance. The study is very significant because it is based on over 198,000 respondents from a wide range of industries such as health care, baking, sales, manufacturing, education, hospitality, and call centers. The authors found significant correlations among satisfaction, engagement, and outcomes such as better customer loyalty, turnover, profitability, safety, and productivity.

Since this study was published, Gallup has continued the practice of conducting large meta-analyses, with data from across the globe. In the most recent one reported on their website at time of writing, published in 2016, they replicate and extend the findings published in the 2002 study.[14] The most recent meta-analysis indicates that business units in the top quartile outperform units in the bottom quartile by a large margin. For example, they report 20 percent higher levels of productivity and 21 percent higher levels of profitability. As in the 2002 study, this one was based on multiple sources of information. The meta-analysis is based on reports by 1.8 million employees working in 82,000 business units across forty-nine industries in seventy-three countries. The implication of these studies is clear: adding value to self, work, and community is highly significant for organizational outcomes.

But adding value has beneficial implications for the person as well. When you are presented with growth opportunities, your level of engagement goes up and your personal satisfaction improves. The impact of growth opportunities cannot be understated. In an extensive review of employee growth, Eduardo Salas and Sallie Weaver report that employees stay in organizations largely because they love to grow and learn.[15] Some of the reasons workers give for staying with a company include career growth, learning, development, exciting work, and challenging work. All of them relate to personal development and engagement, two essential components of transcendence. Employees look to enrich themselves intellectually and socially through their jobs.

When employees are offered growth opportunities, they report a series of beneficial outcomes: improved overall well-being, less emotional exhaustion, more work–life balance, lower turnover intentions, and enhanced organizational commitment. Development of leadership potential is a fruitful way to stimulate employees and augment their sense of mattering in the organization. The authors report that when members participate in leadership training they make a positive impact on three levels: self, peers, and organization. Leaders who train in the art of mattering improve followers' motivations, goal commitments, performances, and self-evaluations. They also encourage prosocial and citizenship behaviors in the workplace.[16]

This research supports our claim that we must nurture the capacity to add productive and relational value at the same time. We must encourage the acquisition of technical as well as relational skills. As Salas and Weaver observe, employees must be experts not only in their technical domain but also in teaming skills such as communication, coordination, and cooperation: "Therefore, developmental opportunities must focus not only on enhancing intrapersonal competence but also on developing interpersonal competence."[17]

Denise Barber, the steelworker we met earlier, provided a first-person account of the importance of occupational and intellectual growth. Although she enjoyed the work at the mill and the interaction with colleagues, she studied to get a university degree for future options. "You look through all my textbooks you won't find a clean one, because I keep them up in the cab with me," she said.[18] She appreciated the opportunity to advance her qualifications and to be involved at work. She helped her peers with emotional issues at home and with working conditions. Denise was on the executive board of their union. She was proud not only to contribute to her professional development through higher education but also to add value to her coworkers. She helped them with psychological support and with occupational benefits and protections. She added productive and relational value. Denise promoted her own growth and the well-being of her peers in the mill. She was heavily involved in the workplace, and she loved it because she felt like she mattered. The more involved she was, the more she mattered. Her experience is emblematic of what happens through employee involvement.

Empirical studies confirm what Denise felt. Involvement works because it meets three fundamental needs: autonomy, competence, and connection. By asserting ourselves we practice autonomy and self-determination. By learning we become more competent, and by relating to others in reciprocal ways we form bonds of solidarity. Denise asserted herself through her union work, improved her competence through advanced education, and nurtured a community through her informal support to coworkers. Denise practiced the essentials of self-determination theory. The more workers enjoy autonomy, competence, and belonging at work, the more benefits they derive, psychologically and physically.

Meeting these basic human needs also enhances motivation and performance. Two comprehensive reviews of self-determination at work, published in 2017 in the *Annual Review of Organizational Psychology and Organizational Behavior*[19] and in 2016 in the *Journal of Management*,[20] demonstrate the many personal and organizational benefits that accrue from meeting these essential needs. From the first review – coauthored by the founders of the theory, Edward Deci and Richard Ryan, along with Anja Olafsen – we learn that the satisfaction of autonomy, competence and belonging is crucial for personal and organizational well-being. When these psychological needs are met, autonomous motivation, emotional health, physical wellness, and organizational performance improve.

The authors provide ample evidence and international data to support their conclusion. For example, in the Netherlands, job autonomy predicted profitability among 3,000 companies. When teachers in China and Gambia were supported by their supervisors in meeting basic psychological needs, they were happier and more intrinsically motivated. In contrast, in Canada, when teachers felt coerced by administrators, they displayed more signs of burnout and lower levels of autonomous motivation. In Norway, managers' support of basic psychological needs induced more motivation among employees and resulted in fewer psychosomatic symptoms and lower levels of emotional depletion, intent to quit, and absenteeism. In the United States, a manufacturing company showed that managerial support for autonomy predicted better work engagement and less desire to quit. Also in the United States, two banking companies in New York reported that company efforts to meet basic psychological needs resulted in higher wellness and productivity.

The second review, published in the *Journal of Management*, included ninety-nine empirical studies with 119 different samples of participants. The authors report that the satisfaction of all three needs – autonomy, competence, and connection – related negatively to role stressors, job insecurity, and work–family conflict. In other words, the more satisfaction, the fewer problems. Fulfilment of competence and autonomy also related negatively to emotional demands and workload. In addition, basic needs were positively related to leader and organizational variables such as fairness. Each of the three basic needs were positively related to employee well-being, affective commitment to the workplace, motivation, and per-formance. Taken as a whole, these two reviews, based on dozens of studies, across multiple industries and countries demonstrate that the more we learn, connect, and express our autonomy, the better we feel and the greater the workplace becomes.

Learning, connecting, and exercising our agency are healthy ways to stay involved at work. Employee involvement has been promoted through participatory decision-making, empowering practices, self-managing teams, employee ownership, and gain sharing. As in the case of self-determination theory, empirical studies across two dozen countries and multiple industries demonstrate that involvement generates personal bene-fits and positive organizational outcomes.[21] Some performance indicators for the company include better financial returns, prosocial behaviors, innovation, improved safety, and climate of trust. When it comes to the individual worker, work satisfaction and overall well-being go up with level of involvement.

Involvement is also crucial because it is related to meaning-making.[22] The more active you are in crafting your job, and the more opportunities management provides to exercise autonomy, the more likely you are to experience meaning, purpose, and significance. When you craft your own job you modify it to suit your passion and strengths.[23] You can alter the nature of the task you do or the quality of the relationships with coworkers. You can reframe the job to derive more pleasure and satisfaction from it.

The level of meaning you experience is a function of what you bring to the job and what the environment affords. An oppressive context can neutralize the most creative urges; but the most supportive climate cannot produce meaning without personal agency. Both of us have worked in a variety of sectors, in four countries, over a period of forty years each. We have worked as teachers in schools, counselors in universities and rehabilitation hospitals, clinicians, consultants in nonprofit organizations, professors, and administrators. It is clear: context matters, and personality matters. We have witnessed the interaction between personality and context time and again.

For over a decade now, the University of Miami has been our second home. Ora was a professor there for seven years, and Isaac was first dean of the School of Education and Human Development and later vice provost for institutional culture. We have met people with incredible talent who have crafted their jobs regardless of status and rank.

Marilyn de Narvaez, who gave us permission to use her name, served as the receptionist at the School of Education and Human Development for decades. While her job might have been stereotypically characterized as monotonous and boring, she transformed it into much more than getting phone calls and directing traffic. She perfected the art of small talk and the practice of warm greetings. She just knew how to wish you a good day, how to crack a joke, how to console a distressed student, and how to inquire about your ailing relative. She organized a gift exchange, kept track of birthdays, and operated a digital billboard for goods and services. She got you supplies and made sure you posted your office hours on your door. She clearly redefined her job into much more than answering phone calls and directing students and parents to the advising office. Marilyn was usually the last staff member to leave the office at night, and Isaac had to remind her to go home around 6:30 pm, long after the rest of the staff was gone. Marilyn did not let her job description get in the way of her creativity and vitality. Funny, friendly, and feisty, she saw her job as creating a climate of warmth for students, parents, faculty, and staff.

Crafting your job to build on your strengths, motives, and passion is a way to transcend the requirements of the job itself; it is a way to matter.

The synergy of strengths, motives, and passion results in meaning and mattering. Some people redefine tasks to make them more meaningful; others reconfigure relationships. There is a lot of evidence that meaningful work benefits worker well-being, life satisfaction, and meaning in life.[24] Job crafting and a meaningful occupation contribute to personal and organizational performance.

Sources

Naturally, some people are more motivated than others to add value to themselves and others.[25] But when you dig deeper into why they are active or passive, you discover that their early efforts were either thwarted or rewarded. We all live in an ecosystem that either encourages or suppresses our drive to perform. Charles Duhigg provides ample evidence of that in his 2016 book *Smarter Faster Better*.[26] Motivated by a personal quest to improve his own productivity, Duhigg, a former reporter for the *New York Times* and winner of the Pulitzer Prize, set out to investigate the sources of performance and productivity. Among many other places, his research took him to the Bay Area in California. There he found invaluable lessons on culture and productivity from two vastly different industries: car manufacturing and information technology.

In his book, Duhigg shares the story of Rick Madrid, who used to work for the Fremont plant of GM. Madrid had worked there for twenty-seven years, prior to the plant closing in 1982. Two years later, the plant was about to reopen, but with a twist. Instead of GM running the show, it was going to be a partnership between Toyota and GM. The Fremont plant had closed because it had a reputation as one of the most inefficient car-making facilities in the world. Rick Madrid knew this firsthand. Every attempt he had made to improve operations were summarily ignored by his superiors. He had come up with innovative ways to make production more efficient, but, as a line worker, he did not have the authority to make the changes by himself. All he could do was to make recommendations, which were discounted time and again. Madrid experienced the exact opposite of mattering.

When he was interviewed in 1984 by the new car manufacturer for a job, he was asked by one of the Japanese executives what he did not like about his job while he worked for GM. Madrid basically shared experiences of helplessness and invisibility. No matter what he suggested, there was never proper follow-up. Needless to say, he got frustrated, alienated, and disenchanted with the job. As Duhigg put it, "nobody ever asked him his opinion or cared what he thought."[27] Nobody valued his views, and nobody cared about him. Nothing could be more demoralizing.

But the new partnership between GM and Toyota was going to change production and, with it, the sense of mattering for Madrid. The new company, now called NUMMI, New United Motor Manufacturing, Inc., would take great interest in what frontline workers had to say. Madrid realized this when he was offered the job in 1984 and sent to Japan to observe the Toyota system. In the old GM system, nobody ever stopped the production line because it cost the company a lot of money, about $15,000 per minute of stoppage. This meant that if you saw a problem with the car being assembled, you put a mark on it, and the vehicle would be disassembled and rebuilt again later. Although workers could stop the assembly line, the culture was such that nobody dared do it. In Japan, the opposite was true. If you saw a problem, you stopped the assembly line, fixed the problem, called your superiors, and everyone learned from the operational problem. Workers in Japan were encouraged to stop the assembly line to learn from mistakes and inefficiencies. Everybody was invested in getting it right. If there was a problem, you learned from it. The voice of workers mattered. Everyone felt that their voices were heard. Their views mattered. This was a complete revelation for Rick Madrid.

When NUMMI started operations in the old Fremont plant in December 1984, workers were instructed to stop production every time they detected a problem. Every worker could pull the andon cords, which were hanging by their stations, to signal there was a problem. Instead of pushing ahead and ignoring the problem, or hoping someone else would fix it later, employees in the assembly line were encouraged to pull the andon cords to investigate what was wrong. At first, workers were hesitant. Since most workers had been employed there before under GM management, the idea of pulling the cord was anathema to them. The memory of the old system was still very fresh. Pulling the cord meant incredible losses, for which they, the workers, would be made responsible. But the Japanese new partners insisted on stopping the assemble line every time there was a learning opportunity. The Toyota managers knew that the worker closest to the problem was the best person to solve it. This approach not only made workers feel in control but also increased productivity in the long term. Instead of costly repairs at the end of the line, fixes would now be made along the way.

Eventually, performance would improve noticeably – and improve it did! Duhigg reports that by 1986, two years after the plan had reopened, productivity in Fremont was higher than any other GM facility. Moreover, it was more than twice as productive as the old GM Fremont operation. In addition, absenteeism had dropped dramatically, from 25 percent under the former management to 3 percent under NUMMI. Instead of many labor disputes, management and workers cooperated to increase perform- ance and preserve employee well-being. NUMMI had made a promise to the union not to lay off workers if at all possible. During recessions the top executives cut their pay instead of laying off auto workers. Grievance procedures were hardly ever invoked. The Rick Madrid in NUMMI was very different from the Rick Madrid under GM management. Rick's voice was heard, he felt in control, he contributed to excellence, and he felt like he mattered. NUMMI fostered a culture of mattering. The plant went on to receive the J.D. Power award for top quality.

A few miles west of Fremont, Duhigg explored the culture at one of the giants of our times, Google. Duhigg shares how Google learned the importance of culture for performance. His investigation took him to the People Analytics division. There he learned about Project Aristotle, which was all about understanding team functioning and performance. People Analytics spent countless hours examining team composition, leadership styles, personality profiles, and background similarities, but nothing seemed to explain why some teams were more effective than others. It was not the characteristics of individual members that would hold the key to excellence but rather group norms.

Group norms consist of repeatable patterns of behavior, such as how people relate to one another, how they deal with disagreements, and how often they talk about their personal lives. A norm is an unwritten rule of what's permissible. There are norms that make some group members coalesce and others recoil. In some teams psychological safety fosters a climate of respect, while in others sarcasm reigns supreme.

After an exhaustive study, People Analytics came to concur with the findings of Amy Edmondson of Harvard, who claimed that psychological safety is a must for high-performing teams.[28] Team members must be allowed to fail and to share frustrations without fear of negative repercus- sions. Google found what Edmondson had discovered and what MIT, Carnegie Mellon, and Union College researchers had demonstrated in their *Science* paper: social sensitivity and relational value are what is indispensable for team performance, not the level of intelligence or tech- nical acumen of individual members.

Being a leader in the application of science, Google translated the findings into actionable advice for its workforce: leaders should refrain from interrupting colleagues; they should summarize what they heard to make sure they got it right; and they should afford all members of the group an opportunity to speak. As it turned out, the relational value that each member contributed to the team was key to the productive value of the team.

If pulling the andon cords at GM was sacrilegious, imagine shutting down Facebook. Even worse, imagine being an intern shutting down Facebook. The name of the summer intern was Ben Maurer. In 2008, he was working on preventing the site from crashing when he accidently triggered a crash himself. The way Sheryl Sandberg, Facebook's COO, tells it, in "Silicon Valley, an outage is one of the biggest debacles a company can face."[29] Yet, the company did not reprimand Ben. Instead, they hired him. Sandberg and others understood that, to become a resilient company, Facebook must learn from mistakes. Sandberg is a big proponent of organizational growth, which, she argues, cannot happen without learning from errors. She encourages teams to discuss missteps and analyze them the way the National Transportation Safety Board investigates airplane crashes. In a climate of fear, you can't prevent crashes. This was a very painful lesson that NASA had to learn, not once but twice.

Records show that the explosion of the *Challenger* and *Columbia* space shuttles were preventable. On both occasions, in 1986 and 2003, respectively, engineers had misgivings but were either ignored or discouraged to disclose crucial safety information.

Bob Ebeling and Roger Boisjoly, engineers at Morton Thiokol, knew that unusually cold temperatures may cause the O-ring seals in the solid rocket boosters of *Challenger* to malfunction.[30] They knew because they were part of the team that built these parts. Worried that the low temperatures in Florida might impede proper functioning of the seals, they pleaded with their superiors and with NASA to delay the launch. The evening before the launch, Ebeling told his wife, in desperation, "It's going to blow up."[31] Despite repeated attempts to halt the launch, Ebeling's request was ignored by superiors and NASA officials. On January 28, 1986, at 11:39 am, EST, Ebeling's nightmare became a reality. Seventy-three seconds into its flight, *Challenger* broke apart, killing its five astronauts and two payload specialists.

Interviewed thirty years later, Bob Ebeling was still haunted by the tragic images. Although he blamed himself for not arguing the case strongly enough, a presidential commission blamed NASA for poor decision-making. The investigation revealed that earlier warnings from Morton Thiokol were ignored by NASA. President Reagan was eager to mention the successful launch at his State of the Union address that evening, and NASA was eager to please Reagan. At a fundamental level, people in NASA refused to hear the concerns and had even threatened Morton Thiokol to change contractors. As Boisjoly later stated to Lesley Stahl of *60 Minutes*, "I was there, I felt the pressure."[32] The disaster was preventable, and it was all about fear. The contractors feared NASA would end the contract. NASA officials were afraid to disappoint their superiors with another delay, and NASA superiors did not want to disappoint President Reagan. Multiple opportunities to add value, by preventing the loss of life, were missed.

Fast forward to 2003, when Rodney Rocha, a NASA engineer, harbored concerns about a piece of foam that broke away from the fuel tank of the space shuttle *Columbia*.[33] The whitish piece of foam struck the left wing. On January 21, five days after liftoff, over two dozen engineers from NASA congregated to evaluate the potential damage the foam had caused in the left wing. Because video images were blurry, the group decided to request additional pictures from American spy satellites or major telescopes. They nominated Rocha to make the request for additional images from the shuttle mission managers. Rocha made at least half a dozen requests to managers, but he was repeatedly turned down. The *New York Times* reported that LeRoy Cain, the flight director, considered it to be a "dead issue." An investigation revealed that mission managers actively resisted the requests for additional images. Rocha had begged to obtain additional imagery from several superiors, but to no avail. Like Bob Ebeling in 1986, he was growing increasingly worried and exasperated by the lack of response from managers. And just like Bob Ebeling, he was right to be worried. On February 1, 2003, upon reentering Earth's atmosphere, *Columbia* disintegrated, killing all seven crew members.

Challenger and *Columbia* were preventable disasters. The inability to hear voices of dissent caused catastrophic loss of life. Ebeling and Rocha were not whispering. They were nearly shouting their concerns – not to one but to several superiors. The commission to investigate the *Columbia* disaster determined that NASA had a broken safety culture. People in the lower ranks were made to feel that they did not matter. Dangerous groupthink among senior officials took hold. They convinced themselves that everything was alright. Fourteen lives were lost, and many of the survivors, including some of the hardworking engineers, suffered post-traumatic stress disorder.

Rick Madrid went from being an apathetic worker who drank alcohol during his shift to being one of the hardest-working people at NUMMI. What happened? In the GM culture of the past, no one listened to people like him. In the NUMMI culture, Rick and his coworkers were heard, encouraged to speak, and treated with respect. At Google, People Analytics confirmed what research had revealed earlier: social sensitivity and a climate of psychological safety made all the difference. At Facebook, Sheryl Sandberg goes around their various departments extolling the virtues of failure. These findings could not have come too soon to NASA, which could have used a better culture years earlier.

Strategies

Denise Barber and Rick Madrid add value to work and the world in different ways. Rick is focused on productive value: building reliable cars. Denise produces steel. But both understand that nothing can be accomplished without relational value and bonds of solidarity.

The strategies we propose to increase value in the workplace fall into two categories: actions you can take to add more productive and relational value to your own work; and things you can do to help others do the same.

What Can I Do to Add Value to Work?

Some of us rejoice in the feeling of accomplishment. We derive neurotic pleasure from putting a check mark on our to-do list: Yes, we finally finished the book! Hooray, I sent my boss the proposal he requested! These are positive feelings that come after the work is done, but there is a lot of research showing that positive emotions can actually lead to creativity in the first place.[34] Positive emotions can be powerful drivers of relational and productive value. As Shawn Achor put it in *The Happiness Advantage*, "fun also leads to bottom-line results."[35] Tal Ben Shahar and Angus Ridgway argue that the best way to lead, and to succeed, is to be happy, not the other way around.[36]

If you want to be more creative and innovative at work, you need to find ways to indulge in positive emotions. In many cases, this involves importing the pleasure we derive from our avocation to our vocation. Our hobbies bring us joy because they engulf us in a state of flow. The artisan loses sense of time while shaping ceramics, while the pianist becomes one with the instrument and the musical notes. I, Isaac, can spend hours writing a humor piece, laughing at my own lines, and revising the column twenty times before I actually send it to *Miami Today* for publication. I find the brainstorming process of humor writing satisfying in itself. The more I laugh, the better I feel and the more humorous connections I can make in my head.

We were in Israel attending a conference when I got an email from Michael Lewis, the editor of *Miami Today*, with the subject heading *you won an award; no joke*. When the National Newspaper Association gave me an award in 2015 for a satirical column, I wrote on David Beckham and his epic struggle to bring a soccer team to Miami, I was completely surprised. I had been writing humor for my personal pleasure. The fact that people laughed at my columns was the icing on the cake. Upon notification of the award, I had two thoughts. The first one was: *that is really cool*. The second was my late Jewish mother would have been disappointed that the award was only for second place.

What started as a hobby turned into an interesting experiment. I was having a lot of fun, and I said to Ora: what if we combined humor and science to educate people about health and happiness? Countless hours of marital discord later, we published a trilogy: *The Laughing Guide to Well-Being*; *The Laughing Guide to Change*; and *The Laughing Guide to a Better Life*.[37] Innumerable arguments later, we also produced an online platform, Fun for Wellness (www.funforwellness.com), consisting of humor, vignettes, and interactive challenges to promote health and happiness. We have since evaluated the intervention and published the results in the scientific literature; a lot of productive value materialized from the love of laughter.

Although the two of us can argue endlessly about the merits of ideas and how best to express them, we do enjoy poking fun at each other and working together. But fun is only one of the positive emotions that help us produce value. Interest, curiosity, and engagement are also powerful drives.

The fact that positive emotions can expand our horizons led Barbara Fredrickson to postulate the Broaden-and-Build Theory of Positive Emotions. She claims that positive emotions such as joy, fun, love, and interest "broaden people's momentary thought-action repertoires and build their enduring personal resources, ranging from physical and intellectual resources to social and psychological resources."[38] Joy, she argues, instigates the urge to play, to push limits, and be more creative.

Interest, in turn, leads people to explore and acquire new information. She offers compelling evidence that positive affect leads to innovative cognitive patterns and creative ways of thinking. With the help of evocative film clips, in one study she induced joy, contentment, fear and anger. Participants in the control condition were exposed to an emotionally neutral clip. Following each film they measured creativity in the various groups. Those in the joy and contentment conditions exhibited more creativity in a test than those in the neutral condition. Participants exposed to the two negative emotions performed less creatively than the other two groups.

Evidence for the link between positive emotions and creativity extends beyond the laboratory. In a recent field study conducted in New Zealand with 658 young adults, participants recorded their mood and level of creativity for thirteen consecutive days.[39] The results showed that creative days were filled with vigor, enthusiasm, energy, and engagement. Interestingly, happy and relaxed days were also reported as creative, but to a lesser extent. The difference between happy and relaxed on one hand and engaged and enthusiastic on the other is the level of emotional activation. The latter are "high activation" positive emotions, while the former are "medium or low activation." What this means is that people are more likely to be creative when they experience both positive and high activation emotions. The authors also found that negative emotions were either unrelated to or detrimental to creativity. Lending support to this conclusion, a comprehensive meta-analysis linking mood with creativity found that overall positive emotions such as feeling elated and enthusiastic were especially likely to engender creativity.[40] Since positive mood is related to innovation and productive value, the question is how to cultivate this state of affairs. There is an extensive literature on how to enhance positive affect.[41] Key strategies include:

- Nurture social relationships
- Practice kindness
- Seek flow experiences
- Express gratitude
- Savor good experiences
- Find meaning in daily activities
- Recognize and apply your strengths
- Laugh often
- Love often

So far we have dealt with productive value, but there are definite ways to increase relational value as well. Although recognizing someone for a job well done is crucial for mattering, in the workplace there are countless missed opportunities to celebrate colleagues. People are not recognized for their efforts, and personal accomplishments go unnoticed. A friend of ours recently told us that his boss only replies to him via email when revisions are needed. When our friend gets it right, he never hears from his boss. He learned that silence means he did a good job. This is a very sad state of affairs. Instead of celebrating and acknowledging good work, bosses just ignore you. We can tell from our own observations working in multiple industries that this is the norm. Superiors take for granted the work of their employees, feeding a sense of invisibility. This is the exact opposite of mattering. If you want to enhance mattering at work, you'd better invest in relational value and stop ignoring the efforts of your colleagues. Mattering depends on providing a sense of worth and appreciation for a job well done. If your workers perform well, failing to congratulate them may be costlier than cleaning up after a bad job. In a "We Culture" we have the responsibility to add productive and relational value. We must reject dismissive treatment and build a supportive, effective, and reflective culture.

What Can I Do to Help Others Add Value to Work?

As noted earlier, bullying and marginalization are widespread in the workplace. Instead of belonging, many managers promote exclusion. Judging from international data, instead of growth many workers experience alienation and disengagement.[42] At work, mattering must be based on a culture of *support, effectiveness*, and *reflectiveness* – what we called in Chapter 8 a SER culture. When these three conditions are met, acts of injustice and intimidation are called out, offenders are reprimanded or fired, and policies to prevent fear and foster mattering are enacted. A culture of mattering cannot rely only on the single heroic act of a courageous leader. The whole organization must buy into it.[43]

When Harvard professors Robert Kegan and Lisa Lahey studied in depth organizations with a healthy culture, they discovered that what characterizes them is the fact that they are "an everyone culture," a culture where every single employee counts, where all voices are heard.[44]

In the BET I CAN model, thoughts can be used to challenge negative stereotypes and create a new story about the potential of minorities. Interactions, in turn, can be leveraged to connect and communicate with all employees. Kegan and Lahey found, time and again, that a climate of support enabled organizations to excel. Similar to Sheryl Sandberg's efforts to learn from mistakes, organizations with exceptional cultures demand from their people to learn from personal and collective blunders. They accomplish this by rewarding honesty and transparency. They encourage communication of errors in an effort to learn. Leaders spend countless hours coaching and mentoring junior colleagues. They understand that bonds of connection help people grow. People are not punished for their mistakes. On the contrary, they are praised for their openness and willingness to learn. But this cannot be achieved in a climate of fear. NASA could have prevented two catastrophic disasters had it promoted a climate of safety as opposed to fear.

A safe workplace – what Kegan and Lahey call *home* – is both an intrinsic good and a means to an end. It is an intrinsic good because it fosters humane relationships: people feel valued and have opportunities to add value. They feel like they belong. But belonging, they claim, also affords everyone an opportunity to learn, take risks, and challenge the status quo. Mattering helps one feel secure and pursue growth. The Harvard researchers call the growth orientation *edge*. This is what we call a reflective culture, an ethos of learning and questioning. When we have a secure base, we are confident to explore new horizons, just like infants did in the attachment studies.

Like us, Kegan and Lahey identify a third leg to the stool of organizational excellence: *groove*. For them, groove signifies efficient practices. We call this the pursuit of effectiveness, which cannot be attained without habits and norms. Communicating often and clearly, and learning from mistakes as they occur, the way Toyota does, are habits. For people to add value to work, they must feel safe, challenged, and heard. Kegan and Lahey propose the principles of *home*, *groove*, and *edge*. We recommend parallel tenets: *support*, *effectiveness*, and *reflectiveness*. The metaphors are different, but both point to the three essential components of a successful culture: a sense of belonging, productivity, and the pursuit of growth. It is no coincidence that these three pillars of organizational mattering correspond to the columns of self-determination theory: relationships, autonomy, and competence. Theories and evidence converge on the soul of mattering at work: we want to belong, learn, and make a difference.

PART V

Community

CHAPTER 10

Mattering in the Community

We knew it. The moment Panchita swung the axe to split wood, our students would burst into an uproarious laughter.[1] The video never failed to make them laugh. Although there is seemingly nothing unusual about women chopping wood, especially if they live in a rural area with a wood stove and no central heating, there is something quite special and surprising about a 100-year-old doing so. This is what our students found both humorous and endearing.

It may not seem unusual either for Panchita's son, Tommy, to ride his bike to visit his mother every day – except that Tommy is eighty years old and he rides with the stamina of a twenty-year-old. Our students loved watching Panchita and Tommy engage in vigorous physical activity. It was both startling and charming. Panchita, who lives in the Nicoya Peninsula of Costa Rica, is featured in the Blue Zones Project.[2] The Blue Zones are parts of the world with a significant proportion of centenarians. Sardinia in Italy, Okinawa in Japan, Loma Linda in California, and the Nicoya peninsula in Costa Rica are some of them.

At 100, Panchita is a fountain of joy and vitality. Although she lives in very modest quarters and lacks many amenities we may take for granted, she is healthy and happy. She gets up at 4 am every morning, sweeps the floors, cooks, chops wood, and collects eggs, fruits, and vegetables from her garden. But perhaps most importantly, she receives many visitors every day. By 8 am Tommy is there. Later on family and friends come to help her with various chores around the house. Even though Panchita lives by herself, she is surrounded by a community of caring people. She is valued by folks in her family and village. Despite her old age she still has a role to play. She must look after herself and she must attend to her visitors. She is senior advisor and cheerleader to neighbors and relatives alike. With little food for herself, she shares what she has among friends and strangers. She has just about enough to get by, with no money for extras. Yet she has a generous spirit and a contagious laughter. Her warmth is engulfing and her optimistic nature uplifting.

In distilling the features that make centenarians unique, Dan Buettner emphasizes a sense of belonging, close relationships with family and friends, and a caring community. In addition to a healthy diet and physical activity, feeling like they matter to family and friends is crucial for their longevity. Feeling valued in the community is essential for health and happiness. Panchita and her co-centenarians live mostly in "We Cultures." These are communities where young and old care about the self *and* others, about feeling valued *and* adding value, about rights *and* responsibilities, and about wellness *and* fairness. In contrast, in "Me Cultures" people focus mostly on the self and on their own right to feel valued and experience wellness. As we shall see, members of "We Cultures" are happier and healthier, and they live longer and better lives. In these communities, mattering is not just about the self but about everyone. Respect is not just a right but also a responsibility; and the ultimate goal of a good life is not just wellness but also fairness. Those of us who live in "Me Cultures" pay a hefty price.

Signs

The late Seymour Sarason, of Yale University, observed that all of us "yearn to be part of a larger network of relationships that would give greater expression to our needs for intimacy, diversity, usefulness, and belongingness."[3] In these four words – intimacy, diversity, usefulness, and belongingness – Sarason captured a universal need. Panchita felt useful and had close, intimate relationships with her family and neighbors. She belonged to her village. Like her, many centenarians featured in the Blue Zones enjoyed close and warm connections. In Okinawa, people joined *Moais*, close circle of friends who accompany them through thick and thin. In Loma Linda, California, Seventh-Day Adventists belonged to a supportive religious community where members cared for one another. In Sardinia, extended families provided for many of the needs of their members. Communities of belonging celebrate with you your achievements, and grieve with you your losses.[4] As Cicero observed, "friendship improves happiness and abates misery, by the doubling of our joy and the dividing of our grief."[5]

Recently, Isaac's team in the Office of Institutional Culture at the University of Miami conducted focus groups with students to learn about their experiences of belonging on campus. Graduate and undergraduate students provided rich descriptions of what it means to belong to the University of Miami. They told us that they have a sense of belonging when they are treated like they matter, respected as equals, cared for, welcomed, affirmed, and wanted. Students expressed a need to be understood, to be treated kindly, and to be included regardless of diverse identities. In their own words, they said that they felt *valued, heard, recognized, respected by peers and faculty, supported, included, accepted,* and that their *opinions matter* and *they have a voice.*

In a 2018 review of effective psychological interventions in *Psychological Review,* Gregory Walton from Stanford and Timothy Wilson from the University of Virginia note that "people want to feel connected to others: to be accepted and included, to be valued members of social groups, and to contribute positively to the lives of others."[6] In the last five decades since Sarason conceptualized a psychological sense of community, scores of studies have documented the beneficial effects of feeling needed, useful, and loved by family and friends. Among the positive correlates of sense of community and social support we find psychological well-being, physical well-being, resilience, resistance to disease, longevity, vitality, and happiness.[7] Just as belonging and mattering are good for us, social isolation and marginalization are toxic for us. When we are lonely and disconnected we tend to become depressed, despondent, and sick.[8] The COVID-19 pandemic has aggravated exponentially the loneliness that many people already experienced.

Some communities are organically supportive. It is part of their tradition and culture to provide informal safety nets. This was the elixir in many Blue Zones. The close physical proximity with frequent face-to-face contact satisfied many of their members' needs. There is human warmth, physical touch, and emotional support. Today, these traditional communities are harder to come by. As Sarason claimed, most of us "do not feel needed in our community and we rarely if ever seriously think about how we can contribute to the solution of its problems."[9] When natural communities fail to provide a sense of mattering, we have to be deliberate about creating better ones.

Belonging is not the sole province of geography though. People belong to multiple communities based on common identities and interests. These can transcend physical boundaries. They can be formed on the basis of ethnicity, race, disability, gender, language, profession, or passion. Researchers now talk about multiple senses of community.[10] You may not derive a great sense of community from your workplace but may feel very close to a community of joggers. Your neighborhood may not be very warm and friendly, but your church might be.

How do Blue Zones, college students, churches, and supportive neighborhoods all around the world do it? What do they have in common? How do they nurture a sense of community? How do they create a sense of belonging? John McKnight and Peter Block, seasoned community builders, refer to these competent and caring communities as *abundant communities*.[11] In their view, such cohesive communities have three properties:

- They focus on the *gifts* of its members
- They nurture *associational life*
- They *welcome* friends and strangers

In mattering language, gifts are about adding value; a welcoming attitude is about making you feel valued; and associations are about the process of exchange. Communities with these properties nurture certain capacities that foster belonging: kindness, generosity, cooperation, forgiveness, and acceptance of fallibility. The last one is especially important because it is difficult, if not impossible, to belong when our vulnerabilities are in the closet. Partial belonging is not fully authentic.[12] As McKnight and Block put it:

> We discover the abundance of our community not only when our gifts are acknowledged, but also when our sorrows are revealed. We make them public. They become community knowledge. Making our gifts and sorrows explicit makes them available for sharing. The range and variety of the sorrows we bear gives us the fuel for community and connectedness.[13]

Sharing a vulnerability is giving a gift to others because it grants us permission to be human.

A foundational tenet of the abundant community is that all of us have gifts: of the head, the heart, or the hand. For gifts to have meaning, they must be exchanged. When we create spaces for capacities and vulnerabilities to be shared, we give life to a sense of belonging. We bring our full person to the table. Associations afford people an opportunity to exchange strengths and weaknesses, sorrow and joy, resilience and fallibility.

Panchita embodied the property of hospitality. She welcomed strangers with open arms and sounds of joy. This is what we call being an inclusive host. Welcoming strangers is all about creating a space for diversity. Hospitality creates the condition for curiosity and conversation. The invitation to talk and the friendly touch create, in turn, the conditions for intimacy and belonging.

Friendship and trust emerge in communities where people balance association with similar and different people. Robert Putnam from Harvard captured this dual need in the distinction between bonding and bridging social capital.[14] The former refers to association with like-minded people. The latter to connections with people from other backgrounds. When Isaac used to get together with friends from his native Córdoba (Argentina) in Miami to play soccer, he was building bonding social capital. He strengthened the connections with people of similar background. But when he went to boarding school in Israel and shared a room with a teen from Iraq and another from Yemen, that was bridging social capital. He had seemingly little in common with them, but they all shared a common space and built relationships.

Not surprisingly, communities that balance bridging with bonding are healthier and stronger. They achieve better outcomes in terms of population health, education, and safety. We lived near Toronto for nine years. Toronto is a pretty integrated city. We now have been in Miami for fourteen years. Miami is a pretty segregated city, along cultural, ethnic, racial, and economic lines. There is a lot of bonding going on in Miami; bridging, not so much. In Toronto, mixed-race couples are everywhere, and multicultural communities coexist in greater harmony. When you compare the two cities in terms of safety, Miami is six times more dangerous.[15] In terms of education, Toronto ranks number 10 out of 240 cities worldwide. Miami ranks 118. When it comes to tolerance toward minorities, Toronto ranks 73 out of 266 comparison cities. Miami ranks 189. One area in which Miami towers over Toronto is GDP per capita. Miami is ranked 16 out of 263 and Toronto 92, but the problem is that Miami is also the most unequal city in the United States.[16] The state of Florida ranks 46 out of 51 in terms of inequality. The Gini coefficient for Florida, used to estimate economic inequality, is 0.48.[17] For Ontario it is much lower: 0.33.[18] Miami may be stronger in terms of GDP, but the vast inequality keeps groups apart. When it comes to the rate of volunteerism, a good proxy for bridging social capital, Miami comes dead last in the United States.[19] When it comes to caring cities, Miami ranks 93 out of 100.[20]

If you live in Miami, like we do, you may be surrounded by wonderful friends. You may be able to create a caring community among a small circle of compatriots. But if you care about what happens outside your inner circle, there is reason to be concerned. When groups feel marginalized on account of inequality or exclusion, like many in Miami and around the world do, mattering goes down.

Significance

Following Seymour Sarason, David Chavis and David McMillan formulated a clear theory of psychological sense of community consisting of four components: membership, influence, integration and fulfilment of needs, and shared emotional connection.[21] Their definition states that "sense of community is a feeling that members have of belonging, a feeling that members matter to one another and to the group, and a shared faith that members' needs will be met through their commitment to be together."[22] Once they proposed this model, it was not long before other community psychologists tested the impact of sense of community on well-being.

In one of the first studies to explore that connection, Bill Davidson and Patrick Cotter conducted interviews in South Carolina and Alabama with three samples consisting of 151, 399, and 442 people, respectively.[23] They used a survey of sense of community consisting of items such as "I feel like I belong here" (tapping into *feeling valued*) and "I feel I can contribute to city politics if I want to" (tapping into *adding value*). They also measured the well-being of participants by asking them about their levels of happiness, worrying, and coping. Davidson and Cotter report that across all three samples a significant and positive relationship between sense of community and subjective well-being was found. Since that study was published in 1991, multiple others have confirmed the positive association between high sense of community and various forms of happiness and health.[24]

In a comprehensive review of mattering in the community, Gordon Flett documents the many positive effects of feeling like you matter – and the negative consequences of feeling like you don't.[25] His review focuses on two populations: people with disabilities and adolescents. The first group was shown to experience significant challenges in achieving a sense of mattering. This is not surprising, given that many persons with disabilities face social and environmental barriers to participation.

For teens, a sense of mattering in the community is crucial for healthy development. The more teens feel like they matter, the better their academic records and engagement in school, the higher their levels of participation in community events, and the lower the risk of suicide. Conversely, the lower the sense of mattering, the higher the risk of delinquency and suicidal ideation.

While lack of mattering is detrimental to all adolescents, there is evidence that minority youth carry an extra burden since stigma and prejudice get in the way of feeling valued. In his wonderful book *Our Kids: The American Dream in Crisis*, Robert Putnam describes the challenges and opportunities faced by teens in his native Port Clinton, Ohio, in the 1950s.[26] Through a series of interviews and mounds of social science data, Putnam describes what it was like for low-income and Black teens to grow up in a mostly White small community.

Jesse and Cheryl were two Black kids who went to school with Putnam. They were the only African American students in his class. They came from families who had escaped violence in Southern states. Jesse's family had to leave Mississippi after his sister was killed. In Cheryl's case, the family had to leave Tennessee following a conflict between her father and a White man. They both came from tightly knit families where both parents worked: the fathers in manual labor and the mothers in cleaning. Jesse and Cheryl excelled in academics. They both obtained graduate degrees and had successful careers in public education. While they succeeded in overcoming racial barriers in the 1950s, it was not without wounds, especially to their sense of mattering.

Jesse was a very popular kid, a tremendous athlete, and a natural leader. He recalls with delight that he defeated Putnam when running for student council. But despite all his popularity and grit, he was not unscathed. As Jesse confided in Putnam years later, "the hardest part was not being accepted as a human being. Some people would like you, but others would ostracize you when you never did anything to them."[27]

Cheryl was a smart, determined young woman. She benefited from the educational opportunities afforded to her in Port Clinton. She recalls with emotional pain the fact that, after school, White kids all but ignored her. While at school they interacted across racial lines, outside of school there was zero contact with White kids. One of her White friends, while walking on the street with her mother, refused to acknowledge Cheryl: "She acted like she didn't even know who I was. I was really hurt by that." She goes on to say that "as an African American student in the graduating class of 1959, I participated in but never felt part of the student body."[28] As Putnam noted, "her sense of not belonging still haunts Cheryl, when she looks back on Port Clinton."[29]

The experiences that Jesse and Cheryl recount left indelible marks in their minds. Even though they were highly popular, smart, resilient, and well-adjusted, they were excluded and marginalized. Unfortunately, the promise of the American dream for Black kids still rings hollow to many.

Discrimination and racial prejudice have deep and enduring impacts on the lives of minority youth. A 2018 meta-analysis on the effects of racial and ethnic discrimination on the well-being of adolescents proves the point.[30] The study, which covered 214 empirical investigations based on 91,338 unique adolescents, showed significant detrimental outcomes. Among youth, greater perceptions of racial discrimination were associated with greater psychological distress, more depression and internalizing symptoms, poorer self-esteem, lower academic engagement and achievement, less motivation in school, increase in aggressive behaviors, risky sexual behavior and substance use, and greater engagement with deviant peers.

Discrimination and prejudice send a clear message that some people are valued more than others. This inequality of worth can be created by a number of social identifiers: money, race, class, education, disability, gender orientation, looks, language, or ethnic origin. The ones with more money, conventional beauty, education, or privilege possess more social status. Low social status causes stress, and stress leads to poor quality of life.[31] Racial discrimination also leads to increased stress and internalized oppression.[32]

In a series of groundbreaking epidemiological studies, Richard Wilkinson and Kate Pickett have shown the deleterious impact of inequality at the state, national, and international levels. The results can be seen in their 2018 book *The Inner Level: How More Equal Societies Reduce Stress, Restore Sanity and Improve Everyone's Well-Being.* With the tremendous rise in inequality in the last two decades, status differences have been exacerbated. As they observe, "greater inequality makes money more important as a key to status and a way of expressing your 'worth' . . . . The larger the disparities in income, the bigger the differences in lifestyles which express class position, and the more invidious and conspicuous inferior status feels."[33]

People with low economic status suffer not just from material deprivation but from worth deprivation as well. Wilkinson and Pickett write that "outward wealth is so often seen as if it was a measure of inner worth. And as greater inequality makes social position more visible, we come to judge each other more by status. With more social evaluation anxieties, problems of self-esteem, self-confidence and status insecurity become more fraught."[34]

Wilkinson and Pickett offer compelling evidence that status differences are not only injurious to those at the bottom but to everyone. They review, for instance, responses to the following question: *Some people look down on me because of my job situation or income.* In a sample of over 35,000 people across thirty-one countries, researchers found that status anxiety increased as income decreased. This was true for all countries surveyed. Not surprisingly, those at the top of the social hierarchy worried less about social status than those at the bottom. However, status anxiety was more elevated across all income levels in more unequal countries. In other words, big income differences create more status anxiety for everyone in unequal societies. In the sample of thirty-one countries, social anxiety was highest in unequal countries like Portugal and Poland and lowest in more equal countries like Denmark, Sweden, and Norway.

It is not just social anxiety that increases with inequality but rates of mental illness as well. The data presented by them show that in more equal countries, like Japan and Germany, fewer than one in ten people had experienced any type of mental illness the year before. In Australia and the United Kingdom, the rate was more than one in five, and in the United States more than one in four. Looking at income differences within the United Kingdom, men at the bottom quintile of income were thirty-five times more likely to experience depression than people at the top. Comparing forty-five states within the United States, those with relative low income inequality, such as Iowa, Minnesota, and Wisconsin, had about a third the rate of depression experienced in high-inequality states such as Alabama and Mississippi. In an international study, rates of schizophrenia were much higher in unequal countries. Based on the UNICEF index, the United States, the most unequal of rich countries, has the lowest levels of child well-being. Japan and Norway, among the most equal, have the highest.[35]

Family well-being in general is especially affected by inequalities. In rich countries like the United Kingdom, recent trends toward more inequality have resulted in serious negative consequences, especially for learning outcomes of poor kids.[36] In 2016, rates of infant mortality were increasing in the United States, especially in Texas, where cuts in funding to maternity clinics had taken place.

In a paper published in the September 2016 issue of *Obstetrics and Gynecology*, researchers reported an increase in maternal mortality rates in the United States.[37] Excluding California and Texas, which were analyzed separately, the rate of maternal mortality in forty-eight states, and Washington DC went up by 26.6 percent from 18.8 per 100,000 in the year 2000 to 23.8 in 2014. To put this in context, among thirty-one countries in the Organization for Economic Cooperation and Development, the United States ranks thirtieth, only ahead of Mexico. California experienced a decline, owing to concerted efforts to tackle the problem, but Texas experienced a sudden increase in recent years. In Texas, the rate of maternal mortality almost doubled between 2010 and 2014. It went from 18.6 to 35.8 per 100,000 births. Although African American women in Texas account for only 11 percent of all births, they suffered 29 percent of all cases of maternal death in the state. The dramatic increase in maternal death coincided with cuts in family planning budgets. These resulted in the closing of eighty-two clinics in the state.

In a more recent investigation published in July 2018 by *USA Today*, the US rate of maternal deaths per 100,000 births went up considerably in the last two decades.[38] Whereas it stood close to 17 in 1990 it was 26.4 in 2015. In the same time period, the rate has gone down in Germany, France, and Japan, where the rate is between 6 and 9 per 100,000. This time period coincides with unprecedented increasing inequality in the country. Michael Marmot makes the point that "sixty-two countries have lower lifetime risks of maternal deaths than the US."[39]

The average rate in the United States, however, belies the dire situation in some states. In Louisiana, the rate of maternal mortality is 58.1 per 100,000 births. In Georgia it is 48.4. In California, the rate is 4, twelve times lower than in Georgia and almost fifteen times lower than in Louisiana. In Texas, the most recent *USA Today* data show a rate of 34.5. It is interesting to note the contrast between California and Texas, where the former invested in prevention and the latter cut funding for maternal health care.

The correspondence between increase in inequality and rise in mental illness, maternal death, and child problems around the world cannot be ignored. As Danny Dorling put it in *The Equality Effect*, "when countries become very unequal, it becomes easier to view other human lives as being less valuable."[40] Elsewhere in the book Dorling also writes that "living with more equality makes you resistant to treating others as inferiors or superiors and so creates increased respect all around .... Growing up under a regime of high inequality can make many feel that they themselves are worth less."[41] Having lived many years in Argentina, Israel, the United States, Canada, and Australia, Isaac can attest to the accuracy of his statement. Many of his Argentinian and US friends cannot understand what it is like to live in a country like Canada, where health care is provided to all, free of charge, and where public education, from elementary to college, is high quality and accessible to all.

Equality permeates social relationships too. In Australia, it was natural to strike up a conversation with the clerk at the post office or with the bank teller. Social distance is shorter when economic distance is shorter. Class barriers are lower in societies where economic fences are lower. In other words, equality is felt not only in your pocket but also in your psyche.

The studies discussed so far in this chapter have dealt with the effects of exclusion, discrimination, and economic inequality, all of which can diminish your sense of mattering and your personal worth, especially if you are poor or a minority.[42] But there is another way to look at mattering in the community. What exclusion, marginality, and inequality have in common is that they are forms of injustice. When a person is devalued for reasons outside of his or her control – such as race, ethnicity, poverty, or disability – the person is the subject of unfair treatment. Withholding respect on account of race, gender orientation, disability status, or income amounts to lack of fairness.[43]

Curious about the impact of fairness and justice on life satisfaction, Isaac and his colleague Salvatore Di Martino conducted an international comparative study.[44] Using the Social Justice Index (SJI) devised by the Bertelsmann Stiftung Institute in Germany and the Life Satisfaction measure used by Gallup, we assessed the relationship between justice and life satisfaction in twenty-eight countries of the European Union between 2008 and 2017. The SJI consists of several dimensions, including poverty prevention, equitable education, labor market inclusion, social cohesion and nondiscrimination, health, and intergenerational justice.[45] Life satisfaction was measured by Gallup[46] using the following question: *Please imagine a ladder, with steps numbered from 0 at the bottom to 10 at the top. The top of the ladder represents the best possible life for you and the bottom of the ladder represents the worst possible life for you. On which step of the ladder would you say you personally feel you stand at this time?*

Similar to the work of Wilkinson and Pickett, we found that the level of social justice significantly predicted levels of life satisfaction. But going beyond their analyses, we demonstrated this relationship using a more comprehensive measure of justice. We also found that social capital, a measure of participation in the community, was highly predictive of life satisfaction as well. This lends support to the claim that a sense of community improves the well-being of its members. When we get involved in the community we have an opportunity to add value and feel valued, with lasting positive effects, as we will see in the case of Brian.

Brian is 27 years old. To make a living, he works as a security guard in two different jobs. He lives with his mother and was proud to have been admitted into the police academy. His parents went through a divorce, and his dad died while he was in high school. He went through a rough period, but he is now in a good place, training to become a police officer. Between job and study, Brian finds time to volunteer at a drop-in center for homeless youth. There he connected with a particular youngster. This is his account of working with a young person:

> He got in a little trouble with the law and ended up in jail, and I never once judged him .... I think we kinda bonded in a really positive way. So the last time I talked to him, I found out that he actually applied himself and went back to school .... I wasn't there to change every kid that went through that door there, but [if] I could have impact on one kid then that just makes me want to volunteer more and just give something to the community.

Brian is a participant in the Canadian Futures Study, which investigates the lives of hundreds of emerging adults. As the authors of the study observe, "volunteering experiences can build on each other and encourage greater engagement over time by developing a sense of competence and identity."[47] It turns out that the sense of mastery and positive identity associated with volunteering brings many positive returns, to Brian, and to the millions of people who help in the community in various ways. One of the lead authors of the Canadian Futures Study is Mike Pratt, Isaac's former colleague in Canada. Mike, a developmental psychologist, partnered with our friend Mark Pancer, a social psychologist, to study civic engagement of youth and emerging adults (ages eighteen to thirty). Mark, the author of *The Psychology of Citizenship and Civic Engagement*, conducted an extensive review of the research and documented the many positive outcomes associated with making a difference in the community. In his book, Mark quotes from many of the participants in his studies. One of the youth who had worked with young kids as a literacy tutor shared how she felt:

> *Just the fact that I was getting involved outside of the high-school community . . . that I was actually within my community where I am from and I could actually see what I was doing was making a difference . . . that was a big deal.*[48]

Many of the participants relayed stories of increased confidence and self-esteem. Helping others increased their life satisfaction and meaning in life. The feeling of making a difference is an expression of the satisfaction derived from self-efficacy, sense of mastery, empowerment, and human agency. Civic engagement is one of the most efficient ways to cultivate a "We Culture" among the next generation. Once you acquire this habit as a teenager, the research shows that most people stick with it for life. Once a helper, always a helper.

Citizenship enhances social responsibility. It moves people from a selfish focus on feeling valued to adding value, from claiming rights to upholding responsibility. In short, Mark Pancer shows how participation in prosocial activities increases the five Cs: confidence, competence, caring, connection, and character.

Engagement builds the good and prevents the bad. Participation in prosocial activities such as community service or religious groups was shown to prevent the use of alcohol in youth. Similarly, involvement in extracurricular activities is associated with reduced rates of drug use. The same goes for delinquent behavior. The more civic engagement there is, the less participation in antisocial groups. In pretty much every domain of life, civic activity protects the participant against risks of dropping out of school, premature sexual encounters, and lighting a cigarette, among other things.

When it comes to mental health, extracurricular activities prevent both internalizing problems (such as depression and anxiety) and externalizing disorders (such as bullying and aggression). But the positive outcomes are not the sole province of youth. Adults also benefit from participation in civic affairs. Mark Pancer, also a lead researcher in Better Beginnings Better Futures, a community-based project designed to improve the educational, social, emotional, and physical development of children in Ontario, documented the impact the program had on the adult volunteers. A woman Mark calls Anna described the transition from being isolated in the community to getting involved with the project as a radical positive change in her life. She was isolated at home with nothing to do, until she joined a parents group. Then she got involved with other committees. Before she knew it she was also doing outreach work in the community as well.

> The first few months with the project felt amazing – very amazing. Very empowering, which was a word I didn't know back then, but I do now. I loved it – I still do. Breaking the isolation was a big factor for me. It changed my personality drastically ... Having what I had to say in the Newsletter was a big to-do for me. Being accessible to the principal and to the teachers, being known by the vice-principal. Being known and feeling important that way has been really good .... I've learned a lot of skills, too.[49]

Thanks to Better Beginnings, Anna felt like she mattered, and the more she mattered to others, the more competent and proud she felt. Like Anna, adults who volunteer and make a difference in the community grow in self-confidence and find renewed meaning in life.

Pancer reviews a number of studies in which participation in community affairs affected not only health but also longevity. In a number of investigations, those who were actively involved in the community lived longer than those who volunteered infrequently or not at all. Like Anna, participants in these studies felt like they mattered, and this feeling enhanced their well-being.

This was precisely the conclusion that Jane Piliavin and Erica Siegl arrived at in their study on the benefits of volunteering in the Wisconsin Longitudinal Study.[50] According to the two researchers, mattering mediates the connection between volunteering and well-being. They discovered this through the use of longitudinal data. The study started in 1957, when a third of all graduating seniors in high school in Wisconsin, 10,317 in total, were surveyed. Participants were interviewed again in 1975, 1992, and 2004. The results showed not only that volunteering predicted well-being and self-reported physical health but that the effects were influenced by the feeling of mattering. The authors hypothesized that "well-being should result from volunteering by making people feel that they matter in the world."[51] This was precisely what they found. They conclude that "volunteering increases psychological well-being in part because it leads people to feel that they have an important role in society and that their existence is important."[52] In short, feeling valued and adding value are the secret sauce of volunteering. This is what increases physical and psychological well-being.

Mark uses his own research in Canada as well as studies from all over the world to show that volunteering has positive effects on physical and mental health, self-efficacy, resilience, capacity building, and quality of life. He also notes that volunteering is most impactful on people who are at-risk of developing problems due to isolation or poverty. There is no question that adding value to the community is a multiplier of health and happiness for the volunteers. But the benefits extend beyond individuals. Entire organizations, communities, and nations reap the benefits of social capital.

When participants are properly represented in the governing bodies of programs, organizations, and communities, systems work better. For example, when residents have a say, the quality of local services improve, accessibility improves, and utilization goes up. When people like Anna express their voice in programs like Better Beginnings, the programs are more responsive. Instead of being driven by professionals removed from the community, the programs are co-led by experts in the subject matter (education, child development, health) and experts in living in the community (parents, teachers, neighbors). Success requires an amalgam of both sets of expertise.

Neighborhoods with higher rates of civic participation enjoy a greater sense of community, lower rates of crime, and citizens who are happier and healthier. The salutary ripple effects of civic engagement bubble up all the way to the level of nations. In summarizing the research, Pancer observed that countries with higher levels of civic engagement report better mental and physical health and reduced rates of disease, psychiatric conditions, crime, and suicide. In addition, they are more prosperous financially and better governed, and their children are healthier.[53]

Sources

The sense of mattering we experience in communities is a function of the personality of their inhabitants and the norms of that particular culture. Cultures that promote inclusion nudge individuals to be fair, caring, and compassionate. Cultures that ignore power differentials pretend that we are all the same and that we all experience identical privilege. Cultures that infringe on people's rights to a psychologically safe environment enable bullying. Personality and culture interact all the time.

Inclusive cultures consist of people who demonstrate caring and norms that actively promote belonging (think Panchita's neighbors). *Insensitive cultures* lack any sort of accountability for people who allow themselves to demean others (think Trump mocking a journalist with a disability). *Ignorant cultures* consist of clueless people and vague norms (think stereotype threat). We can easily spot the first and second types because inclusive or marginalizing behaviors are obvious and explicit; you know when you are being included, and you know when you are being mocked. But many settings fall into the third category, ignorant cultures. In the latter, implicit biases are at play but difficult to detect. They are just too subtle. Few people actively exclude, ostracize, mock, or marginalize others in the community, but every interaction is suffused with stereotypes, microaggressions, status comparisons, and dynamics of dominance and submission.[54] Unconscious biases have real effects on people, even if imperceptible to the naked eye.

Inclusive communities build on the human need to belong. From an evolutionary point of view, we need others to survive and thrive.[55] Groups protect us from enemies and promote our flourishing. Inclusive cultures, be they groups of friends, religious organizations, or neighborhood associations maintain norms that make you feel welcome and safe. People greet you with a warm smile, ask you about your life, invite you to share some time together, and help you in times of need.

Communities of mattering know a few tricks.[56] They organize themselves into small groups so that nobody can get lost in the crowd. They also meet frequently, face-to-face, and create networks of support. They call each other often, share meals together, celebrate milestones, and have lots of formal and informal interactions. They understand the need to participate, so they give their members meaningful roles to play, such as leading a religious ceremony or a group activity. They also ask people to tell their stories. Some religious organizations ask members to share their spiritual biography with a small circle. The community also creates a common story: how it came about, what it stands for, and why it exists. Inclusive communities also share common values, secular or religious. *But most importantly, they treat one another as equals. A fundamental source of mattering in communities is the fact that our worth is upheld and never questioned.* We love these communities because they suppress status anxiety. We are accepted unconditionally. The practice of equality enhances mattering, reduces status anxiety, and promotes well-being.

We are attracted to people and places that make us feel welcome, safe, and valued. This is borne out by the research. The evidence shows that more egalitarian places foster more trust and sense of community among neighbors. But this ideal state of affairs is hard to come by.[57] Susan Fiske, professor of psychology at Princeton, documents the ubiquitous effects of inequality and status comparisons in her book *Envy Up, Scorn Down: How Status Divides Us.*[58] When it comes to mattering, what makes the culture in the United States mostly ignorant is that we deny or minimize the existence of class differences. As she observed, "comparisons up and down the status system divide us from each other. What is most disturbing is that we persist in denying what ails us."[59] Regardless of our beliefs about equality and class distinctions, the powerful scorn the weak and blame them for their misfortune. But it is not just poor people who suffer from stereotypes by the powerful; the elderly and people with disabilities are also regarded as inferior and incompetent. The message is clear: if you are vulnerable, you are worth less.

Since we humans are comparing machines, and comparisons seem natural, we are constantly perturbed by our social standing. According to Fiske, "people are obsessed by admiration and neglect, envy and scorn, the world over. We are divided from each other by the often correlated differences between power (resources) and status (prestige). Elites within the United States and Americans in the world evoke envy and run the risk of scorning those who are less well off."[60]

Both envy and scorn diminish a sense of mattering. Since all social systems entail inequality, envy and scorn are pervasive. The accentuation of class differences observed in the popular media, and perpetuated in communities and the workplace, affect the envious in powerful ways: they feel inferior, ashamed, deprived, bitter, and frustrated.

On account of money, position, beauty, race, fame, education, or prestige, some people have more power than others. Power, in turn, increases teasing, exploitation, stereotyping, and sexual harassment. Fiske concludes that multiple studies demonstrate that power-holders behave with self-serving scorn.

It won't surprise you to learn that scorn scars the scorned, but it also scars the scornful as they become insensitive, exploitive, and selfish. The way the scornful becomes sick, Fiske argues, is through mechanisms associated with anger and hostility, creating a boomerang effect. The way scorn and other kinds of stigma damage the scorned is through physiological responses to stress that undermine immune system functions and heart health. Stress is responsible for the release of cortisol in the body, which over time can lead to serious physical and mental health problems. Cortisol is an equal opportunity aggressor, though: it affects the scornful and the scorned alike. The more devalued you are, the more cortisol is released into the bloodstream and the worse your outlook.

Envy harms the envied because they are the target of hostility and discrimination. Fiske notes that certain out-groups who succeed in business, such as Jews, Asians, middle-class Blacks, and career women, are often the subject of envy. People often see these groups as competent but cold. The envious also suffer because they experience lack of control, resentment, and hostility. In general, lower status generates performance anxiety, and, since most of us are forever interacting with people who are superior to us in some fashion, this is a pretty serious threat to the well-being of the envious.

In light of the insecurity created by growing inequalities, people search for comfort in their in-group and blame out-groups for their misfortune. The findings come from laboratory experiments, field studies, community research, and international comparisons. The evidence is very compelling that lack of fairness leads some people to feel devalued in relationships, at work, and in the community. In Fiske's words, "unfairness distresses some of us because inequality is not just about income – or at least its effects are not. It is about damage to well-being, to feelings of control, self-esteem, belonging, trusting, and understanding."[61] She argues that inequality leads to insecurity, which, in turn, channels comparisons and resentment about unfairness.

The outcome of these inequalities and comparisons is that all of us, collectively, matter less, but the poor suffer disproportionally more than the rest. Linda Tirado, whom we met earlier, experienced the scornful look of her bosses and welfare officers. She worked multiple jobs, tried to go to school, and strove to build a better future, but she was blamed for her poverty and misfortune. She was the subject of scorn and disregard. Her humanity was diminished by people who were ignorant of the impact of their actions. When White supremacists chant, as they did in Virginia in August 2017, "Jews will not replace us," they are not exactly fostering social harmony. Sometimes, insults are direct and aimed at a person, like Linda Tirado, or a group, such as Jews or Blacks. But in many cases the assault on mattering is subtle and the source hard to recognize. Instead of a person or group, it is the system, the entire culture, that makes us feel stressed and as if we do not matter. Black people have been disproportionally harmed by these insults, as recently documented in Ijeoma Oluo's book *So You Want To Talk About Race,* Ibram Kendi's *How To Be An Anti-Racist,* John Powell's *Racing to Justice,* Robin DiAngelo's *White Fragility,* and Isabel Wilkerson's *Caste.*[62]

Strategies

The "Me Culture" we inhabit celebrates individuals for their achievements, but it also blames them for their misfortune. The answer to problems, it suggests, is often more therapy; more self-improvement; more wellness. While therapy can obviously help, it does have its limits. For therapy or any kind of intervention to work, it must shift the discourse from "Me" to "We." Otherwise, we seek wellness without fairness, and we risk blaming the victim. In psychology, this is an occupational hazard.

Balance Wellness with Fairness

As noted in Chapter 5, thirty years ago Isaac argued that psychologists were unwittingly complicit in supporting an unfair state of affairs.[63] Though well-meaning, psychologists often defined social problems in intrapsychic terms. Social anxiety stemming from inequality was reframed as intrapersonal conflict to be cured with talking therapies. Although many therapies illuminated the dark process that caused so much pain, they also obscured the sources of status anxiety. It was all about coping and adjusting the person to the situation. It was rarely about challenging the situation to benefit the person.

The picture Isaac portrayed in 1989 has not entirely changed in the intervening years. As William Davis put it recently in *The Happiness Industry,* "there has been a growing unease with the way in which notions of happiness and well-being have been adopted by policy-makers and managers. The risk is that this science ends up blaming ... individuals for their own misery, and ignores the context that has contributed to it."[64] When we lose sight of context, the sources and cures reside strictly within the person.[65]

To be sure, it is not just physical or psychological fitness that impacts health but also fairness. Communities where fairness is as important as wellness produce better individual and social outcomes: better health, longevity, life satisfaction, education, tolerance, trust, mental health, and happiness. These societies do not require individuals to suffer for the benefit of the collective. On the contrary, they live better lives because they benefit from fairness themselves.

Nations that invest in public institutions are the ones that benefit the private citizen the most.[66] They do that in two ways: collectively and psychologically. Collectively, they invest in the public good – education, health care, unemployment benefits, maternity leave, paid vacations, and minimum wage. They guarantee a minimum level of need satisfaction while curtailing inequality. Psychologically, there is less stress stemming from comparisons across vast divides. The evidence clearly supports the promotion of a "We Culture"; it is healthier and saner.

Leverage emotions. When it comes to feelings, making other people feel valued is a wonderful way to make *you* feel valued. The gift of dignity will boost not only the other person's feelings but yours as well. Generosity is a proven shortcut to positive emotions. The more you help others feel valued and appreciated, the more you help yourself.[67] Gratitude will also accomplish the same outcome. If you are looking for an emotional tonic, write a letter to a former teacher expressing your gratitude for what he or she did for you. Be specific. Mention particular things he or she did on your behalf. Practice gratitude and generosity liberally. They are happiness accelerators.

Challenge false assumptions. When it comes to thoughts, it's crucial to challenge negative assumptions. Since the "Me Culture" dominates contemporary discourse, many people end up stressed and depressed because they blame themselves. The "Me Culture" does not provide a language to understand their plight in liberating ways.[68] The only available narrative is *I'm not successful enough, smart enough, wealthy enough, popular enough, and sexy enough.* The same reasoning leads some people to act out their frustrations. The "me" narrative excludes considerations of privilege and inequality. It promotes a focus on the self, on rights, and on wellness. When these don't materialize we turn inwards or outwards, blaming ourselves or others.[69]

If you are the object of demeaning treatment or the subject of stereotype threat, you need to question the validity of these claims. If you have been the subject of abuse, you might experience self-blame.[70] Children often blame themselves for their parents' problems.[71] Self-blame is a common struggle, only aggravated by abuse of power.[72] In social interactions, the tyranny of hierarchy can make you feel inferior. In all these situations it is crucial to place responsibility where it belongs: the abuser, the power grabber, the system of inequality; and yet, some people internalize oppression and blame themselves.

The social environment is always talking to us. Signs of wealth and prestige are everywhere. Some people wear fancier clothes. Others drive luxury cars.

Some flaunt their education or connection to famous people. Some will treat you with disdain. Others will invoke racial stereotypes. Subtle or overt, the environment is constantly serving us cues. You need to play detective to spot cues that diminish your sense of worth.

Perhaps the major assumption that needs to be challenged is that the world is mostly a just place. According to this belief, if you end up in poverty, you probably did something to deserve it. If your neighbors are filthy rich, they probably did something right. The belief in a just world is a well-known psychological phenomenon: it brings order where there is chaos; it explains the nature of things.[73] A corollary of this belief is that people always get what they deserve. If they succeed it's because either they are smart (ability) or they worked hard (effort). If they fail it's because they are either incompetent or lazy. While simple and persuasive, this narrative is false. A myriad of factors, other than ability and effort, impact success or failure. Chief among them is privilege, which translates into opportunities to develop ability and work ethic. To deny the impact of opportunities on talent development is to be blind to the effects of cognitive stimulation and socialization.

To make this point clear, let's imagine two friends, John and Greg. Both were born with the same level of intelligence and both work equally hard in school, but there is a big difference in their education. John attends an elite private school, whereas Greg goes to an under-resourced public school. Since he was a young age, John's parents enrolled him in Kumon and chess lessons. They also hired a tutor to help him with French. He took violin lessons and participated in the Boy Scouts. His family took him on study trips. His parents inculcated in him aspirations to go to an Ivy League School. When it came time to apply to college, he took a few courses to improve his SAT score.

Greg, in contrast, came from a poor background. His parents understood the need for a good education and always encouraged him to succeed, but he never had the opportunities afforded to John. While Greg applied himself in school, his counselors encouraged him to enroll in a technical or vocational college. Not knowing any better, he did. Greg never had the breaks John had, and, although both worked very hard, John's parents knew how to open doors that were always closed for Greg.

Upper-middle-class parents specialize in opportunity hoarding.[74] They do all they can to secure a good fortune for their children. Parents from poor backgrounds also do all they can, but, since they lack resources and don't know how to work the system, their kids are deprived of prospects that wealthier families take for granted.

Increasing economic inequalities have made the rich richer and the poor poorer.[75] By any measure, from the ratio of CEO/laborer pay to the wealth of the top 1 percent, the inequality gap has grown exponentially in the last thirty years. In the United States, the wealthiest 1 percent make more than 20 percent of all the income in the nation.[76] While the rich have been getting richer, people in the lowest quintile have remained stagnant for the last fifty years. When it comes to the difference in pay between CEOs and production workers, in 1965 the ratio was 18 to 1. In the year 2000 it peaked at 411 to 1. The ratio in 2011 was between 209 to 1 and 231 to 1. And yet, despite all this evidence of inequality, millions of people, including those who suffer from the status quo, ardently defend it.[77]

John Jost, a professor of psychology at New York University, set out to study this phenomenon. He wanted to understand "why do some women feel that they are entitled to lower salaries than men, why do people stay in harmful relationships, and why do some African-American children come to believe that white dolls are more attractive and desirable than black dolls? Why do people blame victims of injustice and why do victims of injustice sometimes blame themselves?"[78]

In a series of experimental and field studies, Jost found that people justify inequalities and injustices because they want to minimize cognitive tension, uncertainty, and social conflict. In the absence of an alternative narrative, people tend to believe that the system is fair and just the way it is. Had they challenged the status quo, there would have been too much dissonance. After all, they were told since a young age that the American dream is there for the taking. Jost has labeled this phenomenon *system justification*.

When Jost studied the responses of disadvantaged groups to injustice, he found that many of them justified the status quo by internalizing an inferior view of themselves.[79] He also found that system justification was associated with increased levels of depression and low self-esteem among minorities. Jost's findings are in line with research showing that victims of abuse often blame themselves for the trauma, increasing their suffering, depression, and post-traumatic stress.[80]

Taken as a whole, the belief in a just world, system justification theory, and self-blame research show that people often acquiesce to the status quo, even when it's patently unfair and unjust. We must be aware of our unconscious predilection to side with power and the status quo, even when we are personally victimized by the system. As Jost observed, "system justification can lead us to deny and excuse aspects of our society – such as the ever-widening gap between rich and poor."[81]

Write a New Story

Creating a new narrative about ourselves and the social system can trigger change. If you feel devalued and you become depressive or aggressive, you can author a new story to become reflective instead. There are a few ways to compose an emancipatory narrative. Start by literally writing down what you value in life. What values and principles guide your behavior? This exercise alone has psychological benefits because it aligns your goals with your behaviors and values.[82] Next, recall an instance where you were helpful to other people. What did you do? How did other people respond? How did others made you feel valued? In moments of self-blame, it is useful to reflect on all the good deeds you have done for others. Do an inventory of your strengths. What gifts do you bring to the community? This is helpful because there is evidence that writing about positive experiences enhances physical and psychological well-being.[83]

Consider also how injustice has affected your life and how you can challenge the perpetrators. Shine a light on fairness. Imagine how an organization or a community can engage in fair practices. How can people participate in decisions affecting their lives? How can you use your voice? How can you exercise choice?

If you feel devalued, ask yourself where this is coming from. What social mores have you internalized that make you feel inadequate? Do you belong to a minority group that is stigmatized? Do you tend to internalize feelings of inferiority projected onto you by others with more power and prestige? Feelings of mattering have personal and social bases. You must examine both. What family and social dynamics have made you feel valued or devalued? What is the dominant discourse in society about people with your identity? Is your identity respected or is it denigrated?

Build Community

A great way to take action is to join others to create a caring community, fight injustice, and promote fairness. This in itself may be a revolutionary act in the "Me Era." After all, you are supposed to be self-sufficient, independent, and strong. But you cannot build a "We Culture" on your own. You have to partner with others in either existing organizations or in new ones. Whether you join an established community or lead the creation of one, there are eight roles you need to embrace, and they form the acronym I VALUE IT.[84]

Inclusive host: To make people feel that they matter, you have to behave like an inclusive host. When you join a team to build a community or an organization, the best thing you can do is to make sure everyone feels a sense of community and belonging. People must feel welcome and experience psychological safety. Behaviorally, you do this by giving everyone a chance to introduce themselves and express their wishes; and you show interest in their lives and aspirations. People may not remember the contents of a meeting very well, but they will not forget whether they were treated with kindness or neglect.

Visionary: Being a visionary does not require being grander than life. It simply means establishing a clear vision of the work you want to do together and what goals you wish to accomplish as a collective. You may want to create a community garden, a book club, a support group, an environmental collective, or a human rights organization. Regardless of the focus, it helps to create a compelling vision that will remind people why they are all together in this. It will also prevent mission drift. As Lewis Carroll said, "if you don't know where you are going, any road will get you there."[85] You can become a visionary by simply asking the group the following question: *what value are we adding to the community?* The answer to that question is your vision.

Asset Seeker: A great way to make sure your partners feel valued is by building on their strengths. Whatever your project is, invite others to use their talents to contribute to it. Some will contribute gifts of the head, others of the heart or hand.[86] You can facilitate the use of strengths by assigning roles that build on people's expertise and interests.

Listener: Attentive listening makes people feel valued and gives them an opportunity to add value by expressing their opinions. You can facilitate voice and choice by creating norms of respectful listening.

Unique solution finder: If you want your partners to remain engaged in your community project, you must move from "admiring the problem" to "solving it." Many willing partners drop out because they are tired of talking instead of doing.

Evaluator: If you want to know if your group is really adding value to the community, you have to engage in some form of evaluation. Healthy organizations evaluate not only the outcomes but also the process. They ask questions such as *Have we achieved our goals? Have we made progress toward our ultimate aim? Is the process inclusive and participatory? Have community members expressed their voice?*

Implementer: Whatever project you have embarked on to increase mattering in the community, you have to move from planning to implementation.

What concrete steps are you taking as a group to address lack of mattering, lack of fairness, or lack of wellness?

Trend setter. People enjoy creating new ventures. They take pride in adding value to the community. Once you have done that, work with others to set a trend, and not just a passing fad. Make sure your community efforts are sustainable and scalable.

Mattering through Social Change

She did not expect the Facebook post to go viral, but it did. Although she had a vast social media presence already, the impact of her post was unprecedented. While the message was meant to console a suffering community, it went on to congeal a social movement. It had struck a chord. A whole group of people were feeling like their lives did not matter. This is why Alicia Garza's post, written after the acquittal of George Zimmerman over the death of Trayvon Martin, resonated with millions of Black people.[1] The last part of her post in July 2013 read as follows: "I continue to be surprised at how little Black lives matter . . . .Black people. I love you. I love us. Our lives matter."[2] Garza penned the original message, but two of her friends, Patrisse Cullors and Opal Tometi, helped to disseminate the call to action.[3]

Patrisse Cullors, a Los Angeles native, had met Garza in 2005 at a conference for organizers. Cullors, who studied religion and philosophy at UCLA, had been an organizer for LGBTQ causes. Later she became a special projects director at the Ella Baker Center for Human Rights in Oakland, California. Based on Garza's post, Cullors created the #BlackLivesMatter hashtag. The two women started promoting the message, but they needed more help. Opal Tometi, an immigration organizer in Brooklyn, volunteered to spread the word through social media platforms. The rest, as they say, is history (or herstory).[4]

The Black Lives Matter (BLM) movement gathered exponential momentum in Ferguson after the killing of another unarmed Black man, Michael Brown, by White police officer Darren Wilson, on August 9, 2014. On November 22, 2014, just two days before a grand jury decided not to prosecute Wilson, two police officers were dispatched in Cleveland to investigate a possible shooting situation. The person alleged to be shooting was a child, Tamir Rice, a twelve-year-old Black boy, using a toy gun.[5] The police officers had not been told that this may be a child, and the officers believed that they were responding to an active shooting scenario. As they arrived on the scene, Tamir was still pretending to shoot with his toy gun. The officers killed him. Unfortunately, Trayvon Martin, Michael Brown, and Tamir Rice were not the only Black youth killed by police since the creation of BLM. Several more deaths, including those of George Floyd, Breonna Taylor, and Ahmaud Arbery, gave rise to global protests against anti-Black racism and placed the BLM movement at the center of it all.

Garza, who grew up Alicia Schwartz, was raised by her African American mother and her Jewish stepfather. Although her family was not especially political, she was already showing interest in activism in middle school: she participated in a campaign to inform students about contraceptives. Her passion for activism was later manifested in various causes. In an interview in 2018 she said that the BLM movement grew out of the realization that Black people were looking to channel their frustration into something useful that could transform, as she put it, "our conditions, and change the way things are."[6]

Her choice of words is very informative because, to add value to a community, it is not enough to deal with the symptoms. We must seek to change the very conditions that lead to suffering and marginalization in the first place. In this chapter we explore the dynamics of adding value to the community, the origins, the consequences, and the best strategies. Garza and her colleagues chose a path that involves wellness with fairness. They are trying to build a "We Community." As we shall see, some efforts to build community embrace wellness without fairness: a typical "Me" approach. Others foster wellness with various degrees of fairness, getting closer to the "We" approach we advocate for. But before we get to strategies, we explore the signs, significance, and sources of making a difference in the community and society.

Signs

On Sunday, May 15, 2016, we held the first South Florida meeting for individuals and family members affected by FSH, a particular type of muscular dystrophy. We were pleased to host this meeting at our home in Miami. Eleven people were in attendance, including June Kinoshita, executive director of the FSH Society, who traveled to Miami especially for this meeting.

We were a diverse bunch: women and men, young and not so young, from various professional backgrounds, having varying levels of impairment due to FSH. Some of us, like Ora, were diagnosed long ago, while others had recently learned that they have FSH. Despite these differences and the fact that most of us had never met before, two hours seemed to fly by. We introduced ourselves and shared our FSH journeys – stories that spoke of struggles and challenges but also of strengths and resilience.

A woman spoke for the first time in public about her disability. A young couple was worried about the future, since the condition is genetic and progressive. The group was extremely supportive and provided a safe space where frustrations could be vented, jokes could be made, and meaning could be created. Not everyone wanted to share to the same extent, but all felt part of a community with common struggles. Albeit this was a temporary community, many people enjoyed the camaraderie, feeling valued and adding value. Everyone felt like they mattered to the group.

People also shared practical information regarding providers, equipment, and ways of addressing challenges. June Kinoshita spoke about the work of the FSH Society and relayed some research highlights. The consensus at the end of the meeting was that knowing others with the same diagnosis is an important source of emotional and instrumental support. At people's request, Ora sent out a list with names and contact details so that folks can keep in touch.

For a few years now we have hosted meetings of these families in our home and at national conferences, where we run workshops. It is a unique and rare opportunity for families to share how they make meaning of the situation and how they come up with solutions to everyday challenges, from mobility to employment to parenting. Unless your family is affected by it, few people can understand what it is like to cope with the challenges of FSH. We exchanged ideas that can help all of us deal with a tough situation. We feel useful when we talk with others about how to confront the situation with optimism and realism.

Ora is very interested in well-being for people with disabilities, both as someone who uses a motorized wheelchair due to FSH and as a psychologist and former professor with expertise in the field. There is no doubt that the progressive, at times unpredictable, nature of FSH can present formidable challenges to well-being. It is also true, however, that it is possible to live a meaningful and productive life, disability and all. Savoring positive experiences, counting our blessings, and cultivating meaningful relationships with others are all conducive to well-being. So is contributing to the life of others and involving ourselves in something we are passionate about. There are losses and hardships, for sure, but also opportunities for deep relationships, meaningful endeavors, and good times.

Community building with people with disabilities is especially important since disability can be a very isolating experience. If it's not the physical
barriers, it's the psychological block of expressing vulnerability. In the
larger community, persons with disabilities are often seen as unable to
add value to the community, which is utterly and completely untrue but
which elicits the common risks associated with stereotype threat.[7] Like
many others who participate in these meetings, both of us feel that, in
a small way, we are making a difference in this community.

In *The Psychology of Citizenship and Civic Engagement*, our friend Mark
Pancer noted that "making a difference" was one of the most common
motivations shared by volunteers and activists in hundreds of interviews
that his research team conducted.[8] Indeed, his book is full of references to
that refrain. There are plenty of signs that individuals all over the world
willingly give of their time and money to help others in need. For example,
in the United States alone, about 30 percent of the population volunteer,
which is close to 77 million people. Over the past fifteen years, people in
the United States volunteered close to 120 billion hours. This amounts to
$2.8 trillion.[9] On average, they volunteer about thirty-two hours per year,
which amounts to 7.9 billion hours of service. In terms of money, this is the
equivalent of $184 billion.[10] Reports indicate that people of all ages and all
racial and ethnic backgrounds volunteer.[11]

People volunteer in all sorts of associations. We volunteer with the FSH
Society and other organizations dealing with disabilities. Many do so with
parent–teacher associations, Boy and Girl Scouts, religious organizations,
museums, schools, and hospitals.

During disasters it is not uncommon for many people to donate money.
After the 2010 Haiti earthquake, NGOs and charities collected $4 billion.[12]
The Red Cross alone collected close to $500 million.[13]

While many people contribute time and money to civic organizations
and relief efforts, others engage in political processes to effect social change.
This is what drew so many African Americans to the BLM movement.
Scholar Barbara Ransby claims that it is not only social conditions that lead
to the emergence of social movements but human agency as well. In her
2018 book *Making All Black Lives Matter: Reimagining Freedom in the 21st
Century,* she argues that

> There is always a set of conditions and circumstances that set the stage for
> movements to emerge. Some of that stage-setting is historical, having little
> to do with activists and organizers themselves but rather with the political
> and economic climate and an array of social realities beyond their immedi-
> ate control. But then there is human agency: what we as human beings, as

oppressed people, as conscientious allies of the oppressed, do (or don't do) in response to the conditions and circumstances we encounter.[14]

It is a testament to the human spirit that African Americans and other oppressed groups throughout history have fought to regain their dignity in the face of relentless denigration. In the case of Blacks in the United States, there has been a concerted effort to vilify their culture as the culprit of social problems. In her book *From #BlackLivesMatter to Black Liberation*, Keeanga-Yamahtta Taylor argues:

> There are constant attempts to connect the badges of inequality, including poverty and rates of incarceration, to culture, family structure, and the internal lives of Black Americans .... How else could the political and economic elite of the United States (and its colonial predecessors) rationalize enslaving Africans at a time when they were simultaneously championing the rights of men and the end of monarchy and establishing freedom, democracy, and the pursuit of happiness as the core principles of this new democracy?[15]

Blaming the victim has been a favorite strategy of elites over centuries. As Taylor points out, "explanations for Black inequality that blame people for their own oppression transforms material causes into subjective causes. The problem is not racial discrimination in the workplace or residential segregation: it is Black irresponsibility, erroneous social mores, and general bad behavior."[16]

That is how society quiets its conscience when four million Black children live in poverty, close to a quarter of a million Black people lost homes in the foreclosure crisis, and about a million Black people are in jail.[17] But like Garza, Cullors, and Tomati, many others seek wellness with fairness in community organizations, social movements, and government policies.[18]

Significance

Depending on social and political dynamics, the pain associated with feeling devalued can lead to social progress or decay. When civil rights activists organized to pass legislation to advance the well-being of Blacks, and when people with disabilities advocated for the passage of the Americans with Disabilities Act, social progress was achieved.[19] These were fights for fairness mounted by people without power. But when certain groups in power feel threatened, instead of creating bridges of belonging they erect walls of exclusion. Instead of extending wellness to all, they hoard opportunities.[20] They are quick to abandon *bridging* social capital in favor of extreme *bonding*. When that happens, we end up with populist nationalism, xenophobia, prejudice, and racial intolerance.[21]

As Francis Fukuyama claimed in his 2018 book *Identity: The Demand for Dignity and the Politics of Resentment*, "demand for recognition of one's identity is a master concept that unifies much of what is going on in world politics today. It is not confined to the identity politics practiced on university campuses, or to the White nationalism it has provoked, but extends to broader phenomena such as the upsurge of old-fashioned nationalism."[22] By his own analysis, there are two main forces converging on the rise of nationalism: economic inequality and the politics of resentment. The economic recession of 2008, occasioned by the reckless practices of the elite, resulted in economic displacement of many. Around the globe people lost their homes, their jobs, and their dignity. But instead of directing their anger toward the source of the problem – the captains of the financial industrial complex – the victims of the recession, aided and abetted by opportunistic political leaders, blamed foreigners. Instead of questioning the very system that led to catastrophic results and holding their leaders accountable, aggrieved groups turned their anger toward immigrants and minorities.[23]

Many people like Trump used the time-honored tradition of deflecting blame onto scapegoats and powerless groups. Fukuyama called this phenomenon the politics of resentment. This is when a leader mobilizes followers by telling them that their "dignity had been affronted, disparaged, or otherwise disregarded." He further argues that this "resentment engenders demands for public recognition of the dignity of the group in question. A humiliated group seeking restitution of its dignity carries far more emotional weight than people simply pursuing their economic advantage."[24]

The two most recent examples of nationalistic surge were the election of Donald Trump and Brexit. But global instances abound: the National Front in France, the Alternative for Germany, the Freedom Party in Austria, and the Party for Freedom in the Netherlands. When it comes to populist leaders, Putin in Russia, Erdoğan in Turkey, Bolsonaro in Brazil, Orbán in Hungary, and Duterte in the Philippines join Trump in the league of nationalists. Fukuyama makes it clear that in all these cases, the leaders fomented politics of resentment by telling followers that their dignity had been trampled upon by foreigners, minorities, or other countries. What all these illustrations demonstrate is that feeling devalued can lead to deleterious consequences for society as a whole, especially when resentment is fueled for political purposes. Throughout history, we have seen how masses can be manipulated into acquiescence and hatred. When inequality of means meets inequality of respect, we end up with a volatile situation.[25]

Mattering, through civic participation, makes people, organizations, neighborhoods, and nations healthier and happier. But, we should note, not all forms of civic participation come easy or without a struggle. Social improvement often requires conflict. Participation in civic affairs is a necessary condition, but not all forms of engagement lead to transformative results. Some actually result in the fortification of the status quo, which is inimical to millions of people. This is why it's important to make a distinction between amelioration and transformation.[26] The former refers to minor social reforms aimed to soothe the pain created by a system of injustice. The latter refers to fundamental changes in the system of injustice itself.

While not all human suffering can be directly tied to injustice, a lot of it can, and when injustice is known to cause pain, exclusion, marginalization, poverty, and discrimination we need transformative, not just ameliorative, engagement. Some of the work we do with the FSH Society is ameliorative in nature – we try to help other families deal with a difficult situation – but not all the hardships associated with muscular dystrophy can be traced back to the impairment itself. A lot of suffering is occasioned by a disabling society that excludes people with disabilities: lack of accessible transportation, lack of accommodations in the workplace, discrimination, exclusion.

Helping people to cope with a disability is important and necessary, but it is also insufficient. More radical changes are needed. This is why social movements emerge. What applies to disabilities goes for poverty as well. We can teach people living in poverty job skills, but we must also attend to the conditions that caused so much poverty in the first place. The same for gender discrimination. Women can learn how to assert themselves, like Anna did in the Better Beginnings project, but that should not replace the elimination of gender discrimination in the workplace. The same goes for racial segregation. Black and Latinx children must achieve the highest level of education they can, but grit and resilience are not enough: we also need fairness in access to educational opportunities.

In the case of people with disabilities, it took a social movement to create the Americans with Disabilities Act (ADA) to remove many of the social barriers that prevented them from participation in society. As Ora noted in her earlier book *Motherhood and Disability: Children and Choices*:

Empowerment for groups that have been marginalized and denied opportunities does not happen as a result of spontaneous enlightenment by the majority group. It was women, rather than men, who brought to the forefront the oppressive factors that constricted their lives; just as leaders from within disadvantaged minority groups challenged White privilege. In the same vein, it was the bold and tireless work of disabled activists that began to challenge public perspectives on disability. The work of these activists, most notably in Britain and the US, illuminated the magnitude of marginalization and oppression suffered by disabled individuals.[27]

The ADA, a major step in the emancipation of people with disabilities, was the result of activism, not charity. In the United States, the creation of the Independent Living Movement in the 1960s supported self-determination of people with disabilities, while grassroots coalitions fought for legal gains in the courts. A precursor of the ADA, which was signed into legislation in 1990, was the Rehabilitation Act, which was fought for by people in wheelchairs, with canes and guide dogs, often chained to buses to protest their lack of access. It took thousands of people with disabilities, many engaged in civil disobedience, to pass both pieces of legislation.[28]

In the United Kingdom, the Union of the Physically Impaired Against Segregation (UPIAS) fought militantly to remove barriers and create enabling environments. They demanded affordable and accessible housing, better educational opportunities, and accessible transportation. Without them, they claimed, social services are no more than cosmetic amelioration. The UPIAS engaged in a militant form of civic engagement. Protest and acts of civil disobedience take courage, but without them social change never happens. Part of the manifesto of UPIAS illustrates the distinction between amelioration and transformation we invoke. It reads as follows:

> We reject the whole idea of "experts" and professionals holding forth on how we should accept our disabilities, or giving learned lectures about the psychology of impairment. We already know what it feels like to be poor, isolated, segregated, done good to, stared at, and talked down to – far better than any able-bodied expert. We as a union are not interested in descriptions of how awful it is to be disabled. What we are interested in is the ways of changing the conditions of life, and thus overcoming the disabilities which are imposed on top of our physical impairments by the way this society is organized to exclude us.[29]

As Frederick Douglass famously argued in a speech in 1857, "power concedes nothing without a demand." On the same occasion he claimed that "if there is no struggle, there is no progress."[30] Douglass was addressing the issue of Black liberation, but his words are as fresh and applicable today as they were over a century and a half ago.

Every major accomplishment for human liberation in recent memory – the passage of the ADA, civil rights legislation, gay marriage, women's suffrage – has been achieved through struggle. This is why we must make a distinction between amelioration and transformation.[31] While the former is very important, without the latter we are bound to treat symptoms instead of root causes. Both types of action increase mattering, but a passion for amelioration should not detract from the need for transformation.[32] Working within the status quo is much simpler, but it is often when we challenge inequality, oppression, and discrimination that long-term gains are achieved. We must enhance wellness, but not at the expense of fairness.

To make all social action significant and meaningful we suggest, as noted in the Introduction to the book, the concept of *wellfair*, which combines *well*ness with *fair*ness. Whereas wellness is often the target of ameliorative efforts, fairness is the object of transformative ones. *Wellfair* calls for the indivisibility of wellness and fairness, of happiness and justice, of effort and opportunities. *Wellfair* challenges the duality of internal or external change, of personal improvement or social betterment. We must actively embrace the "and"; we must repudiate the "either/or." *Wellfair* calls for meaningful and lasting improvement of the human condition through complementary processes of dealing with inevitable pain and eradicating socially created pain: learning how to thrive as an individual and as a collective. The best way to add value to ourselves and to the world, we argue, is through *wellfair* strategies that eliminate either/or strategies. We must support people with disabilities in their struggle today, but we must also remove barriers for full participation. We must teach people how to cope with inimical conditions and create opportunities for them to be involved in social change at the same time. We realize that today most resources go toward individualistic wellness approaches, but in the absence of fairness models we are destined to forever react to problems without a chance of preventing them in the first place.[33]

In the United States, the lack of fairness in social policy manifested itself in the disproportionate number of Black and Latinx deaths due to COVID-19. These populations suffer from many preexisting conditions, the result of policies that neglected both their wellness and their need for fairness.[34] The pandemic further demonstrates the flaws on relying exclusively on individualistic solutions such as personal responsibility. In places where the "Me Culture" reigns supreme, we saw parties with hundreds of people mingling in close range without any face covering. Prototypical exemplars of a hedonic and egotistical culture, these people were concerned, first and foremost, with their personal freedom and their right to be happy.[35] Adding insult to injury, Trump exploited the debate over masks to fuel the politics of resentment, imploring citizens to "liberate" states where democratic governors were demanding face covering.[36] In the United States, the pandemic exposed the fact that government policies promoted neither wellness nor fairness. Had we espoused a "We Culture," people would have engaged in mutual responsibility as opposed to reckless behavior. We would not have pitted personal liberty against collective wellness. Instead, we would have strived to reach a balance between adding value to self and adding value to others. The colossal failure of the United States to respond appropriately to the pandemic reminds us that the "Me Culture" is wholly incapable to dealing effectively with collective problems.[37] For as long as mattering is defined as the personal right to feel valued and be happy, we will continue to fail as a society. We can only hope that a new generation will balance the right to feel valued with the responsibility to add value, not just to the self but to others. We can only hope that government policy will foster not only individual wellness but also social fairness. In a healthy society, there cannot be wellness for all without fairness for all.[38]

Sources

From the age of twelve until I was sixteen years old, I, Isaac, was very active in a Jewish youth movement in Córdoba, Argentina. This was roughly between 1971 and 1976. There was more than one Jewish movement in town, but I was drawn to the most activist and progressive one – partly because I felt comfortable there, and partly because it was the most popular one among my friends. The movement, called Amos, after the prophet, espoused strong social justice values. We learned there about the history of social justice in Jewish thought and dreamt of making Aliyah, "ascending" to Israel. We planned on joining a kibbutz (collectivist farm) and strengthening the progressive movement in Israel. Tnuat Amos, as it was known by its Hebrew name, was well structured, with multiple weekly activities, from study groups to Friday night discussions, Shabbat activities, sport events, and movie nights. With time, I became a leader in the movement, and Tnuat Amos became not my second but my first home. I spent a lot of time there debating social issues, talking about values, planning theater productions, preparing activities for the younger cohort, and playing lots of soccer. It was a one-stop shop for extracurricular activities. I felt valued, and I had plenty of opportunities to add value.

Perhaps because my parents had died when I was eight years old and at the time I was living only with my two older siblings, I had less adult supervision than the rest of the kids. That meant I had plenty of time to devote to Tnuat Amos. My schoolwork inevitably suffered, but I gained much in terms of the five Cs of civic engagement: confidence, competence, connection, character, and caring.

Pancer identifies several factors that lead to civic engagement of the sort I had in Tnuat Amos. He talks about individual and systemic factors. He identifies social influence, values, and need satisfaction as some of the reasons people engage in communal affairs. I checked all three. My closest friends and my sister were part of the movement, I identified with its values, and there were lots of gains to be made by joining: friends, activities, girls, soccer. Albeit important, these motives were insufficient to join the movement. As Pancer observes, the system must offer appealing programs, a sense of community, and norms of reciprocity and social responsibility.[39] Tnuat Amos provided all of that and more. In these heady days, we were getting ready to change the world. We all developed a strong sense of identity with the cause, which was offering us a healthy counterculture. Instead of dancing, we were learning. Instead of shopping, we were educating the younger generation. We always looked down on teens who wasted time frivolously in parties. We had a world to change, and we could not afford distractions. There was always one more book to read, one more activity to prepare.

All the protective factors that Mark Pancer identified in his book were present in Tnuat Amos: the development of a strong sense of community, the belief in prosocial values, positive identity formation, and the cultivation of leadership skills. But none of these protective elements could shield us from persecution. Anti-Semitism in Argentina was on the rise, and the military was getting ready to stage a coup. The repression of dissent was brutal and often fatal. Tnuat Amos became the perfect target: we were young, leftist, and Jewish. We opposed the military, participated in demonstrations, and showed solidarity with the Argentinian people.

You may be thinking that we were way too young to participate in political demonstrations. After all, we were only in our teens. And you would be right to think this – but when there is so much oppression all around you, it is hard to remain indifferent. The situation came to a boil in 1975, when some of our friends who had participated in demonstrations were either killed or "disappeared." If you distributed a pamphlet opposing the government, it was enough reason to shoot first and ask questions later. Eventually, we learned that paramilitary groups "disappeared" 30,000 people – many of them young, many of them Jewish – in what came to be known as the dirty war.[40]

The situation created divisions within Tnuat Amos. Many of our senior leaders, in their late teens and early twenties, felt that as Argentinians we had a duty to join the resistance. We had to fight state terrorism. Others thought that, as Jews, our moral obligation was to move to Israel and contribute to the building of a progressive state. This division resulted in a massive exodus of our leaders. They joined local movements and abandoned Zionist ideals. My sister Miriam was one of them. She joined a resistance organization with her husband in 1975. After that, she went missing for months. I had already moved to Israel in January 1976, when rumors circulated that she was in jail. Nobody knew for sure.

Then, in March 1976, all of a sudden, she appeared on TV at a press conference. She had been pushed into a deal with the devil. The choices were to repent on TV or end up at the bottom of the River Plate, like many others. She chose the former, and so she was exiled instead of executed. That was the last time that she was seen in public for seven years: we didn't know whether she was dead or alive. My sister's story later became the subject of a documentary, *Cuentas del Alma*, which more or less translates into Soulful Reflections. In it, she describes the tremendous pressure that she felt to join a clandestine organization to oppose the regime. Peer pressure is a very effective tactic to get people to do all kinds of things. In her case, it resulted in a series of traumatic events. Nobody can deny that my sister had agency, and she could have said no to deeper and more dangerous involvement in politics. She acknowledged that much in the documentary. But it is also true that, as a 21-year-old, it was hard for her to say no to her husband, who led the charge. This is a reminder that joining a social cause can be a dangerous proposition. How much to push for change? How deeply to get involved? What is at stake? In Argentina, these were questions of life or death.

The last few months of 1975 were extremely dangerous. More than once, when there were rumors that the police was planning a raid, we had to rush to Amos to burn "subversive" books or throw them down the drain. I still remember walking away from our locale trying to find a drain big enough on the street to dump books.

During these tumultuous times the younger members of Amos felt deserted. Our senior leaders had all but abandoned us. I remained loyal to the Zionist ideal of moving to Israel, and – along with a few friends and supportive parents – we called the Jewish Agency to help us. In a matter of weeks we organized a move to Israel. We fled Argentina in January 1976, but many friends remained behind. That year the police made a few visits to my brother Mario, who was not involved in politics at all but who was harassed nonetheless. He also packed his bags and moved to Israel that summer. Two months after I had arrived in Israel we heard that my sister had been jailed and that she had appeared on TV. That started a frantic search that lasted seven years. We eventually found her in Paraguay in 1983. A few months later she joined my brother and me in Israel.

I moved to Israel with my girlfriend, Vivi Solodky, whose parents were very supportive of our move. My girlfriend's sister, Monica, like mine, deserted Zionist ideals and joined the local opposition. Monica and her husband, Hugo Donemberg, stayed in Argentina. On April 29, 1976, a right-wing death squad knocked on the door of their apartment.[41] They kidnapped Hugo and told Monica, who was pregnant at the time, to say goodbye to him because she was never going to see him again. Monica was whisked away by her parents and arrived in Israel, pregnant, a few days later. Hugo was never found.

He was not the only friend who was killed. Alejandra Jaimovich, a school friend, was apprehended in June 1976 at the age of seventeen and killed a few weeks later in detention.[42] Ricardo Levin, brother-in-law of my best friend, Beto Chucrel, was killed during a demonstration. Hugo, Alejandra, and Ricardo were the victims of state terrorism closest to me, but there were thousands who suffered a similar fate. Democracy returned to Argentina in 1983, but not before scores of young people had been tortured or killed. Fascism and anti-Semitism took a toll on all of us. It is estimated that 12 percent of the victims were Jewish.[43]

All of us wanted to make a difference in our country. We wanted democracy over dictatorship, freedom over oppression, prosperity over poverty. Many of our friends paid with their lives. Many others still live with traumatic memories. Families were destroyed. Alejandra's parents, Luis and Elena Jaimovich, went through hell as people demanded bribes from them in exchange for leads.[44] People exploited their desperation and often fabricated leads just to get money. Our own aunt, Eusebia Kotliroff, who raised us after my parents' death, recriminated herself for "allowing" this to happen. She felt guilty that she did not prevent my sister's involvement in politics. Luckily, my aunt had a chance to see my sister alive, seven years after the famous press conference.

The encounter with my sister was as dramatic and unexpected as her disappearance and her reappearance on TV. On a Saturday in late 1983, the phone rang in our apartment in Ramat Gan in Israel. Ora and I had been recently married. Ora picked up the phone and thought that it was a wrong number. Someone was speaking in Spanish. She nearly hung up when she realized that the person at the other end of the line might be my sister. She yelled, "Isaac, run to the phone." Like a bullet, I shot to the phone, and there she was, on the other end of line, alive. We spoke for a few moments, and I was able to ascertain that it was her, that she was fine, and that years of agony had come to an end. She could not share much on the phone though. She was afraid that she was under surveillance, and she never knew when someone might be listening. She had crossed the border from Paraguay to Brazil to make the phone call.

Miriam knew our phone number because we were asked to send her a letter. My brother Mario had initiated contact with a human rights lawyer in Argentina. Through his auspices we were able to establish contact with our sister. At first, we were told to send her a letter with our contact information. Several months passed by without a reply. Then, all of a sudden, the phone call.

Ora was supporting Aunt Eusebia, who nearly fainted, when Miriam arrived in the Ben Gurion Airport in Tel Aviv. All our family was there. At the time, there was a wide window where family members could see their loved ones approach the exit. Due to security reasons the window was eventually blocked, but at the time we could see our relatives and friends get closer and closer. There she was, after seven years of doubt, fears, and trauma – we had recovered her. No sooner did Miriam settle in our place than she decided to stay in Israel.

Since she was forced to repent on TV, she was told by the military that her former comrades wanted nothing to do with her and that it would be dangerous for her to establish any communication with family or friends. She was sent to exile in Paraguay with $50 and an assumed identity: Analía Rosales. When Ora and I met, Ora had asked me about my family. You can imagine her surprise when I responded that my parents had died when I was eight years old and that I did not know whether my sister was dead or alive.

In thinking about the sources of civic and political involvement, parents, peers, religious congregation, and school exert great influence on our first forays into community participation.[45] Values are important too. If we get our needs satisfied, we are likely to stay engaged, but to sustain our involvement we must assume a meaningful role, create a sense of community, and find purpose in our actions. In democratic societies, political engagement does not render you at risk. In totalitarian regimes, as we saw in Argentina, it brings you close to a bullet. To defend democracy in dictatorships a great deal of courage is required. To fight for freedom in oppressive regimes is dangerous. We have to thank all those who came before us for the freedoms we enjoy. As we write this, the world celebrates the hundredth anniversary of the birth of Nelson Mandela, one of these giants who made the world a better place.

Like Mandela, Dr. Martin Luther King Jr., Gandhi, Rosa Parks, and Ella Baker showed great determination and courage. In many cases, the personal price was enormous. Mandela spent twenty-seven years in prison; Dr. King was assassinated. In many ways, these role models embodied the struggle for fairness, and throughout history there have always been heroes ready to stand up to power and injustice. While the historical record is full of examples, now there seems to be evidence that morality is a basic psychological need.

In a series of studies published in 2019, Mike Prentice and his colleagues showed that the need to experience moral feelings was as strong as the desire for autonomy, competence, relatedness, and self-esteem. Moral feelings were defined as the extent to which participants (1) experienced a strong sense of moral fulfilment, (2) felt they were a good person, (3) embodied moral values, and (4) thought that they did the right thing. In addition to demonstrating that the presence of moral sentiments was a human need, moral need satisfaction was also "positively correlated with flourishing." In a similar vein, the study showed that "morality positively predicted both positive affect and quality of life."[46] Taken as a whole, Prentice's studies provide evidence that people value making a contribution and behaving ethically. This moral impulse complements the other factors identified by Pancer as sources of civic engagement: peer and family influence, value congruence, need satisfaction, norms of social responsibility, effective organizational structures, sense of community, and engaging programs.

As we shall see in the next section, not all forms of civic engagement lead to similar outcomes. Some types reinforce the societal status quo, while others challenge it. Some civic organizations reinforce a "Me Culture"; others aim to create a "We Culture." Civic participation is generally a positive attribute of communities, and, as we saw in Prentice's research, people have a need to do the right thing. However, we should be cautious not to engage in settings that blame the victim and render structures of injustice unaltered.

Strategies

When Anu Partanen moved to the United States from Finland, she was excited to join her American boyfriend and start a family in New York.[47]

She was thrilled to become part of a culture of ingenuity, entrepreneurship, and awesome achievements in business, education, science, and the arts. She was intrigued by the American dream. She had been a journalist in Finland, without plans to leave the country, until she met Trevor, an American writer with whom she fell in love. Trevor would find the dark and long Finnish winters too harsh, whereas Anu could get used to American weather and culture. The decision was made; they would marry and live together in the United States.

Coming from Finland in 2010, which at the time was ranked by *Newsweek* as the best country in the world, Partanen was in a position to reflect on the virtues and vices of both countries.[48] In 2018, Finland was again at the top of international rankings, this time as the happiest country in the world. The United States, in contrast, was ranked eighteenth, down four places from 2017.[49] Partanen's reflections on both cultures can help us understand the sources of mattering in the community. Her analysis points to two key factors affecting levels of mattering in the community: *cultural discourse* and *material resources.*

The cultural discourse in America is that, if you work hard enough, the sky is the limit. This narrative is reinforced daily by stories of fame and fortune. Embedded in these stories is the insidious message that these people succeed because of their high levels of motivation, grit, determination, and perseverance. Athletes train day and night; entrepreneurs get up at 4 am and work ninety hours per week. Although Partanen found the stories inspiring, she also found them depressing. In America, the message goes, if you don't succeed it is entirely your fault. After all, Oprah Winfrey came from humble beginnings, and she made billions. The same with Tony Robbins. These stories penetrate the popular psyche.

The inevitable comparison between your own sorry state and the fortune of celebrities leave you depressed and anxious about your abilities. The perception that you can make it in America, regardless of your background, and the reality that you have not yet made it creates a lot of inner tension. Ceaseless comparisons remind you that you're not there yet.[50] There is a big gap between the actual and the ideal. This chasm causes stress and anxiety.[51] In comparison to all the other people at work, in the community, and the media who seem to have made it, you're far from success. A culture that extols individual achievement and suppresses consideration of privilege is bound to deflate the sense of mattering of those who, for whatever reason, have not yet prospered.[52]

In a context of vast inequalities, constant comparisons, garnished with self-blame, form a recipe for disaster. You end up feeling devalued, by yourself and others. Partanen went through this process herself, blaming her inadequacies for not adjusting well to America. She went from upward comparisons to status anxiety to self-blame to low sense of personal worth. You don't have to be Finnish – or any kind of immigrant – to succumb to these forces. Millions of people suffer from this sequence of events. But this is not the whole story.

Material resources also make a big difference in mattering. In Finland, Partanen had all her basic needs met by the government. She enjoyed great universal health care, went to school in the best educational system in the world, and had great work benefits, such as five weeks of paid vacation. Her pregnant friends enjoyed ten months of paid maternity leave. For sure, people paid more taxes in Finland, but everyone had excellent medical care, free education, and more than satisfactory pension plans. In contrast, in the United States, millions of people live below the poverty line, have no health insurance whatsoever, cannot afford to take maternity leave, and cannot secure quality childcare.

Since the United States is supposed to be the land of opportunity and the American dream, you are to make it on your own first and then pay for all these necessities yourself. But for many, looking after health insurance and paying for day care and private school is not a dream but a nightmare. As Partanen compared the levels of stress between her American and Finnish friends, she was stunned by the level of strain of the former and the comfort of the latter.

Partanen suffered not just from status anxiety but from material worries as well. Whereas Finland offered great help to new parents like herself, the American system turned out to be a complicated patchwork of private day care and medical providers. Unless you have a lot of family support, in America you're on your own: trying to go back to work after six weeks of unpaid maternity leave, finding decent day care, and making sense of medical bills. These hassles characterize middle-class life, but if you are poor you can multiply these stressors tenfold. In Finland, the government will help you while you are out of work. In the United States, unemployment benefits will take you below the poverty line real fast.

It is not just nice or nasty people who make you feel that you matter or don't. It is not just dreadful bosses, like the one Linda Tirado had, or White supremacists who make you feel unwanted; it is the entire system that makes you feel like you don't matter.

Partanen makes it clear that both Nordic and American cultures want to promote liberty and expressive individualism. They both want you to pursue your goals. The big difference is that Nordic countries invest in social systems to enable social mobility, whereas the American model wants you to take student loans, pay for private day care, and get some form of health insurance. The former frees you up to pursue your dreams; the latter encumbers you with debt and worry. Social mobility, to wit, is worse in the United States than in most other developed countries.[53]

Intrigued by the different routes to happiness taken by Nordic and American cultures, Partanen consulted Lars Trägårdh, who had come to the United States for college from Sweden. He obtained a PhD in history from UC Berkeley and taught college in the United States for several years. When it was time to raise a family, Lars decided to return to Sweden. Partanen asked him why he chose to leave the United States. Trägårdh's answers reflect the cultural discourse of comparison and competition, on one hand, and the material resources required to raise children on the other. He observed that in Sweden kids are allowed to be kids, whereas in New York his friends are fretting about having their four-year-olds tested in school. In a context of constant comparison and competition starting early in life, the chances of feeling bad about yourself multiply. Trägårdh wanted to protect his kids from that environment. (Sweden, by the way, is ranked ninth in terms of happiness, way ahead than the United States.)

But it was not just cultural reasons that sent him back to Sweden. The public schools left much to be desired, and the cost of private education became prohibitive. His friends back in New York complain about the cost of private education and college. In his view, it is impossible to foster social mobility without investments in schools, health, and communities. Unless you do that, "you're going to end up with inequality, gated communities, collapse of trust, a dysfunctional political system. All these things you see now in the United States."[54]

When social problems emerge, like the ones listed by Trägårdh, Finns respond very differently from Americans. Finns demand social change, whereas Americans expect personal development. As Partanen observed, when Finns perceive an injustice, they

> are quick to demand real changes that improve their external circumstances. Where an American today might be inclined to turn inward, meditate, and nurture positive thinking, a Finn is going to go yell at the politicians until something gets fixed. No one would recommend that we all go around focusing only on our problems and challenges.[55]

What Americans need, according to Partanen, is quite simple: a living wage, day care, affordable health care, quality education, and paid vacations.[56] The absence of any one of these resources can be devastating.

Economic scarcity, for example, is going to focus the mind so intently on that particular need that we end up neglecting others. Ironically, this creates a vicious cycle where the lack of economic resources prevents us from doing other things that would help us get out of poverty, such as better financial planning or getting an education. Just as a lack of food prevents us from thinking about the benefits of a healthier diet, a lack of time to complete assignments prevents us from thinking about better time management. As we saw earlier, this is the scarcity effect.

Scarcity has the effect of focusing the mind singularly on unfulfilled needs. "For the hungry, that need is food. For the busy it might be a project that needs to be finished. For the cash-strapped it might be this month's rent payment; for the lonely, a lack of companionship."[57] Scarcity creates a lock in our psyche. This is how economist Sendhil Mullainathan from Harvard and psychologist Eldar Shafir from Princeton describe the phenomenon. We return to what we lack time and again, preventing us from focusing on other things that are good for us and that could prevent our predicament in the first place. This results in *tunneling*, or reduced bandwidth. Fasting on Yom Kippur reduces bandwidth. Living in poverty for a while limits cognitive resources. Loneliness results in limited bandwidth as much as hunger. The lonely focuses on social connections and the hungry on food. The busy person also suffers from reduced mental capacity.

The paradoxical nature of scarcity is that it creates more of itself. If you are struggling with paying the rent, you may not have a lot of headspace to plan expenses more carefully. Mullainathan and Shafir call it a *bandwidth tax*. You are deficient on something, so much so that you fail to make a plan how to get out of it. Scarcity perpetuates scarcity – what they call the *scarcity trap*. This explains why busy people remain busy, why the lonely remains lonely, and why poor people have a hard time getting out poverty. Scarcity leads us to focus so much on one thing, working hard for instance to pay the rent, that we neglect other areas of life which could help us in the long run. If I'm short on time, focusing on a deadline can help me finish the project by tomorrow, but I'm neglecting other things that can help me in the long run, such as better planning. Running short on cash leads me to get a short-term loan with high interest rates. If I had more time to plan and fewer emergencies, I could think of getting a loan with better interest rates, but the pressing need leads people to make decisions that are not necessarily helpful in the long run.

For the poor in particular, scarcity is a big problem. Not only do they work multiple jobs to pay the bills, but they are often exploited by lenders who charge exorbitant interest rates. High interest rates only deepens their plight. Unexpected emergencies, such as the cost of medication for a sick child, forces them to get another high interest loan, since they have no savings. This treadmill impacts not only their economic well-being but their interpersonal, communal, and physical well-being as well. When you work multiple shifts there is no time to do homework with your kids or read them a bedtime story, let alone volunteer in the community or visit a friend.

Lack of time and lack of headspace are two reasons why poor people refrain from participating in community events. But status anxiety plays a role as well, especially in unequal countries. Civic engagement is much lower in high inequality states.[58] The reason for this is that people are afraid to interact with others and to be judged. Poor people live with a constant stereotype threat. This is why people avoid socially threatening situations and refrain from participating in community life.

Poverty affects people materially, socially, cognitively, and psychologically. "Poverty means scarcity in the very commodity that underpins almost all other aspects of life."[59] You are always juggling balls, and you go from one crisis to the next because you don't have enough slack. There is no buffer zone. You feel easily overwhelmed, worrying about the next bill. The result of this scarcity is diminished ways to feel valued in the family, at work, and in the community. To understand the daily routine of poor people, Mullainathan and Shafir ask us to imagine ourselves distracted, with lack of sleep, unable to think lucidly. This is a difficult psychological tax to contend with.

Linda Tirado offers a first-person account of living in poverty and scarcity in the United States: juggling two jobs in restaurants where your bosses treat you like dirt, walking miles from job to job to avoid the cost of transportation, spending your free day looking for a better job, getting home to a decrepit rental, trying to fix the plumbing, dealing with unscrupulous landlords, and worrying about your kid's toothache. You live from crisis to crisis, just trying to keep your head above water. Tirado writes that her mind is always preoccupied with sudden termination of jobs, reduced working hours, childcare, and a million chores.[60] Any of us, under similar stressors, would succumb to these circumstances. The contextual forces would impose a bandwidth tax on any of us. We would also tunnel on the immediate needs and find no time or headspace to nourish ourselves or to feel like we matter.

There is overwhelming evidence that mattering derives from feeling valued, useful, and appreciated. The more resources we have – time, money, relationships, calmness, mental clarity – the more opportunities we have to interact with others in the community in ways that would make us feel like we matter. On the other hand, scarcity of any kind – time, education, health, money, relationships, or peace of mind – will interfere with our ability to participate meaningfully in the community, minimizing opportunities for mattering.

Scarcity, material and cultural, are more prevalent in unequal societies. Although the poor are especially afflicted by scarcity, income differences affect all of us. Large income inequality is associated with lower levels of trust and higher levels of stress.[61]

How, then, do we change society? How do we go about shifting the cultural paradigm from "Me" to "We"? There are two BET I CAN drivers of change that can help: *Awareness* and *Next Steps*. The first principle of Awareness is *know the issue*.

Know the Issue

The issue at stake is two different approaches to mattering, "Me" and "We," with two different modes of intervention. The "Me Culture" endorses ameliorative solutions, whereas the "We Culture" espouses trans-formative ones. These are two very different routes to mattering in the community. Amelioration is an effort to fix symptoms without getting to the root cause of the problem. It seeks to put on a Band-Aid and to demand individual change to adapt to external conditions. Instead of eradicating the source of the problem it seeks to alleviate the pain caused by it. Think of pay equity for women. It is much better to do away with bias and discrimination than to teach women how to be assertive and demand equal pay. Think of health care. It is far superior to make sure that everyone is provided universal and preventive health care rather than treating people in the emergency room when it's too little too late. The same goes for poverty. Societies with policies that reduce levels of poverty and inequality are healthier than those that expect the poor to lift themselves by their bootstraps.

In all these cases, the transformative option requires changes in fairness. The ameliorative choice requires people to adjust to unjust conditions, to learn wellness techniques. The "Me" paradigm relies on ameliorative cures; the "We" approach relies on transformative solutions that challenge power differentials and oppressive systems. Whereas the former focuses on the acquisition of personal skills such as assertiveness and mindfulness, the latter seeks to empower citizens to take control over their lives and end exploitation.

As Chief Judge of the United States Court of Appeals for the District of Columbia from 1962 to 1978, David L. Bazelon often commented on social issues.[62] In an address to correctional psychologists, he gave a poignant example of the difference between ameliorative and transformative approaches. He told the audience that "in considering our motives for offering you a role, I think you would do well to consider how much less expensive it is to hire a thousand psychologists than to make even a miniscule change in the social and economic structure."[63]

Since many people confuse amelioration with transformation, it is crucial to know which is which. Otherwise we think we are improving the community when in fact we are reinforcing the status quo through interventions that never challenge injustice and never address root causes. Linda Stout, founder of the Piedmont Peace Project in North Carolina, contends that people often confuse social change with social service. People end up treating symptoms instead of root causes. She argues that it is tempting to react to the nearest emergency instead of looking at systemic causes. Stout knows the difference between amelioration and transformation. She worked with poor people on voter registration and literacy and with LGBTQ groups on civil rights. She saw firsthand the limitations of Band-Aid approaches. She states that "people often think social service . . . is all that is needed to fix things. This kind of service is important, but it falls short of changing the systemic oppression that is the root of the problem. Social service is not the same as organizing people for social change. Providing services does not result in social change."[64] If we are to heed Linda Stout's warning, we must shift the paradigm from social services to social change, and from amelioration to transformation.

While amelioration seeks to treat the victims of the system, transformation seeks to change the system itself. We should resist the temptation to dismiss this as fringe activist talk. Similar views were expressed by the US Institute of Medicine in a landmark report. Its authors recommend the endorsement of a "social environmental approach to health and health intervention." The co-chairs of the committee wrote:

> Societal-level phenomena are critical determinants of health . . . Stress, insufficient financial and social supports, poor diet, environmental exposures, community factors and characteristics, and many other health risks may be addressed by one-to-one intervention efforts, but such efforts do little to address the broader social and economic forces that influence these risks.[65]

The Institute of Medicine is challenging the narrow focus on downstream individual factors such as lifestyle and biochemical sources of illness. Instead, it is advocating for upstream approaches that include changes in health-care policies, housing support, and educational opportunities. These societal changes improve not only health but mattering as well – and for them to take place, power must be contested. Those who resist universal health care must be confronted. Those who oppose adequate minimum wage must be challenged. These issues go to the heart of mattering as a citizen. No amount of resilience, grit, mindfulness, and assertiveness training can replace the dignity granted by access to basic human rights. Immediately following the passage of civil rights legislation in the United States, there was significant improvement in the cardiovascular health of African American women.[66]

It is worth noting that governments and corporate elites reward reformers, not transformers. Advocates of amelioration are always seen in a favorable light, whereas champions of transformation are regarded as troublemakers. It makes sense, since the latter question structures of power and the elite that benefit from them. In his 2018 book *Winners Take All: The Elite Charade of Changing the World*, Anand Giridharadas investigates the way in which plutocrats, financiers, and defenders of the status quo construct grandiose narratives of change that are ameliorative at best and damaging at worst.[67] The ruling elite embrace thinkers who frame social and political problems as personal problems and who focus on the victim of injustice as opposed to the perpetrator. They prefer to talk about poverty instead of injustice or inequality. They refrain from confrontational talk. Gatekeepers such as publishers, editors, and curators for TED Talks and the Aspen Institute shape solutions to social problems this way.

Instead of the feminist motto that the "personal is political," the most admired solutions today are those that make the political personal. In other words, if you suffer from discrimination and sexism, the best you can do is to develop "coping strategies" as opposed to challenging inequality. This is what we called earlier *It's all in your head*. The second way to ingratiate yourself as a thinker with the elite is to propose solutions that focus on the victim and not the perpetrator. You can empathize with the victim and offer them training to become more resilient, but never question the legitimacy of powerholders. Giridharadas observes that if you want to become a thought leader, your job is to convince the public that systemic problems are really personal problems. He argues that it is a question of focus. If you want to ingratiate yourself with protectors of the status quo, your job is to concentrate on personal deficiencies, not structural ones. He claims:

It is possible to look at a street corner in Baltimore and zoom in on low-hanging pants as the problem. It is possible to zoom out and see the problem as overpolicing and a lack of opportunity in the inner city. It is possible to zoom out further and see the problem as the latest chapter in a centuries-long story of the social control of African Americans.[68]

If you want to rub shoulders with the elite defending the status quo, your narrative must zoom in on the person. Zooming out is too threatening.

Elites love a reformer. They are the embodiment of the ameliorative approach. Amelioration is asocial and apolitical. It aims to improve the world through personal effort devoid of power struggles. With help from psychology, today we see a retreat from efforts to improve wellness through social change.[69] Instead, we see a thriving industry of inward-looking therapies in the form of mindfulness and the cultivation of grit and resilience. These are no doubt necessary but insufficient conditions for mattering. We practice mindfulness meditation in our family and see the value of perseverance. Many people embrace these approaches because they are very seductive. You can meditate anywhere, and you can practice impulse control in just about every realm of life, from eating to shouting. What's more, they work.[70] However, they don't work for everyone, and they don't solve all the problems we face. Because of the scarcity effect, some people just do not have the headspace to devote time and effort to mindfulness. Ask Linda Tirado if she had mental space for this sort of thing. With multiple jobs, no money for rent, no transportation, and all the indignities associated with being poor, her hard drive is full. For people like Linda to experience wellness, she needs a heavy dose of fairness in her life.

Know Yourself

Now that we have explored the issue, the first principle of *awareness*, we should follow the command *know yourself.* Depending on their status in society, people will relate differently to the status quo. If they are privileged, they will likely extol the virtues of hard work and merit. They might even behave in entitled ways, as has been amply demonstrated.[71] They will definitely invest in their wellness and expect to feel valued by society. In some cases, they will accentuate class differences through the purchase of material goods and shiny objects. Their economic superiority will be bolstered. Inequality works for them. Since they are privileged, they benefit from the "Me Culture" and have no interest in challenging it. But if they think that material goods and an obsession with their worth is their ticket to happiness, they're in for a big surprise. It may feel good momentarily to buy more toys or to demand respect on account of their privilege, but research has found that this is not the ticket to meaning and mattering.[72]

For people who are not privileged, the "Me Culture" will hit them especially hard, since they will feel devalued. If they are poor, Black, disabled, or elderly, they will experience the double whammy of economic disadvantage and psychological devaluation.

In theory, looking after yourself, claiming your rights, and demanding respect are all good things. But in the absence of balancing forces they degenerate into selfishness and entitled behavior. The four essential ingredients of the "Me Culture" – self, rights, wellness, and feeling valued – must be tempered with a focus on others, responsibility, fairness, and adding value.

The shift from "Me" to "We" starts with being aware of your status in society – your relative privilege. Since the current approach to mattering focuses on wellness without fairness, a useful goal is to find out how wellness and fairness impact your feelings of worth in the community. If you feel valued, respected, and appreciated, ask yourself what wellness skills help you achieve that state; and what fairness dynamics support your sense of mattering. Wellness skills include emotional intelligence, empathy, and social sensitivity. Fairness dynamics include resources you have access to, power to claim your piece of the pie, and voice and choice.

Make a plan. Fighting for a fair system can bring about benefits for you and others. There is evidence that political activism leads to improved psychological well-being.[73] Activism enhances a sense of control over your life and combats helplessness and hopelessness. It is an empowering way to change the cues, not just in your immediate environment but in society at large. To improve our sense of mattering in the community and support others in their quest, we must join a cause. As we shall see next, mattering is not a spectator sport. We must participate in the process of creating a culture where *we all have the right* and *responsibility to feel valued* and *add value, to self* and *others, to experience wellness* and *fairness.*

To improve mattering for all in the community, we have to *make a plan.* There are three essential steps to transformative change in the community: *join, organize,* and *reflect.* To *make it stick,* this three-step plan must include a sustainability strategy, which comes from simply making sure that everyone in the process feels valued and has an opportunity to add value.

Join in ways that matter. Transformative change in the community requires collective effort.[74] Social change is the quintessential team sport.

You must join an organization, a government, or a social movement to create lasting change. When you join an organization to pursue a social cause, such as advancing the rights of people with disabilities or securing universal health care, you have two key responsibilities: to make sure everyone *within* the organization feels valued and adds value; and to make sure your partners *outside* the organization also feel valued and add value. In short, your job is to ascertain that everyone matters, your peers within and your partners without.

Coalition building, network creation, and collaborative solutions require that all partners feel like they matter. Without them, you are lost. In books like *Join the Club*, *Forces for Good*, and *Principles for Social Change*,[75] authors document the imperative of building networks in efforts to improve social conditions. It is a sine qua non.

You may think that joining a group or a social movement is all about the external cause. After all, you share similar values – no need to worry about the people within the organization because they all join voluntarily to pursue the common good. Big mistake! You cannot treat people within the organization as if they don't matter because you are all engaged in some bigger good. As reviewed in Chapter 8, the most effective teams are those in which people are socially responsive to others and take turns to participate. The best teams also had a higher proportion of women.[76] Ironically, women are sometimes marginalized in social change movements.

Linda Stout of the Piedmont Peace Project, whom we met earlier in this chapter, grew up in disadvantage. She was poor and did not have the type of education she wanted. Among her activist peers she was different. She was lesbian in a mostly straight culture. As an activist, she knew that opposing the police and the government would not be easy. What she was not prepared for was the marginalization she would experience within progressive social movements. Although she was a superb organizer and advocate for the poor, she had a harder time with her partners than with outside opponents. This is how Linda expressed her disappointment:

> Usually without intending it or seeing it, middle-class progressive people behave in ways that disempower low-income and working class folks; Whites do the same to people of color, men to women and heterosexuals to gay, lesbian and bisexual folks.[77]

Ijeoma Oluo[78] shares similar concerns when social justice movements privilege one identity over others, dismissing the rights of groups with less power and privilege. Activists and agents of social change do not check their psychological needs at the door. Treating them in dismissive ways is intrinsically wrong and extrinsically stupid. No coalition is built on animosity and marginalization of players. You do not need to be the leader in a group to care about the feelings of people in the organization. That would be narrow-minded. Everyone has a role in making sure that people within the settings feel like they matter, that people you partner with also feel valued and respected, and, ultimately, that the people whose lives you are trying to improve feel like they matter, both in the process and in the outcomes of change.

If you join a group just to get flattery, you may diminish its efforts. If you expect other people to do the "nurturing" work you are shortsighted. It is incumbent on all agents of change to guarantee the sense of mattering of activists. Do not expect just women to do the caring work or some committee to look into the touchy-feely stuff. Mattering is real, its consequences are real, and ignoring it is tantamount to wanting activists to act like robots.

Organize in ways that balance process with outcomes. Jonathan Smucker was brought up on a Mennonite farm close to the small town of Bird-In-Hand in Lancaster County, Pennsylvania. His family was quite conservative, and his life revolved around family and church services, which he attended a few times a week. Jonathan was not a particularly good student. By his own account, he spent way too much time playing video games and watching television. He had no knowledge of politics or sensitivity to issues of social injustice. But his background as a Mennonite would cause him to read the Bible, first as an obligation and later out of interest. He discovered that social and economic justice was a central theme in the Bible and that "Jesus Christ had apparently spouted off about it two thousand years ago. And apparently it got him killed."[79]

Jonathan was inspired by the prophets who challenged the rich and powerful and stood next to the poor and the oppressed. According to Jonathan, reading the gospels he found "a front-and-center emphasis on social justice in the here and now, but at church I heard mostly about individual salvation for a select few in the hereafter."[80]

His insights from biblical passages would soon give rise to a life of activism. Following various projects, Jonathan found himself in the middle of the Occupy movement, demanding justice for the 99 percent and decrying the power of the 1 percent. Despite its momentum, Occupy disappointed him and many others who saw an opportunity to build coalitions to create a power base. There was so much emphasis on participatory processes that few outcomes were ever achieved. On its face, participatory democracy is a good thing. Participation is about voice and choice, the royal path to mattering. But in true "Me Culture" fashion, the process was all about the interests of a few individuals and small groups and not really about accomplishing political goals that would benefit everyone in society.

Like Jonathan, many activists were disillusioned with the inward gaze of Occupy. The refusal to compromise led many to drop out. The precious identity of the activists, and some small factions within the movement, took priority over coalition and network building. People were demanding the right to be heard without being willing to take responsibility for action. In Australia, some of our colleagues would call this type of gathering a "talk fest." One of our colleagues here in Miami often says that "we've admired the problem long enough." Time and energy are finite resources, and, after interminable meetings with no clear direction, Occupy just dissipated, vanished.

The right to be heard, an unquestionable part of mattering, can be taken to extremes. Occupy was an extreme case of people wanting to feel valued for their opinions. This was done to such an extent that little or no attention was paid to the demands and strategies that come with the responsibility to add value, not just to the participants but to all members of society, and especially the folks who are marginalized. The wellness of the process took precedence over the fairness of the outcomes.

The state of Kerala in India provides an example where political parties and social movements managed to keep their eye on the ball. Multiple pressure groups have worked together and separately to achieve concessions for the working poor. For over a century now, the struggle to make Kerala fair and just for women and children has resulted in enviable results. Although the activists came from many corners, including labor unions and political parties, they managed to create a common set of demands that produced results. The good of the whole prevailed over the particular interests of sectarian groups. Some of the policy changes made include land reform, income equalization, legislation to improve social security and pensions, free primary and secondary education, access to price-controlled food, enhanced participation of women in the workforce, and enforcement of labor laws for children and youth. Although at first it seemed that these massive investments in public services would hamper economic prosperity, this has not been the case.[81]

Kerala does much better than the rest of India on many indicators of human development. For example, 98 percent of children aged six to fourteen in Kerala are in school, compared to 80 percent in India. Literacy for women aged fifteen to forty-nine is 93 percent in Kerala and only 55 percent in the rest of the country. When it comes to people living below the poverty line, the rate is 20 percent in Kerala, compared to 37 percent in India. In 2004–2005, the median income per person in Kerala was 80 percent higher than in the rest of the nation. Kerala has the highest Human Development Index score in India, 0.712 in 2015; the highest life expectancy, at seventy-seven years; and the highest literacy rate, at 93.91 percent in 2011. It also has the highest sex ratio: 1,084 women per 1,000 men. In terms of homicides, Kerala has the lowest rate among Indian states, with 1.1 per 100,000 in 2011. The infant mortality rate in Kerala is much lower than in India: 13 per 1,000 and 65 per 1,000 live births, respectively.[82]

Kerala also boasts excellent results in many public health indices such as better immunization rates and lower indices of cholera and malaria than the rest of the country. In addition, Kerala is considered healthier than many states in the United States, which lacks a universal health-care program.[83] In light of its very effective promotion of breast-feeding programs (over formula), the United Nations Children's Fund (UNICEF) and the World Health Organization (WHO) have designated Kerala the world's first baby-friendly state. It is worth noting that all these changes do not just derive from the supply side. The poor majority has been educated on what to demand – and demand they have.

The Kerala case is interesting because it started investing in human development and quality of life before it experienced economic growth. Many skeptics thought that these voluminous investments in public health and social services would cost the economy greatly, but it turns out that there is not a trade-off between quality of life and economic growth. On the contrary.

Focused attention on results helped social movements, human service organizations, nonprofits, and government officials to achieve better levels of wellness and fairness for all people in Kerala. This was a very political and transformative process. Lives were saved because of the power struggles mounted by women and labor unions. The focus was not on what the powerless can do better (power poses, mindfulness) but on what the powerful can do differently (land reform, universal health care, free education, pension plans).

Reflect to learn from experience. PICO (Pacific Institute of Community Organizations) was founded in 1972 by Father John Baumann, a Jesuit priest.[84] Baumann had learned community organizing in Chicago before moving to California, where PICO got started. The organization changed its name to Faith in Action in 2018 to reflect its national, faith-based nature. Faith in Action consists of forty-four affiliated federations and eight statewide networks operating in 150 cities in seventeen states. This is a community-organizing network that brings citizens together to demand social cures and not just mind cures. It advocates for more resources for children, families, and people with addictions. It also mobilizes people to reduce crime and help people in poor neighborhoods.

Faith in Action is very successful in engaging its members and volunteers. More than a million families and a thousand congregations participate in action-oriented campaigns. They work to hold corporations accountable, increase voter turnout, eliminate racial and economic discrimination, and pass legislation to improve affordable housing, education, health care, and the criminal justice system. It mobilizes citizens for rallies, facilitates town halls, gathers information, leverages the media, and confronts politicians with difficult questions.

The list of its accomplishments is impressive.[85] Among many other successes, it led a $190 million public bond initiative for school infrastructure in California, prompted Minneapolis to stop school suspensions for nonaggressive behavior, secured $9 million for the treatment and prevention of substance abuse, defeated a proposal by the mayor of Indianapolis to build a new prison and immigration detention center, and supported law enforcement reform in many communities.

Faith in Action believes that "everyone belongs and that our fates are bound up with one another's."[86] It balances a good interpersonal process with a focus on tangible gains. Parallel to the three steps offered here, *join, organize*, and *reflect*, Faith in Action follows three principles:

- Social power is built on the strength of interpersonal relationships
- Empowerment can only be realized through organizing
- Empowerment must be grounded in a dialectic of action and reflection

The last and crucial principle is about reflection. Faith in Action learns from successes and failures. Some important lessons in organizing derive from Occupy and Kerala. Occupy failed because it valued a participatory process more than a focused approach on results. The people of Kerala won major concessions and massive investments in human development because they came together in broad-based coalitions. Faith in Action knows how to engage people, how to keep them involved, and how to achieve resources for the community.

Another lesson from Occupy is the inability to compromise and find common ground. The purity of identity movements gets in the way of building a strong power base. In an effort to overcome this fatal shortcoming, a group of activist, scientists, writers, and artists got together in

Toronto in 2015 to devise a common platform for transformative change. Mindful of the sectarian trap, participants spent considerable time creating a joint vision of a better and greener Canada.[87] Naomi Klein, author and activist, was given the task of summarizing the proceedings of the event into a common manifesto. That was the birth of the *Leap Manifesto* – a transformative platform.[88] Subtitled *A Call for a Canada Based on Caring for the Earth and One Another*, the manifesto demands social, economic, and environmental justice as preconditions to improving the wellness of all Canadians, including marginalized communities such as indigenous peoples. The document is a call to correct crimes of the past, address pressing issues of the moment, and protect the well-being of future Canadians.

The visions articulated in the manifesto and in Faith in Action are clearly aligned with a "We Culture." They balance rights with responsibilities, to present and future generations; emphasize the need to care for one another and renounce parochial interests for the common good; and put fairness on par with wellness. These expressions of a better society could not have been achieved without some hard-won lessons about what constitutes a good process, one that balances participation with action.

Similar to effective teams and organizations, social movements need to have a culture that is supportive, effective, and reflective. Despite the diversity of founding members and organizations in the *Leap Manifesto*, ranging from climate change coalitions to labor unions to scientists to Black Lives Matter Toronto, there was a concerted effort to reach common ground. Hundreds of organizations endorsed the manifesto, and thousands of Canadians signed it. The ability to see the common good as superseding the narrow interests of any one group is an expression of mattering at a global scale. Unlike Occupy, there was a deliberate effort to reach consensus to enable productive action. The *Leap Manifesto* generated a great deal of activism throughout Canada and was influential in the 2015 elections. There are now Leap chapters all over Canada, with international interest growing.

Fairness to past, present, and future generations is one of the defining issues of our times. We will not be able to achieve wellness for all until transformative action is taken. Responsibility must be taken for crimes of the past and for unfair burdens placed on future generations. This dictum reaches beyond Canada. It applies to atrocities against Aboriginal peoples all over the world, against Blacks in the United States, and against other oppressed minorities. Our kids and grandkids are destined to inherit an

uninhabitable planet if urgent action is not taken. The *Leap* platform calls
for intergenerational justice in the form of climate action. The authors
propose a series of steps to stop the reliance on fossil fuels and an extractive
economy, and they show how to pay for it. When it comes to economic
justice, they want to build on an experiment in Manitoba and other parts
of the world where universal basic income (UBI) is guaranteed. Recent
analysis of UBI show that it is financially viable and socially beneficial.[89] It
is a bold proposal, one that can inspire action for transformative change.
The beginning of the manifesto reads as follows:

> The Truth and Reconciliation Commission has acknowledged shocking
> details about the violence of Canada's near past. Deepening poverty and
> inequality are a scar on the country's present. And Canada's record on
> climate change is a crime against humanity's future.
>
> These facts are all the more jarring because they depart so dramatically
> from our stated values: respect for Indigenous rights, internationalism,
> human rights, diversity, and environmental stewardship.
>
> Canada is not this place today – but it could be.
>
> We could live in a country powered entirely by renewable energy, woven
> together by accessible public transit, in which the jobs and opportunities of
> this transition are designed to systematically eliminate racial and gender
> inequality. Caring for one another and caring for the planet could be the
> economy's fastest growing sectors. Many more people could have higher
> wage jobs with fewer work hours, leaving us ample time to enjoy our loved
> ones and flourish in our communities.[90]

In a poem published in 1772, Voltaire popularized an Italian proverb: *Le
meglio è l'inimico del bene* – The perfect is the enemy of the good.[91] The
Leap Manifesto is not perfect, but it is a pretty good vision of what
mattering can look like in the community. Ideological purists who settle
for nothing less than perfect may achieve greatness in theory but never in
action. Mattering is too important to wait for perfection. In the end, life is
not about your right to feel valued for the brilliance of your ideas but about
your right *and* responsibility to feel valued *and* add value, to yourself *and*
others. This is the only way in which everyone can experience wellness *and*
fairness, in the present *and* the future.

Notes

Introduction

1. Fredrickson, B. (2013). *Love 2.0: How our supreme emotion affects everything we feel, think, do, and become.* Penguin.
2. Elliott, G. (2009). *Family matters: The importance of mattering to family in adolescence.* Wiley-Blackwell; Flett, G. (2018). *The psychology of mattering: Understanding the human need for significance.* Academic Press; Rosenberg, M., & McCullough, B. C. (1981). Mattering: inferred significance and mental health among adolescents. *Research in Community Mental Health, 2,* 163–182.
3. Case, A., & Deaton, A. (2020). *Deaths of despair and the future of capitalism.* Princeton; Dixon, A. L. (2007). Mattering in the later years: older adults' experiences of mattering to others, purpose in life, depression, and wellness. *Adultspan Journal, 6,* 83–95; Flett, G. L., & Heisel, M. J. (2020). Aging and feeling valued versus expendable during the COVID-19 pandemic and beyond: A review and commentary of why mattering is fundamental to the health and well-being of older adults. *International Journal of Mental Health and Addiction.* Advance online publication. https://doi.org/10.1007/S11469-020-00339-4; McGowan, P., Sasaki, A., D'Alessio, A., Dymov, S., Labonte, B., Szyf, M., Turecki, G., & Meaney, M. (2009). Epigenetic regulation of the glucocorticoid receptor in human brain associates with childhood abuse. *Nature Neuroscience, 12*(3), 342–348, https://doi.org/10.1038/nn.2270; Redmond, R. A., & Barrett, A. E. (2015). The link between functional limitations and depressive symptoms: the explanatory role of self-conceptions. *Society and Mental Health, 5,* 33–48; Wight, R. G., LeBlanc, A. J., Meyer, I. H., & Harig, F. A. (2015). Internalized gay ageism, mattering, and depressive symptoms among midlife and older gay-identified men. *Social Science and Medicine, 147,* 200–208.
4. Applebaum, A. (2020). *Twilight of democracy: The seductive lure of authoritarianism.* Doubleday; Fukuyama, F. (2018). *Identity: The demand for dignity and the politics of resentment.* Farrar, Straus and Giroux; Leary, M., Kowalski, R., Smith, L., & Phillips, S. (2003). Teasing, rejection, and violence: Case studies of the school

shootings. *Aggressive Behavior, 29,* 202–14; Lind, M. (2020). *The new class war: Saving democracy from the managerial elite.* Penguin.

5. Hedegaard, H., Curtin, S., & Warner, M. (2018). *Suicide mortality in the United States, 1999–2017* (NCHS Data Brief No. 330). Centers for Disease Control and Prevention. www.cdc.gov/nchs/data/databriefs/db330-h.pdf.

6. World Health Organization. (2017). *Depression and other common mental disorders: Global health estimates.* www.who.int/mental_health/manage ment/depression/prevalence_global_health_estimates/en/.

7. Weinberger, A. H., Gbedemah, M., Martinez, A. M., Nash, D., Galea, S., & Goodwin, R. D. (2018). Trends in depression prevalence in the USA from 2005 to 2015: Widening disparities in vulnerable groups. *Psychological Medicine, 48* (8), 1308–1315. https://doi.org/10.1017/S0033291717002781.

8. Gallup. (2017). *State of the Global Workforce.* Gallup Press.

9. Harari, Y. N. (2018). *21 lessons for the 21st Century.* Spiegel & Grau; Moghaddam, F. M. (2019). *Threat to democracy: The appeal of authoritarianism in an age of uncertainty.* American Psychological Association.

10. Diamond, L. (2015). Facing up to the democratic recession. *Journal of Democracy, 26*(1), 141–155.

11. Applebaum. *Twilight of democracy.*

12. Fukuyama. *Identity.*

13. Moghaddam. *Threat to democracy.*

14. Twenge, J., & Campbell, K. (2013). *The narcissism epidemic: Living in the age of entitlement.* Atria.

15. Sheskin, M. (2018, March 27). The inequality delusion: Why we've got the wealth gap all wrong. *New Scientist.* www.newscientist.com/article/mg23731710-300-the-inequality-delusion-why-weve-got-the-wealth-gap-all-wrong/.

16. IPCC. (2018). *Global warming of 1.5°C.* www.ipcc.ch/sr15/.

17. Lind. *The new class war;* Moghaddam. *Threat to democracy;* Wilkerson, I. (2020). *Caste: the origins of our discontents.* Random House.

18. Applebaum. *Twilight of democracy.*

19. Heumann, J. (2020). *Being Heumann: An unrepentant memoir of a disability rights activist.* Beacon Press; Kendi, I. X. (2019). *How to be an antiracist.* One World.

20. Kendi. *How to be an antiracist;* Oluo, I. (2019). *So you want to talk about race.* Seal Press.

21. Wilkerson. *Caste.*

22. DiAngelo, R. (2018). *White fragility: Why it's so hard for White people to talk about racism.* Beacon Press.

23. Ford, T., Reber, S., & Reeves, R. (2020, June 16). Race gaps in COVID-19 deaths are even bigger than they appear. Brookings. www.brookings.edu/bl og/up-front/2020/06/16/race-gaps-in-covid-19-deaths-are-even-bigger-than-t hey-appear/.

24. Oluo. *So you want to talk about race*; Prilleltensky, I. (2003). Understanding and overcoming oppression: Towards psychopolitical validity. *American Journal of Community Psychology, 31,* 195–202; Prilleltensky, I., Gonick, L. (1996). Polities change, oppression remains: On the psychology and politics of oppression. *Political Psychology, 17,* 127–147.

25. Flett. *The psychology of mattering.*

26. Grenville-Cleave, B., Guðmundsdóttir, D. G., Huppert, F. A., King, V., Roffey, D., Roffey, S., & de Vries, M. W. (2020). *Creating the world we want to live in: How positive psychology can build a brighter future.* Routledge.

27. Di Martino, S., & Prilleltensky, I. (2020). Happiness as fairness: The relationship between national life satisfaction and social justice in EU countries. *Journal of Community Psychology.* Advance online publication. https://doi.org/10.1002/jcop.22398; Wilkinson, R., & Pickett, K. (2018). *The inner level: How more equal societies reduce stress, restore sanity and improve everyone's well-being.* Penguin.

28. Bernard, M. E. (Ed.). (2013). *The strength of self-acceptance: Theory, practice, and research.* Springer.

29. Ryan, R., & Deci, E. (2017). *Self-determination theory: Basic psychological needs in motivation, development, and wellness.* Guilford.

30. Pileggi Pawelski, S., & Pawelski, J. O. (2018). *Happy together: Using the science of positive psychology to build love that lasts.* Penguin.

31. Benson, G., & Lawler III, E. E. (2016). Employee involvement: Research foundations. In M. J. Grawitch and D. Ballard (Eds.), *The psychologically healthy workplace: Building a win win environment for organizations and employees* (pp. 13–33). American Psychological Association; Steger, M. F. (2017). Creating meaning and purpose at work. In L. G. Oades, M. F. Steger, A. Delle Fave, and J. Passmore (Eds.), *The Wiley Blackwell Handbook of the psychology of positivity and strengths-based approaches at work* (pp. 60–81). John Wiley & Sons.

32. Block, P. (2009). *Community: The structure of belonging.* Berrett-Koehler; Christens, B. D. (2019). *Community power and empowerment.* Oxford.

33. Prilleltensky, I. (2019). Mattering at the intersection of psychology, philosophy, and politics. *American Journal of Community Psychology, 1*(19). https://doi.org/10.1002/ajcp.12368.

34. Friedman, T. (2020, July 28). If our masks could speak. *The New York Times.* www.nytimes.com/2020/07/28/opinion/coronavirus-masks.html; Lévy, B-H. (2020). *The virus in the age of madness.* Yale.

35. Leonhardt, D. (2020, August 6). The unique U.S. failure to control the virus. *The New York Times.* www.nytimes.com/2020/08/06/us/coronavirus-us.html.

36. Storr, W. (2018). *Selfie: How we became so self-obsessed and what it's doing to us.* Picador.

37. Prilleltensky, I. (2012). Wellness as fairness. *American Journal of Community Psychology, 49*, 1–21. https://doi.org/10.1007/s10464-011-9448-8.

38. Case & Deaton. *Deaths of despair*; Di Martino & Prilleltensky. Happiness as fairness; Partanen, A. (2016) *The Nordic theory of everything: In search of a better life*. HarperCollins; Wilkinson & Pickett. *The inner level*.

39. Harari. *21 lessons*; Lowery, A. (2018). *Give people money: How a universal basic income would end poverty, revolutionize work, and remake the world*. Crown.

1 The Mattering Wheel

1. Brontë, C. (1847). *Jane Eyre: An autobiography*. Service & Paton (p. 236).

2. James, W. (1890). *The principles of psychology*. Cosimo (pp. 293–294).

3. Crocker, J., Canevello, A., & Brown, A. (2017). Social motivation: Costs and benefits of selfishness and otherishness. *Annual Review of Psychology, 68*, 299–325; Elliott, G. (2009). *Family matters: The importance of mattering to family in adolescence*. Wiley-Blackwell; Flett, G. (2018). *The psychology of mattering: Understanding the human need for significance*. Academic Press; Grant, A., & Gino, F. (2010). A little thanks goes a long way: Explaining why gratitude expressions motivate prosocial behavior. *Journal of Personality and Social Psychology* 98(6), 946–955; Reece, A., Yaden, D., Kellerman, G., Robichaux, A., Goldstein, R., Schwartz, B., Seligman, M., & Baumeister, R. (2019). Mattering is an indicator of organizational health and employee success. *Journal of Positive Psychology*. Advance online publication. https://doi.org/10.1080/17439760.2019.1689416.

4. Chippendale, T. (2013). Factors associated with depressive symptoms among elders in senior residences: The importance of feeling valued by others. *Clinical Gerontologist, 36*(2), 162–169; Newberger Goldstein, R. (2013). Feminism, religion, and "mattering." *Free Inquiry, 34*(1), 22–27; Newberger Goldstein (2016, March 16). The Mattering Instinct, *Edge*. www.edge.org/conversation/rebecca_newberger_goldstein-the-mattering-instinct; Williams, K. (2007). Ostracism. *Annual Review of Psychology, 58*, 425–452.

5. Picciolini, C. (2015). *Romantic violence: Memoirs of an American skinhead*. Goldmill Group.

6. American Psychological Association. (2012). *APA survey finds feeling valued at work linked to well-being and performance*. www.apa.org/news/press/releases/2012/03/well-being.aspx; Brown, S., & Brown, R. (2015). Connecting prosocial behavior to improved physical health: Contributions from the neurobiology of parenting. *Neuroscience & Biobehavioral Reviews, 55*, 1–17; Danner, D., Snowdon, D., & Friesen, W. (2001). Positive emotions in early life and longevity: Findings from the nun

study. *Journal of Personality and Social Psychology*, 80(5), 804–813; Halusic, M., & King, L. (2013). What makes life meaningful: Positive mood works in a pinch. In K. Markman, T. Proulx & M. Indberg (Eds.), *The psychology of meaning* (pp. 445–464). American Psychological Association; Lavelock, C., Griffin, B., Worthington, E., Benotsch, E., Lin, Y., Greer, C., Garthem R., Coleman, J., Hughes, C., Davis, D., & Hook, J. (2016). A qualitative review and integrative model of gratitude and physical health. *Journal of Psychology and Theology*, *44*, 55–86; Midlarsky, E., Kahana, E., & Belser, A. (2015). Prosocial behavior in late life. In D. Schroeder & W. Graziano (Eds.), *The Oxford handbook of prosocial behavior* (pp. 415–432). Oxford; Park, C. (2013). The meaning making model: A framework for understanding meaning, spirituality, and stress-related growth in health psychology. *European Health Psychologist*, *15*(2), 40–47; Steger, M. (2012). Experiencing meaning in life: Optimal functioning at the nexus of spirituality, psychopathology, and well-being. In P. T. Wong (Ed.), *The human quest for meaning: Theories, research, and applications* (2nd ed., pp. 165–184); Erlbaum. Wood, A., Froh, J., & Geraghty, A. (2010). Gratitude and well-being: A review and theoretical integration. *Clinical Psychology Review*, *30*, 890–905.

7. Crocker, Canevello & Brown. Social motivation, 315–316.

8. Danner, D., Snowdon, D., & Friesen, W. (2001). Positive emotions in early life and longevity: Findings from the nun study. *Journal of Personality and Social Psychology*, *80*(5), 804–813.

9. Ibid., 809.

10. Elliott. *Family matters*, 2.

11. Ibid., 119.

12. Keltner, D. (2016). *The power paradox: How we gain and lose influence*. Penguin; Prilleltensky, I. (2008). The role of power in wellness, oppression, and liberation: The promise of psychopolitical validity. *Journal of Community Psychology*. *36*, 116–136; Prilleltensky, I., & Fox, D. (2007). Psychopolitical literacy for wellness and justice. *Journal of Community Psychology*, *35*, 793–806.

13. Prilleltensky, I. (2012). Wellness as fairness. *American Journal of Community Psychology*, *49*, 1–21. https://doi.org/10.1007/s10464-011-9448-8; Prilleltensky, I., & Nelson, G. (2002). *Doing psychology critically: Making a difference in diverse settings*. Palgrave/Macmillan.

14. Storr, W. (2018). *Selfie: How we became so self-obsessed and what it's doing to us*. Picador; Twenge, J., & Campbell, K. (2013). *The narcissism epidemic: Living in the age of entitlement*. Atria.

15. Biglan, A. (2015). *The nurture effect: How the science of human behaviour can improve our lives and the world*. New Harbinger; Grenville-Cleave, B., Guðmundsdóttir, D. G., Huppert, F. A., King, V., Roffey, D., Roffey, S., & de Vries, M. W. (2020). *Creating the world we want to live in: How positive*

psychology can build a brighter future. Routledge; Kanat-Maymon, Y., Roth, G., Assor, A., & Reizer, A. (2012). Conditional regard in close relationships. In P. Shaver & M. Mikulincer (Eds.), *Meaning, mortality, and choice: The social psychology of existential concerns* (pp. 235–251). American Psychological Association; Prilleltensky, I., Nelson, G., & Peirson, L. (Eds.). (2001). *Promoting family wellness and preventing child maltreatment: Fundamentals for thinking and action*. University of Toronto.

16. Williams, K., Forgas, J., & von Hippel, W. (Eds.). (2005). *The social outcast: ostracism, social exclusion, rejection, and bullying*. Psychology Press.

17. Nelson, G., & Prilleltensky, I. (Eds.). (2010). *Community psychology: In pursuit of liberation and well-being* (2nd ed.). Palgrave/Macmillan; Prilleltensky, O. (2009). Critical psychology and disability studies: Critiquing the mainstream, critiquing the critique. In D. Fox, I. Prilleltensky, & S. Austin (Eds.), *Critical Psychology: An Introduction* (2nd ed., pp. 250–266); Sage. Wilkerson, *Caste*.

18. Case, A., & Deaton, A. (2020). *Deaths of despair and the future of capitalism*. Princeton; Klein, E. (2020). *Why we're polarized*. Simon & Schuster; Lind, M. (2020). *The new class war: Saving democracy from the managerial elite*. Penguin.

19. Gallup. (2017). *State of the Global Workforce*. Gallup Press.

20. Leary, M. (2005). Sociometer theory and the pursuit of relational value: Getting to the root of self-esteem. *European Review of Social Psychology, 16* (1), 75–111 (p. 82).

21. Fowers, B. (2015). *The evolution of ethics: Human sociality and the emergence of ethical mindedness*. Palgrave/Macmillan; Markman, D., Proulx, T. & Lindberg, M. (Eds.). (2013). *The psychology of meaning*. American Psychological Association; Newberger Goldstein, R. (2014). *Plato at the Googleplex*. Pantheon; Reece, Yaden, Kellerman, Robichaux, Goldstein, Schwartz, Seligman & Baumeister, Mattering is an indicator of organizational health and employee success; Schroeder, D., & Graziano, W. (Eds.). (2015). *The Oxford handbook of prosocial behavior*. Oxford.

22. Yunus, M. (2007). *Creating a world without poverty*. Public Affairs.

23. Bandura, A. (2001). Social cognitive theory: An agentic perspective. *Annual Review of Psychology, 52*, 1–26; Bandura, A. (Ed.). (1995). *Self-efficacy in changing societies*. Cambridge.

24. Prilleltensky, I. (2016). *The laughing guide to well-being: Using humor and science to become happier and healthier*. Rowman and Littlefield; Prilleltensky, I., & Prilleltensky, O. (2006). *Promoting well-being: Linking personal, organizational, and community change*. Wiley.

25. Storr. *Selfie*.

26. Mullainathan, S., & Shafir, E. (2013). *Scarcity: Why having too little means so much*. Henry Holt.

27. Elliott. *Family matters*; Grant & Gino. A little thanks goes a long way.

28. Crocker, Canevello & Brown. Social motivation, 303–304.

29. Kanat-Maymon, Roth, Assor & Reizer. Conditional regard in close relationships; Keltner. *The power paradox.*

30. Felitti, V. J., Anda, R. F., Nordenberg, D., Williamson, D. F., Spitz, A. M., Edwards. V., Koss, M., & Marks, J. (1998). Relationship of childhood abuse and household dysfunction to many of the leading causes of death in adults: The Adverse Childhood Experiences (ACE) Study. *American Journal of Preventive Medicine, 14*(4), 245–258.

31. Ibid., 253.

32. Leary, M. (2005). Sociometer theory and the pursuit of relational value: Getting to the root of self-esteem. *European Review of Social Psychology, 16* (1), 75–111; Riva, P., & Eck, J. (Eds.). (2016). *Social exclusion: Psychological approaches to understanding and reducing its impact.* Springer; Williams, Forgas & von Hippel. *The social outcast.*

33. Kessler, R., & Bromet, E. (2013). The epidemiology of depression across cultures. *Annual Review of Public Health, 34,* 119–138.

34. Twenge & Campbell. *The narcissism epidemic.*

35. Engel, P. (2014, May 25). Divorce rates around the world. *Business Insider,* www .businessinsider.com/map-divorce-rates-around-the-world-2014-5; Hawkley, L., & Cacioppo, C. (2010). Loneliness matters: A theoretical and empirical review of consequences and mechanisms. *Annals of Behavioral Medicine, 40*(2), 218–227; Parker-Pope, T. (2008, October 27). Love, sex, and the changing landscape of infidelity. *The New York Times.* www.nytimes.com/2008/10/28/health/28well .html; Perissinotto. C., Stijacic Cenzer I., Covinsky, K., (2012). Loneliness in older persons: A predictor of functional decline and death. *Archives of Internal Medicine, 172*(14):1078–1084; Sorenson, S., & Garman, K. (2013, June 11). How to tackle US employees' stagnating engagement. *Business Journal.* http://news.gal lup.com/businessjournal/162953/tackle-employees-stagnating-engagement.aspx.

36. European Risk Observatory. (2014). *Calculating the cost of work-related stress and psychosocial risks.* European Agency for Safety and Health at Work. http s://osha.europa.eu/en/publications/calculating-cost-work-related-stress-and-psychosocial-risks; Gallup. (2014). *State of the American Workplace.* Gallup.

37. Payne, K. (2017). *The broken ladder: How inequality affects the way we think, live, and die.* Penguin; Putnam, R. (2001). *Bowling alone: The collapse and renewal of American community.* Simon & Schuster; Putnam, R. (2015). *Our kids: The American dream in crisis.* Simon & Schuster; Stiglitz, J. (2013) *The price of inequality.* Norton.

38. Dorling, D. (2017). *The equality effect: Improving life for everyone.* New Internationalist; Global Happiness Council. (2018). *Global happiness policy report* 2018. https://s3.amazonaws.com/ghc-2018/UAE/; Marujo, H., &

Neto, L. (Eds.). (2014). *Positive nations and communities.* Springer; Pickett, K., & Wilkinson, R. (2010). *The spirit level: Why greater equality makes societies stronger.* Bloomsbury.

39. Block, P. (2009). *Community: The structure of belonging.* Berrett-Koehler; Levy, B., & Sidel, V. (Eds.). (2006). *Social injustice and public health.* Oxford; Marmot, M. (2015). *The health gap: The challenge of an unequal world.* Bloomsbury; McKnight, J., & Block, P. (2010). *The abundant community: Awakening the power of families and neighborhoods.* Berrett-Koehler; Nelson, G., & Prilleltensky, I. (Eds.). (2010). *Community psychology: In pursuit of liberation and well-being* (2nd ed.). Palgrave/Macmillan.

40. Achor, S. (2010). *The happiness advantage.* Crown; Kegan, R., & Lahey, L. (2016). *An everyone culture: Becoming a deliberately developmental organization.* Harvard Business School. Sisodia, R., Wolfe, D., & Sheth, J. (2014). *Firms of endearment: How world class companies profit from passion and purpose.* Pearson.

2 Feeling Valued

1. Yoshino, K. (2007). *Covering: The hidden assault on our civil rights.* Random House.
2. Ainsworth, M., Blehar, M., Waters, E., & Wall, S. (1978). *Patterns of attachment: A psychological study of the strange situation.* Erlbaum.
3. Bowlby, J. (1969). *Attachment and loss: Vol 1. Attachment.* Basic Books; Bowlby, J. (1973). *Attachment and loss: Vol 2. Separation: Anxiety and anger.* Basic Books.
4. Mikulincer, M., & Shaver, P. (2007). *Attachment in adulthood: Structure, dynamics, and change.* Guilford.
5. Shaver, P., & Mikulincer, M. (2012). An attachment perspective on coping with existential concerns. In P. Shaver & M. Mikulincer (Eds.), *Meaning, mortality, and choice: The social psychology of existential concerns* (pp. 291–307). American Psychological Association (p. 291).
6. Ibid., 291.
7. Mikulincer & Shaver. *Attachment in adulthood,* 370.
8. Robles, T., & Kane, H. (2014). The attachment system and physiology in adulthood: Normative processes, individual differences, and implications for health. *Journal of Personality, 82*(6), 515–527.
9. Schlossberg, N. K. (1989). Marginality and mattering: Key issues in building community. *New Directions for Student Services, 48,* 5–15.
10. Baumeister, R., & Leary, M. (1995). The need to belong: Desire for interpersonal attachments as a fundamental human motivation. *Psychological Bulletin, 117*(3), 497–529 (p. 498).

11. Ibid., 498.
12. Fowers, B. (2017). The deep psychology of eudaimonia and virtue: Belonging, loyalty, and the anterior cingulate cortex. In D. Carr, J. Arthur, & K. Kristjansson (Eds.), *Varieties of virtue ethics* (pp. 199–216). Palgrave/Macmillan.
13. Baumeister & Leary. The need to belong, 508.
14. Hawkley, L., & Cacioppo, C. (2010). Loneliness matters: A theoretical and empirical review of consequences and mechanisms. *Annals of Behavioral Medicine, 40*(2), 218–227; Riva, P., & Eck, J. (Eds.). (2016). *Social exclusion: Psychological approaches to understanding and reducing its impact.* Springer.
15. Yeginsu, C. (2018, January 17). U.K. appoints a minister for loneliness. *The New York Times.* www.nytimes.com/2018/01/17/world/europe/uk-britain-loneliness.html.
16. Baumeister & Leary. The need to belong, 517.
17. Gallo, C. (2016). *The storyteller's secret.* St Martin's Press (p. 43).
18. Gollwitzer, M, & van Prooijen, J. (2016).Psychology of justice. In C. Sabbagh & M. Schmitt (Eds.), *Handbook of social justice theory and research* (pp.61–82). Springer.
    Miller, D. T. (2001). Disrespect and the experience of injustice. *Annual Review of Psychology, 52,* 527–553.
19. Lieberman, M. (2013). *Social: Why our brains are wired to connect.* Random House.
20. Sun, L. (2013). *The fairness instinct.* Prometheus.
21. McFarland, S., Brown, D., & Webb, M. (2013). Identification with all humanity as a moral concept and psychological construct. *Current Directions in Psychological Science, 22*(3), 194–198.
22. Riva & Eck. *Social exclusion.*
23. Berger, R. (2013). *Introducing disability studies.* Lynne Rienner; Prilleltensky, O. (2004). *Motherhood and disability: Children and choices.* Palgrave/Macmillan.
24. Tirado, L. (2014). *Hand to mouth: Living in bootstrap America.* Penguin (p. 26).
25. Albrecht, G., & Devlinger, P. (1999). The disability paradox: High quality of life against all odds. *Social Science and Medicine, 48*(8), 977–988.
26. Twenge, J., & Campbell, K. (2013). *The narcissism epidemic: Living in the age of entitlement.* Atria.
27. Sapolsky, R. (2004). Social status and health in humans and other animals. *Annual Review of Anthropology, 33,* 393–418; Sapolsky, R. (2018). *Behave: The biology of humans at or best and worst.* Penguin; Sun, L. (2013). *The fairness instinct.* Prometheus.
28. Eisenberg, N., & Lieberman, M. (2005). Why it hurts to be left out: The neurocognitive overlap between physical and social pain. In K. Williams,

J. Forgas, & W. von Hippel (Eds.), *The social outcast: Ostracism, social exclusion, rejection, and bullying* (pp. 109–130). Psychology Press; MacDonald, G., Kingsbury, R., & Shaw, S. (2005). Adding insult to injury: Social pain theory and response to social exclusion. In K. Williams, J. Forgas, & W. von Hippel (Eds.), *The social outcast: Ostracism, social exclusion, rejection, and bullying* (pp. 77–90). Psychology Press.

29. Sapolsky, R. (2004). Social status and health in humans and other animals. *Annual Review of Anthropology, 33,* 393–418; Sapolsky. *Behave*; Shwartz, M. (2007, March 7). Robert Sapolsky discusses physiological effects of stress. *Stanford Report,* https://news.stanford.edu/news/2007/march7/sapolskysr-03 0707.html.

30. Mahadevan, N., Gregg, A.P., Sedikides, C., & De Waal-Andrews, W. G. (2016). Winners, losers, insiders, and outsiders: Comparing hierometer and sociometer theories of self-regard. *Frontiers of Psychology, 7*(334). https://doi .org/10.3389/fpsyg.2016.00334.

31. Williams, Forgas & von Hippel. *The social outcast.*

32. Payne, K. (2017). *The broken ladder: How inequality affects the way we think, live, and die.* Penguin.

33. Wesselman, E., Grzybowsky, M., Steakley-Freeman, D., DeSouza, E., Nezlek, J., & Williams, K. (2016). Social exclusion in everyday life. In P. Riva and J. Eck (Eds.), *Social exclusion: Psychological approaches to understanding and reducing its impact* (pp. 3–23). Springer.

34. Riva & Eck. *Social exclusion*; Williams, Forgas & von Hippel. *The social outcast.*

35. Bernstein, M. E. (2016). Research in social psychology: consequences of short- and long-term social exclusion. In P. Riva and J. Eck (Eds.), *Social exclusion: Psychological approaches to understanding and reducing its impact* (pp.51–72). Springer.

36. Leary, M., Kowalski, R., Smith, L., & Phillips, S. (2003). Teasing, rejection, and violence: Case studies of the school shootings. *Aggressive Behavior, 29,* 202–14

37. Williams, K. (2007). Ostracism. *Annual Review of Psychology, 58,* 425–452 (p. 44).

38. Ibid.

39. Bernstein. Research in social psychology; Williams. Ostracism.

40. Kendi, I. X. (2019). *How to be an antiracist.* One World; Oluo, I. (2019). *So you want to talk about race.* Seal Press; Wilkerson, I. (2020). *Caste: the origins of our discontents.* Random House.

41. Miller. Disrespect and the experience of injustice; Sun, L. (2013). *The fairness instinct.* Prometheus; Wesselman, Grzybowsky, Steakley-Freeman, DeSouza, Nezlek, & Williams. Social exclusion in everyday life.

42. Wilkerson, *Caste*.
43. Howard, L., & Cordes, C. (2010). Flight from unfairness: Effects of perceived injustice on emotional exhaustion and employee withdrawal. *Journal of Business Psychology*, *25*, 409–428; Sabbagh, C., & Schmitt, M. (Eds.). (2016). *Handbook of social justice theory and research*. Springer.
44. Tirado. *Hand to mouth*.
45. Miller. Disrespect and the experience of injustice.
46. Gollwitzer & van Prooijen. Psychology of justice.
47. Fiske, S. (2011). *Envy up, scorn down: How status divides us*. Russel Sage; Mahadevan, Gregg, Sedikides & De Waal-Andrews. Winners, losers, insiders, and outsiders.
48. Case, A., & Deaton, A. (2020). *Deaths of despair and the future of capitalism*. Princeton; Graham, C. (2017). *Happiness for all? Unequal hopes and lives in pursuit of the American dream*. Princeton.
49. Norton, M., & Ariely, D. (2011). Building a better America – One wealth quintile at a time. *Perspectives on Psychological Science*, *6*, 9–12.
50. Payne. *The broken ladder*, 42.
51. Case & Deaton. *Deaths of despair*; Wilkinson, R., & Pickett, K. (2018). *The inner level: How more equal societies reduce stress, restore sanity and improve everyone's well-being*. Penguin.
52. Payne. *The broken ladder*, 78.
53. Dorling, D. (2017). *The equality effect: Improving life for everyone*. New Internationalist; Pickett, K., & Wilkinson, R. (2010). *The spirit level: Why greater equality makes societies stronger*. Bloomsbury.

3 Adding Value

1. Baumeister, R. (1991). *Meanings of life*. Guilford; Prilleltensky, I. (2014). Meaning-making, mattering, and thriving in community psychology: From co-optation to amelioration and transformation. *Psychosocial Intervention*, *23*, 151–154.
2. Gollwitzer, M, & van Prooijen, J. (2016).Psychology of justice. In C. Sabbagh & M. Schmitt (Eds.), *Handbook of social justice theory and research* (pp. 61–82). Springer.
3. McKnight, J, & Block, P. (2010). *The abundant community: Awakening the power of families and neighborhoods*. Berrett-Koehler.
4. Ryan, R., & Deci, E. (2017). *Self-determination theory: Basic psychological needs in motivation, development, and wellness*. Guilford.
5. Mikulincer, M., & Shaver, P. (2007). *Attachment in adulthood: Structure, dynamics, and change*. Guilford; Twenge, J., & Campbell, K. (2013). *The narcissism epidemic: Living in the age of entitlement*. Atria.

6. Biglan, A. (2015). *The nurture effect: How the science of human behaviour can improve our lives and the world*. New Harbinger.

7. Bandura, A. (2001). Social cognitive theory: An agentic perspective. *Annual Review of Psychology, 52*, 1–26.

8. Bandura, A. (Ed.). (1995). *Self-efficacy in changing societies*. Cambridge; Gancarczyk, A., Czekierda, K., & Luszczynska, A. (2014). Associations between self-efficacy and health outcomes among cardiac patients: A systematic review. *Bulletin of the European Health Psychology Society, 16*. www.ehps.net/ehp/index.php/contents/article/view/520/513; Maddux, J. (2009). Self-efficacy: The power of believing you can. In S. Lopez & C. Snyder (Eds.), *Handbook of positive psychology* (pp. 335–344). Oxford.

9. Myers, N.D., Prilleltensky, I., Hill, C.R., & Feltz, D.L. (2017). Well-being self-efficacy and complier average causal effect modeling: A substantive-methodological synergy. *Psychology of Sport & Exercise, 30*, 135–144; Maddux. Self-efficacy.

10. Frankl, V. (2002). *Man's search for meaning*. Beacon Press.

11. Costin, V., & Vignoles, V. L. (2020). Meaning is about mattering: Evaluating coherence, purpose, and existential mattering as precursors of meaning in life judgments. *Journal of Personality and Social Psychology, 118*(4), 864–884. https://doi.org/10.1037/pspp0000225

12. Steger, M. (2012). Making meaning in life. *Psychological Inquiry, 23*, 381–385.

13. Baumeister. *Meanings of life*.

14. Mandela, N. (2013). *Long walk to freedom*. Little, Brown, and Company.

15. Heumann, J. (2020). *Being Heumann: An unrepentant memoir of a disability rights activist*. Beacon Press.

16. Clark Hine, D. (2013, May 31). Parks, Rosa. *Oxford African American Studies Center*. https://doi.org/10.1093/acref/9780195301731.013.34629.

17. Watkins, M. (2019). *Mutual accompaniment and the creation of the commons*. Yale.

18. Heintzelman, S., & King, L. (2014). Life is pretty meaningful. *American Psychologist, 69*, 561–574.

19. Steger. Making meaning in life; Costin & Vignoles. Meaning is about mattering.

20. Reich, R. (2018). *The common good*. Knopf.

21. Marmot, M. (2015). *The health gap: The challenge of an unequal world*. Bloomsbury; Partanen, A. (2016) *The Nordic theory of everything: In search of a better life*. HarperCollins.

22. Watkins. *Mutual accompaniment and the creation of the commons*.

23. Grant, A. (2013). *Give and take: Why helping others drives our success*. Penguin.

24. Reich, R. (2018). *The common good*. Knopf.

25. Mikulincer, M. (1994). *Human learned helplessness*. Plenum; Pryce, C., Azzinnari, D., Spinelli, S., Seifritz, E., Tegethoff, M., & Meinlschmidt, G.

(2011). Helplessness: A systematic translational review of theory and evidence for its relevance to understanding and treating depression. *Pharmacology & Therapeutics, 132,* 242–267.

26. Liu, R., Kleiman, E., Nestor, B., & Cheek, S., (2015). The hopelessness theory of depression: A quarter century in review. *Clinical Psychology: Science and Practice, 22,* 345–365.

27. Mikulincer. *Human learned helplessness.*

28. Marmot, M. (2004). *The status syndrome.* Times Books.

29. Fiske, S. (2011). *Envy up, scorn down: How status divides us.* Russell Sage.

30. Keltner, D. (2016). *The power paradox: How we gain and lose influence.* Penguin.

31. DiAngelo, R. (2018). *White fragility: Why it's so hard for White people to talk about racism.* Beacon Press.

32. Ibid.

33. Kendi, I. X. (2019). *How to be an antiracist.* One World; Marmot. *The health gap*; Mullainathan, S., & Shafir, E. (2013). *Scarcity: Why having too little means so much.* Henry Holt.

34. Case, A., & Deaton, A. (2020). *Deaths of despair and the future of capitalism.* Princeton; Payne, K. (2017). *The broken ladder: How inequality affects the way we think, live, and die.* Penguin.

35. Keltner. *The power paradox,* 141.

4 Ways to Matter

1. Prilleltensky, I., & Prilleltensky, O. (2019). *The laughing guide to a better life: Using humor and science to improve yourself, your relationships, and your surroundings.* Rowman and Littlefield; Prilleltensky, O., & Prilleltensky, I. (2019). *The laughing guide to change: Using humor and science to master your behaviors, emotions, and thoughts.* Rowman and Littlefield.

2. Myers, N. D., Dietz, S., Prilleltensky, I., Prilleltensky, O., McMahon, A., Rubenstein, C. L., & Lee, S. (2018). Efficacy of the fun for wellness online intervention to promote well-being actions: A secondary data analysis. *Games for Health Journal, 7*(4), 1–15. Myers, N. D., Prilleltensky, I., Hill, C. R., & Feltz, D. L. (2017). Well-being self-efficacy and complier average causal effect modeling: A substantive-methodological synergy. *Psychology of Sport & Exercise, 30,* 135–144. https://dx.doi.org/10.1016/j.psychsport.2017.02.010; Myers, N. D., Prilleltensky, I., Prilleltensky, O., McMahon, A, Dietz, S., & Rubenstein, C. L. (2017). Efficacy of the fun for wellness online intervention to promote multidimensional well-being: A randomized controlled trial. *Prevention Science, 18,* 984–994. https://doi:10.1007/s11121-017-0779-z.

3. Myers, N. D., McMahon, A., Prilleltensky, I., Lee, S., Dietz, S., Prilleltensky, O., et al. (2020). Effectiveness of the fun for wellness web-based behavioral intervention to promote physical activity in adults with obesity: A randomized controlled trial. *Journal of Medical Internet Research, 4*(2), e15919. https://formative .jmir.org/2020/2/e15919/.

4. Prilleltensky, I., McMahon, A., Myers, N., Prilleltensky, O., Dietz, S., Scarpa, M., Lee, S., Pfeiffer, K., Bateman, A., & Brincks, A. (2020). An exploration of the effectiveness of the Fun for Wellness online intervention to promote health in adults with obesity: A randomized controlled trial. *Journal of Prevention and Health Promotion. 1–28.* https://doi.org/10.1177/2632077020968737.

5. Wansink, B. (2014). *Slim by design: Mindless eating solutions.* Harper Collins; Thaler, R., & Sunstein, C. (2008). *Nudge: Improving decisions about health, wealth, and happiness.* Yale.

6. Bandura, A. (1977). Self-efficacy: toward a unifying theory of behavioral change. *Psychological Review, 84*(2), 191–215; Bandura, A. (2000). Exercise of human agency through collective efficacy. *Current directions in psychological science, 9*(3), 75–78; Merluzzi, T. V., Pustejovsky, J. E., Philip, E. J., Sohl, S. J., Berendsen, M., & Salsman, J. M. (2019). Interventions to enhance self-efficacy in cancer patients: A meta-analysis of randomized controlled trials. *Psycho-Oncology, 28*(9), 1781–1790; Schmitt, M. M., Goverover, Y., DeLuca, J., & Chiaravalloti, N. (2014). Self-efficacy as a predictor of self-reported physical, cognitive, and social functioning in multiple sclerosis. *Rehabilitation psychology, 59*(1), 27–34.

7. Koestner, R., Lekes, N., Powers, T. A., & Chicoine, E. (2002). Attaining personal goals: Self-concordance plus implementation intentions equals success. *Journal of Personality and Social Psychology, 83*(1), 231–244. https://doi .org/10.1037//0022-3514.83.1.231; Sheldon, K. M. (2014). Becoming oneself: The central role of self-concordant goal selection. *Personality and Social Psychology Review, 18*(4), 349–365; Sheldon K. M., & Elliot A. J. (1999). Goal striving, need-satisfaction, and longitudinal wellbeing: The self-concordance model. *Journal of Personality and Social Psychology, 76,* 482–497.

8. Conzemius, A., O'Neill, J., & Commodore, C. (2005). *The power of SMART goals.* Solution Tree; Ericsson, A., & Pool, R. (2017). *Peak: Secrets from the new science of expertise.* Houghton, Mifflin, Harcourt.

9. Achtziger, A., Gollwitzer, P. M., & Sheeran, P. (2008). Implementation intentions and shielding goal striving from unwanted thoughts and feelings. *Personality and Social Psychology Bulletin, 34*(3), 381–393. https://doi.org/10.1177/0146167207311201; Adriaanse, M. A., Gollwitzer, P. M., De Ridder, D. T. D., De Wit, J. B. F., & Kroese, F. M. (2011). Breaking habits with implementation intentions: A test of underlying processes. *Personality and Social Psychology Bulletin, 37,* 502–513. https:// doi.org/10.1177/0146167211399102; Friedman, S., & Ronen, S. (2015). The effect of implementation intentions on transfer of training: Effect of implementation

intentions on training transfer. *European Journal of Social Psychology*, *45*(4), 409–416. https://doi.org/10.1002/ejsp.2114.

10. Gollwitzer, P. M. & Sheeran, P. (2006). Implementation intentions and goal achievement: A meta-analysis of effects and processes. *Advances in Experimental Social Psychology*, *38*, 69–119; Gollwitzer, P. M. (1999). Implementation intentions: Strong effects of simple plans. *American Psychologist*, *54*(7), 493–503. https://doi.org/10.1037/0003-066X.54.7.493; Gollwitzer, P. M. (2014). Weakness of the will: Is a quick fix possible? *Motivation and Emotion*, *38*(3), 305–322. https://doi.org/10.1007/s11031-014-9416-3; Oettingen, G. (2014). *Rethinking positive thinking: Inside the new science of motivation*. Current.

11. Norcross, J. C. (2012). *Changeology: 5 steps to realizing your goals and resolutions*. Simon & Schuster.

12. Watson, D. L. & Tharp, R. G. (2014). *Self-directed behavior: Self-modification for personal adjustment* (10th ed.). Cengage Learning.

13. Clear, J. (2018). *Atomic habits: An easy and proven way to build good habits and break bad ones*. Penguin; Duhigg, C. (2014). *The power of habit*. Random House.

14. Prilleltensky & Prilleltensky. *The laughing guide to change*.

15. Danner, D., Snowdon, D., & Friesen, W. (2001). Positive emotions in early life and longevity: Findings from the nun study. *Journal of Personality and Social Psychology*, *80*(5), 804–813; Fredrickson, B. (2004). The broaden-and-build theory of positive emotions. *Philosophical Transactions of the Royal Society B: Biological Sciences*, *359*(1449), 1367–1377; Gloria, C., & Steinhardt, M. (2016). Relationships among positive emotions, coping, resilience and mental health. *Stress and Health*, *32*(2), 145–156.

16. Arakawa, D. & Greenburg, M. (2007). Optimistic managers and their influence on productivity and employee engagement in a technology organization: Implications for coaching psychologists. *International Coaching Psychology Review*, *2*, 78–89; Biswas-Diener, R. (2010). *Practicing positive psychology coaching*. John Wiley & Sons; Lopez, S. J., Pedrotti, J. T., & Snyder, C. R. (2015). *Positive psychology: The scientific and practical explorations of human strengths*. (3rd ed.). Sage; Seligman, M., Steen, T., Park, N., & Peterson, C. (2005). Positive psychology progress: empirical validation of interventions. *American Psychologist*, *60*(5), 410–421.

17. Lomas, T., Froh, J. J., Emmons, R. A., & Mishra, A. (2014). Gratitude interventions: A review and future agenda. In A. Parks & Stephen M. Schueller (Eds.), *Handbook of positive psychological interventions* (pp. 3–19). Wiley-Blackwell.

18. Emmons, R. A., & McCullough, M. E. (2003). Counting blessings versus burdens: An experimental investigation of gratitude and subjective well-being in daily life. *Journal of Personality and Social Psychology*, *84*(2), 377–389. https://doi.org/10.1037/0022-3514.84.2.377.

19. Bryant, F. & Veroff, J. (2006). *Savoring: A new model of positive experience.* Earlbaum; Smith, J. L., Harrison, P. R., Kurtz, J. L., & Bryant, F. B. (2014). Nurturing the capacity to savor: Interventions to enhance the enjoyment of positive experiences. In A. C. Parks, & S. M. Schueller (Eds.), *The Wiley Blackwell handbook of positive psychological interventions* (pp. 42–65). Wiley-Blackwell.

20. Lyubomirsky, S. (2007*). The how of happiness: The new approach to getting the life you want.* Penguin.

21. Brooks, D. (2019). *The second mountain: The quest for a moral life.* Random House;
Slotter, E., & Ward, D. (2015). Finding the silver lining. *Journal of Social and Personal Relationships, 32*(6), 737–756.

22. Bower, J., Moskowitz, J., & Epel, E. (2009). Is benefit finding good for your health? *Current Directions in Psychological Science, 18*(6), 337–341; Roepke, A., & Nezu, A. M. (2015). Psychosocial interventions and posttraumatic growth: A meta-analysis. *Journal of Consulting and Clinical Psychology, 83*(1), 129–142.

23. First People. (n.d.). *Native American Legend.* Retrieved June 15, 2020, from www.firstpeople.us/FP-Html-Legends/TwoWolves-Cherokee.html.

24. Garland, E. L., Fredrickson, B., Kring, A. M., Johnson, D. P., Meyer, P. S., & Penn, D. L. (2010). Upward spirals of positive emotions counter downward spirals of negativity: Insights from the broaden-and-build theory and affective neuroscience on the treatment of emotion dysfunctions and deficits in psychopathology. *Clinical Psychology Review, 30*(7), 849–864; Nolen-Hoeksema, S., Wisco, B., & Lyubomirsky, S. (2008). Rethinking rumination. *Perspectives on Psychological Science, 3*(5), 400–424; Zawadzki, M. (2015). Rumination is independently associated with poor psychological health: Comparing emotion regulation strategies. *Psychology & Health, 30*(10), 1146–1163. https://doi.org/10.1080/08870446.2015.1026904.

25. Bonanno, G., & Burton, C. (2013). Regulatory flexibility. *Perspectives on Psychological Science, 8*(6), 591–612; Brackett, M. A., Mayer, J. D., & Warner, R. M. (2004). Emotional intelligence and its relation to everyday behavior. *Personality and Individual Differences, 36*, 1387–1402; Brackett, M. A., Rivers, S. E., & Salovey, P. (2011). Emotional intelligence: Implications for personal, social, academic, and workplace success. *Social and Personality Psychology Compass, 5*, 88–103; Brown, K. W. and Ryan, R. M. (2015) A self-determination theory perspective on fostering healthy self-regulation from within and without. In S. Joseph (Ed.), *Positive psychology in practice: Promoting human flourishing in work, health, education, and everyday life* (pp. 139–158). John Wiley & Sons; Kashdan, T., Barrett, L., & McKnight, P. (2015). Unpacking emotion differentiation. *Current Directions in Psychological Science, 24*(1), 10–16.

26. Arch, J. J., & Craske, M. G. (2006). Mechanisms of mindfulness: Emotion regulation following a focused breathing induction. *Behaviour Research Therapy*, *44*, 1849–1858. https://doi.org/10.1016/j.brat.2005.12.007; Chambers, R., Gullone, E., & Allen, N. B. (2009). Mindful emotion regulation: An integrative review. *Clinical Psychology Review*, *29*, 560–572. https://doi.org/10.1016/j.cpr.2009.06.005; Germer, C., & Neff, K. (2013). Self-compassion in clinical practice. *Journal of Clinical Psychology*, *69*(8), 856–867; Hayes, S. C, Pistorello, J., & Levin, M. (2012). Acceptance and commitment therapy as a unified model of behavior change. *The Counseling Psychologist*, *40*(7), 976–1002; Kabat-Zinn, J. (2005). *Full catastrophe living: Using the wisdom of your body and mind to face stress, pain and illness* (15th anniversary ed.). Bantam Dell.

27. Germer & Neff. Self-compassion in clinical practice; Robins, C. J., Keng, S. L., Ekblad, A. G., & Brantley, J. G. (2012), Effects of mindfulness-based stress reduction on emotional experience and expression: A randomized controlled trial. *Journal of Clinical Psychology*, *68*, 117–131. https://doi.org/10.1002/jclp.20857.

28. Beck, J. S. (2011). *Cognitive behavior therapy: Basics and beyond* (2nd ed.). Guilford.
    Beck, A., & Haigh, E. (2014). Advances in cognitive theory and therapy: The generic cognitive model. *Annual Review of Clinical Psychology*, *10*, 1–24; Burns, D. (1999). *10 days to self-esteem*. New York: Quill; Dobson, D., & Dobson, K. S. (2009). *Evidence-based practice of cognitive-behavioral therapy*. Guilford.

29. Greenberger, D., & Padesky, C. (1995). *Mind over mood: Changing how you feel by changing the way you think*. Guilford.

30. Larsson, A., Hooper, N., Osborne, L., Bennett, P., & McHugh, L. (2016). Using brief cognitive restructuring and cognitive defusion techniques to cope with negative thoughts. *Behavior Modification*, *40*(3), 452–482.

31. Beck. *Cognitive behavior therapy*; Prilleltensky & Prilleltensky. *The laughing guide to change*.

32. Siegel, D. J. (2010). *Mindsight: The new science of personal transformation*. Bantam; Williams, M., & Penman, D. (2011). *Mindfulness: An eight-week plan for finding peace in a frantic world*. Rodale.

33. Combs, G., & Freedman, J. (2012). Narrative, post-structuralism, and social justice: Current practices in narrative therapy. *The Counseling Psychologist*, *40*, 1033–1060; McLean, K. C., Pasupathi, M., & Pals, J. L. (2007). Selves creating stories creating selves: A process of self-development. *Personality and Social Psychology Review*, *11*, 262–278. https://doi.org/10.1177/108886830 7301034; Meichenbaum, D. (2012). *A Roadmap to resilience*. Institute Press.

34. Steele, C. (2010). *Whistling Vivaldi: How stereotype affect us and what we can do*. Norton; Yoshino, K. (2007). *Covering: The hidden assault on our civil rights*. Random House .

35. Pals, J. L. (2006). Narrative identity processing of difficult life experiences: Pathways of personality development and positive self-transformation in adulthood. *Journal of Personality, 74*, 1079–1110; Walton, G. M., & Wilson, T. D. (2018). Wise interventions: Psychological remedies for social and personal problems. *Psychological Review, 125*(5), 617–655. http://dx .doi.org/10.1037/rev0000115; White, M., & Epston, D. (1990). *Narrative means to therapeutic ends* (1st ed.). Norton.
36. Morgan, A. (200). *What is narrative therapy?* Dulwich Center.
37. Morrison, T. (2019). *The source of self-regard.* Knopf.
38. Harris, R. (2009). *ACT made simple: An easy-to-read primer on acceptance and commitment therapy.* New Harbinger Publications; Harris, R. (2011). *The confidence gap: A guide to overcoming fear and self-doubt.* Trumpeter Books; Hayes, S. C, Pistorello, J., & Levin, M. (2012). Acceptance and commitment therapy as a unified model of behavior change. *The Counseling Psychologist, 40* (7), 976–1002.
39. Bonanno & Burton. Regulatory flexibility.
40. Baney, J. (2004). *Guide to interpersonal communication.* Pearson Prentice Hall; Ivey, A., Ivey, M., & Zalaquett, C. (2010). *Intentional interviewing and counseling: Facilitating client development in a multicultural society* (7th ed.). Cengage Learning.
41. Glaser, S. & Glaser, P. A. (2006). *Be quiet be heard: The paradox of persuasion.* Communication Solutions Publishing.
42. Baney. *Guide to interpersonal communication*; Johnson. D. W., & Johnson, F. P. (2012). *Joining together: Group dynamics and group skills* (11th ed.). Pearson.
43. Brown, B. (2015). *Daring greatly: How the courage to be vulnerable transforms the way we live, love, parent, and lead.* Avery.
44. Canevello, A., & Crocker, J. (2010). Creating good relationships: Responsiveness, relationship quality, and interpersonal goals. *Journal of Personality and Social Psychology, 99*(1), 78–106. https://doi.org/10.1037/a0018186.
45. McGonigal, K. (2012). *The willpower instinct: How self-control works, why it matters, and what you can do to get more of it.* Penguin.
46. Ariely, D. (2009). *Predictably irrational: The hidden forces that shape our decisions.* Harper Collins.
47. Asch, S. E. (1956). Studies of independence and conformity. A minority of one against a unanimous majority. *Psychological Monographs, 70*(9), 1–70; Cialdini, R. (1993). *Influence: The psychology of persuasion.* Quill; Martins, C. M. & Vallen, B. (2014). The impact of holiday eating cues on self-regulatory bolstering for dieters and non-dieters. *Psychology & Health, 29* (4), 999–1013. https://doi.org/10.1080/08870446.2014.900682; Thaler & Sunstein. *Nudge.*

48. Andreassen, C. S., Pallesen, S., & Griffiths, M. D. (2017). The relationship between addictive use of social media, narcissism, and self-esteem: Findings from a large national survey. *Addictive Behaviors, 64,* 287–293. https://doi.org /10.1016/j.addbeh.2016.03.006; De Vries, D. A., & Kuhne, R. (2015). Facebook and self-perception: Individual susceptibility to negative social comparison on Facebook. *Personality and Individual Differences, 86,* 217–221. https://doi.org/10.1016/j.paid.2015.05.029; Hawi, N. S., & Samaha, M. (2017). The relations among social media addiction, self-esteem, and life satisfaction in university students. *Social Science Computer Review. 35*(5), 576–586. https:// doi.org/10.1177/0894439316660340; Vogel, E. A., Rose, J. P, Roberts, L. R., & Eckles, K. (2014). Social comparison, social media, and self-esteem. *Psychology of Popular Media Culture, 3*(4), 206–222.

49. Wansink, B. (2014). *Slim by design: Mindless eating solutions.* HarperCollins.

50. Lobel, T. (2014). *Sensation: The new science of physical intelligence.* Simon & Schuster; Ulrich, R. (1984). View through a window may influence recovery from surgery. *Science, 224,* 420–421.

51. Duhigg, C. (2016). *Smarter faster better: The transformative power of real productivity.* Random House.

52. Dolan, P. (2014). *Happiness by design: Change what you do, not how you think.* Hudson Street Press.

53. Brooks. *The second mountain.*

54. Prilleltensky, I. (1997). Values, assumptions, and practices: Assessing the moral implications of psychological discourse and action. *American Psychologist, 52*(5), 517–535; Prilleltensky, I. (2018). The road to mattering: challenging the status quo, promoting wellness and fairness. In F. Bemak and R. Conyne (Eds.), *Journeys to professional excellence* (11–22). Sage; Prilleltensky, I. (2019). Mattering at the intersection of psychology, philosophy, and politics. *American Journal of Community Psychology,* 1–19. https://doi.org/10.1002/ajcp.12368.

55. Cramer, P. (2006). *Protecting the self: Defense mechanisms in action.* Guilford; Diehl, M., Chui, H., Hay, E. L., Lumley, M. A., Grühn, D., & Labouvie-Vief, G. (2014). Change in coping and defense mechanisms across adulthood: Longitudinal findings in a European American sample. *Developmental Psychology, 50*(2), 634–648. https://doi.org/10.1037/a0033619; Freud, A. (1967). *The ego and the mechanisms of defense.* (Revised ed.). International Universities Press; Luft, J. (1969). *Of human interaction: The Johari model.* Mayfield Publishing; Metzger, J. A. (2014). Adaptive defense mechanisms: function and transcendence. *Journal of Clinical Psychology, 70*(5), 478–488. https://doi.org/10 .1002/jclp.22091; Sala, M., Testa, S., Pons, F., & Molina, P. (2015). Emotion regulation and defense mechanisms. *Journal of Individual Differences,36*(1), 19–29.

56. Brown. *Daring greatly;* Brown, B. (2017). *Braving the wilderness: The quest for true belonging and the courage to stand alone.* Random House.

57. Prilleltensky, I. (1994). *The morals and politics of psychology: Psychological discourse and the status quo*. State University of New York Press.
58. Gable, S. L., Gonzaga, G. C., & Strachman, A. (2006). Will you be there for me when things go right? Supportive responses to positive event disclosures. *Journal of Personality and Social Psychology, 91*(5), 904–917. https://doi.org/10.1037.0022-3514.91.5.904.
59. Norcross. *Changeology*; Watson & Tharp. *Self-directed behavior*.
60. Prilleltensky. *The laughing guide to well-being*.
61. Clear. *Atomic habits*.

5 Mattering through Mastery

1. Tough, P. (2012). *How children succeed: Grit, curiosity, and the hidden power of character*. Houghton Mifflin Harcourt (pp. 142–143).
2. Ibid.
3. Ibid., 145.
4. Duckworth, A. (2016). *Grit: The power of passion and perseverance*. Scribner (p. 91).
5. Brooks, D. (2015). *The road to character*. Random House (p. 131).
6. Ibid., 131.
7. Ibid.
8. Ericsson, A., & Pool, R. (2017). *Peak: Secrets from the new science of expertise*. Houghton, Mifflin, Harcourt.
9. Ibid., 95–96.
10. Rowson, J. (2019). *The moves that matter: A chess grandmaster on the fame of life*. Bloomsbury (Loc. 519).
11. Csikszentmihalyi, M., Khosla, S., & Nakamura, J. (2017). Flow at work. In L. G. Oades, M. F. Steger, A. Delle Fave, and J. Passmore (Eds.), *The Wiley Blackwell Handbook of the psychology of positivity and strengths-based approaches at work* (pp. 99–109). John Wiley & Sons.
12. Ericsson & Pool. *Peak*.
13. Ibid.
14. Ibid.
15. Duckworth, A. (2016). *Grit: The power of passion and perseverance*. Scribner.
16. Bandura, A. (Ed.). (1995). *Self-efficacy in changing societies*. Cambridge; Bandura, A. (2000). Exercise of human agency through collective efficacy. *Current Directions in Psychological Science, 9*(3), 75–78; Chaudhary, R., Rangnekar, S., & Barua, M. K. (2013). Engaged versus disengaged: The role of occupational self-efficacy. *Asian Academy of Management Journal, 18*(1), 91–108; Maddux, J. (2009). Self-efficacy: The power of believing you can. In S. Lopez & C. Snyder (Eds.), *Handbook of positive psychology* (pp. 335–344). Oxford;

Stajkovic, A., Bandura, A., Locke, E., Lee, D., & Sergent, K. (2018). Test of three conceptual models of influence on the big five personality traits and self-efficacy on academic performance: A meta-analytic path-analysis. *Personality and Individual Differences, 120,* 238–245; Usher, E. L., Li, C. R., Butz, A. R., & Rojas, J. P. (2019). Perseverant grit and self-efficacy: Are both essential for children's academic success? *Journal of Educational Psychology, 111*(5), 877–902.

17. Haimovitz, K., & Dweck, C. (2017). The origins of children's growth and fixed mindsets: new research and a new proposal. *Child Development, 88*(6), 1849–1859.

18. Myers, N.D., Dietz, S., Prilleltensky, I., Prilleltensky, O., McMahon, A., Rubenstein, C.L., & Lee, S. (2018). Efficacy of the fun for wellness online intervention to promote well-being actions: A secondary data analysis. *Games for Health Journal, 7*(4), 1–15; Myers, N.D., Prilleltensky, I., Hill, C. R., & Feltz, D. L. (2017). Well-being self-efficacy and complier average causal effect modeling: A substantive-methodological synergy. *Psychology of Sport & Exercise, 30,* 135–144. https://dx.doi.org/10.1016/j.psychsport.2017.02.010.

19. Dweck, C. (2016, January 13). What having a "growth mindset" actually means. *Harvard Business Review.* https://hbr.org/2016/01/what-having-a-gro wth-mindset-actually-means; Haimovitz & Dweck. The origins of children's growth and fixed mindsets.

20. Ericsson & Pool. *Peak.*

21. Phillips, K. A., Vaillant, G. E., & Schnurr, P. (1987). Some physiologic antecedents of adult mental health. *The American Journal of Psychiatry, 144,* 1009–1013. https://doi.org/10.1176/ajp.144.8.1009.

22. Ibid.

23. Baumeister, R., Tierney, J. (2011). *Willpower: Rediscovering the greatest human strength.* Penguin; McGonigal, K. (2012). *The willpower instinct: How self-control works, why it matters, and what you can do to get more of it.* Penguin.

24. Moffitt, T., Arseneault, L., Belsky, D., Dickson, N., Hancox, R., Harrington, H., Houts, R., Poulton, R., Roberts, B., Ross, S., Sears, M., Thomson, W., & Caspi, A. (2011). A gradient of childhood self-control predicts health, wealth, and public safety. *PNAS, 108*(7), 2693–2698. (p. 2693).

25. Biglan, A. (2015). *The nurture effect: How the science of human behaviour can improve our lives and the world.* New Harbinger.

26. Meaney, M., & Szyf, M. (2005). Environmental programming of stress responses through DNA methylation: Life at the interface between a dynamic environment and a fixed genome. *Dialogues in Clinical Neuroscience, 7*(2), 103–123.

27. McGowan, P., Sasaki, A., D'Alessio, A., Dymov, S., Labonte, B., Szyf, M., Turecki, G., & Meaney, M. (2009). Epigenetic regulation of the glucocorticoid receptor in human brain associates with childhood abuse. *Nature Neuroscience, 12*(3), 342–348. https://doi:10.1038/nn.2270.

28. McGill. (2009, February 22). *Childhood trauma has life-long effect on genes and the brain.* www.mcgill.ca/newsroom/channels/news/childhood-trauma-has-life-long-effect-genes-and-brain-104667.

29. Fisher, P., Frenkel, T., Noll, L., Berry, M., & Yockelson, M. (2016). Promoting healthy development via a two-generation translational neuroscience framework: The filming interactions to nurture development video coaching program. *Child Development Perspectives, 10*(4), 251–256. https://doi.org/10.1111/cdep.12195.

30. Mackler, J., Kelleher, R., Shanahan, L., Calkins, S, Keane, S., & O'Brien, M. (2015). Parenting stress, parental reactions, and externalizing behavior from ages 4 to 10. *Journal of Marriage and Family, 77*(2), 388–406. https://doi.org/10.1111/jomf.12163.

31. Tough, P. (2016). *Helping children succeed: What works and why.* Houghton Mifflin Harcourt; Tough, P. (2019). *The years that matter most: How college makes or breaks us.* Houghton Mifflin Harcourt.

32. Hanushek, E. (2016). What matters for student achievement. *Education Next, 16*(2). www.educationnext.org/what-matters-for-student-achievement/.

33. Gould, E. (2012). U.S. lags behind peer countries in mobility. *Economic Policy Institute.* www.epi.org/publication/usa-lags-peer-countries-mobility/; Graham. *Happiness for all?*

34. Weis, L., & Fine, M. (2012). Critical bifocality and circuits of privilege: Expanding critical ethnographic theory and design. *Harvard Educational Review, 82*(2), 173–202.

35. DiAngelo, R. (2018). *White fragility: Why it's so hard for White people to talk about racism.* Beacon Press; Kendi, I. X. (2019). *How to be an antiracist.* One World.

36. Sen, A. (2009). *The idea of justice.* Harvard; Nussbaum, M. (2011). *Creating capabilities: The human development approach.* Harvard.

37. Nausbaum. *Creating capabilities.* Loc. 351.

38. Ibid., Loc. 407.

39. Mullainathan, S., & Shafir, E. (2013). *Scarcity: Why having too little means so much.* Henry Holt.

40. Tough. *The years that matter most.*

41. Dorfman, A., & Mattelart, A. (1971). *Para leer al Pato Donald (How to read Donald Duck).* Ediciones Universitarias de Valparaiso; Dorfman, A., & Mattelart, A. (1975). *How to read Donald Duck.* International General.

42. Fox, D., & Prilleltensky, I., & Austin, S. (Eds.). (2009). *Critical Psychology: An Introduction* (2nd ed.). Sage; Prilleltensky, I. (2008). The role of power in wellness, oppression, and liberation: The promise of psychopolitical validity. *Journal of Community Psychology, 36,* 116–136.

43. Prilleltensky, I. (1989). Psychology and the status quo. *American Psychologist, 44,* 795–802.

44. Prilleltensky, I. (1994). *The morals and politics of psychology: Psychological discourse and the status quo.* State University of New York Press.

45. Braginsky, D. D. (1985). Psychology: Handmaiden to society. In S. Koch & D. E. Leary (Eds.), *A century of psychology as science* (pp. 880–891). McGraw-Hill.

46. Giridharadas, A. (2018). *Winners take all: The elite charade of changing the world.* Knopf.

47. Chapman, B., & Sisodia, R. (2015). *Everybody matters: The extraordinary power of caring for your people like family.* Penguin; Mackey, L., & Sisodia, R. (2014). *Conscious capitalism.* Harvard Business Review; Schlossberg, N. K. (1989). Marginality and mattering: Key issues in building community. *New Directions for Student Services, 48,* 5–15.

48. Marmot, M. (2015). *The health gap: The challenge of an unequal world.* Bloomsbury.

49. DiAngelo. *White fragility;* Kendi. *How to be an antiracist;* Payne, K. (2017). *The broken ladder: How inequality affects the way we think, live, and die.* Penguin; Twenge, J. M. (2014). *Generation Me: Why today's young Americans are more confident, assertive, entitled – and more miserable than ever before* (2nd ed.). Atria; Twenge, J., & Campbell, K. (2013). *The narcissism epidemic: Living in the age of entitlement.* Atria; Wilkinson, R., & Pickett, K. (2018). *The inner level: How more equal societies reduce stress, restore sanity and improve everyone's well-being.* Penguin.

50. Tirado, L. (2014). *Hand to mouth: Living in bootstrap America.* Penguin (p. 26).

51. Yoshino, K. (2007). *Covering: The hidden assault on our civil rights.* Random House.

52. Oluo, I. (2019). *So you want to talk about race.* Seal Press.

53. Heumann, J. (2020). *Being Heumann: An unrepentant memoir of a disability rights activist.* Beacon Press.

54. Andrews, W., & McFeely, W. (Eds.). (1997). *Narrative of the life of Frederick Douglass, An American slave, written by himself.* Norton; Gladwell, M. (2019). *Talking to strangers: What people should know about the people we don't know.* Little, Brown and Company.

55. Brown, N., Lomas, T., & Eiroa-Orosa, F. J. (Eds.). (2018). *The Routledge international handbook of critical positive psychology.* Routledge; Burkeman, O. (2019, May 14). The second mountain by David Brooks: Review – A self-help guide to escaping the self. *The Guardian.* www.theguardian.com/books/2019/may/14/the-second-mountain-quest-for-moral-life-david-brooks-review; Schwartz, A. (2018, January 8). Improving ourselves to death: What the self-help gurus and their critics reveal about our times. *The New Yorker.* www.newyorker.com/magazine/2018/01/15/improving-ourselves-to-death; Shulevitz,

J. (2016, May 4). Review of Grit. *The New York Times.* www.nytimes.com/20
16/05/08/books/review/grit-by-angela-duckworth.html.

56. De Vogli, R., Brunner, E., & Marmot, M. G. (2007). Unfairness and the
social gradient of metabolic syndrome in the Whitehall II study. *Journal of
Psychosomatic Research, 63*(4), 413–419; De Vogli, R., Ferrie, J. E.,
Chandola, T., Kivimaki, M., & Marmot, M. G. (2007). Unfairness and
health: Evidence from the Whitehall II study. *Journal of Epidemiology and
Community Health, 61,* 513–518; Elovainio, M., Kivimaki, M., & Vahtera, J.
(2002). Organizational justice: Evidence of a new psychosocial predictor of
health. *American Journal of Public Health, 92*(1), 105–108.

57. Corning, P. (2011). *The fair society.* Chicago University Press; Tornblom, K.,
& Vermunt, R. (Eds.). (2007). *Distributive and procedural justice: Research
and social applications.* Ashgate; Vermunt, R., & Steensma, H. (2016).
Procedural justice. In C. Sabbagh & M. Schmitt (Eds.), *Handbook of social
justice theory and research* (pp.219–236). Springer.

58. Ibid.

59. Prilleltensky (2008). The role of power in wellness, oppression, and liberation;
Prilleltensky, I., Prilleltensky, O., & Voorhees, C. (2007). Psychopolitical
validity in the helping professions: Applications to research, interventions,
case conceptualization, and therapy. In C. Cohen, and S. Tamiami (Eds.),
Liberatory psychiatry: Towards a new psychiatry (pp. 105–130). Cambridge.

60. De Vogli, Brunner & Marmot. Unfairness and the social gradient of
metabolic syndrome in the Whitehall II study; De Vogli, Ferrie, Chandola,
Kivimaki & Marmot. Unfairness and health; Elovainio, Kivimaki & Vahtera.
Organizational justice.

61. Mehta, J. (2014, June 20). Deeper learning has a race problem. *Education
Week.* http://blogs.edweek.org/edweek/learning_deeply/2014/06/deeper_lear
ning_has_a_race_problem.html.

62. Fiske, S. (2011). *Envy up, scorn down: How status divides us.* Russell Sage.

63. Steele, C. (1997). A threat in the air: How stereotypes shape intellectual
identity and performance. *American Psychologist, 52*(6), 613–629 (p. 614).

64. Ibid., 614.

65. Ibid., 620.

66. Steele, C. (2010). *Whistling Vivaldi: How stereotype affect us and what we can
do.* Norton (p. 216).

67. Yeager, D. S., Walton, G. M., Brady, S. T., Akcinar, E. N., Paunesku, D.,
Keane, L., Kamentz, D., Ritter, G., Duckworth, A., Urstein, R., Gomez, E.,
Markus, H., Cohen, G., & Dweck, C. (2016, May 31). Teaching a lay theory
before college narrows achievement gaps at scale (E3342). *PNAS Plus.* www
.pnas.org/cgi/doi/10.1073/pnas.1524360113.

68. Ibid.

69. Walton, G. M., & Cohen, G. L. (2011). A brief social belonging intervention improves academic and health outcomes of minority students. *Science, 331,* 1447–1451.
70. Walton, G. M., Logel, C., Peach, J., Spencer, S., & Zanna, M. P. (2015). Two brief interventions to mitigate a "chilly climate" transform women's experience, relationships, and achievement in engineering. *Journal of Educational Psychology, 107*(2), 468–485.
71. Yeager, Walton, Brady, Akcinar, Paunesku, Keane, Kamentz, Ritter, Duckworth, Urstein, Gomez, Markus, Cohen & Dweck. Teaching a lay theory before college narrows achievement gaps at scale (E3347).
72. Andreassen, C. S., Pallesen, S., & Griffiths, M. D. (2017). The relationship between addictive use of social media, narcissism, and self-esteem: findings from a large national survey. *Addictive Behaviors, 64,* 287–293. https://doi.org /10.1016/j.addbeh.2016.03.006; Damour, L. (2019). *Under pressure: Confronting the epidemic of stress and anxiety in girls.* Ballantine; Hibbs, J., & Rostain, A. (2019). *The stressed years of our lives: Helping your kind survive and thrive during their college years.* St. Martin's; Vogel, E. A., Rose, J. P, Roberts, L. R., & Eckles, K. (2014). Social comparison, social media, and self-esteem. *Psychology of Popular Media Culture, 3*(4), 206–222.

6 Mattering through Self-Regard

1. Bernard, M. E. (Ed.). (2013). *The strength of self-acceptance: Theory, practice, and research.* Springer; Patterson, T. G., & Joseph, S. (2013). Unconditional positive regard. In M. G. Bernard (Ed.), *The strength of self-acceptance: Theory, practice, and research* (pp. 93–106). Springer; Rogers, C. (1961). *On becoming a person: A therapist's view of psychotherapy.* Houghton Mifflin.
2. Bosson, J., & Swann, W. B., Jr. (2009). Self-esteem: Nature, origins, and consequences. In R. Hoyle & M. Leary (Eds.), *Handbook of individual differences in social behavior* (pp. 527–546). Guilford; Eromo, T. L., & Levy, D. A. (2017). The rise, fall, and resurgence of "self-esteem": A critique, reconceptualization, and recommendations. *North American Journal of Psychology, 19*(2), 255–303; Pyszczynski, T. & Kesebir, P. (2013). An existential perspective on the need for self-esteem. In V. Zeigler-Hill (Ed.), *Self-Esteem* (pp. 124–143). Psychology Press.
3. Rosenberg, M. (1965). *Society and the adolescent self-image.* Princeton (p. 25).
4. Prilleltensky, O. (2004). *Motherhood and disability: Children and choices.* Palgrave/Macmillan (p. 125).
5. Ibid., 125.
6. Ibid., 126.

7. Pyszczynski & Kesebir. An existential perspective on the need for self-esteem.

8. Orth, U., & Robins, R. (2014). The development of self-esteem. *Current Directions in Psychological Science, 23*(5), 381–387; Trzesniewski, K. H., Donnellan, M. B., Moffitt, T. E., Robins, R. W., Poulton, R., & Caspi, A. (2006). Low self-esteem during adolescence predicts poor health, criminal behavior, and limited economic prospects during adulthood. *Developmental Psychology, 42*, 381–390.

9. Bosson & Swann. Self-esteem; MacDonald, G., & Leary, M.R. (2011). Individual differences in self-esteem. In M. R. Leary and J. P. Tangley (Eds.), *Handbook of self and identity* (2nd ed., pp. 354–377). Guilford.

10. Buss, A. (2012). *Pathways to individuality: Evolution and development of personality traits.* American Psychological Association; Di Paula, A., & Campbell, J. (2002). Self-esteem and persistence in the face of failure. *Journal of Personality and Social Psychology, 83*(3), 711–724.

11. Mahadevan, N., Gregg, A.P., Sedikides, C., & De Waal-Andrews, W. G. (2016). Winners, losers, insiders, and outsiders: Comparing hierometer and sociometer theories of self-regard. *Frontiers of Psychology,* 7:334. https://doi .org/10.3389/fpsyg.2016.00334.

12. Brown, J. D. (2010). High self-esteem buffers negative feedback: Once more with feeling. *Cognition and Emotion, 24*, 1389–1404.

13. Erol, R. Y., & Orth, U. (2017). Self-esteem and the quality of romantic relationships. *European Psychologist, 21*, 274–283; Holden, C., Zeigler-Hill, V., Shackelford, T., & Welling, L. (2018). The impact of relationship-contingent self-esteem on mate retention and reactions to threat. *Personal Relationships, 25*(4), 611–630; Hoplock, L., Stinson, D., Marigold, D., & Fisher, A. (2019). Self-esteem, epistemic needs, and responses to social feedback. *Self and Identity,* 18(5), 467–493.

14. Hoplock, Stinson, Marigold & Fisher. Self-esteem, epistemic needs, and responses to social feedback, 470.

15. Holden, Zeigler-Hill, Shackelford & Welling. The impact of relationship-contingent self-esteem on mate retention and reactions to threat; Erol & Orth. Self-esteem and the quality of romantic relationships.

16. El Ghaziri, N., & Darwiche, J. (2018). Adult self-esteem and family relationships. *Swiss Journal of Psychology, 77*(3), 99–115.

17. Baumeister, R. F., Campbell, J. D., Krueger, J. I., & Vohs, K. D. (2003). Does high self-esteem cause better performance, interpersonal success, happiness, or healthier lifestyles? *Psychological Science in the Public Interest, 4*, 1–44; Diener, E., & Diener, M. (1995). Cross-cultural correlates of life satisfaction and self-esteem. *Journal of Personality and Social Psychology: Personality Processes and Individual Differences, 68*, 653–663; Eromo & Levy. The rise, fall, and resurgence of "self-esteem."

18. Fredrickson, B. (2009) *Positivity*. Three Rivers, Lyubomirsky, S., Sheldon, K., & Schkade, D. (2005). Pursuing happiness: The architecture of sustainable change. *Review of General Psychology, 9*(2), 111–131; Seligman, M. (2011). *Flourish: A visionary new understanding of happiness and well-being*. Free Press; Seligman, M. E. P. (2002). *Authentic happiness*. Free Press.

19. Diener, E., & Biswas-Diener, R. (2008). *Happiness: Unlocking the mysteries of psychological wealth*. Blackwell Publishing; Fredrickson, B., & Kurtz, L. (2011). Cultivating positive emotions to enhance human flourishing. In S. I. Donaldson, M. Csikzentmihalyi & J. Nakamura (Eds.), *Applied positive psychology: Improving everyday life, health, schools, work, and society* (pp. 35–47). Routledge.

20. Orth, U., & Robins, R. (2013). Understanding the link between low self-esteem and depression. *Current Directions in Psychological Science, 22*(6), 455–460. https://doi.org/10.1177/0963721413492763; Rosenberg. *Society and the adolescent self-image*; Sowislo, J. F., & Orth, U. (2013). Does low self-esteem predict depression and anxiety? A meta-analysis of longitudinal studies. *Psychological Bulletin, 139*, 213–240.
https://doi.org/10.1037/a0028931.

21. Zeigler-Hill, V. (2013). The importance of self-esteem. In V. Zeigler-Hill (Ed.), *Self-Esteem* (1–20). Psychology Press.

22. Pyszczynski & Kesebir. An existential perspective on the need for self-esteem, 131.

23. Baumeister, Campbell, Krueger & Vohs. Does high self-esteem cause better performance interpersonal success, happiness, or healthier lifestyles?; Twenge, J. M. (2014). *Generation Me: Why today's young Americans are more confident, assertive, entitled – and more miserable than ever before* (2nd ed.). Atria; Twenge, J., & Campbell, K. (2013). *The narcissism epidemic: Living in the age of entitlement*. Atria.

24. California Task Force to Promote Self-Esteem and Personal and Social Responsibility. (1990). *Toward a state of self-esteem*. California State Department of Education.

25. Twenge. *Generation Me*.

26. Baumeister, R., & Vohs, K. (2018). Revisiting our reappraisal of the (surprisingly few) benefits of high self-esteem. *Perspectives on Psychological Science, 13*(2), 137–140.

27. Baumeister, Campbell, Krueger & Vohs. Does high self-esteem cause better performance interpersonal success, happiness, or healthier lifestyles?

28. Orth, U., Robins, R., Widaman, K., & King, L. (2012). Life-span development of self-esteem and its effects on important life outcomes. *Journal of Personality and Social Psychology, 102*(6), 1271–1288; Sowislo & Orth. Does low self-esteem predict depression and anxiety?; Swann, W. B., Chang-Schneider, C., &

McClarty, K. L. (2007). Do people's self-views matter? Self-concept and self-esteem in everyday life. *American Psychologist*, 62, 84–94.

29. Rosenberg. *Society and the adolescent self-image.*

30. Trzesniewski, Donnellan, Moffitt, Robins, Poulton, & Caspi. Low self-esteem during adolescence predicts poor health, criminal behavior, and limited economic prospects during adulthood, 385.

31. Orth, Robins, Widaman & King. Life-span development of self-esteem and its effects on important life outcomes, 1283.

32. Rosenberg. *Society and the adolescent self-image*, 62.

33. Ibid., 62.

34. Jordan, C. H. & Zeigler-Hill, V. (2013). Fragile self-esteem: The perils and pitfalls of (some) high self-esteem. In V. Zeigler-Hill (Ed.), *Self-Esteem* (pp. 80–98). Psychology Press; Swann, Chang-Schneider & McClarty. Do people's self-views matter? Self-concept and self-esteem in everyday life; Zeigler-Hill. The importance of self-esteem.

35. Baumeister, Campbell, Krueger & Vohs. Does high self-esteem cause better performance interpersonal success, happiness, or healthier lifestyles? 2.

36. Bosson, J. K., Lakey, C. E., Campbell, W. K., Zeigler-Hill, V., Jordan, C. H., & Kernis, M. H. (2008). Untangling the links between narcissism and self-esteem: A theoretical and empirical review. *Social and Personality Psychology Compass*, 2, 1415–1439; Brummelman, E., Thomaes, S., & Sedikides, C. (2016). Separating narcissism from self-esteem. *Current Directions in Psychological Science*, 25(1), 8–13; Eromo & Levy. The rise, fall, and resurgence of "self-esteem"; Zeigler-Hill, V., Holden, C. J., Southard, A. C., Noser, A. E., Enjaian, B., & Pollock, N. C. (2016). The dark sides of high and low self-esteem. In V. Zeigler-Hill & D. K. Marcus (Eds.), *The dark side of personality: Science and practice in social, personality, and clinical psychology* (pp. 325–340). American Psychological Association.

37. Kernis, M. H. (2003). Optimal self-esteem and authenticity: Separating fantasy from reality. *Psychological Inquiry*, 14, 83–89; Park, L. E., & Crocker, J. (2008). Contingencies of self-worth and responses to negative interpersonal feedback. *Self & Identity*, 7, 184–203; Zeigler-Hill, Holden, Southard, Noser, Enjaian, & Pollock. The dark sides of high and low self-esteem.

38. Jordan & Zeigler-Hill. Fragile self-esteem: The perils and pitfalls of (some) high self-esteem, 80.

39. Crocker, J. & Parker, L. E. (2011). Contingencies of self-worth. In M. R. Leary and J. P. Tangley (Eds.), *Handbook of self and identity* (2nd ed., pp. 309–326). Guilford; Lakey, C., Hirsch, J., Nelson, L., & Nsamenang, S. (2014). Effects of contingent self-esteem on depressive symptoms and suicidal behavior. *Death Studies*, 38(9), 563–570; Park, L. E., & Maner, J. K. (2011). Does self-threat promote social connection? The role of self-esteem and contingences of

self-worth. *Journal of Personality and Social Psychology, 96,* 203–271; Ryan, R. M., & Brown, K. W. (2006). What is optimal self-esteem? The cultivation and consequences of contingent vs. true self-esteem as viewed from the self-determination theory perspective. In M. H. Kernis (Ed.), *Self-esteem issues and answers: A sourcebook of current perspectives* (pp. 125–131). Psychology Press.

40. Park, L. E., Crocker, J., & Kiefer, A. K. (2007). Contingencies of self-worth, academic failure, and goal pursuit. *Personality and Social Psychology Bulletin, 33,* 1503–1517.
    Wouters, S., Thomaes, S., Colpin, H., Luyckx, K., & Verschueren, K. (2018). How does conditional regard impact well-being and eagerness to learn? An experimental study. *Psychologica Belgica, 58*(1), 105–114. https://doi.org/10.5334/pb.401.

41. Kernis, M. H. (2003). Toward a conceptualization of optimal self-esteem. *Psychological Inquiry, 14,* 1–26; Ryan & Brown. What is optimal self-esteem?; Vonk, R., & Smit, H. (2012). Optimal self-esteem is contingent: intrinsic versus extrinsic and upward versus downward contingencies. *European Journal of Personality, 26*(3), 182–193.

42. Crocker & Parker. Contingencies of self-worth.

43. Epstein, R. (2001, January 1). The prince of reason: An interview with Albert Ellis. *Psychology Today.* www.psychologytoday.com/us/articles/200101/the-prince-reason.

44. Ellis, A., & Harper, R. A. (1961). *A guide to rational living.* Prentice-Hall.

45. Bernard. *The strength of self-acceptance*; Kim, S., & Gal, D. (2014). From compensatory consumption to adaptive consumption: The role of self-acceptance in resolving self-deficits. *Journal of Consumer Research, 41*(2), 526–542; Patterson, T. G., & Joseph, S. (2013). Unconditional positive regard. In M. G. Bernard (Ed.), *The strength of self-acceptance: Theory, practice, and research* (pp. 93–106). Springer.

46. Neff, K. D. (2009). The role of self-compassion in development: A healthier way to relate to oneself. *Human Development, 52,* 211–214; Neff, K. D. (2011). *Self-compassion: The proven power of being kind to yourself.* William Morrow; Neff, K. D. (2012). The science of self-compassion. In C. Germer & R. Siegel (Eds.), *Compassion and wisdom in psychotherapy* (pp. 79–92). Guilford.

47. Germer, C., & Neff, K. (2019). *Teaching the mindful self-compassion program: A guide for professionals.* Guilford; Neff, K. D., & Germer, C. (2017). Self-compassion and psychological wellbeing. In E. Seppala (Ed.), *Oxford Handbook of Compassion Science* (pp. 371–386). Oxford; Warren, R., Smeets, E., & Neff, K. D. (2016). Self-criticism and self-compassion: Risk and resilience for psychopathology. *Current Psychiatry, 15*(12), 18–32.

48. Neff, K. D. (2011). Self-compassion, self-esteem, and well-being. *Social and Personality Compass, 5,* 1–12; Neff, K. D., & Vonk, R. (2009). Self-

compassion versus global self-esteem: Two different ways of relating to oneself. *Journal of Personality, 77*, 23–50.

49. Crocker, J., Karpinski, A., Quinn, D. M., & Chase, S. (2003). When grades determine self-worth: Consequences of contingent self-worth for male and female engineering and psychology majors. *Journal of Personality and Social Psychology, 85*, 507–516.

50. CBS News. (2019, October 23). Lady Gaga's mom on witnessing her daughter's "turn" in mental health. www.cbsnews.com/news/lady-gaga-mom-cynthia-germanotta-on-witnessing-daughters-turn-in-mental-health/.

51. Broderick, P. C., & Blewitt, P. (2020). *The life span: Human development for helping professionals* (5th ed.). Pearson; Harter, S., (2012). *The construction of the self: Developmental and sociocultural foundations* (2nd ed.). Guilford.

52. Orth & Robins. The development of self-esteem.

53. Bosson & Swann. Self-esteem; DeHart, T., Pena, R., & Tennen, Z. (2013). The development of explicit and implicit self-esteem and their role in psychological adjustment. In V. Zeigler-Hill (Ed.), *Self-Esteem* (99–123). Psychology Press.

54. Bowlby, J. (1969). *Attachment and loss: Vol 1. Attachment.* Basic Books; Bowlby, J. (1973). *Attachment and loss: Vol 2. Separation: Anxiety and anger.* Basic Books; Thompson, R. A. (2016). Early attachment and later development: Reframing the questions. In J. Cassidy & P. R. Shaver (Eds.), *Handbook of attachment: Theory, research, and clinical applications* (pp. 330–365). Guilford.

55. Belsky, J., & Pluess, M. (2009). Beyond diathesis stress: Differential susceptibility to environmental influences. *Psychological Bulletin, 135*(6), 885–908; Vaughn, B. E. (2016). Attachment and temperament as intersecting developmental products and interacting developmental contexts throughout infancy and childhood. In J. Cassidy & P. R. Shaver (Eds.), *Handbook of attachment: Theory, research, and clinical applications* (pp. 202–222). Guilford.

56. Broderick & Blewitt. *The life span*; Harter. *The construction of the self*; Keizer, R., Helmerhorst, K., & Van Rijn-van Gelderen, O. (2019). Perceived quality of the mother–adolescent and father–adolescent attachment relationship and adolescents' self-esteem. *Journal of Youth and Adolescence, 48*(6), 1203–1217.

57. Biglan, A. (2015). *The nurture effect: How the science of human behaviour can improve our lives and the world.* New Harbinger; Putnam, R. (2015). *Our kids: The American dream in crisis.* Simon & Schuster.

58. Putnam. *Our kids.*

59. Ibid.

60. Bosson & Swann. Self-esteem; Broderick & Blewitt. *The life span.*

61. Allen, J. P. (2016). The multiple facets of attachment in adolescence. In J. Cassidy & P. R. Shaver (Eds.), *Handbook of attachment: Theory, research,*

and clinical applications (pp. 415–365). Guilford; Thompson. Early attachment and later development.

62. Broderick & Blewitt. *The life span.*
63. Harter. *The construction of the self.*
64. Ibid.
65. Leary. Sociometer theory and the pursuit of relational value, 88.
66. Broderick & Blewitt. *The life span;* Harter. *The construction of the self.*
67. Rogers. *On becoming a person.*
68. Ryan & Brown. What is optimal self-esteem? 127.
69. Assor, A., & Tal, K. (2012). When parents' affection depends on child's achievement: Parental conditional positive regard, self-aggrandizement, shame and coping in adolescents. *Journal of Adolescence, 35,* 249–260.
70. Roth, G., Assor, A., Niemiec, C. P., Ryan, R. M., & Deci, E. L. (2009). The emotional and academic consequences of parental conditional regard: comparing conditional positive regard, conditional negative regard, and autonomy support as parenting practices. *Developmental Psychology, 45,* 1119–1142.
71. Wouters, S., Doumen, S., Germeijs, V., Colpin, H., & Verschueren, K. (2013). Contingencies of self-worth in early adolescence: The antecedent role of perceived parenting. *Social Development, 22*(2), 242–258.
72. Otterpohl, N., Lazar, R., & Stiensmeier-Pelster, J. (2019). The dark side of perceived positive regard: When parents' well-intended motivation strategies increase students' test anxiety. *Contemporary Educational Psychology, 56,* 79–90.
73. Wuyts, D., Vansteenkiste, M., Soenens, B., & Assor, A. (2015). An examination of the dynamics involved in parental child-invested contingent self-esteem. *Parenting, 15*(2), 55–74.
74. Harvard Graduate School of Education. (2014). *The children we mean to raise: The real messages adults are sending about values.* https://mcc.gse.harvard.edu /reports/children-mean-raise.
75. Biglan. *The nurture effect.*
76. Brummelman, Thomaes & Sedikides. Separating narcissism from self-esteem; Brummelman, E., Thomaes, S., Nelemans, S., Orobio de Castro, B., Overbeek, G., & Bushman, B. (2015). Origins of narcissism in children. *Proceedings of the National Academy of Sciences of the United States of America 112*(12), 3659–3662;
Brummelman, E., Nelemans, S., Thomaes, S., & Orobio de Castro, B. (2017). When parents' praise inflates, children's self-esteem deflates. *Child Development, 88*(6), 1799–1809.
77. Brummelman, E., Thomaes, S., Nelemans, S., Orobio de Castro, B., & Bushman, B. (2015). My child is God's gift to humanity: Development and validation of the Parental Overvaluation Scale (POS). *Journal of Personality and Social Psychology, 108*(4), 665–79 (p. 666).

78. Brummelman, Thomaes & Sedikides. Separating narcissism from self-esteem (p. 9).

79. Brummelman, E., & Thomaes, S. (2017). How children construct views of themselves: A social-developmental perspective. *Child Development, 88*(6), 1763–1773; Brummelman, Nelemans, Thomaes & Orobio de Castro. When parents' praise inflates, children's self-esteem deflates; Brummelman, Thomaes, Nelemans, Orobio de Castro, Overbeek & Bushman. Origins of narcissism in children.

80. Park & Crocker. Contingencies of self-worth and responses to negative interpersonal feedback.

81. Beck, J. S. (2011). *Cognitive behavior therapy: Basics and beyond* (2nd ed.). Guilford; Donohue, W., & Fisher, J. (2012). *Cognitive behavior therapy: Core principles for practice*. John Wiley & Sons.

82. Ryan, R., & Deci, E. (2017). *Self-determination theory: Basic psychological needs in motivation, development, and wellness*. Guilford.

83. Ryan & Brown. What is optimal self-esteem?

84. Jordan & Zeigler-Hill. Fragile self-esteem: The perils and pitfalls of (some) high self-esteem, 91.

85. Norcross, J. C. (2012). *Changeology: 5 steps to realizing your goals and resolutions*. Simon & Schuster; Watson, D. L. & Tharp, R. G. (2014). *Self-directed behavior: Self-modification for personal adjustment* (10th ed.). Cengage Learning.

86. Neff, K., & Germer, C. (2018). *The mindful self-compassion workbook: A proven way to accept yourself, build inner strength, and thrive*. Guilford.

87. Biglan, A., Hayes, S., & Pistorello, C. (2008). Acceptance and commitment: implications for prevention science. *Prevention Science, 9*(3), 139–152; Harris, R. (2009). *ACT made simple: An easy-to-read primer on acceptance and commitment therapy*. New Harbinger Publications.

88. Hayes, S. C., Strosahl, K. D., & Wilson, K. G. (2012). *Acceptance and commitment therapy* (2nd ed.). Guilford; Larsson, A., Hooper, N., Osborne, L., Bennett, P., & McHugh, L. (2016). Using brief cognitive restructuring and cognitive defusion techniques to cope with negative thoughts. *Behavior Modification, 40*(3), 452–482.

89. Harris. *ACT made simple*; Harris, R. (2011). *The confidence gap: A guide to overcoming fear and self-doubt*. Trumpeter Books; Hayes, S., & Smith, S. (2005). *Get out of your mind and into your life: The new acceptance and commitment therapy*. New Harbinger.

90. Neff. *Self-compassion: The proven power of being kind to yourself.*

91. Neff & Germer. *The mindful self-compassion workbook.*

92. Germer & Neff. *Teaching the mindful self-compassion program.*

93. Breines, J. G., & Chen, S. (2012). Self-compassion increases self-improvement motivation. *Personality and Social Psychology Bulletin, 38*(9), 1133–1143; Kelliher Rabon, J., Sirois, F. M., & Hirsch, J. K. (2018). Self-compassion and suicidal behavior in college students: Serial indirect effects via depression and wellness behaviors. *Journal of American College Health, 66*(2), 114–122; MacBeth, A., & Gumley, A. (2012). Exploring compassion: A meta-analysis of the association between self-compassion and psychopathology. *Clinical Psychology Review, 32,* 545–552; Marsh, I. C., Chan, S. W., & MacBeth, A. (2018). Self-compassion and psychological distress in adolescents – a meta-analysis. *Mindfulness, 9*(4), 1011–1027; Stutts, L. A., Leary, M. R., Zeveney, A. S., & Hufnagle, A. S. (2018). A longitudinal analysis of the relationship between self-compassion and the psychological effects of perceived stress. *Self and Identity, 17*(6), 609–626; Zessin, U., Dickhauser, O., & Garbade, S. (2015). The relationship between self-compassion and well-being: A meta-analysis. *Applied Psychology: Health and Well-Being, 7*(3), 340–364; Zhang, J., Chen, S., Tomova Shakur, T., Bilgin, B., Chai, W., Ramis, T., & Manukyan, A. (2019). A compassionate self is a true self? Self-compassion promotes subjective authenticity. *Personality and Social Psychology Bulletin, 45*(9), 1323–1337.
94. Neff, K. D. (2011). Self-compassion, self-esteem, and well-being. *Social and Personality Compass, 5,* 1–12; Neff, K. D., & Vonk, R. (2009). Self-compassion versus global self-esteem: Two different ways of relating to oneself. *Journal of Personality, 77,* 23–50.
95. Neff, K. D., & Beretvas, S. N. (2013). The role of self-compassion in romantic relationships. *Self and Identity, 12*(1), 78–98.

7 Mattering in the Inner Circle

1. Pileggi Pawelski, S., & Pawelski, J. O. (2018). *Happy together: Using the science of positive psychology to build love that lasts.* Penguin.
2. Gottman, J. M, & Gottman, J. (2017). The natural principles of love. *Journal of Family Theory & Review, 9*(1), 7–26; Gottman, J. M., & DeClaire, J. (2001). *The relationship cure: A 5 step guide to strengthening your marriage, family, and friendships.* Crown; Gottman, J. M., & Silver, N. (2000). *The seven principles for making marriage work.* Three Rivers.
3. Gottman, J., Schwartz Gottman, J., Abrams, D., & Carlton Abrams, R. (2019). *Eight dates: Essential conversations for a lifetime of love.* Workman.
4. Ibid.
5. Brown, B. (2015). *Daring greatly: How the courage to be vulnerable transforms the way we live, love, parent, and lead.* Avery.

6. Vermunt, R., & Steensma, H. (2016). Procedural justice. In C. Sabbagh & M. Schmitt (Eds.), *Handbook of social justice theory and research* (pp. 219–236). Springer.

7. Lee, Gary R., DeMaris, A., Bavin, S., Sullivan, R. (2001). Gender differences in the depressive effect of widowhood in later life. *Journal of Gerontology: Psychological Sciences.* *56*(1): S56.https://doi.org/10.1093/geronb/56.1.s56 ; Streeter, J. L. (2020). Gender differences in widowhood in the short-run and long-run: Financial, emotional, and mental wellbeing. *The Journal of the Economics of Ageing, 17,* 100258. https://doi.org/10.1016/j.jeoa.2020.100258; Umberson, D., Wortman, C., & Kessler, R. C. (1992). Widowhood and depression: Explaining long-term gender differences in vulnerability. *Journal of Health and Social Behavior, 33*(1), 10–24.

8. Fredrickson, B. (2013).*Love 2.0: How our supreme emotion affects everything we feel, think, do, and become.* Penguin; Gable, S. (2011). Affiliation and stress. In S. Folkman (Ed.), *The Oxford handbook of health, stress, and coping* (pp. 86–100). Oxford; Kroenke, C., Kubzansky, L., Schernhammer, E., Holmes, M., & Kawachi, I. (2006). Social networks, social support, and survival after breast cancer diagnosis. *Journal of Clinical Oncology: Official Journal of the American Society of Clinical Oncology, 24*(7), 1105–1111;
Pinker, S. (2014). *The village effect: How face-to-face contact can make us healthier and happier.* Random House.

9. Diener, E. & Biswas-Diener, R. (2008). *Happiness: Unlocking the mysteries of psychological wealth.* Blackwell Publishing.

10. Hawkley, L., & Cacioppo, C. (2010). Loneliness matters: A theoretical and empirical review of consequences and mechanisms. *Annals of Behavioral Medicine, 40*(2), 218–227; Holt-Lunstad, J. (2017). The potential public health relevance of social isolation and loneliness: Prevalence, epidemiology, and risk factors. *Public Policy & Aging Report, 27*(4), 127–130; Holt-Lunstad, J., Smith, T., Baker, M., Harris, T., & Stephenson, D. (2015). Loneliness and social isolation as risk factors for mortality: A meta-analytic review. *Perspectives on Psychological Science, 10*(2), 227–237. https://doi.org/10.1177/1745691614568352.

11. Fredrickson. *Love 2.0.,* 3.

12. Waldinger, R., & Schulz, M. (2016). The long reach of nurturing family environments: Links with midlife emotion-regulatory styles and late-life security in intimate relationships. *Psychological Science, 27*(11), 1443–1450.

13. Hamblin, (2015, December 30). The physiological power of altruism. *The Atlantic.* www.theatlantic.com/health/archive/2015/12/altruism-for-a-better-body/422280/.

14. Powdthavee, N. (2008). Putting a price tag on friends, relatives, and neighbours: Using surveys of life satisfaction to value social relationships. *Journal of Socio-Economics, 37*(4), 1459–1480.

15. Pinker. *The village effect.*

16. Kroenke, Kubzansky, Schernhammer, Holmes & Kawachi. Social networks, social support, and survival after breast cancer diagnosis.

17. Park, N., Oates, S., & Schwarzer, R. (2013). Christopher Peterson: "Other people matter." *Applied Psychology: Health and Well-Being, 5*(1), 1–4. https://doi.org/10.1111/aphw.12007.

18. Fredrickson. *Love 2.0.,* 4.

19. Brown, *Daring greatly.*

20. Lieberman, M. (2013). *Social: Why our brains are wired to connect.* Random House.

21. Mikulincer, M., & Shaver, P. (2007). *Attachment in adulthood: Structure, dynamics, and change.* Guilford.

22. Lyubomirsky, S. (2007*). The how of happiness: The new approach to getting the life you want.* Penguin.

23. Gottman & DeClaire. *The relationship cure*; Gottman & Silver. *The seven principles for making marriage work.*

24. Fredrickson. *Love 2.0.*; Gottman, Schwartz Gottman, Abrams & Carlton Abrams. *Eight dates*; Pileggi Pawelski & Pawelski. *Happy together.*

25. Prilleltensky, I. (2016). *The laughing guide to well-being: Using humor and science to become happier and healthier.* Rowman and Littlefield.

26. Prilleltensky, I., & Prilleltensky, O. (2019). *The laughing guide to a better life: Using humor and science to improve yourself, your relationships, and your surroundings.* Rowman and Littlefield.

27. Gable, S. L., Gonzaga, G. C., & Strachman, A. (2006). Will you be there for me when things go right? Supportive responses to positive event disclosures. *Journal of Personality and Social Psychology, 91*(5), 904–917. https://doi.org/10.1037.0022 -3514.91.5.904; Gable, S. L., Reis, H. T., Impett, E. A., & Asher, E. R. (2004). What do you do when things go right? The intrapersonal and interpersonal benefits of sharing positive events. *Journal of Personality and Social Psychology, 87* (2), 228–245 https://doi.org/10.1037/0022-3514.87.2.228.

28. Glaser, S. & Glaser, P. A. (2006). *Be quiet be heard: The paradox of persuasion.* Communication Solutions Publishing. Farmer, R. F., & Chapman, A. L. (2016). *Behavioral interventions in cognitive behavior therapy: Practical guidance for putting theory into action* (2nd ed.). American Psychological Association.

8 Mattering in Teams

1. Bowe, J., Bowe, M., & Streeter, S. (Eds.). (2001). *Gig: Americans talk about their jobs.* Three Rivers Press.

2. Ibid., 253.

3. Ibid., 256.

4. Ibid., 265–266.

5. Kegan, R., & Lahey, L. (2016). *An everyone culture: Becoming a deliberately developmental organization.* Harvard Business School.

6. Ibid., 15.

7. Edmondson, A. C. (2012). *Teaming: How organizations learn, innovate, and compete in the knowledge economy.* Jossey-Bass (p. 2).

8. Zhou, J., & Hoever, I. (2014). Research on workplace creativity: A review and redirection. *Annual Review of Organizational Psychology and Organizational Behavior, 1,* 333–359.

9. Edmondson, A. C. (2012). *Teaming: How organizations learn, innovate, and compete in the knowledge economy.* Jossey-Bass (p. 2); Edmondson, A. C. (2019). *The fearless organization: Creating psychological safety in the workplace for learning, innovation and growth.* Wiley.

10. Dutton, J. E., Debebe, G., & Wrzesniewski, A. (2016). Being valued and devalued at work: A social valuing perspective. In B. A. Bechky & K. D. Elsbach (Eds.), *Qualitative Organizational Research: Best Papers from the Davis Conference on Qualitative Research* (p. 9–51). Information Age Publishing.

11. Ibid., 21.

12. Ibid., 25.

13. Ibid., 12.

14. Ashkanasy, N., & Dorris, A. (2017). Emotions in the workplace. *Annual Review of Organizational Psychology and Organizational Psychology, 4,* 67–90; Driskell, J., Salas, E., & Driskell, T. (2018). Foundations of teamwork and collaboration. *American Psychologist, 73*(4), 334–348; Edmondson. *Teaming*; Edmondson. *The fearless organization*; Mitchell, T. (2018). A dynamic, inclusive, and affective evolutionary view of organizational behavior. *Annual Review of Organizational Psychology and Organizational Behavior, 5,* 1–19; Reece, A., Yaden, D., Kellerman, G., Robichaux, A., Goldstein, R., Schwartz, B., Seligman, M., & Baumeister, R. (2019). Mattering is an indicator of organizational health and employee success. *The Journal of Positive Psychology.* Advance online publication. https://doi.org/10.1080/17439760.2019.1689416; Worline, M., & Dutton, J. (2017). *Awakening compassion at work: The quiet power that elevates people and organizations.* Berrett-Koehler.

15. Bell, S. T., Brown, S. G., Colaneri, A., & Outland, N. (2018). Team composition and the ABC's of teamwork. *American Psychologist, 73*(4), 349–362.

16. Bowe, Bowe & Streeter. *Gig,* Loc. 283.

17. Robinson, S., Wang, W., & Kiewitz, C. (2014). Coworkers behaving badly: the impact of coworker deviant behavior upon individual employees. *Annual Review of Organizational Psychology and Organizational Psychology, 1,* 123–143.

18. Keltner, D. (2016). *The power paradox: How we gain and lose influence.* Penguin.

19. Ibid., 85–86.

20. Ballard, D., & Grawitch, M. J. (2016). Concluding remarks: Into the future. In M. J. Grawitch, and D. Ballard (Eds.), *The psychologically healthy workplace: Building a win win environment for organizations and employees* (257–262). American Psychological Association (p. 258).

21. Pierce, J. L., Gardner D. G, Cummings, L. L., & Dunham, R. B. (1989). Organization-based self-esteem: Construct definition, operationalization, and validation. *Academy of Management Journal, 32,* 622–648.

22. Jung, A. K., & Heppner, M. J. (2017). Development and validation of a Work Mattering Scale (WMS).*Journal of Career Assessment, 25*(3), 467–483.

23. Flett, G. (2018). *The psychology of mattering: Understanding the human need for significance.* Academic Press.

24. Sears, L., Shi, Y., Coberley, C., & Pope, J. E. (2013). Overall well-being as a predictor of health care, productivity, and retention outcomes in a large employer. *Population Health Management, 16*(6), 397–405.

25. Harrison, P. L., Pope, J. E., Coberley, C., & Rula, E. (2012). Evaluation of the relationship between individual wellbeing and future health care utilization and cost. *Population Health Management, 15*(6), 325–330.

26. Prilleltensky, I., Dietz, S., Zopluoglu, C., Clarke, A., Lipsky, M., & Hartnett, C. (2020). Assessing a culture of mattering in a higher education context. *Journal for the Study of Postsecondary and Tertiary Education, 5,* 58–104. https://doi.org/10.28945/4539.

27. Prilleltensky, I., Dietz, S., Zopluoglu, C., Clarke, A., Lipsky, M., & Hartnett, C. (2019, July 18–21). *Promoting and measuring a culture of mattering in higher education.* Presented at the World Congress of Positive Psychology, Melbourne, Australia.

28. Worline & Dutton. *Awakening compassion at work.*

29. Colquitt, J., & Zipay, K. (2015). Justice, fairness, and employee reactions. *Annual Review of Organizational Psychology and Organizational Behavior, 2,* 75–99.

30. Ferris, D., Chen, M., & Lim, S. (2017). Comparing and contrasting workplace ostracism and incivility. *Annual Review of Organizational Psychology and Organizational Behavior, 4,* 315–338.

31. Sonnentag, S. (2014). Dynamics of well-being. *Annual Review of Organizational Psychology and Organizational Behavior, 2,* 261–293.

32. Morrison, E. (2014). Employee voice and silence. *Annual Review of Organizational Psychology and Organizational Behavior, 1,* 173–197.

33. American Psychological Association. (n.d.). *Workplace bullying.* www .apaexcellence.org/resources/special-topics/workplace-bullying.

34. Yamada, D. C., Duffy, M., & Berry, P. A. (2018). Workplace bullying and mobbing: Definitions, terms, and when they matter. In M. Duffy and D. C. Yamada (Eds.), *Workplace bullying and mobbing in the United States* (pp. 3–24). Praeger.

35. Bowe, Bowe & Streeter. *Gig*, Loc. 709 and 745.

36. Mitchell, T. (2018). A dynamic, inclusive, and affective evolutionary view of organizational behavior. *Annual Review of Organizational Psychology and Organizational Behavior, 5*, 1–19 (p. 9).

37. Namie, G. (2018). Foreword. In M. Duffy and D. C. Yamada (Eds.), *Workplace bullying and mobbing in the United States* (pp. ix–xi). Praeger(p. ix).

38. Ibid., xi.

39. Reich, R. (2018). *The common good*. Knopf.

40. Sisodia, R. (2017). Foreword. In Worline, M., & Dutton, J. (2017). *Awakening compassion at work: The quiet power that elevates people and organizations* (pp. ix–xiii). Berrett-Koehler (p. ix).

41. Ibid., xiii.

42. Prilleltensky, I., & Prilleltensky, O. (2006). *Promoting well-being: Linking personal, organizational, and community change*. Wiley.

43. Chapman, B., & Sisodia, R. (2015). *Everybody matters: The extraordinary power of caring for your people like family*. Penguin; Quinn, R. (2015). *The Positive Organization*. Berrett-Koehler; Sisodia, R., Wolfe, D., & Sheth, J. (2014). *Firms of endearment: How world class companies profit from passion and purpose*. Pearson.

44. Kegan & Lahey. *An everyone culture*.

45. University of Miami. (2020, June 13). https://umculture.miami.edu/um/.

46. University of Miami. (2017, May 10). *University of Miami named one of America's best employers by Forbes*. https://news.miami.edu/stories/2017/05/um-named-one-of-americas-best-employers-by-forbes.html.

47. Bond, F. W., Lloyd, J., Flaxman, P. E., & Archer, R. (2016). Psychological flexibility and ACT at work. In R. D. Zettle, S. C. Hayes, and A. Biglan (Eds.), *The Wiley handbook of contextual behavioral science* (pp. 459–482). John Wiley & Sons.

48. Harris, R. (2011). *The confidence gap: A guide to overcoming fear and self-doubt*. Trumpeter Books.

49. Biglan, A., Hayes, S., & Pistorello, C. (2008). Acceptance and commitment: implications for prevention science. *Prevention Science, 9*(3), 139–152; Harris, R. (2009). *ACT made simple: An easy-to-read primer on acceptance and commitment therapy*. New Harbinger Publications; Hayes, S. C., Strosahl, K. D., & Wilson, K. G. (2012). *Acceptance and commitment therapy* (2nd ed.). Guilford.

50. Bond, F. W., Lloyd, J., Flaxman, P. E., & Archer, R. (2016). Psychological flexibility and ACT at work. In R. D. Zettle, S. C. Hayes, and A. Biglan

(Eds.), *The Wiley handbook of contextual behavioral science* (pp. 459–482). John Wiley & Sons.

51. Porath, C. (2014, November 19). Half of employees don't feel respected by their bosses. *Harvard Business Review*. https://hbr.org/2014/11/half-of-employees-dont-feel-respected-by-their-bosses.

52. Ashkanasy & Dorris. Emotions in the workplace; Sonnentag. Dynamics of well-being.

53. Kegan & Lahey. *An everyone culture*; Prilleltensky & Prilleltensky. *Promoting well-being*; Worline & Dutton. *Awakening compassion at work*.

54. Goleman, D., & Davidson, R. (2017). *Altered states: Science reveals how meditation changes your mind, brain, and body*. Avery.

55. Porath. Half of employees don't feel respected by their bosses.

56. Rogers, K. (2018, July–August). Do your employees feel respected? *Harvard Business Review*. https://hbr.org/2018/07/do-your-employees-feel-respected.

57. Nelson, B. (2016). You get what you reward: A research-based approach to employee recognition. In M. J. Grawitch, and D. Ballard (Eds.), *The psychologically healthy workplace: building a win win environment for organizations and employees* (157–179). American Psychological Association.

58. Ibid., 159.

59. Ibid.

60. Edmondson. *Teaming*, 118.

61. Driskell, J., Salas, E., & Driskell, T. (2018). Foundations of teamwork and collaboration. *American Psychologist*, 73(4), 334–348 (p. 341).

62. Lacerenza, C. N., Marlow, S. L., Tannenbaum, S. I., & Salas, E. (2018). Team development interventions: evidence-based approaches for improving teamwork. *American Psychologist*, 73(4), 517–531 (p. 528).

63. Rogers. Do your employees feel respected?

9 Mattering through Performance

1. Bannister, R. (2014). *Twin tracks: The autobiography*. The Robson Press.

2. Ibid., Loc. 4468.

3. Ibid., Loc. 1478.

4. Ibid., Loc. 1500.

5. Gawande, A. (2007). *Better: A surgeon's notes on performance*. Picador.

6. Melville, H. (1853). *Bartleby, the scrivener: A story of Wall-Street*. SMK Books.

7. Bowe, J., Bowe, M., & Streeter, S. (Eds.). (2001). *Gig: Americans talk about their jobs*. Three Rivers Press. (Loc. 975)

8. Williams Woolley, A., Chabris, C. F., Pentland, A., Hashmi, N., & Malone, T. W. (2010). Evidence for a collective intelligence factor in the performance of human groups. *Science, 330*, 686–688.

9. Bailey, C., & Madden, A. (2016). What makes work meaningful-or-meaningless? *MIT Sloan Management Review, 57*(4), 53–61; Smith, E. E. (2017). *The power of meaning: Finding fulfillment in a world obsessed with happiness.* Broadway Books; Steger, M. F. (2017). Creating meaning and purpose at work. In L. G. Oades, M. F. Steger, A. Delle Fave, and J. Passmore (Eds.), *The Wiley Blackwell handbook of the psychology of positivity and strengths-based approaches at work* (pp. 60–81). John Wiley & Sons.

10. Csikszentmihalyi, M., Khosla, S., & Nakamura, J. (2017). Flow at work. In L. G. Oades, M. F. Steger, A. Delle Fave, and J. Passmore (Eds.), *The Wiley Blackwell handbook of the psychology of positivity and strengths-based approaches at work* (pp. 99–109). John Wiley & Sons.

11. Grant, A. (2008). The significance of task significance: Job performance effects, relational mechanisms, and boundary conditions. *Journal of Applied Psychology, 93*(1), 108–124. https://doi.org/10.1037/0021-9010.93.1.108.

12. Ibid., 119.

13. Harter, J. K., Schmidt, F. L., & Hayes, T. L. (2002). Business-unit-level relationship between employee satisfaction, employee engagement, and business outcomes: A meta-analysis. *Journal of Applied Psychology*, 87, 268–279. https://doi.org/10.1037//0021-9010.87.2.268.

14. Gallup. (n.d.). *Gallup Q12 Meta-Analysis Report.* https://news.gallup.com/re ports/191489/q12-meta-analysis-report-2016.aspx.

15. Salas, E., & Weaver, S. J. (2016). Employee growth and development: cultivating human capital. In M. J. Grawitch, and D. Ballard (Eds.), *The psychologically healthy workplace: Building a win win environment for organizations and employees* (pp. 59–86). American Psychological Association.

16. Ibid.

17. Ibid., 77.

18. Bowe, Bowe & Streeter. *Gig*, Loc. 968.

19. Deci, E., Olafsen, A., & Ryan, R. (2017). Self-determination theory in work organizations: The state of a science. *Annual Review of Organizational Psychology and Organizational Behavior, 4*, 19–43.

20. Van den Broeck, A., Lance Ferris, D., Chang, C. & Rosen, C., (2016). A review of self-determination theory's basic psychological needs at work. *Journal of Management, 42*, 1195–1229. https://doi.org/10.1177/0149206316632058.

21. Benson, G., & Lawler E. E. III, (2016). Employee involvement: Research foundations. In M. J. Grawitch, and D. Ballard, (Eds.), *The psychologically*

healthy workplace: Building a win win environment for organizations and employees (pp. 13–33). American Psychological Association.

22. Steger. Creating meaning and purpose at work.

23. Slemp, G. R. (2017). Job crafting. In L. G. Oades, M. F. Steger, A. Delle Fave, and J. Passmore (Eds.), *The Wiley Blackwell handbook of the psychology of positivity and strengths-based approaches at work* (pp. 342–365). John Wiley & Sons; Wrzesniewski, A., Berg, J. M., & Dutton, J. E. (2010, June). Turn the job you have into the job you want. *Harvard Business Review,* 114–117.

24. Schwartz, B. (2015). *Why we work.* Simon & Schuster/TED; Steger. Creating meaning and purpose at work.

25. Grant, A. (2013). *Give and take: Why helping others drives our success.* Penguin.

26. Duhigg, C. (2016). *Smarter faster better: The transformative power of real productivity.* Random House.

27. Ibid., 141.

28. Edmondson, A. C. (2012). *Teaming: How organizations learn, innovate, and compete in the knowledge economy.* Jossey-Bass.

29. Sandberg, S., & Grant, A. (2017). *Option B: Facing adversity, building resilience, and finding joy.* Knopf (p. 145).

30. Feldman, C. (2016, January 28). *NASA's Challenger mistakes.* CBS News. www .cbsnews.com/news/60-minutes-overtime-nasa-challenger-mistakes/.

31. Berkes, H. (2016, January 28). *30 years after explosion, Challenger engineer still blames himself.* NPR. www.npr.org/sections/thetwo-way/2016/01/28/464744 781/30-years-after-disaster-challenger-engineer-still-blames-himself.

32. Feldman. *NASA's Challenger mistakes.*

33. Glanz, J., & Schwartz, J. (2003, September 26). Dogged engineer's effort to assess shuttle damage. *The New York Times.* www.nytimes.com/2003/09/26/ us/dogged-engineer-s-effort-to-assess-shuttle-damage.html.

34. Baas, M., De Dreu, C. K. W., & Nijstad, B. A. (2008). A meta-analysis of 25 years of mood-creativity research: *Hedonic tone, activation, or regulatory focus? Psychological Bulletin, 134,* 779–806. https://dx.doi.org/10.1037/a0012 815; Conner, T. S., & Silva, P. (2015). Creative days: A daily diary study of emotion, personality, and everyday creativity. *Psychology of Aesthetics, Creativity, and the Arts 9*(4), 463–470. https://doi.org/10.1037/aca0000022.

35. Achor, S. (2010). *The happiness advantage.* Crown (p. 45).

36. Ben Shahar, T., & Ridgway, A. (2017). *The joy of leadership: How positive psychology can maximize your impact in a challenging world.* John Wiley & Sons.

37. Prilleltensky, O., & Prilleltensky, I. (2019). *The laughing guide to change: Using humor and science to master your behaviors, emotions, and thoughts.* Rowman and Littlefield; Prilleltensky, I., & Prilleltensky, O. (2019). *The*

laughing guide to a better life: Using humor and science to improve yourself, your relationships, and your surroundings. Rowman and Littlefield; Prilleltensky, I. (2016). *The laughing guide to well-being: Using humor and science to become happier and healthier.* Rowman and Littlefield.

38. Fredrickson, B. (2009). *Positivity.* Three Rivers (p. 219).
39. Conner & Silva. Creative days: A daily diary study of emotion, personality, and everyday creativity.
40. Baas, De Dreu & Nijstad. A meta-analysis of 25 years of mood-creativity research: Hedonic tone, activation, or regulatory focus?
41. Prilleltensky & Prilleltensky. *The laughing guide to change.*
42. Rothmann, S. (2017). Employee engagement. In L. G. Oades, M. F. Steger, A. Delle Fave, and J. Passmore (Eds.), *The Wiley Blackwell handbook of the psychology of positivity and strengths-based approaches at work* (pp. 317–341). John Wiley & Sons.
43. Brafford, A. (2017). *Positive professionals: Creating high-performing profitable firms through the science of engagement.* American Bar Association.
44. Kegan, R., & Lahey, L. (2016). *An everyone culture: Becoming a deliberately developmental organization.* Harvard Business School.

10 Mattering in the Community

1. Blue Zones. (n.d.). *Living longer in Costa Rica.* Retrieved June 13, 2020, from www.bluezones.com/2011/12/living-longer-in-costa-rica/.
2. Buettner, D. (2008). *The Blue Zones: Lessons for living longer from the people who've lived the longest.* National Geographic.
3. Sarason, S. B. (1988). *The psychological sense of community: Prospects for a community psychology.* Brookline Books (p. 3).
4. Buettner. *The Blue Zones.*
5. Brainy Quote. (n.d.). Marcus Tullius Cicero quotes. Retrieved June 13, 2020, from www.brainyquote.com/quotes/marcus_tullius_cicero_130785.
6. Walton, G. M., & Wilson, T. D. (2018). Wise interventions: Psychological remedies for social and personal problems. *Psychological Review, 125*(5), 617–655.
7. Fisher, A. T., Sonn, C. C., & Bishop, B. J. (Eds.). (2002). *Psychological sense of community: Research, applications, and implications.* Plenum; Hystad, P., & Carpiano, R. (2009). Sense of community-belonging and health behavior change in Canada. *Journal of Epidemiology and Community Health, 66,* 277–283; Lombard, J., & Brown, S. (2014). Neighborhoods and social interaction. In R. Cooper, E. Burton, and C. Cooper, (Eds.), *Wellbeing and the environment: Wellbeing: A complete reference guide, Volume II* (pp. 91–118). Wiley-Blackwell; Painter, C. V. (2013). *Sense of belonging: Literature*

review. Citizen and Immigration Canada; Pinker, S. (2014). *The village effect: How face-to-face contact can make us healthier and happier*. Random House.

8. Hawkley, L., & Cacioppo, C. (2010). Loneliness matters: A theoretical and empirical review of consequences and mechanisms. *Annals of Behavioral Medicine, 40*(2), 218–227; Perissinotto. C., Stijacic Cenzer I., & Covinsky, K., (2012). Loneliness in older persons: A predictor of functional decline and death. *Archives of Internal Medicine, 172*(14): 1078–1084.

9. Sarason. *The psychological sense of community,* 2.

10. Mannarini, T., Talo, C., Mezzi, M., & Procentese, F. (2018). Multiple senses of community and acculturation strategies among migrants. *Journal of Community Psychology, 46,* 7–22.

11. McKnight, J, & Block, P. (2010). *The abundant community: Awakening the power of families and neighborhoods*. Berrett-Koehler.

12. Brown, B. (2017). *Braving the wilderness: The quest for true belonging and the courage to stand alone*. Random House.

13. McKnight & Block. *The abundant community,* 69.

14. Putnam, R. (2001). *Bowling alone: The collapse and renewal of American community*. Simon & Schuster.

15. Teleport. (2020, June 13). https://teleport.org/compare/toronto-and-miami-vs-/.

16. Bloomberg. (2016, October 5). https://www.bloomberg.com/news/articles/2016-10-05/miami-is-the-newly-crowned-most-unequal-city-in-the-u-s).

17. List of US States by Gini coefficient. (2020, June 13). In Wikipedia. https://en.wikipedia.org/wiki/List_of_U.S._states_by_Gini_coefficient.

18. Conference Board. (2020). *Income inequality*. https://www.conferenceboard.ca/hcp/provincial/society/income-inequality.aspx?AspxAutoDetectCookieSupport=1.

19. National Service. (2020, June 13). *City rankings by volunteer rate*. https://www.nationalservice.gov/vcla/city-rankings-volunteer-rate.

20. New Times (Miami). (2016, December 27). *Study: Miami is a bleak, heartless wasteland where no one cares about you*. www.miaminewtimes.com/news/study-miami-is-a-bleak-heartless-wasteland-where-no-one-cares-about-you-9020430.

21. McMillan, D. W., & Chavis, D. M. (1986). Sense of community: A definition and theory. *Journal of Community Psychology, 14,* 6–23.

22. Ibid., 9.

23. Davidson, W., & Cotter, P. (1991). The relationship between sense of community and subjective well-being: A first look. *Journal of Community Psychology, 19,* 246–253.

24. Fisher, Sonn & Bishop. *Psychological sense of community*; Hystad & Carpiano. Sense of community-belonging and health behavior change in Canada; Lombard & Brown. Neighborhoods and social interaction; Painter. *Sense of belonging*.

25. Flett, G. (2018). *The psychology of mattering: Understanding the human need for significance.* Academic Press.

26. Putnam, R. (2015). *Our kids: The American dream in crisis.* Simon & Schuster.

27. Ibid., 16.

28. Ibid., 16.

29. Ibid., 18.

30. Benner, A., A., Wang, Y., Shen, Y., Boyle, A. E., Polk, R., & Cheng, Y. (2018). Racial/ethnic discrimination and well-being during adolescence: A meta-analytic review. *American Psychologist, 73*(7), 855–883.

31. De Botton, A. (2008). *Status anxiety.* Random House; Marmot, M. (2004). *The status syndrome.* Times Books.

32. Kendi, I. X. (2019). *How to be an antiracist.* One World; Oluo, I. (2019). *So you want to talk about race.* Seal Press.

33. Wilkinson, R., & Pickett, K. (2018). *The inner level: How more equal societies reduce stress, restore sanity and improve everyone's well-being.* Penguin (p. 23).

34. Ibid., 25.

35. Ibid.

36. Dorling, D. (2017). *The equality effect: Improving life for everyone.* New Internationalist.

37. MacDorman, M., Declercq, E., Cabral, H., & Morton, C. (2016). Recent increases in the U.S. maternal mortality rate. *Obstetrics & Gynecology, 128*(3), 447–455.

38. Young, A. (2018, July 27). Deadly deliveries. *USA Today.* www.usatoday.com/in-depth/news/investigations/deadly-deliveries/2018/07/26/maternal-mortality-rates-preeclampsia-postpartum-hemorrhage-safety/546889002/#iwasreallyscared.

39. Marmot. *The health gap,* 36.

40. Dorling. *The equality effect,* 107.

41. Ibid., 22.

42. Case, A., & Deaton, A. (2020). *Deaths of despair and the future of capitalism.* Princeton; Graham, C. (2017). *Happiness for all? Unequal hopes and lives in pursuit of the American dream.* Princeton.

43. Wilkerson, I. (2020). *Caste: the origins of our discontents.* Random House.

44. Di Martino, S., & Prilleltensky, I. (2020). Happiness as fairness: The relationship between national life satisfaction and social justice in EU countries. *Journal of Community Psychology, 48*(6), 1997–2012. https://doi.org/10.1002/jcop.22398.

45. Bertelsmann-Stiftung. (2017). *Social Justice in the EU – Index Report 2017.* www.bertelsmann-stiftung.de//en/publications/publication/did/social-justice-in-the-eu-index-report-2017-1.

46. Gallup. (n.d.). *Understanding how Gallup uses the Cantril Scale.* www.gallup.com/poll/122453/understanding-gallup-uses-cantril-scale.aspx.

47. Pratt, M. W., & Matsuba, M. K. (2018). *The life story, domains of identity, and personality development in emerging adulthood.* Oxford (p. 264).

48. Pancer, S. M. (2015). *The psychology of citizenship and civic engagement.* Oxford (p. 95).

49. Ibid., 111–112.

50. Piliavin, J. A., & Siegl, E. (2007). Health benefits of volunteering in the Wisconsin Longitudinal Study. *Journal of Health and Social Behavior, 48,* 450–464.

51. Ibid., 453.

52. Ibid., 460.

53. Pancer. *The psychology of citizenship and civic engagement.*

54. Fiske, S. (2011). *Envy up, scorn down: How status divides us.* Russell Sage; Kendi. *How to be an antiracist*; Oluo. *So you want to talk about race.*

55. Lieberman, M. (2013). *Social: Why our brains are wired to connect.* Random House.

56. McKnight & Block. *The abundant community*; Putnam, R., & Feldstein, L. (2003). *Better together: Restoring the American community.* Simon & Schuster; Rosenberg, T. (2011). *Join the club: How peer pressure can transform the world.* Norton; Vogl, C. (2016). *The art of community: Seven principles for belonging.* Berrett-Koehler.

57. Dorling. *The equality effect*; Payne, K. (2017). *The broken ladder: How inequality affects the way we think, live, and die.* Penguin; Wilkinson & Pickett. *The inner level.*

58. Fiske. *Envy up, scorn down.*

59. Ibid., 3.

60. Ibid., 12.

61. Ibid., 164.

62. DiAngelo, R. (2018). *White fragility: Why it's so hard for White people to talk about racism.* Beacon Press; Kendi. *How to be an antiracist*; Oluo. *So you want to talk about race*; Powell, J. A. (2012). *Racing to justice.* Indiana University Press; Wilkerson. *Caste.*

63. Prilleltensky, I. (1989). Psychology and the status quo. *American Psychologist, 44,* 795–802.

64. Davis, W. (2015). *The happiness industry: How the government and big business sold us well-being.* Verso (pp. 5–6).

65. Di Martino, S., Eiroa-Orosa, F. J., & Arcidiacono, C. (2017). Community psychology's contributions on happiness and well-being: Including the role of context, social justice, and values in our understanding of the good life. In N. J. L. Brown, T. Lomas, & F. J. Eiroa-Orosa (Eds.), *The Routledge international handbook of critical positive psychology* (pp. 99–118). Routledge.

66. Case & Deaton. *Deaths of despair*; Dorling. *The equality effect*; Partanen, A. (2016) *The Nordic theory of everything: In search of a better life*. HarperCollins; Wilkinson & Pickett. *The inner level*.

67. Crocker, J., Canevello, A., & Brown, A. (2017). Social motivation: Costs and benefits of selfishness and otherishness. *Annual Review of Psychology*, *68*, 299–325; Grant, A. (2013). *Give and take: Why helping others drives our success*. Penguin.

68. Glantz, K., & Bernhard, G. (2018). *Self-evaluation and psychotherapy in the market system*. Routledge.

69. Brown. *Braving the wilderness*.

70. Sigurvinsdottir, R., & Ullman, S. E. (2015). Social reactions, self-blame, and problem drinking in adult sexual assault survivors. *Psychology of Violence*, *5*(2), 192–198. http://dx.doi.org/10.1037/a0036316.

71. Miller, L. E., Howell, K. H., & Graham-Bermann, S. A. (2014). Developmental changes in threat and self-blame for preschoolers exposed to intimate partner violence. *Journal of Interpersonal Violence*, *29*(9), 1535–1553.

72. Zahn, R., Lythe, K. E., Gethin, J. A., Green, S., Deakin, J. F., Young, A. H., & Moll, J. (2015). The role of self-blame and worthlessness in the psychopathology of major depressive disorder. *Journal of Affective Disorders*, *186*, 337–341. https://doi.org/10.1016/j.jad.2015.08.001.

73. Ellard, J. H., Harvey, A., & Callan, M. J. (2016). The justice motive: History, theory, and research. In C. Sabbagh & M. Schmitt (Eds.), *Handbook of social justice theory and research* (pp. 127–145). Springer; Hafer, C. L., & Sutton, R. (2016). Belief in a just world. In C. Sabbagh & M. Schmitt (Eds.), *Handbook of social justice theory and research* (pp. 145–160). Springer.

74. Currid-Halkett, E. (2017). *The sum of small things: A theory of the aspirational class*. Princeton; Reeves, R. (2017). *Dream hoarders: How the American Upper Middle Class is leaving everyone else in the dust, why that is a problem, and what to do about it*. Brookings Institution Press.

75. Graham. *Happiness for all?*

76. Payne. *The broken ladder*.

77. Sabadish, N., & Mishel. L. (2012). *Pay and the top 1%: How executive compensation and financial-sector pay have fueled income inequality*. Issue Brief. Economic Policy Institute. www.epi.org/publication/ib331-ceo-pay-top-1-percent/.

78. Jost, J. (2017). *A theory of system justification: Is there a nonconscious tendency to defend, bolster and justify aspects of the societal status quo?* Psychological Science Agenda: Science Brief. www.apa.org/science/about/psa/2017/06/system-justification.aspx.

79. Jost, J., Banaji, M., & Nosek, B. A. (2004). A decade of system justification theory: Accumulated evidence of conscious and unconscious bolstering of the status quo. *Political Psychology*, *25*(6), 881–919.

80. Okur, P., Pereda, N., Van Der Knaap, L., & Bogaerts, S. (2018). Attributions of blame among victims of child sexual abuse: Findings from a community simple. *Journal of Child Sexual Abuse, 28*(3), 301–317.

81. Jost. *A theory of system justification.*

82. Schmeichel, B. J., & Vohs, K. (2009). Self-affirmation and self-control: Affirming core values counteracts ego depletion. *Journal of Personality and Social Psychology, 96*(4), 770–782.

83. Burton, C. M., & King, L. A. (2004). The health benefits of writing about intensely positive experiences. *Journal of Research in Personality, 38*(2), 150–163.

84. Prilleltensky, I., & Prilleltensky, O. (2006). *Promoting well-being: Linking personal, organizational, and community change.* Wiley.

85. Brainy Quote. (n.d.). Lewis Carroll. Retrieved July 2, 2020, from www .brainyquote.com/quotes/lewis_carroll_165865.

86. Langhout, R. D. (2015). Considering community psychology competencies: A love letter to budding scholar-activists who wonder if they have what it takes. *American Journal of Community Psychology, 55*(3–4), 266–278. https:// doi.org/10.1007/s10464-015-9711-5.

11 Mattering through Social Change

1. Harris-Perry, M. (2016, June 27). Why #BlackLivesMatter's Alicia Garza won't support Hillary Clinton. *Elle.* www.elle.com/culture/career-politics/news/a37 416/alicia-garza-black-lives-matter-hillary-clinton/; Hunt, E. (2016, September 2). Alicia Garza on the beauty and the burden of Black Lives Matter. *The Guardian.* www.theguardian.com/us-news/2016/sep/02/alicia-garza-on-the-beauty-and-the-burden-of-black-lives-matter.

2. Lowery, W. (2017, January 17). Black Lives Matter: Birth of a movement. *The Guardian.* www.theguardian.com/us-news/2017/jan/17/black-lives-matter-birth-of-a-movement.

3. Cobb, J. (2016, March 14). Where is Black Lives Matter headed? *The New Yorker.* www.newyorker.com/magazine/2016/03/14/where-is-black-lives-matter-headed

4. Garza, A. (2014). A herstory of the #BlackLivesMatter movement. In J. Hobson (Ed.), *Are all the women still White?* (pp. 23–28). SUNY Press.

5. Lowery. Black Lives Matter.

6. Sheppard, E. (2018, April 19). "I am not ready to give up this country without a fight": Black Lives Matter co-founder Alicia Garza on the future of America. *Yahoo! Life.* www.yahoo.com/lifestyle/alicia-garza-interview-120028361.html.

7. Hughes, B. (2009). Disability activisms: social model stalwarts and biological citizens. *Disability & Society, 24*(6), 677–688.

8. Pancer, S. M. (2015). *The psychology of citizenship and civic engagement.* Oxford.

9. National Service. (n.d.). *Volunteering in America.* Retrieved June 14, 2020, from www.nationalservice.gov/serve/via/demographics.

10. Joseph, M. (2017, January 31). America does not have enough volunteers. *Huffpost.* www.huffingtonpost.com/marc-joseph/america-does-not-have-eno_b_9032152.html.

11. Patterson, T. (2018, July 20). Stats reveal how many Americans volunteer and where. *CNN.* www.cnn.com/2018/07/19/us/volunteering-statistics-cfc/index.html.

12. Attkisson, S. (2010, April 22). Haiti Earthquake aid: Nearly $15 billion in donations. *CBS News.* www.cbsnews.com/news/haiti-earthquake-aid-nearly-15-billion-in-donations.

13. Sullivan, L. (2015, June 3). In search of the Red Cross' $500 million in Haiti relief. *NPR.* www.npr.org/2015/06/03/411524156/in-search-of-the-red-cross-500-million-in-haiti-relief.

14. Ransby, B. (2018). *Making all black lives matter: Reimagining freedom in the 21st century.* University of California Press (p. 11).

15. Taylor, K. T. (2016). *From #BlackLivesMatter to Black liberation.* Haymarket Books (p. 23).

16. Ibid., 24.

17. Looman, M. D., & Carl, J. D. (2015). *A country called prison: Mass incarceration and the making of a new nation.* Oxford; Powell, J. A. (2012). *Racing to justice.* Indiana University Press; Taylor. *From #BlackLivesMatter to Black liberation.*

18. Thomas, D., & Zuckerman, A. (2018). Black Lives Matter in community psychology. *Community Psychology in Global Perspective, 4*(2), 1–8.

19. Heumann, J. (2020). *Being Heumann: An unrepentant memoir of a disability rights activist.* Beacon Press.

20. Currid-Halkett, E. (2017). *The sum of small things: A theory of the aspirational class.* Princeton; DiAngelo, R. (2018). *White fragility: Why it's so hard for White people to talk about racism.* Beacon Press; Reeves, R. (2017). *Dream hoarders: How the American upper middle class is leaving everyone else in the dust, why that is a problem, and what to do about it.* Brookings Institution Press.

21. Wilkerson, I. (2020). *Caste: the origins of our discontents.* Random House.

22. Fukuyama, F. (2018). *Identity: The demand for dignity and the politics of resentment.* Farrar, Straus and Giroux (Loc. 114).

23. Applebaum, A. (2020). *Twilight of democracy: The seductive lure of authoritarianism.* Doubleday.

24. Fukuyama. *Identity*, Loc. 196.

25. Wilkerson. *Caste.*

26. Nelson, G., Kloos, B., & Ornelas, J. (Eds.). (2014). *Community psychology and community mental health: Towards transformative change.* Oxford.

27. Prilleltensky, O. (2004). *Motherhood and disability: Children and choices.* Palgrave/Macmillan (p. 10).

28. Heumann. *Being Heumann.*

29. Barnes, C. (1998). The social model of disability: A sociological phenomenon ignored by sociologists? In T. Shakespeare (Ed.), *The disability reader: Social science perspectives* (pp. 65–78). Cassell (p. 68).

30. Blackpast. (2007, January 25). *1857 – Frederick Douglas.* https://blackpast.org /1857-frederick-douglass-if-there-no-struggle-there-no-progress.

31. Riemer, M., Reich, S., Evans, S., Nelson, G., & Prilleltensky, I. (Eds). (2020). *Community psychology: In pursuit of liberation and wellbeing* (3rd ed.). Macmillan.

32. Nelson, Kloos & Ornelas. *Community psychology and community mental health.*

33. Prilleltensky, I., & Nelson, G. (2002). *Doing psychology critically: Making a difference in diverse settings.* Palgrave/Macmillan; Riemer, Reich, Evans, Nelson & Prilleltensky. *Community psychology.*

34. Ford, T., Reber, S., & Reeves, R. (2020, June 16). Race gaps in COVID-19 deaths are even bigger than they appear. Brookings. www.brookings.edu/blog/up-front/ 2020/06/16/race-gaps-in-covid-19-deaths-are-even-bigger-than-they-appear/.

35. Lévy, B-H. (2020). *The virus in the age of madness.* Yale.

36. Applebaum. *Twilight of democracy.*

37. Leonhardt, D. (2020, August 6). The unique U.S. failure to control the virus. *The New York Times.* www.nytimes.com/2020/08/06/us/coronavirus-us.html.

38. Prilleltensky, I. (2012). Wellness as fairness. *American Journal of Community Psychology, 49,* 1–21. https://doi.org/10.1007/s10464-011-9448-8.

39. Pancer. *The psychology of citizenship and civic engagement.*

40. Dirty War. (2020, June 14). In Wikipedia. https://en.wikipedia.org/wiki/ Dirty_War.

41. Iton Gadol. (2014, June 29). *Israel/Desaparecidos.* http://itongadol.com/no ticias/val/79708/israel-desaparecidos-monica-bard-junto-a-sus-nietas-brind o-homenaje-a-su-esposo-hugo-donemberg-desaparecido-en-1976.html.

42. Oliva, A. (2013). La infinita busqueda de Alejandra Jaimovich. *Causa Cordoba.* http://causacordoba.blogspot.com/2013/09/la-infinita-busqueda-de-alejandra.html.

43. KKL-JNF. (2014, July 3). *Remembering the Argentine Jewish Disappeared in Memoria Forest.* www.kkl-jnf.org/about-kkl-jnf/green-israel-news/june-14/ar gentina-disappeared-memoria-israel/.

44. Oliva. La infinita busqueda de Alejandra Jaimovich.

45. Campbell, D. E. (2013). Social networks and political participation. *Annual Review of Political Science, 16,* 33–48; Erikson, E., & Occhiuto, N. (2017). Social networks and macrosocial change. *Annual Review of Sociology, 43,* 229–248; McAdam, D. (2017). Social movement theory and the prospects

for climate change activism in the United States. *Annual Review of Political Science, 20,* 189–208.

46. Prentice, M., Jayawickreme, E., Hawkins, A., Hartley, A., Furr, R. M., & Fleeson, W. (2019). Morality as a basic psychological need. *Social Psychological and Personality Science, 10*(4), 449–460 (p. 454). https://doi.org/10.1177% 2F1948550618772011.

47. Partanen, A. (2016) *The Nordic theory of everything: In search of a better life.* HarperCollins.

48. Foroohar, R. (2010, August 16). The best countries in the world. *Newsweek.* www.newsweek.com/best-countries-world-71817.

49. World Happiness Report. (2018). *World Happiness Report 2018.* http://world happiness.report/ed/2018/.

50. Graham, C. (2017). *Happiness for all? Unequal hopes and lives in pursuit of the American dream.* Princeton.

51. Case, A., & Deaton, A. (2020). *Deaths of despair and the future of capitalism.* Princeton.

52. Giridharadas, A. (2018). *Winners take all: The elite charade of changing the world.* Knopf.

53. Graham. *Happiness for all?*

54. Partanen. *The Nordic theory of everything,* Loc. 4601.

55. Ibid., 4552

56. Ibid.

57. Mullainathan, S., & Shafir, E. (2013). *Scarcity: Why having too little means so much.* Henry Holt (p. 7).

58. Wilkinson, R., & Pickett, K. (2018). *The inner level: How more equal societies reduce stress, restore sanity and improve everyone's well-being.* Penguin.

59. Mullainathan & Shafir. *Scarcity,* 150.

60. Tirado, L. (2014). *Hand to mouth: Living in bootstrap America.* Penguin.

61. Glantz, K., & Bernhard, G. (2018). *Self-evaluation and psychotherapy in the market system.* Routledge; Gonick, L., & Kasser, T. (2018). *Hyper-capitalism: The modern economy, its values, and how to change them.* The New Press.

62. Berger, M. (1993, February 21). David Bazelon dies at 83; Jurist had wide influence. *The New York Times.* www.nytimes.com/1993/02/21/us/david-bazelon-dies-at-83-jurist-had-wide-influence.html.

63. Caplan, N., & Nelson, S. (1973). On being useful: The nature and consequences of psychological research on social problems. *American Psychologist, 28,* 199–211 (p. 210).

64. Stout, L. (1996). *Bridging the class divide and other lessons for grassroots organizing.* Beacon Press (p. 106).

65. Smedley, B. D., & Syme, S. L. (Eds.). (2000). *Promoting health: Interventions strategies from social and behavioral research.* National Academy Press

66. House, J., Schoeni, R., Kaplan, G., & Pollack, H. (2008). The health effects of social and economic policy: The promise and challenge for research and policy. In R. Schoeni, J. House, G. Kaplan & H. Pollack (Eds.), *Making Americans healthier: Social and economic policy as health policy* (pp. 3–26). Russell Sage Foundation.

67. Giridharadas. *Winners take all.*

68. Ibid., 97.

69. Brown, N., Lomas, T., & Eiroa-Orosa, F. J. (Eds.). (2018). *The Routledge international handbook of critical positive psychology.* Routledge; Davis, W. (2015). *The happiness industry: How the government and big business sold us well-being.* Verso.

70. Goleman, D., & Davidson, R. (2017). *Altered states: Science reveals how meditation changes your mind, brain, and body.* Avery.

71. DiAngelo. *White fragility*; Keltner, D. (2016). *The power paradox: How we gain and lose influence.* Penguin.

72. Dunn, E., & Norton, M. (2013). *Happy money: The science of smarter spending.* Simon & Schuster; Gonick & Kasser. *Hyper-capitalism.*

73. Klar, M., & Kasser, T. (2009). Some benefits of being an activist: measuring activism and its role in psychological well-being. *Political Psychology, 30*(5), 755–777; Parissa, B., & Ozer, E. (2016). Implications of youth activism for health and well-being. In J. Conner and S. M. Rosen (Eds.), *Contemporary youth activism: Advancing social justice in the United States* (pp. 223–244). ABC-CLIO.

74. Christens, B. D. (2019). *Community power and empowerment.* Oxford.

75. Rosenberg, T. (2011). *Join the club: How peer pressure can transform the world.* Norton; Crutchfield, L. R., & McLeod Grant, H. (2008). *Forces for good: The six practices of high-impact nonprofits.* Jossey Bass; Jason, L. A. (2013). *Principles of social change.* Oxford.

76. Williams Woolley, A., Chabris, C. F., Pentland, A., Hashmi, N., & Malone, T. W. (2010). Evidence for a collective intelligence factor in the performance of human groups. *Science, 330*, 686–688.

77. Stout. *Bridging the class divide and other lessons for grassroots organizing*, 89.

78. Oluo, I. (2019). *So you want to talk about race.* Seal Press.

79. Smucker, J. M. (2017). *Hegemony how-to.* AK Press (p. 14).

80. Ibid.

81. Marmot, M. (2015). *The health gap: The challenge of an unequal world.* Bloomsbury.

82. Franke, R., & Chasin, B. (1995). Kerala State: A social justice model. *Multinational Monitor, 16*(7/8); Franke, R., & Chasin, B. (2000). Is the Kerala model sustainable? Lessons from the Past, Prospects for the future. In G. Parayil (Ed.), *Kerala: The development experience* (pp. 16–39). Zed Books; Kannan, K. (2000). Poverty alleviation as advancing basic human

capabilities: Kerala's achievements compared. In G. Parayil (Ed.), *Kerala: The development experience* (pp. 40–65). Zed Books; Kerala (2020, June 14). In Wikipedia. https://en.wikipedia.org/wiki/Kerala.

83. McKibben, B. (1996). The enigma of Kerala. *Utne Reader*, March–April, 103–112. www.utne.com/community/theenigmaofkerala.

84. Faith in Action. (n.d. a). *History*. Faith in Action. Retrieved June 14, 2020. https://faithinaction.org/about-us/history/.

85. Faith in Action. (2015). *2015 Special Report*. https://faithinaction.org/about-us/2015-special-report/.

86. Faith in Action. (n.d. b). *About us*. Faith in Action. Retrieved on June 14, 2020. https://faithinaction.org/about-us/what-is-faith-based-community-organizing/.

87. Klein, N. (2017). *No is not enough*. Haymarket Books.

88. The Leap Manifesto. (n.d.). Sign the manifesto. Retrieved on June 14, 2020, from https://leapmanifesto.org/en/the-leap-manifesto/#manifesto-content.

89. Lowery, A. (2018). *Give people money: How a universal basic income would end poverty, revolutionize work, and remake the world*. Crown.

90. See https://leapmanifesto.org.

91. Voltaire (1833). La Bégueule: Conte moral. In *Voltaire Oeuvres completes*. Leroi (p. 1100).

Index

CPSIA information can be obtained
at www.ICGtesting.com
Printed in the USA
LVHW060512090723
751909LV00004B/164